# Reference Series

## Computer Security Sourcebook

*Basic Information for General Readers about Computer, Internet, and E-mail Security, Including Information about Data Backups, Firewalls, Passwords, Virus Protection, Sensitive Data Encryption, Internet Filtering, E-mail Monitoring and Security, Children's Online Privacy and Security, Privacy Rights and Policies, Online Monitoring, and More*

*Along with a Glossary of Related Terms and Resources for Further Information*

Edited by Wilma R. Caldwell. 514 pages. Index. 2003. 0-7808-0648-4. $68.

A reported 52 percent of U.S. computer users are connected to the Internet, and the *Computer Industry Almanac* expects to see more than 765 million Internet users worldwide by the end of the year 2005. Security concerns associated with the Internet and other advanced technologies are rising. Information on these concerns is often widely scattered.

The *Computer Security Sourcebook* brings together a wide range of facts, figures, and resources to better assist the general reader in navigating today's computer security issues. The book covers the basics of computer, Internet, and e-mail security to help consumers protect themselves from fraud, privacy invasion, hackers, lost data, computer viruses, and other security issues associated with computer use.

## Travel Security Sourcebook

*Basic Information for General Readers about Security Issues Related to Travel, Including Information about Safety in Airports and on Airplanes, Preparing for and Responding to Crises and Emergencies while Traveling Abroad, Avoiding Health Risks, and Protecting Money and Possessions while Traveling*

*Along with Tips for Safe Traveling Related to Children, Students, Women, Businesspeople, and the Elderly, Statistics, a Glossary of Related Terms, and Resources for Further Information*

Edited by Chad T. Kimball. 600 pages. Index. 2003. 0-7808-0617-4. $68.

The *Travel Security Sourcebook* provides the latest information on safeguarding the security of the traveler, including airport and airline safety information, responding to crises and emergencies abroad, preserving one's health during travel in foreign countries, protecting money and possessions while traveling, and other travel security concerns.

Information in this *Sourcebook* will be useful for every type of traveler, including international, domestic, business, and leisure travelers. It will help them prepare for unexpected emergencies and crises as well as the normal occurrences involved with travel, whether by airplane, train, subway, bus, or automobile. Tips on various travel matters as well as sources of assistance are included throughout the book.

# www.omnigraphics.com

# Travel Security
## SOURCEBOOK

*76.00*     *Gn*

# Travel Security
## SOURCEBOOK

*Basic Information for General Readers about
Security Issues Related to Travel, Including
Information about Safety in Airports and on
Airplanes, Preparing for and Responding to
Crises and Emergencies while Traveling
Abroad, Avoiding Health Risks, and Protecting
Money and Possessions while Traveling*

*Along with Tips for Safe Traveling Related to
Children, Students, Women, Businesspeople,
and the Elderly; Statistics, a Glossary of
Related Terms, and Resources for Further
Information*

## Edited by Chad T. Kimball

*Omnigraphics*

615 Griswold Street • Detroit, MI 48226

Bibliographic Note

Because this page cannot legibly accommodate all the copyright notices, the Bibliographic Note portion of the Preface constitutes an extension of the copyright notice.

Edited by Chad T. Kimball

*Security Reference Series*

Chad T. Kimball, *Series Editor*
Peter D. Dresser, *Managing Editor*
Elizabeth Barbour, *Permissions Associate*
Dawn Matthews, *Verification Assistant*
Laura Pleva Nielsen, *Index Editor*
EdIndex, Services for Publishers, *Indexers*

\* \* \*

Omnigraphics, Inc.

Matthew P. Barbour, *Senior Vice President*
Kay Gill, *Vice President—Directories*
Kevin Hayes, *Operations Manager*
Leif Gruenberg, *Development Manager*
David P. Bianco, *Marketing Consultant*

\* \* \*

Peter E. Ruffner, *Publisher*

Frederick G. Ruffner, Jr., *Chairman*

Copyright © 2003 Omnigraphics, Inc.

ISBN 0-7808-0617-4

Library of Congress Cataloging-in-Publication Data

Travel security sourcebook : basic information for general readers about security issues related to travel, including information about safety in airports and on airplanes, preparing for and responding to crises and emergencies while traveling abroad, avoiding health risks, and protecting money and possessions while traveling; along with tips for safe traveling related to children, students, women, businesspeople, and the elderly, statistics, a glossary of related terms, and resources for further information / edited by Chad T. Kimball.--1st ed.
    p. cm.. -- (Security reference series)
Includes bibliographical references and index.
ISBN 0-7808-0617-4
    1. Travel--Safety measures. I. Kimball, Chad T. II. Series.
G151.T675 2003
363.12'07--dc21
                                                                                2003051701

# Table of Contents

## Part II: Protecting Yourself during Crises and Emergencies while Traveling Abroad

## Part III: Protecting Your Health during International Travel

## Part IV: Protecting Money and Possessions while Traveling

## Part V: Other Travel Security Concerns

## Part VI: Additional Help and Information

# Preface

## About This Book

In the wake of the September 11, 2001 terrorist attacks on the World Trade Center and Pentagon, the world is on travel safety alert. The *Travel Security Sourcebook* provides the latest information on safeguarding the security of the traveler including airport and airline safety information, responding to crises and emergencies abroad, and preserving one's health during travel in foreign countries. This *Sourcebook* also includes tips on carrying money; safety in rental cars, trains, and subways; traveling with children; international travel security tips for businesspeople, women, students, and the elderly; a glossary of related terms; and resources for further information.

## How to Use This Book

This book is divided into parts and chapters. Parts focus on broad areas of interest. Chapters are devoted to single topics within a part.

*Part I: Protecting Yourself in Airports and on Aircraft* describes in detail how airport security works, including changes that have been made since the September 11, 2001 terrorist attacks. It also provides tips for protecting yourself at the airport and onboard aircraft, safeguarding baggage, surviving airline emergencies, flying with children and pets, keeping safe if you have a disability, and more.

*Part II: Protecting Yourself during Crises and Emergencies while Traveling Abroad* discusses U.S. government assistance abroad, as well as how to protect yourself from terrorist threats, arrests in foreign countries, and natural disasters.

*Part III: Protecting Your Health during International Travel* provides general health tips for international travel and medical emergencies abroad and discusses specific diseases and health risks to travelers in different regions. Recommendations about insurance and vaccinations are also included.

*Part IV: Protecting Your Money and Possessions while Traveling* offers tips on avoiding home burglary and theft while traveling; safeguarding souvenirs, passports, laptops, and money; and spotting con artists.

*Part V: Other Travel Security Concerns* provides travel safety tips for women, students, children, business travelers, and the elderly. It helps travelers recognize and avoid common methods used by foreign intelligence agents in gathering sensitive information. It also offers advice on safety in rental cars, trains, subways, and cruises.

*Part VI: Additional Help and Information* includes a glossary of travel security-related terms, a listing of resources for obtaining travel warnings, contact information for international embassies, a directory of travel security-related resources, and a listing of references for additional reading.

## Bibliographic Note

This volume contains documents and excerpts from publications issued by the following U.S. government agencies: Animal and Plant Health Inspection Service, U.S. Department of Agriculture; Bureau of Diplomatic Security; Centers for Disease Control and Prevention; Counterintelligence Training Academy, Nonproliferation and National Security Institute, Department of Energy; Division of Public Safety, National Institutes of Health; Federal Aviation Administration; Federal Emergency Management Agency; Federal Trade Commission; National Disaster Education Coalition; Office of the Assistant General Counsel for Aviation Enforcement and Proceedings and its Aviation Consumer Protection; Transportation Security Administration; U.S. Coast Guard; U.S. Department of State; and the U.S. Department of Transportation.

In addition, this volume contains copyrighted documents from the following organizations and individuals: American Red Cross; American Society of Tropical Medicine and Hygiene; Department of Foreign Affairs and International Trade (Canada); Eastman Kodak Company; Educational Directories Unlimited, Inc.; Gary Rhodes; How Stuff Works, Inc.; Insure.com; Plan it Safe Presentations; University of California Education Abroad Program; and the World Health Organization (WHO).

Full citation information is provided on the first page of each chapter. Every effort has been made to secure all necessary rights to reprint the copyrighted material. If any omissions have been made, please contact Omnigraphics to make corrections for future editions.

## *Acknowledgements*

Special thanks to Jacki Bustos, Dawn Matthews, and Elizabeth Bellenir for their editorial assistance, and to Karen Bellenir for her consulting services.

# Part One

# Protecting Yourself in Airports and on Aircraft

# Chapter 1

# *How Airport Security Works*

## *Introduction to How Airport Security Works*

Imagine a terrorist trying to blow up or hijack a plane. What are all of the different techniques that the terrorist might use to get a bomb into position? A terrorist could:

- Plant a bomb in an unsuspecting passenger's luggage.

- Smuggle a bomb in his luggage.

- Strap a bomb or gun onto his body.

- Walk onto the tarmac by hopping a fence, and approach a plane from the ground.

Airport security tries to cut off all of these different routes. In this chapter, you'll learn about the metal detectors and x-ray systems used by airport-security personnel. You will also find out what you definitely can't carry on a plane.

## *Who Are You?*

The first line of security at an airport is confirming your identity. This is done by checking a photo ID, such as your driver's license. If you are traveling internationally, you need to present your passport.

During the check-in process, the attendant asks you a couple of security questions:

- Has your luggage been in your possession at all times?

- Has anyone given you anything or asked you to carry on or check any items for them?

These are very important questions. A tactic used on occasion by terrorists is to hide a bomb inside an unsuspecting person's luggage. Another tactic is to give something, maybe a toy or stuffed animal, to someone who is about to board a plane. That innocent-seeming object may actually be a bomb or other harmful device.

The guidelines and requirements for airport security are established by Civil Aviation Security (CAS), a division of the Federal Aviation Administration. CAS has three main objectives for airport security:

- Prevent attacks on airports or aircraft.

- Prevent accidents and fatalities due to transport of hazardous materials.

- Ensure safety and security of passengers.

FAA agents working under CAS are located at every major airport for immediate response to possible threats. Most major airports also have an entire police force, just like a small town, monitoring all facets of the facility, and require background checks on all airport personnel, from baggage handlers to security-team members, before they can be employed. All airport personnel have photo-ID cards with their name, position and access privileges clearly labeled.

## Step through, Please

The entire perimeter of an airport is secured. A fence restricts access to the runways, cargo-handling facilities, and terminal gates. All public access is channeled through the terminal, where every person must walk through a metal detector, and all items must go through an x-ray machine.

Almost all airport metal detectors are based on pulse induction (PI). Typical PI systems use a coil of wire on one side of the arch as the transmitter and receiver. This technology sends powerful, short bursts (pulses) of current through the coil of wire. Each pulse generates a brief magnetic field. When the pulse ends, the magnetic field reverses polarity, and collapses very suddenly, resulting in a sharp electrical spike. This spike lasts a few microseconds (millionths of a second), and causes another current to run through the coil. This subsequent current is called the reflected pulse and lasts only about 30 microseconds. Another pulse is then sent and the process repeats. A typical PI-based metal detector sends about 100 pulses per second, but the number can vary greatly based on the manufacturer and model, ranging from about 25 pulses per second to over 1,000.

If a metal object passes through the metal detector, the pulse creates an opposite magnetic field in the object. When the pulse's magnetic field collapses, causing the reflected pulse, the magnetic field of the object makes it take longer for the reflected pulse to completely disappear. This process works something like echoes: If you yell in a room with only a few hard surfaces, you probably hear only a very brief echo, or you may not hear one at all. But if you yell into a room with a lot of hard surfaces, the echo lasts longer. In a PI metal detector, the magnetic fields from target objects add their "echo" to the reflected pulse, making it last a fraction longer than it would without them.

A sampling circuit in the metal detector is set to monitor the length of the reflected pulse. By comparing it to the expected length, the circuit can determine if another magnetic field has caused the reflected pulse to take longer to decay. If the decay of the reflected pulse takes more than a few microseconds longer than normal, there is probably a metal object interfering with it.

The sampling circuit sends the tiny, weak signals that it monitors to a device call an integrator. The integrator reads the signals from the sampling circuit, amplifying and converting them to direct current (DC). The DC's voltage is connected to an audio circuit, where it is changed into a tone that the metal detector uses to indicate that a target object has been found. If an item is found, you are asked to remove any metal objects from your person and step through again. If the metal detector continues to indicate the presence of metal, the attendant uses a handheld detector, based on the same PI technology, to isolate the cause.

Many of the newer metal detectors on the market are multi-zone. This means that they have multiple transmit and receive coils, each one at a different height. Basically, it's like having several metal detectors in a single unit.

While you are stepping through the metal detector, your carry-on items are going through the x-ray system. A conveyor belt carries each item past an x-ray machine. X-rays are like light in that they are electromagnetic waves, but they are more energetic, so they can penetrate many materials. The machine used in airports usually is based on a dual-energy x-ray system. This system has a single x-ray source sending out x-rays, typically in the range of 140 to 160 kilovolt peak (KVP). KVP refers to the amount of penetration an x-ray makes. The higher the KVP, the further the x-ray penetrates.

After the x-rays pass through the item, they are picked up by a detector. This detector then passes the x-rays on to a filter, which blocks out the lower-energy x-rays. The remaining high-energy x-rays hit a second detector. A computer circuit compares the pick-ups of the two detectors to better represent low-energy objects, such as most organic materials.

Since different materials absorb x-rays at different levels, the image on the monitor lets the machine operator see distinct items inside your bag. Items are typically colored on the display monitor, based on the range of energy that passes through the object, to represent one of three main categories:

- Organic.
- Inorganic.
- Metal.

While the colors used to signify "inorganic" and "metal" may vary between manufacturers, all x-ray systems use shades of orange to represent "organic." This is because most explosives are organic. Machine operators are trained to look for suspicious items—and not just obviously suspicious items like guns or knives, but also anything that could be a component of an improvised explosive device (IED). Since there is no such thing as a commercially available bomb, IEDs are the way most terrorists and hijackers gain control. An IED can be made in an astounding variety of ways, from basic pipe bombs to sophisticated, electronically-controlled component bombs.

A common misconception is that the x-ray machine used to check carry-on items will damage film and electronic media. In actuality, all modern carry-on x-ray systems are considered film-safe. This means that the amount of x-ray radiation is not high enough to damage photographic film. Since electronic media can withstand much more radiation than film can, it is also safe from damage. However, the CT scanner and many of the high-energy x-ray systems used to examine checked baggage can damage film (electronic media is still safe), so you should always carry film with you on the plane.

Electronic items, such as laptop computers, have so many different items packed into a relatively small area that it can be difficult to determine if a bomb is hidden within the device. That's why you may be asked to turn your laptop or PDA on. But even this is not sufficient evidence since a skilled criminal could hide a bomb within a working electronic device. For that reason, many airports also have a chemical sniffer. This is essentially an automated chemistry lab in a box. At random intervals, or if there is reason to suspect the electronic device that someone is carrying, the security attendant quickly swipes a cloth over the device and places the cloth on the sniffer. The sniffer analyzes the cloth for any trace residue of the types of chemicals used to make bombs. If there is any residue, the sniffer warns the security attendant of a potential bomb.

Now that you have passed through security and are waiting to board your plane, let's see what is happening with your checked baggage.

## Check Your Bags: X-ray Systems

In addition to passenger baggage, most planes carry enormous amounts of cargo. All of this cargo has to be checked before it is loaded. Most airports use one of three systems to do this:

- Medium x-ray systems—These are fixed systems that can scan an entire pallet of cargo for suspicious items.

- Mobile x-ray systems—A large truck carries a complete x-ray scanning system. The truck drives very slowly beside another, stopped truck to scan the entire contents of that truck for suspicious items.

- Fixed-site systems—This is an entire building that is basically one huge x-ray scanner. A tractor-trailer is pulled into the building and the entire truck is scanned at one time.

One old-fashioned method of bomb detection still works as well or better than most hi-tech systems—the use of trained dogs. These special dogs, called K-9 units, have been trained to sniff out the specific odors emitted by chemicals that are used to make bombs, as well the odors of other items such as drugs. Incredibly fast and accurate, a K-9 barks at a suspicious bag or package, alerting the human companion that this item needs to be investigated.

In addition to an x-ray system, many airports also use larger scanners. Let's take a look at those next.

## Check Your Bags: CT Scanners

The first security check that your checked bags go through depends on the airport. In the United States, most major airports have a computer tomography (CT) scanner. A CT scanner is a hollow tube that surrounds your bag. The x-ray mechanism revolves slowly around it, bombarding it with x-rays and recording the resulting data. The CT scanner uses all of this data to create a very detailed tomogram (slice) of the bag. The scanner is able to calculate the mass and density of individual objects in your bag based on this tomogram. If an object's mass/density falls within the range of a dangerous material, the CT scanner warns the operator of a potential hazardous object.

CT scanners are slow compared to other types of baggage-scanning systems. Because of this, they are not used to check every bag. Instead, only bags that the computer flags as "suspicious" are checked. These flags are triggered by any anomaly that shows up in the reservation or check-in process. For example, if a person buys a one-way ticket and pays cash, this is considered atypical and could cause the computer to flag that person. When this happens, that person's checked bags are immediately sent through the CT scanner, which is usually located somewhere near the ticketing counter.

In most other countries, particularly in Europe, all baggage is run through a scanning system. These systems are basically larger versions of the x-ray system used for carry-on items. The main differences are that they are high-speed, automated machines integrated into the normal baggage-handling system and the KVP range of the x-rays is higher.

With all of these detectors, scanners and sniffers, it's pretty obvious that you're not allowed take a gun or bomb on a plane. But what else is prohibited?

## Now Boarding

### *You Can't Take It with You*

There are a number of items that you cannot carry on a plane, and some that can't be packed in your bags, either:

- Explosives: Fireworks, ammunition, sparklers, matches, gunpowder, signal flares.

- Weapons: Guns, swords, pepper spray, mace, martial arts weapons, swords, knives with blades of 4 inches or longer.

- Pressurized containers: Hair spray, oxygen tanks, propane tanks, spray paint, insect repellant.

- Household items: Flammable liquids, solvents, bleach, pool chemicals, flammable perfume in bottles 16 ounces or larger.

- Poisons: Insecticides, pesticides, rat poison, arsenic, cyanide.

- Corrosives: Car batteries, acids, lye, drain cleaner, mercury.

While most of the things that you can't take on board an airplane are fairly obvious (guns, knives, explosives), there are some things that most people wouldn't think about. Who would have thought that a smoke detector could be considered hazardous? If you do transport a hazardous material on a passenger plane without declaring it, you could face a fine of up to $27,500! Make sure you contact the local airport authority if you have any concerns about an item you plan to carry with you on a trip.

Another thing you don't want to carry on a plane is a dark sense of humor. Terrorism is a constant and terrifying threat. This means that any mention of certain words, such as "bomb," "hijack," or "gun," can lead to your immediate removal from the plane and quite possibly your arrest, even if the word is said in jest. Everyone who works in aviation, from flight attendants to security personnel, are trained to react immediately to those words.

# Chapter 2

# *How Have Airport Security Procedures Changed since the September 11, 2001 Terrorist Attacks?*

## *Guidelines for Getting Onboard*

### *Allow Extra Time*

Heightened security measures require more time to properly screen travelers. Travelers should contact their airline to find out how early they should arrive.

### *Check-in*

- A government-issued ID—federal, state, or local—will be requested. Each traveler should be prepared to show ID at the ticket counter and subsequent points, such as at the boarding gate, along with an airline-issued boarding pass.

- Curbside check-in is available on an airline-by-airline basis. Travelers should contact their airline to see if it is available at their airport.

- E-ticket travelers should check with their airline to make sure they have proper documentation. Written confirmation, such as a letter from the airline acknowledging the reservation, may be required to pass through a security checkpoint.

---

This chapter contains text from "Guidelines for getting Onboard," and "Travel Tips," Transportation Security Administration (TSA), downloaded November 2002.

### *Screener Checkpoints*

- Only ticketed passengers are allowed beyond the security checkpoints. (Arrangements can be made with the airlines for non-travelers accompanying children, and travelers needing special assistance to get to the gate.)

- Don't discuss terrorism, weapons, explosives, or other threats while going through the security checkpoint. Don't joke about having a bomb or firearm. The mere mention of words such as "gun," "bomb," etc., can compel security personnel to detain and question you. They are trained to consider these comments as real threats.

- Each traveler will be limited to one carry-on bag and one personal item (such as purse or briefcase). Travelers and their bags may be subject to additional screening at the gate.

- All electronic items—such as laptops and cell phones—are subject to additional screening. Be prepared to remove your laptop from its travel case so that each can be x-rayed separately.

- Limit metal objects worn on your person or clothing.

- Remove metal objects (such as keys, cell phones, change, etc.) prior to passing through the metal detectors to facilitate the screening process. (Putting metal objects in your carry-on bag will expedite the process of going through the metal detector.)

### *At All Times*

- Control all bags and personal items.

- Do not accept any items to carry onboard a flight from anyone unknown to you.

- Report any unattended items in the airport or on an aircraft to the nearest airport, airline, or security personnel.

## Travel Tips

### *Do*

- Allow extra time. Arrive early.

- Please be patient, as the federalization of security at the airports continues.

- Please be vigilant for suspicious activity, and report it to authorities.

- Keep your baggage with you at all times.

- Please review the guidelines for what you *can* take in your carry-on luggage.

- Please remove undeveloped film from your checked baggage, and keep it with you. Failure to remove undeveloped photographic film of all types may result in damage to that film.

- Bring a government-issued photo ID. (If you have photo identification for your children, please bring those as well.)

- Bring your ticket, or a printout of your itinerary for your E-ticket.

- Please prepare your children for the security checkpoints. Advise your children that all bags and toys must go through the x-ray machine. Leave toys at home that could be mistaken for weapons.

- It is recommended that while in line at the checkpoint, please remove your cell phone and pager, take out your keys and change, and put all of them into your carry-on bag. This will save time once you arrive at the metal detector and save everyone time waiting in line.

### *Don't*

- Carry weapons—including guns or knives, in your carry-on luggage.

- Carry prohibited objects like scissors, pocketknives, mace, and corkscrews.

- Joke about terrorism, weapons, or firearms while in the airports or threaten, or appear to threaten passenger screeners. All remarks like this will be taken seriously. This could lead to arrest and/or fines. At a minimum, you may encounter a delay in travel.

# Chapter 3

# *Safety Checklist for Travelers in Airports and Aircraft*

## *Traveler's Checklist*

Safety sense should follow you wherever you go. There are several basic precepts of safe travel which apply to all destinations. These general safety and security tips are offered whether you are traveling for business or pleasure.

## *Pre-Trip Planning*

- Make sure you have 2 forms of identification that are an identical match to your ticket documentation.

- Pay for tickets with a credit card, and carry it with you for confirmation.

- If a packing list will help, put one together.

- Review your baggage, and be familiar with the contents.

- Plan your trip to allow for delays. Arrive at the airport early to avoid the rush, unforeseen parking challenges, and security backlogs.

---

This chapter contains text from "Traveler's Checklist," © 2001 Plan it Safe Presentations, www.planitsafe.com. Reprinted with permission. Also text is excerpted from "Travel Security," *Public Safety News*, Issue 31, December 1996, Division of Public Safety, National Institutes of Health Office of Research Services, http://www.nih.gov/od/ors/newsltrs/psn/psn31.htm.

- Call your air carrier several hours prior to departure to confirm status, determine any restricted items, and learn their security requirements.

- Consider being dropped off at the airport, using a shuttle service or taxi.

- Know how to use your text messaging cell phone option, if you have it.

- Remember to bring your adaptors, i.e. car and re-charger—regardless of whether you think you will need them.

- Always trust your instincts. If something doesn't feel right, avoid it.

- Consider a pre-paid calling card.

### *Planning for Your Safety and Security Begins at Home*

- For the flights, dress in tightly knit natural fibers, such as cotton, denim, leather, or wool.

- Avoid restrictive clothing and synthetic fibers. Cover as much of your body as possible.

- When in doubt, pack black. It's easy to match and hides dirt.

- Reduce to a bare minimum the amount of metal on your person so you aren't held up at the metal detector. Things to consider: belts, key chains, etc.

- Shoes should be low-heeled, laced, leather, or canvas. No nylons, high heels, or slip-ons.

- Wear a safety strap for glasses and always have a back-up pair of glasses or contact lenses as well as medication in your carry-on luggage.

- Carry a small flashlight with you on your person.

- Bring an essentials kit, moist towelettes, reading material, snacks, flight schedule, as well as a CD/tape player.

- Take a copy of prescriptions should you need to have glasses or medication replaced.

- Carry with you a list with your blood type, allergies, medical conditions, and special needs.

- Do not pack sensitive or proprietary information in your checked luggage. Double envelope the material and hand carry it.

- Tag your bags, inside and out, with your business address and telephone number.

- Consider shipping heavy items ahead of you to your destination.

- Seek out pre-departure briefing, and determine what special security precautions should be taken during your trip.

- Do research on the country you will be visiting. Check with the U.S. State Department, Bureau of Consular Affairs and U.S. Customs regarding any special requirements.

- Request from the Embassy of the country you plan on visiting, a list describing customs restrictions or banned materials.

- Learn the basics about the destination country's history, culture, laws, norms, and language. The OK sign—making a circle with the thumb and forefinger—is considered terribly obscene in Spain and Brazil. In Japan, it tells the cashier you want your change in coins. Get educated.

- Carry your international shot record, just in case.

- Do not publicize your travel plans. Leave an itinerary at the office and with a family member, or friend.

- Advise all parties of changes to your travel plans when they occur.

- Make photocopies of your passport, visa, and other important documents. Put copies in your carry-on and checked luggage, and leave one at home and at the office.

- When traveling with someone, always use the buddy system, from the start of your trip to the end.

- Help each other, whenever possible.

### *At the Airport*

- Never leave bags unattended or carry any article given to you by a stranger.

- Only ticketed passengers are allowed past security, so say your goodbye's before you reach the security checkpoint on your way to the gate. Arriving passengers should arrange a meeting point in the main terminal building, not in the gate area.

- Report anything unusual to officials immediately, and cooperate fully with security.

- Follow bags through all security checkpoints, and don't let them out of your sight.

- Always familiarize yourself with emergency equipment and exits, wherever you are.

- Be aware of your surroundings at all times. Look for safe areas to move if there is trouble, look for people paying too much attention to you, and watch for traffic. Remain alert and focused.

### On Board the Aircraft

- Safely secure all carry-on items. Place heavier items under the seat in front of you.

- Use overhead stowage across the aisle so your bags are in view at all times.

- Keep your seat belt fastened at all times while seated.

- Young children should be seated and belted in an airline-approved safety seat.

- On overseas flights, make sure you check under your seat for a life vest.

- Locate and count the rows to the nearest emergency exists and alternates.

- Be familiar with *all* exists. Mentally plan your escape.

- The safest seat might just be the one where you have the most options. For emergency evacuations, the word to remember is "speed."

- Review the safety information card and pay close attention to the demonstration regardless of how many miles you have under your belt.

- Remember the "10 minute rule". For 10 minutes after take-off and 10 minutes before landing be alert.

- Be seated flat-footed with no distractions such as books or CD/tape players.

- Drink plenty of fluids to stay hydrated (at least 8 oz. of water for every hour of flight).

- Bring bottled water and snacks that are appealing at any time.
- Eliminate the intake of caffeine, alcohol, and sleeping pills.
- If you take your shoes off, put them on again before landing.
- If you sit in an emergency exit, you must be physically capable, aware of your responsibilities, and willing to perform all emergency functions. If not, request another seat.
- Ask questions if instructions are not clear, and report anything unusual.
- Follow crew's instructions in case of turbulence and for any and all emergencies.

## What to Know in the Event of an Emergency

- Evacuation slides.
  - Jump feet first into the slide. Do not sit down. Cross arms over chest, elbows in with legs together.
  - High-heeled shoes should be removed if time permits as they can puncture slides.
- Decompression.
  - Pull mask toward you to start the flow of oxygen. Put your mask on first, then assist others.
- Flotation devices.
  - Life vests, life rafts, some seat cushions, and evacuation slides can be used for flotation devices.
  - Do not inflate life vests until instructed by a uniformed crewmember.
- Evacuating the aircraft.
  - Follow the instructions of crewmembers.
  - Stay calm, leave all carry-on items behind, and proceed quickly to an exit.
- Fire or smoke, in-flight or on the ground.
  - If in-flight, cover nose and mouth, and move away from the source of fire and smoke.
  - If on the ground, stay low and proceed to the exit using your predetermined count of rows, the floor-mounted track lighting, and the small flashlight packed in your pocket or purse.

- If outside the aircraft, move away. Help those requiring assistance, but never return to a burning aircraft.

## *Upon Arrival*

- Invest in a good map of the city. Mark your hotel, office, embassies, police and fire stations.

- Make mental notes of alternative routes to your hotel, office, or other significant locations.

- Select a secure hotel. The crew layover facility's security is usually consistent with U.S. standards.

- If you stay at the same hotel on every visit, this can be identified as a routine, so avoid this if possible.

- Consider changing hotels if you are on a protracted visit.

- Use the bellman. Luggage in the "control" of the hotel causes the hotel to be liable for your property.

- Ground floor rooms, rooms close to the elevator core or the stairwells should be avoided.

- Check fire exits and instructions carefully, and if in an earthquake zone, check what to do if one occurs.

- Use the double-lock and identify visitors visually before admitting them.

- If people claiming to be officials ask you to accompany them, ask the hotel management to assist you in verifying their credentials.

- Keep sensitive documents, such as travel plans, with you or in the hotel safe.

- In unfamiliar locations, avoid walking or jogging. If you must walk or jog, vary your schedule.

- Follow local advice on areas to avoid.

- Don't go anywhere near local demonstrations.

- For in-country and international phoning, find out how to make a local call, what types of coins to use, and the procedures for getting a call through.

- Always keep a low profile. Do not wear flashy clothing, company logos, or jewelry.

- Avoid using unofficial or unmarked taxis. Arrange for taxis through your hotel. Have the address of your destination written down in the native language, and carry a hotel card to show the driver for your return trip. Agree on a fare before getting in. If possible, have the hotel negotiate the fare.

- Be careful about what you photograph. Don't photograph police, military, bridges, or communication facilities.

- Consider a GSM (Global System for Mobile Communications) phone to simplify calling in and out of the country.

- In general, be careful about getting into a taxi with other passengers you do not know. If possible, keep your luggage with you. Try to have exact change or small bills.

- If you plan to rent a car, check to see if you must obtain an international driver's permit.

- Park in a well-lit area and as close to a hotel access point as possible.

- Remove all property from the car interior and place it in the trunk.

Be aware and beware. Safety and security risks exist, not only in unfamiliar locations, such as on the airplane, but even in familiar locales. Preparing for a trip means more than packing your clothes. This trip list will help you to keep some important items in mind while you are on the road and in the air.

## Travel Security

### Travel Alert: Laptop Security

Travelers are cautioned about a scam being used by thieves to steal laptop computers at airports. The scam usually involves two persons who look for a victim carrying a laptop computer and approaching a security checkpoint metal detector. The suspects position themselves in front of the unsuspecting passenger. They stall until the victim places the laptop on the conveyor belt. The first suspect then moves through the metal detector quickly. The second suspect sets off the detector and begins a slow process of emptying his/her pockets, removing money and jewelry, etc., for inspection. While this is happening, the first suspect takes the laptop as soon as it appears on the conveyor belt and moves away quickly. When the passenger finally gets through the metal detector, the laptop is gone. The suspect who picked up the computer heads into the gate area and disappears in the crowd. Sometimes there is a third suspect who takes a hand-off from the first suspect and exits the restricted area before the victim even knows what has happened.

To reduce your chances of becoming the victim of this scam:

- Try to avoid lines to enter a metal detector when possible.

- When this is not possible, delay putting your luggage on the conveyor belt until you are sure that you will be the next person through the metal detector.

- As you move through the detector, keep your eyes on the conveyor belt and watch for your luggage and laptop to come through.

- Watch what the people in front of you are picking up.

### Hotel and Motel Security

When staying overnight at a hotel or motel, remember the following:

- Do not allow anyone to loudly announce your room number, especially if traveling alone. Do not give your room number to anyone you do not know well.

- Ask for assistance with your luggage, and have the bellman check the room—including closets and bathroom—before he/she leaves.

- Check the locations of emergency exits and fire extinguishers.

- Do not leave valuables (camera, cash, jewelry, etc.) unsecured in your room. Utilize safe deposit boxes at the hotel/motel.

- Use all auxiliary locking devices on doors and windows. Consider purchasing a portable door lock or portable personal alarm.

- Know the number and location of security.

Remember—your greatest security asset is yourself. Take precautions, keep a low profile, and stay alert to your surroundings at all times.

# Chapter 4

# *Safeguarding Your Baggage*

## *Chapter Contents*

## Section 4.1

# *Tips on Avoiding Baggage Problems*

Office of Aviation Enforcement and Proceedings, Aviation Consumer Protection Division, U.S. Department of Transportation, available online at http://airconsumer.ost.dot.gov/publications/bagtips.htm, last updated July 15, 2002.

Relatively few bags are damaged or lost. However, your chances of encountering this experience can be reduced even further if you follow the advice set out below.

## *Packing*

Avoid putting the following in checked baggage:

- Valuables (cash, jewelry). Don't rely on suitcase locks; they are easily defeated.
- Critical items (medicine, keys, passport, tour vouchers, business papers).
- Irreplaceable items (manuscript, heirlooms).
- Fragile items (camera, eyeglasses, glass containers). If these must be checked, wrap them carefully in padding.
- Perishables.

Carry the above items either:

- On your person, or
- In a small bag that you carry on board.

Even if a bag is not lost, it may be delayed for a day or two. It is wise to put items that you will need during the first 24 hours in a carry-on bag (toiletries, one change of underwear).

Don't overpack checked bags. This puts pressure on the latches, making it easier for them to spring open.

Lock your bags. The locks aren't very effective against pilferage, but they make it harder for the bags to spring open accidentally.

Put a tag on the outside of your baggage with your name, home address, and home and work phone numbers. The airlines provide free stick-on tags. Most carriers also have "privacy tags" which conceal this information from passerby.

Put the same information inside each bag, and add an address and telephone number where you can be reached at your destination city.

Carry-on baggage advice:

- Check with the airline for any limits it has on the size, weight, or number of carry-on bags. (There is no single federal standard.)

- Inquire about your flight; different airplanes can have different limits.

- If you are using more than one airline for a trip, check on all of them.

- A heavy bag which fits in an overhead bin may still cause the bin to exceed its weight limit.

- Don't assume that the flight has unlimited closet space for garment bags; some may have to be checked.

- Don't pack anything in a carry-on bag that could be considered a weapon (for example, scissors, knife).

## *Check-In*

Don't check in at the last minute. Even if you make the flight, your bag may not.

Make sure that you get a claim check for every bag that you check. Don't throw them away until your bags are returned. Not only will you need them if a claim is necessary, but you may need to show them to security upon leaving the baggage-claim area. Don't leave them in the seat-pocket on the airplane.

Verify that the agent checking your bags attaches a destination tag to each one. (Remove tags from previous trips to avoid confusion.) Check to see that these tags show the correct three-letter code for your destination airport.

Know where your bags are checked to. They may be checked only to one of your intermediate stops rather than your final destination if:

- You must clear Customs short of your final destination, or

- You are taking a connecting flight involving two airlines which don't have an interline agreement (for example, Southwest Airlines does not transfer bags to other carriers).

If you have a choice, select flights which minimize the potential for baggage disruption. The likelihood of a bag going astray increases as the following numbers get higher:

1.  Nonstop flights.

2.  Through flights (one or more stops, but no change of aircraft).

3.  Online connections (change of aircraft but not airlines).

4.  Interline connections (change of aircraft and airlines).

Buy "excess valuation" from the airline if your property is worth more than the airline's liability limit. This limit is usually $2,500 per passenger for domestic flights ($1,250 if the flight was before 1/18/2000), or $640 per bag on international trips).

Your chances of recovery can be improved depending on where and how you bought your airline ticket. Some credit card companies and travel agencies offer optional baggage insurance; some others provide it automatically.

## *Claiming Your Bags*

If your bag arrives open, unlocked or visibly damaged, check immediately to see if any of the contents are missing or damaged.

Report any problems to your airline before leaving the airport. Insist that the airline fill out a form and give you a copy, even if they say the bag will be in on the next flight. Get the agent's name and an appropriate telephone number for following up.

It's not unusual for the airline to take your claim checks when you report the problem; simply make sure this is noted on all copies of the report.

Before leaving the airport, ask the airline if they will deliver the bag without charge when it is found. Also ask about an advance or reimbursement for any items you must buy while your bag is missing.

Open your suitcase immediately when you get to where you are staying. Report any damage to contents or pilferage immediately by telephone. Make a note of the date and time of the call, and the name and telephone number of the person you spoke with. Follow up immediately with a certified letter.

# Section 4.2

## *Pack Your Carry-on for Maximal Safety*

"Carry-On Baggage Advice." Reprinted with permission from
www.airsafe.com. © 2000 Todd Curtis. All Rights Reserved.

A reasonable approach to carry-on baggage is keep in mind three
things: think small, think smart, and think safe. Keep in mind the
following points when you pack and you will likely avoid any problems with your carry-on baggage while you are on the aircraft.

### *Think Small*

- The maximum size carry-on bag for most airlines is 45 linear
  inches (the total of the height, width, and depth of the bag).
  Anything larger should be checked.

- No oversize packages or luggage can be stowed onboard.

- Stow only your essentials (such as prescriptions, personal hygiene items, passports, and other documentation) and valuable
  items, such as jewelry or cameras, in your carry-on bag.

### *Think Smart*

- Plan to check more of your baggage and carry less with you in
  the cabin.

- Check with your airline before packing to determine its
  carry-on guidelines regarding the number of items you may
  carry and the maximum size of those items.

- In certain situations the airline may require most or even all of
  your bags to be checked, so be prepared to do so.

### *Think Safe*

- Carry-on items which may fall from overhead bins can injure
  you or other passengers during flight or in the event of an emergency evacuation.

- Head injury risks from overhead baggage:
    - Stow heavy items under the seat in front of you, not overhead.
    - Don't stack items in the overhead storage bin.
- If an emergency evacuation is necessary, leave your carry-on items on the plane. Retrieving personal items may impede the safe evacuation of passengers.
- Remember, be safety conscious when stowing your carry-on items.

## Section 4.3

# *Dangerous Cargo:*
# *What Not to Pack on Airlines*

This section includes "Do Not Pack" and "Don't Pack Light for Your Next Flight!" cited November 2002, from the Federal Aviation Administration, Office of Security and Investigations.

## *Do Not Pack*

Do not pack in luggage or carry on board:

- Fireworks: Signal flares, sparklers or other explosives.
- Flammable liquids or solids: Fuel, paints, lighter refills, matches.
- Household items: Drain cleaners and solvents.
- Pressure containers: Spray cans, butane fuel, scuba tanks, propane tanks, $CO_2$ cartridges, self-inflating rafts.
- Weapons: Firearms, ammunition, gunpowder, mace, tear gas or pepper spray.
- Other hazardous materials: Dry ice, gasoline-powered tools, wet-cell batteries, camping equipment with fuel, radioactive

materials (except limited quantities), poisons, infectious substances.

## Beware

Many common items used everyday in the home or workplace may seem harmless, however, when transported by air, they can be very dangerous. In flight, variations in temperature and pressure can cause items to leak, generate toxic fumes or start a fire.

## It's the Law

You must declare your hazardous materials to the airline, air package carrier, or U.S. Postal Service. Violators of Federal Hazardous Materials Regulations (49 CAR parts 171-180) may be subject to a civil penalty of up to $27,500 for each violation and, in appropriate cases, a criminal penalty of up to $500,000 and/or imprisonment of up to five years.

## Plan Ahead

Hazardous materials are prohibited in checked or carry-on baggage.

There are certain exceptions for personal care, medical needs, sporting equipment, and items to support physically challenged passengers. For example:

- Personal care items: containing hazardous materials (for example, flammable perfume, aerosols) totaling no more than 70 ounces may be carried on board. Contents of each container may not exceed 16 fluid ounces.

- Matches and lighters: may only be carried on your person. However, "strike-anywhere" matches, lighters with flammable liquid reservoirs and lighter fluid are forbidden.

- Firearms and Ammunition: may not be carried by a passenger on an aircraft. However, unloaded firearms may be transported in checked baggage if declared to the agent at check in and packed in a suitable container. Handguns must be in a locked container. Boxed small arms ammunition for personal use may be transported in checked luggage. Amounts may vary depending on the airline.

- Dry ice: (four pounds or less) for packing perishables, may be carried on board an aircraft provided the package is vented.

- Electric wheelchairs: must be transported in accordance with airline requirements. The battery may need to be disconnected, removed, and the terminals insulated to prevent short circuits.

## Don't Pack Light for Your Next Flight

Torches come in many shapes and sizes but all may be dangerous.

Micro torches, soldering tools and utility lighters are powered by flammable gas in a lighter, other gas receptacle or built-in fuel tank. Many of these torches have electronic starters. Some do not have safety devices to prevent accidental ignition. The FAA has investigated several incidents recently where these micro torches either caught fire or exploded during loading aboard passenger aircraft.

Larger torches consist of a torch head (often with a self-igniting switch) that is designed to be attached to a 14-16 ounce container of flammable gas. In two recent incidents involving a fire, these cylinders were packed or shipped with the torch head attached, and the electronic ignitor switch was found to be in the "on" position.

Even if you think your torch is empty, it may still contain flammable gas vapors that could ignite! One passenger checked a toolbox containing a micro torch. The toolbox exploded during loading and injured two airline employees. The passenger claimed he had emptied the torch by running it on high for four hours.

Department of Transportation Hazardous Materials Regulations forbid the carriage of butane or other flammable gas products on passenger aircraft. Do not pack any flammable gas torches in any checked or carry-on baggage.

# Section 4.4

## *Safeguarding Film from X-Rays*

"Baggage X-ray Scanning Effects on Film," updated February 18, 2002. Reprinted courtesy © Eastman Kodak Company. For the most recent information about this topic, visit www.kodak.com.

### *New Baggage Scanning Equipment Can Jeopardize Your Film*

Because your pictures are important to you, this information is presented as an alert to travelers carrying unprocessed film. Over the past two years new Federal Aviation Administration (FAA) -certified explosive detection systems have been used in more than 50 U.S. airports to scan (x-ray) checked baggage. This stronger scanning equipment is also being used in many non-U.S. airports. The new equipment may fog any unprocessed film that passes through the scanner.

The recommendations in this document are valid for all film formats (135, Advanced Photo System, 120/220, sheet films, 400 ft. rolls, EBN in cans, etc).

Note: X-rays from airport scanners don't affect digital camera images or film that has already been processed, i.e. film from which you have received prints, slides, KODAK PHOTO CD Discs, or KODAK PICTURE CD Discs.

### *Suggestions for Avoiding Fogged Film*

X-ray equipment used to inspect carry-on baggage uses a very low level of x-radiation that will not cause noticeable damage to your film. However, baggage that is checked (loaded on the planes as cargo) sometimes goes through equipment with higher energy x-rays. Therefore, take these precautions when traveling with unprocessed film:

- Don't place single-use cameras or unprocessed film in any luggage or baggage that will be checked. This includes cameras that still have film in them.

- If an attendant or security personnel informs you that your carry-on baggage must be stowed with the checked luggage or go through a second scan, you should remove your unprocessed film.

- Have your exposed film processed locally before passing through airport security on your return trip.

- If you're going to be traveling through multiple x-ray examinations (more than 5 times), request a hand search of your carry-on baggage. FAA regulations in the U.S. allow for a hand search of photographic film and equipment if requested. (The FAA provides air travelers in the United States the right to request a non-x-ray inspection of photosensitive products [FAA Reg. 108.17-AIRPLANE OPERATOR SECURITY]. The complete regulation is very informative, but section Part 108.17e is most important to travelers carrying film. Remember that this only applies to air travelers in the United States.) However, non-US airports may not honor this request.

- If you're asked to step aside for a more thorough search of your carry-on baggage, you should be advised that film could be harmed and you should take it out of your luggage.

- Lead-lined bags, available from photo retailers, will weaken the x-radiation on film and reduce potential harm. However, the effectiveness of any particular lead bag depends on the intensity and electric potential of the x-ray generator, the lead's thickness, and the film speed. If you use a lead bag, check with the manufacturer for the effectiveness of their products with airport x-ray devices. The inspection process may be triggered by a lead bag on the scanner screen. In a typical airport surveillance situation, the baggage may be pulled aside for additional inspection.

- Consider shipping unexposed or exposed film through an expedited carrier, but first check with the carrier to determine what package examination procedures they are using.

- Be polite, helpful and patient. Please remember that security personnel are trying to protect the traveling public.

## Corrections Can't Be Made at the Processing Lab

The processing lab cannot separate x-ray fog from camera exposure, and because this type of x-ray fog often appears in patterns, it is impossible to correct this damage in the duplicating or printing process. Therefore, make every effort to keep your film away from baggage scanning devices.

## The X-Ray Scanning Process

There are two types of higher-dose scanners. The first type is similar to a hospital CAT scan and uses a low dose scan followed by a higher-dose scan on specific areas of the baggage. The other type gives a high-dose, full bag scan on the first pass, damaging the film immediately.

Tests indicate that there is significant fogging of unprocessed film when the film sustains a direct hit by the scanner's high-intensity x-ray beam. The faster the film, the more dense the fog stripe. Because the type of equipment at each airport is unknown to the traveler, avoid putting film in your checked baggage.

## X-Ray Fog Appearance

Fog caused by the new baggage scanners is usually more pronounced than fog caused by other means. Fog from the CAT scan type of scanner typically appears as soft-edged bands 1/4 to 3/8 inch (1 to 1.5 cm) wide. Depending on the orientation of the film to the x-ray beam, the banding may be linear or wavy and can run lengthwise or horizontally on the film. It can also undulate, depending on the combination of the angle of exposure and the multiple laps of film on the roll. However, the fog will usually lack the more subtle patterns produced by traditional types of x-ray equipment. The orientation of the fog stripe depends on the orientation of the film relative to the x-ray beam. Additionally, whether this stripe is seen in the photographic print may depend on scene content. Busy scenes with flowers, foliage, etc. may obscure or lessen the perception of x-ray effects.

- On black-and-white negative films: Dark areas in patterns as described above.

- On color-negative films: Dark areas with neutral or brown patterns.

- On color-reversal films (slides): Minus-density area (light patches) with patterns as described above.

Fog from the second type of high-dose scanners affects the whole negative, causing it to appear over-exposed and grainy.

## Other Conditions That Resemble X-Ray Fog

Certain keeping conditions can produce effects that are confused with x-ray fog. However, you can usually distinguish the more common types of x-ray fog by its distinct patterns and increased granularity.

On 35 mm film, reverse-wind streaks are often mistaken for x-ray fog. However, these streaks are more evenly spaced and prominent, and tend to bow outward from the film perforations.

As noted earlier, exposure to the new airport security equipment produces a pronounced band of plus density or minus density (light patches) that lacks the subtle patterns associated with x-ray exposure by other equipment. The fog pattern can resemble typical white-ight fogging that occurs in a defined path, i.e. from pinhole light leaks in equipment. The most defining characteristics of fog caused by the new equipment are the well-bounded width of the bands and a fairly uniform density, with increase in granularity within the band. The banding will typically run continuously through the whole roll, or be broken by patterns from the laps of film in the roll.

## Motion Picture, Professional Films and Special Processes

Travelers probably shouldn't worry about possible x-ray damage when hand-carrying their film unless they are carrying:

- Highly sensitive x-ray or scientific films.

- Film with an IS speed or Exposure Index (E.I.) of 400 or higher.

- Film of any speed which is subjected to x-ray surveillance more than 5 times (the effect of x-ray screening is cumulative).

- Film that is or will be underexposed.(X-ray fog is most noticeable in the lower-exposure range of the film, and underexposed film has more of the image recorded in this range. Therefore, the effects of x-ray exposure may further reduce the quality of underexposed images.)

- Film that you intend to "push process."(Push-processing involves over-development of film to increase the effective speed and density of underexposed images on color-negative and black-and-white films. On color-reversal films [slides], push-processing on underexposed images will decrease the density range. X-ray exposure has the potential to impact the quality of images that will be processed in a push condition.)

In any of these cases, you should request visual inspection of your film and of any cameras containing film. Depending on the format(s) of film you have, carrying a light-tight changing bag may be advisable to help the inspection process. Remember that this is only a guaranteed option in U.S. air travel. Outside of the U.S. you will have to comply with the local standards and regulations.

## Advice to Professional Photographers and Cinematographers

Kodak suggests taking the following precautions when transporting film via the airlines:

- Never ship unprocessed film as checked luggage with commercial airlines. Keep all unprocessed film as carry-on baggage.

- If you plan to hand-carry unprocessed film on an airplane at an international airport, contact the airport security office before your flight and ask if they will conduct a manual inspection.

- Bring a light-tight changing bag in case it is needed.

- Be cautious with film not purchased through Kodak or authorized Kodak dealers. Ask about the source of the film, and consider shooting a test before you use it.

- Lead-lined bags, available from photo retailers, will weaken the x-radiation on film and reduce potential harm. However, the effectiveness of any particular lead bag depends on the intensity and electric potential of the x-ray generator, the lead's thickness, and the film speed. If you use a lead bag, check with the manufacturer for the effectiveness of their products with airport x-ray devices. The inspection process may be triggered by a lead bag on the scanner screen. In a typical airport surveillance situation, the baggage may be pulled aside for additional inspection.

35

# Chapter 5

# *Overview of Flight Safety*

### What to Wear

- Passengers who wear sensible clothing can reduce their chances of serious injury in the unlikely event of an emergency.

- Wear clothes made of natural fabrics such as cotton, wool, denim, or leather. Synthetics may melt when heated.

- Dress to cover as much skin as possible.

- Wear clothing that is roomy, avoiding restrictive clothing.

- Wear low-heeled, leather or canvas shoes.

### Carry-On Baggage

- Think small, think smart, think safe.

- Check with airline on the maximum size and number of carry-on bags allowed.

- Keep essentials such as prescriptions, personal hygiene items, passports, important documents and valuables (jewelry or cameras) in your carry-on bag.

- Plan to check more of your baggage, and carry on less.

---

"Your Trip," Federal Aviation Administration, http://www1.faa.gov/index.cfm/apa/1079, 2002.

- Be safety conscious when stowing baggage.
- Stow heavy items under the seat in front of you, not overhead.
- Don't stack items in the overhead bin.
- Don't be a bin hog.
- Don't overstuff the overhead bin.
- In an emergency evacuation, leave your belongings behind.

## Passenger Safety Information

- Review the passenger safety card before takeoff and landing.
- Listen carefully to the safety briefing.
- Be able to locate emergency exits both in front and behind you. Count the rows between you and the nearest front and rear exits.
- Locate the flotation device.
- Make a mental plan of action in case of emergency.

## Turbulence

Turbulence happens and much of it is unpredicted. And when it does happen, adults and children who are not buckled up can be seriously injured. Indeed, the majority of turbulence-related injuries and deaths occur when the seat belt sign is on.

- Wear your seat belt at all times, turbulence is not always predictable.
- Make sure your seat belt is secured snugly, and low across the hips.
- In non-fatal accidents, in-flight turbulence is the leading cause of injuries to airline passengers and flight attendants.
- Each year, approximately 58 airline passengers in the United States are injured by turbulence while not wearing their seat belts.
- From 1981 through December 1997, there were 342 reports of turbulence affecting major air carriers.
- As a result, three passengers died, 80 suffered serious injuries and 769 received minor injuries.

- At least two of the three fatalities involved passengers who were not wearing their seat belts while the seat belt sign was illuminated.

- Of the 80 passengers who were seriously injured, approximately 73 were not wearing their seat belts while the seat belt sign was illuminated.

- Generally, two-thirds of turbulence-related accidents occur at or above 30,000 feet. In 1997, about half of the accidents occurred above 30,000 feet.

## Child Safety Seats

- FAA strongly recommends the use child safety seats for children under 40 lbs. It is important to check with the airline to see if the child seat will fit the width of the airline seat. While airline seats vary in width, a safety seat no wider than 16" in width should fit most coach seats.

- Ask about discount fares for children under two traveling in a safety seat.

- Purchasing a discounted seat for your child is the only way to guarantee you will be able use a safety seat.

- Ask about the airlines busiest travel times. Avoiding these times make it more likely you will have an empty seat next to you. In many cases, airlines will allow you to place your child infant/toddler in an empty seat next to you.

- Children under 20 lbs should be in a rear-facing seat.

- From 20–40 lbs use a forward-facing seat.

- Place the infant seat in the window seat.

- Ask airlines to arrange for assistance in making connections when traveling with children and a child safety seat.

- Infant seats should not be placed in an aisle seat.

## Exit Row Seating

- You must be physically capable and willing to perform emergency actions when seated in emergency or exit rows. If you are not, ask for another seat.

- Thoroughly familiarize yourself with the emergency evacuation techniques outlined on the written safety instructions. Ask questions if instructions are unclear.

## Cellulars, Laptops, and Computer Games

- The FCC and FAA ban cell phones for airborne use because its signals could interfere with critical aircraft instruments. Radios and televisions are also prohibited.

- Laptops and other personal electronic devices (PEDs) such as hand-held computer games and tape or CD players are also restricted to use above 10,000 feet owing to concerns they could interfere with aircraft instrumentation.

## Unruly Passengers

- Interference with the duties of any crewmember is a violation of federal law.

- Fines could range up to $25,000 per violation in addition to criminal penalties.

- The Federal Bureau of Investigation (FBI), federal enforcement agencies, airlines, crewmembers and the Federal Aviation Administration (FAA) have combined to vigorously pursue prosecution, which has resulted in imprisonment.

## Fire or Smoke

- Use wet napkin or handkerchief over nose and mouth.

- Move away from fire and smoke.

- Stay low.

## Evacuation

- Leave your possessions behind.

- Stay low.

- Proceed to the nearest front or rear exit—count the rows between your seat and the exits.

- Follow floor lighting to exit.

- Jump feet first onto evacuation slide. Don't sit down to slide. Place arms across your chest, elbows in, and legs and feet together. Remove high-heeled shoes.

- Exit the aircraft and clear the area.

- Remain alert for emergency vehicles.

- Never return to a burning aircraft.

# Chapter 6

# *Smart Protection in Small Airplanes*

We all enjoy the convenience, fun, and safety of flying. We also understand that there may be times when our best efforts for a safe flight will be inadequate, and an accident could happen.

While most accidents are minor, and pose no significant risk to the airplane or its occupants, some can result in major injuries or fatalities. However, studies of serious accidents have shown that the proper use of shoulder harnesses—in addition to the safety belt—would reduce major injuries by 88 percent, and reduce fatalities by 20 percent.

## Install Shoulder Harnesses in Small Airplanes

Shoulder harnesses have been required for all seats in small airplanes manufactured since December 12, 1986. If your airplane is not equipped with them, you should obtain kits for installing shoulder harnesses from the manufacturer, or the manufacturer's local sales representative.

## Use the Restraint System Properly

Federal Aviation Administration (FAA) regulations require that safety belts and shoulder harnesses (when installed) be properly worn during landings and takeoffs. If the restraint is not worn properly, it cannot provide full benefits, and can even cause injury in a serious impact.

"Smart Protection in Small Airplanes," U.S. Department of Transportation, and Federal Aviation Administration. http://www.cami.jccbi.gov/AAM-400A/ Brochures/sbelts.html, updated 2002.

Tests have shown that slack in the restraint system should be minimal. In an impact, your body keeps moving until the slack is taken out of the restraint, but then must be abruptly stopped to "catch up" with the airplane. The restraint should be adjusted as tightly as your comfort will permit to minimize potential injuries.

The safety belt should be placed low on your hip bones so that the belt loads will be taken by the strong skeleton of your body. If the safety belt is improperly positioned on your abdomen, it can cause internal injuries. If the safety belt is positioned on your thighs, rather than the hip bones, it cannot effectively limit your body's forward motion.

Shoulder harness systems can use dual shoulder belts, or a single diagonal belt similar to those used in automobiles. The belts should not rub against your head or neck. This is uncomfortable, will discourage use of the shoulder harness, and can also cause neck injuries during an impact.

Single diagonal shoulder belts should be positioned so that the torso's center of gravity falls within the angle formed by the shoulder belt and the safety belt. Otherwise your torso may roll right out of the shoulder belt during an impact, and compromise your protection.

Because the lower end of the shoulder belt is usually fastened to the safety belt buckle or the buckle insert, the safety belt buckle should be positioned on the side of your hip. This differs from the central location of the buckle that is common when only the safety belt is used.

Be sure that the safety belt is installed so that when the buckle is unlatched, both the safety belt and the shoulder belt are released. Also, be sure that the buckle can be unlatched without interference from the seat armrest, aircraft controls, or the interior wall of the airplane.

If the shoulder harness uses dual belts fastened to the safety belt near the center of your body, the shoulder belts will tend to pull the safety belt up off your hip bones. This could cause internal injuries in an impact.

When it is tightened about your hips, the safety belt should be positioned so that it makes an angle of about 55 degrees with the centerline of the airplane.

This allows it to resist the upward pull of the shoulder belts, reducing the risk of internal injury.

Otherwise, a tie-down strap from the buckle to the center-forward edge of the seat may be necessary to resist the upward pull of the shoulder belts.

If your restraint system uses a tie-down strap, adjust it to remove all the slack when the restraint system is used. A properly installed and adjusted tie-down strap is completely safe.

# Chapter 7

# *Be Prepared for Turbulence*

## Turbulence Happens

### *What Is Turbulence?*

Turbulence is air movement that usually cannot be seen or predicted. It can be created by a number of different conditions, including atmospheric pressures, jet streams, mountain waves, cold or warm fronts, or thunderstorms. Turbulence can occur when the sky appears to be clear.

Quick tips:

- Children weighing under 40 pounds are safest when sitting in a certified child restraint system (CRS).

- All other travelers should remain buckled up for the duration of a flight, not just for take-off and landing.

## *Facts about Turbulence*

Current Federal Aviation Administration (FAA) regulations require passengers to be seated with their seat belts properly fastened:

- When the aircraft leaves the gate and until it climbs after take-off;

---

This chapter contains text from "Turbulence Happens," and "Facts about Turbulence" Federal Aviation Administration. Downloaded November 2002.

- During landing until the aircraft reaches the gate and comes to a complete stop;

- Whenever the seat belt sign is illuminated during flight.

In the aftermath of two serious turbulence events in June 1995, the FAA issued a public advisory to airlines urging the use of seat belts at all times when passengers are seated. The FAA concluded that the rules concerning seat belts did not require strengthening but that a public education initiative was necessary to encourage the use of seat belts.

## *Statistics*

- In non-fatal accidents, in-flight turbulence is the leading cause of injuries to airline passengers and flight attendants.

- Each year, approximately 58 airline passengers in the United States are injured by turbulence while not wearing their seat belts.

- From 1981 through December 1997, there were 342 reports of turbulence affecting major air carriers. As a result, three passengers died, 80 suffered serious injuries and 769 received minor injuries.

- At least two of the three fatalities involved passengers who were not wearing their seat belts while the seat belt sign was illuminated.

- Of the 80 passengers who were seriously injured, approximately 73 were not wearing their seat belts while the seat belt sign was illuminated.

- Generally, two-thirds of turbulence-related accidents occur at or above 30,000 feet. In 1997, about half of the accidents occurred above 30,000 feet. The National Transportation Safety Board defines an accident as an occurrence associated with the operation of an aircraft in which any person suffers death or serious injury or in which the aircraft receives substantial damage.

## *Safe Air Travel with Children*

Proper use of an approved child restraint system (CRS) on an aircraft enhances child safety in the event of turbulence or an accident.

The Federal Aviation Administration (FAA) strongly recommends that all children who fly, regardless of their age, use the appropriate restraint based on their size and weight.

*Before You Fly*

- Ensure that your CRS has received FAA approval. Check for a label reading, "This restraint is certified for use in motor vc hicles and aircraft."

- Check the width of your CRS. While airline seats vary in width, a CRS no wider than 16" should fit in most coach seats. Even if the armrests are moved out of the way, a CRS wider than 16" is unlikely to fit properly into the frame of the aircraft seat.

- Ask the airline if they offer a discounted fare for a child traveling in a CRS. Purchasing an airline ticket (discounted or full fare) for your child is the only way to guarantee that you will be able to use a CRS.

- Check with the airline to determine their busiest days and times. By avoiding these times, you are more likely to be on a flight with an empty seat next to you. In many cases, airlines will allow you to seat your child under two years of age in your CRS in the empty airplane seat without having to pay the airline fare for the child. Be sure to ask your airline for its policy regarding an empty seat.

- If you purchase a ticket for your child, reserve adjoining seats. A CRS must be placed in a window seat so it will not block the escape path in an emergency. A CRS may not be placed in an exit row.

- If you need to change planes to make a connecting flight, it can be very challenging to transport a CRS, a child, and luggage through a busy airport. Most airlines will help parents make the connection if they can arrange for assistance in advance.

*Choosing the Correct CRS*

- Always follow the manufacturer's instructions regarding use of the CRS. Do not place a child in a CRS designed for a smaller child. Be sure that shoulder straps come out of the CRS seat back above the child's shoulders. Fasten the aircraft seat belt around the CRS as tightly as possible.

- The FAA recommends that a child weighing:
  - Under 20 pounds be placed in a rear-facing CRS.
  - From 20 to 40 pounds use a forward- facing child restraint. Although the safety technology of forward-facing child restraint systems in aircraft is still developing, cur-rent restraints offer dramatic.
  - Improvements in protection compared to lap-held or unrestrained children.
  - Over 40 pounds may safely use an aircraft seat belt.

*Reminders*

Use an approved CRS when traveling to and from the airport, and when you arrive at your destination.

The safest place for a child on an airplane is in an approved CRS based on the child's weight. While booster seats and harness vests enhance safety in automobiles, they are banned for use during taxi, take-off, and landing. Although they are permissible for use during the cruise portion of flight, they do not afford the same level of protection as a hard-shell CRS.

In the United States, supplemental lap restraints, "belly belts," are banned from use in both automobiles and aircraft.

# Chapter 8

# *Survive a Crash, Hijacking, or Other Airline Emergency*

## Unforeseen Circumstances/Situations

During your travels, it will be most unlikely that you will ever be hijacked, kidnapped, held captive, or become a victim of terrorist or criminal activity. You should be aware; however, that the terrorist and criminal threat varies from country to country, and that sometimes dangerous or unforeseen circumstances may occur. The information provided in the following sections is not meant to alarm you, but is simply provided as guidance.

## Evading Terrorists and Criminals

Get as much information as you can about the threat in your destination before you leave, especially if traveling to a high-risk area.

It is strongly recommended that you contact the State Department for additional information prior to traveling. Recorded messages provide information and travel warnings, if warranted, for most regions of the world.

Develop and implement a security plan upon your arrival.

Do not become complacent in low-risk areas. Situations sometimes change rapidly. In general, terrorists and criminals alike strike

"Dealing with Problems," by the Office of the National Counterintelligence Executive, http://www.nacic.gov/pubs/passport/dealing.html, 1995. Despite the age of this document, readers seeking an understanding of surviving airline emergencies will find this information useful.

when and where they sense their targets to be most vulnerable, and they are most successful when security measures are low, and daily routines are predictable. Vary arrival times, departure times, and routes that you normally take.

Be alert to the possibility of surveillance. If you believe that you are being followed, do not challenge your follower; instead, attempt to mentally note his/her physical characteristics, type of car, license number, etc.

Regarding street crime, never resist armed robbery; it could lead to violence. Always carry some cash to appease muggers who may resort to violence at finding no reward for their efforts. Turn over the small bills that you kept separate. If the robber presses the attack, give up your wallet. If you do not have much money on you, offer something else such as, "I don't have my wallet, here take my jacket." Never pursue a thief; call for help and contact the police.

Promptly report such incidents to security officials at the site where you are or at the nearest U.S. Embassy or Consulate.

## Hijacking/Hostage Situation

- Try to remain calm and alert, and avoid doing anything that might attract undue attention to yourself.

- Comply with orders and instructions without complaining. Keep in mind that what you say and do could impact on others.

- Be as general as possible if questioned, and do not discuss anything that you are obligated to protect.

- Be non-threatening in conversations with your captors, and avoid arguments and physical violence.

- Prepare yourself for experiencing depression, boredom, and frustration because a hostage situation may continue for an indefinite period.

- Try to humanize the event as much as possible. If you need anything ask for it, making your request in a reasonable low-key manner.

- Try to establish a program of mental and physical activity if your situation becomes lengthy and drawn out.

- Above all, rely on your inner resources and think positively.

## What to Do in Case of an Aircraft Emergency

Although the U.S. airline system is the safest in the world, crashes do occur. However, nearly all crashes have survivors. The tips below, courtesy of the FAA, can help ensure that you survive a crash (which causes 10 percent of airline deaths) and the resultant fire and smoke (which causes the other 90 percent). Do not depend upon others. You are your own safety officer. Survival favors the prepared.

## Getting Dressed to Go to the Airport

- Dress casually (slacks, no tight fitting clothes, no skirts) in case you have to climb over obstacles to leave the plane.

- Wear natural fibers. Synthetic clothing, including nylons, burns right through the skin causing severe injury. If you are wearing nylons and have to slide down the emergency chute, the friction could melt the material into your skin.

- Wear bright colors. You can be seen better if you need emergency treatment outside the plane. If you collapse on the ground, you will not be run over by an emergency vehicle.

- Do not wear high-heeled shoes; they could puncture the exit chute.

- Do not wear pierced earrings. The safety vest inflates above the ears. The earrings could puncture the safety vest, losing 50 percent of buoyancy. If you are in cold water, the vest keeps your head above water, helping to retain your body heat. Losing the buoyancy of the vest dramatically increases the chance of body heat loss, and death from hypothermia.

- Wear laced shoes and keep them on during take-off and landing. If preparing for a crash, put your shoes back on. In a crash, loafers may fly off from the G-forces. Avoid walking where there might be debris such as glass, razor-sharp metal shards, or fuel. Also avoid touching the cabin if there is a fire, as the metal would be hot.

- Because the plane is set to a low humidity (between 4 and 15 percent) you dehydrate while in the air. Drink plenty of water or juice at home and before boarding the plane. While in-flight, drink fluids, even if you are not thirsty. Dehydration parches your throat and nasal passages, which will have a hard enough time from the smoke soot. A word of caution: alcohol speeds dehydration.

- Do not take any medication that may slow thinking and reaction time in an emergency (i.e., sedatives) unless prescribed by a physician. Regarding prescription medication, if you are traveling in different time zones, make sure you take your medication according to the number of hours between doses, not by the time on your watch. There is a good chance you could either overdose or underdose.

## *Once in the Aircraft*

- Where to sit: The best place to sit is either on an exit row or within two rows of one. Most people instinctively exit a plane the way they entered. Make sure you know where the closest emergency exits are. Those sitting in exit rows are crucial to everyone's safety. Make sure that those sitting on the exit rows speak and understand English. The FAA requires that they be able-bodied enough to remove the window (it weighs 40–70 pounds) or open the door. If you notice these rules not being followed, you have the right (and obligation) to report the situation to the flight attendants to arrange for a passenger to move to another seat. Removal of the emergency exit window is an important first step in crash survival.

- Be grateful for the tight leg room. It is safer because there is less room to be thrown around.

- Check with the air carrier regarding the number and size of carry-on bags. Put a softer, lighter bag (with no sharp edges) in the top bin. In an emergency, these bins pop open (they are rated for only 3Gs) and contents become projectiles. A heavier bag should be placed under the seat in front of you. In case of an emergency while the plane is still moving, brace your feet against the bag to keep it from traveling under your feet where you might trip in your haste to leave the plane.

- While on the airplane, remember to keep items like your laptop computer near your seat, and not in an overhead compartment away from your view.

- Pay heed to the flight attendant's emergency instructions. All planes (even the same models from the same manufacturers) are configured differently, particularly regarding the location and operation of emergency doors and window. Know where the nearest two exits are; doors can jam because of a crash. Count the number of rows you are away from these exits. When the plane fills up with smoke, visibility is zero. Back up what the attendant says by reading the emergency card in the flap in front of you. Caution: Look before you reach into the pocket. Passengers have been stabbed with discarded hypodermic needles.

- 80 percent of all accidents happen at takeoff and landing. Make sure you are buckled up securely as acceleration and deceleration causes the body to lurch forward and backward, which could cause injury. Never release your seatbelt until the plane comes to a complete stop.

- Keep the seatbelt buckled when seated. Most injuries from air turbulence occur in a split second. 100 percent of the injuries could be eliminated if seatbelts were worn.

- Keep debris off the floor, especially magazines with slick covers, which could cause you to slip when in a hurry.

## *Should the Worst Happen*

- Once the plane comes to a halt, what you do in the first 90 seconds may decide your fate; knowledge of your surroundings is crucial. Never release your seatbelt until the plane comes to a complete stop and you have observed your surroundings. If you find yourself upside down, releasing your seatbelt could prove hazardous.

- The seat cushion floats do not work very well in water because they are unstable and force you to use energy to stay up. Use them until you find a better alternative, such as the exit chute that can serve as a raft. The inflatable safety vests are also good bets as they keep your head above water even if you are unconscious. When making reservations, you should ask the airline for flotation devices for children and infants.

- If traveling with your family, get seats next to each other. Do not leave the lives of loved ones in the hand of panicky strangers.

- Before removing an exit door or window, make sure you see no fire outside. You court disaster by allowing the fire and smoke to draft inside.

- If the window must be removed, sit down to do it. If you stand, the person behind you will be pushing you and the window cannot be brought inside before it releases. Your knees can block panicky passengers until you can move the window.

- Do not come out head first, unless it is a water landing. You could be pushed out, landing on your head. First put out a leg, then your body, then your other leg, thereby maintaining your balance.

- If the plane breaks apart, consider using the new holes as exits.

- There is an emergency rope in the cockpit. If it is the only way out, close the door behind you to block out the smoke, pop out the window, and climb down. This is not the best way to leave the plane, but it might be your only way.

- If the exit chute does not deploy, reach down and pull the handle at the base of the door jamb.

- The steeper the chute, the faster you travel.

- Jump feet first into the center of the slide; do not sit down to slide. Cross your arms across your chest, elbows in, with legs and feet together or crossed. If you try to brace yourself with your hands while traveling downward, severe friction burns can occur.

- There are no exit chutes over the wings on some domestic flights. The pilot will bring the flaps down to enable people to slide off the wing to safety.

- Leave belongings behind. Do not risk your life and the lives of others by slowing down to retrieve things. Do not carry bags out—if they get stuck, even for a few seconds, you are dooming those behind you.

- Move away from the aircraft, fire, and smoke. If possible, help those requiring assistance. Never go back into a burning aircraft.

- Remain alert for emergency vehicles.

# Chapter 9

# *Tips for Flying with Children*

## Getting a Child Ready for a Plane Ride

### *Planning Your Trip*

- Flying during nap time, or overnight is the best.

- Choose a direct flight, if at all possible

- A child under two years of age may ride in an adult's lap, but an approved child safety seat is recommended by the Federal Aviation Administration (FAA).

- Order kid's meals in advance, this option will depend upon the airline that you booked passage with.

- Request a roomier bulkhead.

- Do not request the emergency exit seating row.

---

This chapter contains text from "Getting a Child Ready for a Plane Ride: Here's Some Practical Advice," Federal Aviation Administration (FAA), http://www.faa.gov/fsdo/mia/Children.htm, downloaded 2002, and "A Change is in the Air," by John Wensel in association with FAA, http://www.faa.gov/fsdo/ord/change.htm. "A Change Is in the Air" is a 1995 document which summarizes FAA's Civil Aeromedical Institute's findings regarding the crashworthiness of various types of child restraint systems. The recommendations at the end of this document represent the most current information available on FAA's website. However, FAA recommends that travelers check with the airline regarding the use of child restraint systems before arrival at airport.

## Raising a Frequent Flier

- Present flying as an adventure.

- Tell children ages five and older about the flight two weeks in advance, and remind them a week later, and then the day before.

## Keeping the Flight Day Sane

- Dress your child in bright colors, so he or she is easy to spot in a crowd. Give the child a card with his/her name, phone number, age, medical information, and your name, address, home/cell/beeper phone number in case you become separated. A copy of your flight itinerary is a good idea to have with the child. It's not a bad idea to attach a luggage type tag envelope to the child with all this information.

- Have a current picture photo of the child, preferably a Polaroid the day you're traveling, showing the exact clothing that the child is wearing and how they are dressed. This will aid in quickly reuniting you with your child, should you become separated from them. Small children are quick, and can disappear from you site in the blink of an eye, so keep them very close to you at all times.

- Check your stroller at the gate and not with your luggage, you'll want use it to maneuver through the airport.

- Request preboarding with a baby, but think twice about preboarding with a toddler, who may not want to be confined longer than necessary.

- Bring something new, like books or hand held games for older children, and small toys or picture books for toddlers; you'll want to keep them occupied during the trip. But don't give them or show them what you brought on board for them to play with until after the take off, make it a surprise. Remember a child can only look out the window so long, then they become bored too.

- For infants, the best advice is to feed them well, change them often, and try to plan your trip during their normal nap time, or keep them awake until you board.

- Oh, and don't forget to have fun once you are in the air.

## A Change Is in the Air

Since the article, "Don't Forget the Children," was published in the April 1994 issue of FAA Aviation News, the FAA's Civil Aeromedical Institute (CAMI) completed a study to evaluate whether the FAA regulations regarding crashworthiness requirements for adult passenger seats, and the standards applicable to child restraint systems were consistent for transport category aircraft. The following is a summary of CAMI's findings. Some of the most serious issues identified by CAMI concern child restraints commonly referred to as shield-type booster seats, vest-and harness-type child restraint systems, and belly belts.

[Editors note: Since the time this article was written, the FAA has banned the use of booster seats as well as harness and vest-type child restraint systems aboard all U.S. air carriers. Note that previously, the use of supplemental lap restraints (belly belts) was also banned from use in aircraft.]

### Booster Seats

The shield-type booster seat, in combination with other factors, contributed to an abdominal pressure measurement higher than in other means of protection. As noted in the original article, airline seats are not rigid, and may break over under their own inertia, or when struck by a passenger. This represents a potential source of pressure and force to the occupant of a backless child restraint system. In a typical seat used by an airline, shield-type booster seats do not provide adequate protection from aft row occupant impact forces on the seat back. The movement of the aft row adult passenger may expose the child to an impact from behind, and to being crushed between the airplane seat back and the booster seat shield.

CAMI tests demonstrate that booster seats do not adequately protect children in the air. When an adult-size test dummy was seated behind a break over type seat occupied by a child-size test dummy seated in a shield-type booster seat, the abdominal load was 59.5 pounds per square inch (psi). When the same child-size test dummy was restrained by the seat's lap belt, the abdominal load was 37.6 psi. This represents a 37% reduction in the force applied to a child's abdomen. The FAA believes that there is a relationship between abdominal loading and injury.

## *Vest- and Harness-Type Child Restraint Systems*

Harness-type child restraints tested at CAMI did not provide adequate restraint to prevent a serious impact with a seat back in front of the child occupant, and a rebound impact with the occupant's own seat because of the location of the safety belt anchors for an airplane seat.

In an accident, these systems allow unacceptable levels of body excursion and/or submarining (the occupant's lower body slides underneath the restraint system). The FAA believes that if a child under two falls in the weight use limits (25–50 pounds) recommended by vest and harness manufacturers, the child would be safer in a passenger seat restrained by a lap belt than in a vest- and harness-type device if no other approved systems were available. However, the FAA believes that a child weighing between 20 and 40 pounds would be better protected in a forward facing child restraint system than in a lap belt. In addition. CAMI testing revealed that lap belts provide a superior level of protection for children weighing more than 40 pounds to that provided by harnesses and booster seats.

## *Belt-Positioning Booster Seats*

These seats require shoulder harnesses, and airplanes used in airline operations do not have passenger shoulder harnesses. In addition, in other aircraft that may have shoulder harnesses for passengers, the FAA believes that during an aircraft crash there is a likelihood that a belt-positioning booster seat will shift from the passenger seat, causing a degradation in the performance of that child restraint system.

## *Belly Belts*

These systems allowed the test dummy to make severe contact with the back of the seat in the row in front of the test dummy. The child also may be crushed by the forward bending motion of the adult to whom the child is attached.

## *New Regulations*

The National Highway Traffic Safety Administration (NHTSA) and the FAA developed a common approach to the approval of child restraints during the mid-1980's. Federal Motor Vehicle Safety Standards (FMVSS) No. 213 was amended to provide criteria for the certification of child restraints that were appropriate for both aircraft and automobiles. FMVSS, as revised, is the current U.S. standard used to approve child restraint systems. On July 21, 1994. NHTSA issued an amendment to its standard requiring that belt-positioning booster seats be labeled with a statement that they are not certified for use on aircraft.

On June 9, 1995, the FAA issued a notice of proposed rulemaking that proposes to ban the use of booster seat and vest- and harness-type child restraint systems in aircraft during takeoff, landing, and movement on the surface. Because of the safety issues involved, these child restraint systems should not be used in an aircraft, and if the proposed changes to the rules become effective, they will not be approved for use in aircraft.

### *Recommendations*

Considering the CAMI study, the FAA believes that forward facing child restraint devices are superior to vest- and harness-type devices, booster seats, belly belts, and the holding of children on laps. The FAA recommends:

- The use of a rear facing child restraint system for children weighing under 20 pounds

- And a forward facing system for children weighing between 20 and 40 pounds.

- Children weighing over 40 pounds should use the standard lap belt that is attached to all airline seats.

# Chapter 10

# *Flight Safety for Passengers with Disabilities*

## *Introduction*

For years, access to the nation's air travel system for persons with disabilities was an area of substantial dissatisfaction, with both passengers and the airline industry recognizing the need for major improvement. In 1986 Congress passed the Air Carrier Access Act, requiring the Department of Transportation (DOT) to develop new regulations which ensure that persons with disabilities will be treated without discrimination in a way consistent with the safe carriage of all passengers. These regulations were published in March 1990.

The DOT regulations, referred to here as the Air Carrier Access Rules, represent a major stride forward in improving air travel for persons with disabilities. The rules clearly explain the responsibilities of the traveler, the carriers, the airport operators, and contractors, who collectively make up the system which moves over one million passengers per day. (These rules do not apply to foreign airlines.)

The Air Carrier Access Rules are designed to minimize the special problems that travelers with disabilities face as they negotiate their way through the nation's complex air travel system from origin to destination. This is achieved:

---

"New Horizons Information for the Air Traveler with a Disability," U.S. Department of Transportation, http://www1.faa.gov/acr/dat.htm, updated December 2002.

- By recognizing that the physical barriers encountered by passengers with disabilities can frequently be overcome by employing simple changes in layout and technology.

- By adopting the principle that many difficulties confronting passengers with hearing or vision impairments will be relieved if they are provided access to the same information that is available to all other passengers.

- Through training of all air travel personnel who come in day-to-day contact with persons with disabilities, to understand their needs and how they can be accommodated quickly, safely, and with dignity.

This chapter is designed to offer travelers with disabilities a brief but authoritative source of information about the Air Carrier Access Rules: the accommodations, facilities, and services that are now required to be available. It also describes features required by other regulations designed to make air travel more accessible.

This chapter is structured in much the same sequence as a passenger would plan for a trip: the circumstances he or she must consider prior to traveling, what will be encountered at the airport, and what to expect in the transitions from airport to airplane, on the plane, and then airplane to airport.

## Planning Your Trip

### *The New Traveling Environment*

The Air Carrier Access Rules sweep aside many restrictions that formerly discriminated against passengers with disabilities:

- A carrier may not refuse transportation to a passenger solely on the basis of a disability.

- Air carriers may not limit the number of individuals with disabilities on a particular flight.

- All trip information that is made available to other passengers also must be made available to passengers with disabilities.

- Carriers must provide passage to an individual who has a disability that may affect his or her appearance or involuntary behavior, even if this disability may offend, annoy, or be an inconvenience to crew-members or other passengers.

There are a few exceptions:

- The carrier may refuse transportation if the individual with a disability would endanger the health or safety of other passengers, or transporting the person would be a violation of Federal Aviation Administration (FAA) safety rules.

- If the plane has fewer than 30 seats, the carrier may refuse transportation if there are no lifts, boarding chairs, or other devices available which can be adapted to the limitations of such small aircraft by which to enplane the passenger. Airline personnel are not required to carry a mobility-impaired person onto the aircraft by hand.

- There are special rules about persons with certain disabilities or communicable diseases. These rules are covered in the section entitled "At the Airport."

- The carrier may refuse transportation if it is unable to seat the passenger without violating the FAA Exit Row Seating Rules. See the section "On the Plane."

There are new procedures for resolving disputes:

- All carriers are now required to have a Complaints Resolution Official (CRO) immediately available (even if by phone) to resolve disagreements which may arise between the carrier and passengers with disabilities.

- Travelers who disagree with a carrier's actions toward them can pursue the issue with the carrier's CRO on the spot.

- A carrier that refuses transportation to any person based on a disability must provide a written statement to that person within 10 calendar days, stating the basis for the refusal. The statement must include, where applicable, the basis for the carrier's opinion that transporting the person could be harmful to the safety of the flight.

- If the passenger is still not satisfied, he or she may pursue DOT enforcement action.

### Getting Advance Information about the Aircraft

Travelers with disabilities must be provided information upon request concerning facilities and services available to them. When feasible this information will pertain to the specific aircraft scheduled for a specific flight. Such information includes:

- Any limitations which may be known to the carrier concerning the ability of the aircraft to accommodate an individual with a disability.

- The location of seats (if any) with movable aisle armrests, and any seats which the carrier does not make available to an individual with a disability (e.g., exit rows).

- Any limitations on the availability of storage facilities in the cabin, or in the cargo bay for mobility aids, or other equipment commonly used by an individual with a disability.

- Whether the aircraft has an accessible lavatory.

Normally, advance information about the aircraft will be requested by phone. Any carrier that provides telephone service for the purpose of making reservations or offering general information must provide comparable services for hearing-impaired individuals, utilizing telecommunications devices for the deaf (TDDs), or text telephones (TTs). The TTs shall be available during the same hours that the general public has access to regular phone service. The response time to answer calls on the TT line shall also be equivalent to the response time available to the general public. Charges for the call, if any, shall be the same as charges made to the general public.

### When Advance Notice Can Be Required

Airlines may not require passengers with disabilities to provide advance notice of their intent to travel or of their disability except as provided below. Nonetheless, letting the airline know in advance how they can help you will generally result in a smoother trip.

Carriers may require up to 48 hours advance notice and one hour advance check-in from a person with a disability who wishes to receive any of the following services:

- Transportation for an electric wheelchair on an aircraft with fewer than 60 seats.

- Provision by the carrier of hazardous materials packaging for the battery of a wheelchair or other assistive device.

- Accommodations for 10 or more passengers with disabilities who travel as a group.

- Provision of an on-board wheelchair on an aircraft that does not have an accessible lavatory for persons who can use an inaccessible lavatory but need an on-board chair to do so.

Carriers are not required to provide the following services or equipment, but should they choose to provide them, they may require 48 hours advance notice, and a one hour advance check-in:

- Medical oxygen for use on board the aircraft.
- Carriage of an incubator.
- Hook-up for a respirator to the aircraft's electrical supply.
- Accommodations for a passenger who must travel on a stretcher.

Carriers may impose reasonable, nondiscriminatory charges for these optional services.

Where a service is required by the Rule, the airline must ensure that it is provided if appropriate notice has been given, and the service requested is available on that particular flight. If a passenger does not meet advance notice or check-in requirements, carriers must make a reasonable effort to accommodate the requested service, providing this does not delay the flight.

If a passenger with a disability provides the required notice but is required to fly on another carrier (for example, if the flight is cancelled), the original carrier must, to the maximum extent feasible, provide assistance to the second carrier in furnishing the accommodation requested by the individual.

It must be recognized that even when a passenger has requested information in advance on the accessibility features of the scheduled aircraft, carriers sometimes have to substitute a different aircraft at the last minute for safety, mechanical, or other reasons. It must also be recognized that the substitute aircraft may not be as fully accessible—a condition that may prevail for a number of years. On-board wheelchairs must be available on many aircraft, but it will take a number of years before movable aisle armrests are available on all aircraft with over 30 seats. Similarly, while accessible lavatories must be built into all new wide-body aircraft, they will be put into existing aircraft only when such aircraft are undergoing a major interior refurbishment.

### When Attendants Can Be Required

Carriers may require the following individuals to be accompanied by an attendant:

- A person traveling on a stretcher or in an incubator (for flights where such service is offered).

- A person who, because of a mental disability, is unable to comprehend or respond appropriately to safety instructions from carrier personnel.

- A person with a mobility impairment so severe that the individual is unable to assist in his or her own evacuation from the aircraft.

- A person who has both severe hearing and severe vision impairments which prevent him or her from receiving and acting on necessary instructions from carrier personnel when evacuating the aircraft during an emergency.

The carrier and the passenger may disagree about the applicability of one of these criteria. In such cases, the airline can require the passenger to travel with an attendant, contrary to the passenger's assurances that he or she can travel alone. However, the carrier cannot charge for the transportation of the attendant.

The airline can choose an attendant in a number of ways. It could designate an-off duty employee who happened to be traveling on the same flight to act as the attendant. The carrier or the passenger with a disability could seek a volunteer from among other passengers on the flight to act as the attendant. The carrier could provide a free ticket to an attendant of the passenger's choice for that flight segment. In the end, however, a carrier is not required to find or furnish an attendant.

The attendant would not be required to provide personal service to the passenger with a disability other than to provide assistance in the event of an emergency evacuation. This is in contrast to the case of the passenger that usually travels accompanied by a personal attendant, who would provide the passenger whatever service he or she requests.

If there is not a seat available on the flight for an attendant, and as a result a person with a disability holding a confirmed reservation is denied travel on the flight, the passenger with a disability is eligible for denied boarding compensation.

For purposes of determining whether a seat is available for an attendant, the attendant shall be deemed to have checked in at the same time as the person with the disability.

## At the Airport

### *Airport Accessibility*

Until recently, only those airport facilities designed, constructed, or renovated by or for a recipient of federal funds had to comply with federal accessibility standards. Even at federally-assisted airports, not all facilities and activities were required to be accessible. Examples are privately-owned ground transportation and concessions selling goods or services to the public. [Editor's Note: The accessibility features for over 500 airports are covered in a publication of the Airports Council International entitled *Access Travel: Airports—A Guide to the Accessibility Of Terminals*. It may be obtained by writing the Consumer Information Center, Pueblo, CO 81009.] As a result of the Air Carrier Access rules, and the Americans with Disabilities Act of 1990 (ADA) and implementing regulations, these privately-owned facilities must also be made accessible.

In general, airports under construction or being refurbished must comply with the ADA Accessibility Guidelines (ADAAG) and other regulations governing accessibility in accordance with a timetable established in the ADA. Thus, while there are still many changes to be made, the accessibility of most airports is improving. With few exceptions, the following services should be available in all air carrier terminals within the next few years:

- Accessible parking near the terminal.

- Signs indicating accessible parking, and the easiest access from those spaces to the terminal.

- Accessible medical aid facilities, and travelers aid stations.

- Accessible restrooms.

- Accessible drinking fountains.

- Accessible ticketing systems at primary fare collection areas.

- Amplified telephones and text telephones (TTs) for use by persons with hearing and speech impairments (there must be at least one TT in each terminal in a clearly marked accessible location).

- Accessible baggage, check-in, and retrieval areas.

- Jetways and mobile lounges that are accessible (at airports that have such facilities).

- Level entry boarding ramps, lifts, or other means of assisting an individual with a disability on and off an aircraft.

- Information systems using visual words, letters, or symbols with lighting and color coding, and systems for providing information orally.

- Signs indicating the location of specific facilities and services.

### *Moving through the Airport*

To make travel easier for an individual with a disability, major airports will be required to make the following services accessible under new rules being put into effect in the next several years:

- Shuttle vehicles, owned or operated by airports, transporting people between parking lots and terminal buildings.

- People movers and moving walkways within and between terminals and gates.

All carrier facilities must currently include one accessible route from an airport entrance to ticket counters, boarding locations, and baggage handling areas. These routes must minimize any extra distance that wheelchair users must travel compared to other passengers to reach these facilities. Outbound and inbound baggage facilities must provide efficient baggage handling for individuals with a disability, and these facilities must be designed and operated so as to be accessible. There must be appropriate signs to indicate the location of accessible services.

Carriers cannot restrict the movements of persons with disabilities in terminals, or require them to remain in a holding area or other location while awaiting transportation and other assistance.

Curbside baggage check-in (available only for domestic flights) may be helpful to passengers with a disability.

### *Passenger Information*

Carriers must ensure that individuals with disabilities, including those with vision and hearing impairments, have timely access to the same information provided to other passengers, including (but not limited to) information on:

- Ticketing.

- Scheduled departure times and gates.
- Change of gate assignments.
- Status of flight delays.
- Schedule changes.
- Flight check-in.
- Checking and claiming of luggage.

This information must be made available upon request. A crew member is not required to interrupt his or her immediate safety duties to supply such information.

A copy of the Air Carrier Access Rules must be made available by carriers for inspection upon request at each airport.

As previously noted, any carrier that provides telephone service for the purpose of making reservations or offering general information shall also provide text telephone (TT) service. This service for people with speech and hearing impairments must be available during the same hours that the general public has access to regular phone service, with equivalent response times and charges.

### Security Screening

An individual with a disability must undergo the same security screening as any other member of the traveling public.

If an individual with a disability is able to pass through the security system without activating it, the person shall not be subject to special screening procedures. Security personnel are free to examine an assistive device that they believe is capable of concealing a weapon or other prohibited item. If an individual with a disability is not able to pass through the system without activating it, the person will be subject to further screening in the same manner as any other passenger activating the system.

Security screening personnel at some airports may employ a hand-held device that will allow them to complete the screening without having to physically search the individual. If this method is still unable to clear the individual and a physical search becomes necessary, then at the passenger's request, the search must be done in private.

If the passenger requests a private screening in a timely manner, the carrier must provide it in time for the passenger to board the aircraft. Such private screenings will not be required, however, to a greater extent or for any different reason than for other passengers. However, they may take more time.

## *Medical Certificates*

A medical certificate is a written statement from the passenger's physician saying that the passenger is capable of completing the flight safely without requiring extraordinary medical care.

A disability is not sufficient grounds for a carrier to request a medical certificate. Carriers shall not require passengers to present a medical certificate unless the person:

- Is on a stretcher or in an incubator (where such service is offered).

- Needs medical oxygen during flight (where such service is offered).

- Has a medical condition which causes the carrier to have reasonable doubt that the individual can complete the flight safely, without requiring extraordinary medical assistance during the flight.

- Has a communicable disease or infection that has been determined by federal public health authorities to be generally transmittable during flight.

If the medical certificate is necessitated by a communicable disease (see next section), it must say that the disease or infection will not be communicable to other persons during the normal course of flight, or it shall state any conditions or precautions that would have to be observed to prevent transmission of the disease or infection to others.

Carriers cannot mandate separate treatment for an individual with a disability except for reasons of safety, or to prevent the spread of a communicable disease or infection.

## *Communicable Diseases*

As part of their responsibility to their passengers, air carriers try to prevent the spread of infection or a communicable disease on board an aircraft. If a person who seeks passage has an infection or disease that would be transmittable during the normal course of a flight, and that has been deemed so by a federal public health authority knowledgeable about the disease or infection, then the carrier may:

- Refuse to provide transportation to the person.

- Require the person to provide a medical certificate stating that the disease at its current stage would not be transmittable during the normal course of flight, or describing measures which would prevent transmission during flight.

- Impose on the person a condition or requirement not imposed on other passengers (e.g., wearing a mask).

If the individual has a contagious disease but presents a medical certificate describing conditions or precautions that would prevent the transmission of the disease during the flight, the carrier shall provide transportation, unless it is not feasible to act upon the conditions set forth in the certificate to prevent transmission of the disease.

## Getting on and off the Plane

### The Safety Briefing

FAA regulations require that carrier personnel provide a safety briefing to all passengers before takeoff. This briefing is for the passengers' own safety and is intended for that purpose only.

Carrier personnel may offer an individual briefing to a person whose disability precludes him or her from receiving the information presented in the general briefing. The individual briefing must be provided as inconspicuously and discretely as possible. Most carriers choose to offer this briefing before other passengers board the flight if the passenger with a disability chooses to pre-board the flight. A carrier can present the special briefing at any time before takeoff that does not interfere with other safety duties.

Carriers may not "quiz" the individual about the material presented in the briefing, except to the same degree they quiz all passengers about the general briefing. A carrier cannot take any adverse action against the passenger on the basis that, in the carrier's opinion, the passenger did not understand the safety briefing.

Safety briefings presented to passengers on video screens must have an open caption, or an insert for a sign language interpreter, unless this would interfere with the video or would not be large enough to be seen. This requirement takes effect as old videos are replaced in the normal course of business.

## *Handling of Mobility Aids and Assistive Devices*

To the extent consistent with various FAA safety regulations, passengers may bring on board and use ventilators and respirators, powered by non-spillable batteries. Assistive devices brought into the cabin by an individual with a disability shall not count toward a limit on carry-on items.

Persons using canes and other assistive devices may stow these items on board the aircraft, consistent with safety regulations. Carriers shall permit passengers to stow wheelchairs or component parts of a mobility device under seats, or in overhead compartments.

Carriers must permit one folding wheelchair to be stowed in a cabin closet, or other approved priority storage area, if the aircraft has such areas, and stowage can be accomplished in accordance with FAA safety regulations. If the passenger using it pre-boards, stowage of the wheelchair takes priority over the carry-on items brought on by other passengers enplaning at the same airport (including passengers in another cabin, such as First Class), but not over items of passengers who boarded at previous stops.

When stowed in the cargo compartment, wheelchairs and other assistive devices must be given priority over cargo and baggage, and must be among the first items unloaded. Mobility aids shall be returned to the owner as close as possible to the door of the aircraft (consistent with DOT hazardous materials regulations) or at the baggage claim area, in accordance with whatever request was made by the passenger before boarding.

If the priority storage accorded to mobility aids prevents another passenger's baggage from being carried, the carrier shall make its best efforts to ensure the other baggage arrives within four hours.

On certain aircraft, some assistive devices will have to be disassembled in order to be transported (e.g., electric wheelchairs, other devices too large to fit in the cabin or in the cargo hold in one piece). When assistive devices are disassembled, carriers are obligated to return them to passengers in the condition that the carrier received them (e.g., assembled).

Carriers must transport battery-powered wheelchairs, except where cargo compartment size or aircraft airworthiness considerations do not permit doing so. Electric wheelchairs must be treated in accordance with both DOT regulations for handling hazardous materials, and DOT Air Carrier Access regulations, which differentiate between spillable and non-spillable batteries:

- *Spillable batteries.* If the chair is powered by a spillable battery, the battery must be removed unless the wheelchair can be loaded, stored, secured, and unloaded always in an upright position. When it is possible to load, store, secure, and unload with the wheelchair always in an upright position and the battery is securely attached to the wheelchair, the carrier may not remove the battery from the chair.

- *Nonspillable batteries.* It is never necessary under the DOT hazardous materials regulations to remove a nonspillable battery from a wheelchair before stowing it. There may be individual cases, however, in which a carrier is unable to determine whether a battery is spillable or nonspillable. DOT has issued new rules that require new non-spillable batteries to be marked as such effective September 1995.

  The carrier may remove a particular unmarked battery from the mobility aid if there is reasonable doubt that it is nonspillable, and it cannot be loaded, stored, secured, and unloaded always in an upright position. An across-the-board assumption that all batteries are spillable is not consistent with the Air Carrier Access Rules.

  A nonspillable battery may be removed where it appears to be damaged, and leakage of battery fluid is possible.

- *Determining the battery type.* Compliance with DOT rules on the marking of nonspillable batteries is sufficient to identify a battery as nonspillable for this purpose. In the absence of such markings, carrier personnel are responsible for determining, on a case-by-case basis, whether a battery is nonspillable, taking into account information provided by the user of the wheelchair.

- *Other provisions concerning electric wheelchairs:*

  - The battery of a wheelchair may not be drained.

  - When DOT hazardous materials regulations require detaching the battery from the wheelchair, the carrier shall upon request provide packaging for the battery that will meet safety requirements.

  - Carriers may not charge for packaging wheelchair batteries.

- Carriers may require passengers with electric wheelchairs to check in one hour before flight time.

- If a passenger checks in less than one hour before flight time, the carrier shall make a reasonable effort to carry his or her wheelchair unless this would delay the flight.

- Carriers must allow passengers to provide written instructions concerning the disassembly and assembly of their wheelchairs.

Carriers may not require a passenger with a disability to sign a waiver of liability for damage or loss of wheelchairs or other assistive devices. The carrier may make note of any pre-existing defect to the device.

On domestic trips, carriers' maximum liability for loss, damage, or delay in returning assistive devices is twice the liability limit established for passengers' luggage under DOT regulations. As of 2002, the current limit for liability on assistive devices is $2,500 per passenger (i.e., two times the $1,250 limit for luggage). (As with other passenger baggage, this limit can usually be increased by purchasing Excess Valuation coverage from the airline.) The passenger should also check his or her homeowners or renters insurance to determine whether it provides additional coverage.

This expanded liability does not extend to international trips, where the Warsaw Convention applies. For most international trips (including the domestic portions of an international trip) the current liability is approximately $9.07 per pound for checked baggage and $400 per passenger for unchecked baggage.

### *Boarding and Deplaning*

Properly trained service personnel who are knowledgeable on how to assist individuals with a disability in boarding and exiting must be available if needed. Equipment used for assisting passengers must be kept in good working condition.

Boarding and exiting most medium and large-size jet aircraft is almost always by way of level boarding ramps or mobile lounges, which must be accessible. If ramps or mobile lounges are not used, a lifting device (other than a device used for freight) must be provided to assist persons with limited mobility safely on and off the aircraft.

For certain small aircrafts, at present there are few suitable devices to assist persons with limited mobility in boarding and exiting.

Lifting devices for smaller aircraft are now under development and will be put into place as soon as they become available.

Carriers do not have to hand-carry passengers on and off aircraft with fewer than 30 seats, if this is the only means of getting the person on and off the aircraft. Carrier employees may do so on a strictly voluntary basis.

In order to provide some personal assistance and extra time, the air carrier may offer a passenger with a disability, or any passenger that may be in need of assistance, the opportunity to pre-board the aircraft. The passenger has the option to accept or decline the offer.

On connecting flights, the delivering carrier is responsible for providing assistance to the individual with a disability in reaching his or her connecting flight.

Carriers cannot leave a passenger unattended for more than 30 minutes in a ground wheelchair, boarding chair, or other device in which the passenger is not independently mobile.

## On the Plane

### *Aircraft Accessibility*

Prior to the enactment of the Air Carrier Access Act of 1986, accessibility requirements for aircraft were very limited. The rules implementing that law require that new aircraft delivered after April 1992 have the following accessibility features:

- For aircraft with 30 or more passenger seats:
  - At least one half of the armrests on aisle seats shall be movable to facilitate transferring passengers from on-board wheelchairs to the aisle seat.
  - Carriers shall establish procedures to ensure that individuals with disabilities can readily obtain seating in rows with movable aisle armrests.
  - An aisle seat is not required to have a movable armrest if not feasible, or if a person with a disability would be precluded from sitting there by FAA safety rules (e.g., an exit row).

- For aircraft with 100 or more seats:
  - Priority space in the cabin shall be provided for stowage of at least one passenger's folding wheelchair. (This rule also applies to aircraft of smaller size, if there is a closet large enough to accommodate a folding wheelchair.)

75

- For aircraft with more than one aisle:

  - At least one accessible lavatory (with door locks, call buttons, grab bars, and lever faucets) shall be available which will have sufficient room to allow a passenger using an on-board wheelchair to enter, maneuver, and use the facilities with the same degree of privacy as other passengers.

- Aircraft with more than 60 seats must have an operable on-board wheelchair if

  - There is an accessible lavatory.

  - A passenger provides advance notice that he or she can use an inaccessible lavatory but needs an on-board chair to reach it, even if the aircraft predated the Rule and has not been refurbished (see below).

An aircraft delivered before April 1992 does not have to be made accessible until its interior is refurbished. At that time the relevant accessibility features shall be added.

Airplanes in the commercial fleet have their seats replaced under different schedules depending on the carrier. At the time when all seats are being replaced on an aircraft with 30 or more passenger seats, half of the aisle seats must be equipped with movable aisle armrests. This shall be done on smaller aircraft to the extent it is not inconsistent with structural, weight, balance, operational, or interior configuration limitations.

Similarly, all aircraft undergoing replacement of cabin interior elements or lavatories must meet the accessibility requirements for the affected features, including cabin storage space for a folding wheelchair, and an on-board wheelchair if there is an accessible lavatory (unless prohibited by structural, weight, balance, or configuration limitations).

### Seat Assignments

An individual with a disability cannot be required to sit in a particular seat or be excluded from any seat, except as provided by FAA safety rules, such as the FAA Exit Row Seating Rule. For safety reasons, that Rule limits seating in exit rows to those persons with the most potential to be able to operate the emergency exit and help in an aircraft evacuation. The carrier cannot deny transport, but may deny specific seats to travelers who are less than age 15 or lack the capacity to act without an adult, or who lack sufficient mobility, strength, dexterity, vision, hearing, speech, reading, or comprehension abilities to perform emergency evacuation functions. The carrier may also deny specific seats to persons with a condition or responsibilities, such as caring for small children, that might prevent the person from performing emergency evacuation functions, or cause harm to themselves in doing so.

A traveler with a disability may also be denied certain seats if:

- The passenger's involuntary behavior is such that it could compromise safety of the flight and the safety problem can be mitigated to an acceptable degree by assigning the passenger a specific seat rather than refusing service.

- The seat desired cannot accommodate guide dogs or service animals.

In each instance, carriers are obligated to offer alternative seat locations.

### Service Animals

Carriers must permit dog guides or other service animals with appropriate identification to accompany an individual with a disability on a flight. Identification may include cards or other documentation, presence of a harness or markings on a harness, tags, or the credible verbal assurance of the passenger using the animal.

If carriers provide special information to passengers concerning the transportation of animals outside the continental United States, they must provide such information to all passengers with animals on such flights, not simply to passengers with disabilities who are traveling with service animals.

Carriers must permit a service animal to accompany a traveler with a disability to any seat in which the person sits, unless the animal obstructs an aisle or other area that must remain clear in order to facilitate an emergency evacuation, in which case the passenger will be assigned another seat.

### In-Cabin Service

Air carrier personnel shall assist a passenger with a disability to:

- Move to and from seats as a part of the boarding and exiting process.

- Open packages and identify food (assistance with actual eating is not required).

- Use an on-board wheelchair when available to enable the passenger to move to and from the lavatory.

- Move to and from the lavatory, in the case of a semi-ambulatory person (as long as this does not require lifting or carrying by the airline employee).

- Load and retrieve carry-on items, including mobility aids and other assistive devices stowed on board the aircraft.

Carrier personnel are not required to provide assistance inside the lavatory or at the passenger's seat with elimination functions. The carrier personnel are also not required to perform medical services for an individual with a disability.

### Charges for Accommodations Prohibited

Carriers cannot impose charges for providing facilities, equipment, or services to an individual with a disability that are required by DOT's Air Carrier Access regulations. They may charge for optional services, however, such as oxygen and accommodation of stretchers.

### Personnel Training

Carriers must provide training on passengers with disabilities for all personnel who deal with the traveling public. This training shall be appropriate to the duties of each employee and will be designed to help the employee understand the special needs of these travelers, and how they can be accommodated quickly, safely, and with dignity. The training must familiarize employees with:

- The Department of Transportation's rules on the provision of air service to an individual with a disability.

- The carrier's procedures for providing transportation to persons with disabilities, including the proper and safe operation of any equipment used to accommodate such persons.

- How to respond appropriately to persons with different disabilities, including persons with mobility, sensory, mental, and emotional disabilities.

## Compliance Procedures

Each carrier must have at least one Complaints Resolution Official (CRO) available at each airport during times of scheduled carrier operations. The CRO can be made available by telephone.

Any passenger having a complaint of alleged violations of the Air Carrier Access rules is entitled to communicate with a CRO, who has authority to resolve complaints on behalf of the carrier.

If a CRO receives a complaint before the action of carrier personnel has resulted in violation of the Air Carrier Access rules, the CRO must take or direct other carrier personnel to take action to ensure compliance with the rule. The CRO, however, does not have authority to countermand a safety-based decision made by the pilot-in-command of an aircraft.

If the CRO agrees with the passenger that a violation of the rule occurred, he must provide the passenger a written statement summarizing the facts and what steps if any, the carrier proposes to take in response to the violation.

If the CRO determines that no violation has occurred, he must provide the passenger a written statement summarizing the facts and reasons for the decision or conclusion.

The written statement must inform the interested party of his or her right to pursue DOT enforcement action if the passenger is still not satisfied with the response. If possible, the written statement by the CRO must be given to the passenger at the airport; otherwise, it shall be sent to the passenger within 10 days of the incident.

Carriers shall establish a procedure for resolving written complaints alleging violations of any Air Carrier Access rule provision. If a passenger chooses to file a written complaint, the complaint should note whether the passenger contacted the CRO at the time of the alleged violation, including the CRO's name and the date of contact, if available. It should include any written response received from the CRO. A carrier shall not be required to respond to a complaint postmarked more than 45 days after the date of an alleged violation.

A carrier must respond to a written complaint within 30 days after receiving it. The response must state the airline's position on the alleged violation, and may also state whether and why no violation occurred, or what the airline plans to do about the problem. The carrier must also inform the passenger of his or her right to pursue DOT enforcement action.

Any person believing that a carrier has violated any provision of the rule may report the incident to the following office:

Department of Transportation
Aviation Consumer Protection
Division, C-75
400 Seventh Street, S.W.
Washington, DC 20590

## *In Conclusion*

Our work is not yet done. At the time of publication of this chapter, there remained a number of accessibility issues unresolved. These include:

- Accessible terminal transportation systems.
- Boarding chair standards.
- Accessible lavatories on narrow body aircraft.
- Open captioning for in-flight movies and videos.
- TT service on aircraft.

There are many others.

# Chapter 11

# *Disease Risks on Airlines*

## *Travel by Air: Health Considerations*

The volume of air traffic has risen steeply in recent years. The number of long-distance flights has increased greatly, and the distance that planes can fly non-stop, and therefore the duration of flights, also continues to rise. The passenger capacity of long-distance aircraft is increasing, so that larger numbers of people travel aboard a single aircraft. Frequent travelers now form a substantial proportion of the traveling public. According to the International Civil Aviation Organization, the annual number of flight passengers exceeded 1562 million in 1999 and 1647 million in 2000.

Air travel, particularly long-distance travel, exposes passengers to a number of factors that may adversely affect their health and well-being. Passengers with pre-existing health problems may find that they are more susceptible to these factors. Health risks associated with air travel can be minimized if the traveler plans carefully and takes some simple precautions before, during, and after the flight. An explanation of the various factors that may affect the health and well-being of air travelers follows.

This chapter includes three documents: "Travel by Air: Health Considerations," excerpted from *International Travel and Health*. © 2002 World Health Organization. Reprinted with permission; "Tuberculosis Risk on Aircraft," Centers for Disease Control and Prevention, reviewed July 20, 2000; and, "Guidelines for the Management of Airline Passengers Exposed to Meningococcal Disease," Centers for Disease Control and Prevention, reviewed August 8, 2000.

## *Cabin Air Pressure*

Although aircraft cabins are pressurized, cabin air pressure at cruising altitude is lower than air pressure at sea level. At a typical cruising altitude of 11,000 meters (37,000 feet), air pressure in the cabin is equivalent to that at an altitude of 1,500–2,500 meters (5,000–8,000 feet) above sea level. As a consequence, the available oxygen is reduced and gases within the body expand. The effects of reduced cabin air pressure are usually well tolerated by healthy passengers.

### *Oxygen and Hypoxia*

During all stages of flight, cabin air contains ample oxygen for healthy passengers. However, because cabin air pressure is relatively low, the oxygen saturation of the blood is slightly reduced, leading to mild hypoxia (which is reduced supply of oxygen to the tissues). Passengers with cardiovascular or respiratory disease, or certain disorders of the blood such as anemia or sickle cell disease, may not tolerate hypoxia well. Moreover, the effect of alcohol on the brain is increased by hypoxia.

### *Gas Expansion*

Air expands in all air-filled body cavities as a result of the reduced cabin air pressure. Abdominal gas expansion may cause moderate discomfort, which may be exacerbated by consumption of carbonated beverages and certain vegetables. As the aircraft ascends, air escapes from the middle ear and the sinuses, usually without causing problems. As the aircraft descends, air must be allowed to flow back into the middle ear and sinuses in order to equalize pressure differences ("clearing the ears"). Most discomfort can be alleviated by swallowing, chewing, or yawning; if the problem persists, forceful expiration against a closed nose and mouth will usually help. For infants, feeding or giving a pacifier to stimulate swallowing may reduce the symptoms.

People with ear, nose, and sinus infections should avoid flying because pain and injury may result from the inability to equalize pressure differences. If travel cannot be avoided and problems arise during flight, decongestant nasal drops may be helpful.

Individuals who have recently undergone certain types of surgery should not fly for a period of time because of possible damage resulting from gas expansion.

## Cabin Humidity

The relative humidity in aircraft cabins is low, usually less than 20%. Low humidity may cause discomfort of the eyes, mouth, and nose but presents little risk to health. Discomfort can be alleviated by maintaining good fluid intake before and during the flight, using a skin-moisturizing lotion, using a saline nasal spray to moisturize the nasal passages, and wearing spectacles rather than contact lenses.

## Dehydration

Measures should be taken to prevent dehydration during long flights. Fluid intake should consist of non-alcoholic beverages (water and fruit juices) both before and throughout the flight. As alcohol contributes to dehydration, consumption of alcohol should be restricted, and preferably avoided, before and during the flight.

## Ozone and Cosmic Radiation

The concentration of ozone (triatomic oxygen, $O_3$) and the intensity of cosmic radiation both increase with altitude. Ozone is easily converted to oxygen by heat and various catalytic processes. In modern jet aircraft, almost all ozone in the ambient air is converted to oxygen in the compressors that provide pressurized air for the cabin. During descent, when engine power is low, a build-up of ozone is prevented by catalytic converters. At usual cruising altitudes, the concentration of ozone in the cabin air is negligible.

Cosmic radiation is the sum of solar and galactic radiation. At aviation altitudes, the cosmic ray field consists of high energy-ionizing radiation and neutrons. The atmosphere and the earth's magnetic field are natural shields. Because of the orientation of the magnetic field and the "flattening" of the atmosphere over the North and South Poles, cosmic radiation levels are significantly higher at polar than at equatorial latitudes. The intensity of cosmic radiation increases with altitude and dose rates of 1–3 µSv/hour on short haul routes and 5 µSv/hour on long haul routes are typical. For comparison, the natural background radiation from soil, water and building materials is about 2 mSv per year in most countries. The International Commission on Radiological Protection has set 1 mSv per year as a basic safety standard for the protection of the health of the general public against the dangers arising from additional ionizing radiation.

## *Motion Sickness*

Except in the case of severe turbulence, travelers by air rarely suffer from motion sickness. Travelers susceptible to motion sickness should request a seat over the wing and/or a window seat and keep the motion sickness bag provided readily accessible at all times. If necessary, medication may be taken to prevent motion sickness.

## *Immobility and Circulatory Problems*

Prolonged immobility, particularly when the individual is seated, leads to pooling of blood in the legs, which in turn causes swelling, stiffness, and discomfort.

Circulatory stasis is a predisposing factor for the development of venous thrombosis (blood clots). In the case of air travel, it is possible, but not scientifically proven, that other factors in the flight environment also contribute.

Most venous thrombi do not cause any symptoms and are reabsorbed without any consequences. Occasionally, if a thrombus detaches from the lining of the vein and travels in the bloodstream to the lungs (pulmonary embolism), deep-vein thrombosis may have serious consequences including chest pain, shortness of breath, and even sudden death. This may occur many hours or even days after the formation of the thrombus.

The risk of developing deep-vein thrombosis is very small unless additional pre-existing risk factors for thromboembolism are present. These include:

- Previous history of venous thrombosis or pulmonary embolism.
- Age over 40 years (risk increases with age).
- Use of estrogen therapy (oral contraceptives or hormone replacement therapy).
- Pregnancy.
- Recent surgery or trauma, particularly abdominal or lower limb surgery.
- Cancer.
- Genetic blood-clotting abnormalities.

Some researchers also suggest that, in addition, there may be a risk from tobacco smoking, obesity and varicose veins.

84

It is advisable for people with one or more of these risk factors to seek medical advice before traveling.

*Precautions*

The negative effects of prolonged immobility can be reduced by doing simple exercises at frequent intervals during the flight. Many airlines provide helpful advice on in-flight exercises that stimulate the circulation, reduce discomfort, fatigue and stiffness, and lower the risk of developing venous thrombosis. Wearing properly fitted graduated-compression stockings specially designed for air travel may be helpful. Hand luggage should not be placed where it may restrict movement of the legs and feet. Clothing should be loose and comfortable.

Based on evidence from its post-surgical use for prevention of thrombosis, aspirin is often advised for travelers taking long-distance flights. However, there is a need for research to determine whether aspirin has any protective effect for air travelers. Aspirin should not be used by travelers with medical contraindications, such as bleeding disorders or gastric ulcer, in view of the risk of adverse side-effects. Injection of low-molecular-weight heparin products may be prescribed for some high-risk travelers.

After arrival, the traveler can reduce the effects of the journey by gentle exercise to stimulate the circulation.

## *Jet Lag*

Jet lag refers to the disruption of sleep patterns and other circadian rhythms (the body's internal clock) caused by crossing multiple time zones in a short period of time, for example, when flying east–west or west–east. The adverse effects of jet lag may lead to indigestion, general malaise, insomnia, and reduced physical and mental performance.

There are useful strategies for reducing the effects of jet lag (see below). Travelers who take medication according to a strict timetable (for example, insulin, oral contraceptives) should seek medical advice.

*General Measures to Reduce the Effects of Jet Lag*

- Be well rested before departure and have as much rest as possible during the flight, including short naps. Ensure the same total amount of sleep in every 24 hours when traveling as when staying at home.

- Drink plenty of water and/or juices before and throughout the flight.

- Eat light meals and limit consumption of alcohol before and during the flight.

- Short-acting sleeping pills may be helpful in assisting the adjustment of sleeping should be used only in accordance with medical advice. (Melatonin, at present available in very few countries [sold, but not approved by the Food and Drug Administration, in the USA] is used by some travelers to resynchronize the body's internal clock although its benefit is unproven and side-effects unknown.)

- It is not always appropriate to adjust to local time for short trips. If in doubt, seek specialist advice.

## Psychological Aspects

Despite being an increasingly common mode of transport, travel by air is not a natural activity for human beings. Air travel is frequently accompanied by psychological difficulties. The main problems encountered are stress and fear of flying. These may occur together or separately at different times before and during the period of travel.

### Flight Phobia (Fear of Flying)

A considerable proportion of the general population in industrialized countries experiences some degree of fear of flying. This may have significant adverse effects on personal and professional life.

Flight phobia is often associated with the presence of other phobias, such as claustrophobia and agoraphobia. In addition, anxiety levels may be heightened by the presence of other stress-related factors, personality disorders or an underlying psychiatric disorder. Treatment is based on identification of the cause, and desensitization is the most commonly used intervention.

Travelers who experience fear of flying but are obliged to travel by air should seek medical advice before the journey. The use of tranquillizers or beta-blocking agents may be useful in some cases. Travelers taking tranquillizers should not consume alcohol. The dose of tranquillizer should not prevent arousal of the passenger in case of an emergency.

For longer-term treatment, travelers should be advised to seek specialized treatment to reduce the impact of psychological difficulties associated with air travel. Several airlines offer desensitization training courses to reduce or cure fear of flying.

*Air Rage*

"Air rage" has been only relatively recently recognized as a form of disruptive behavior associated with air travel. It appears to be linked to high levels of general stress but not specifically to flight phobia, and is frequently preceded by excessive consumption of alcohol.

## Travellers with Special Needs

Individual airlines have different policies for the carriage of passengers with medical problems or those with special needs. Examples of commonly used guidelines are as follows.

*Infants*

Air travel is not recommended for infants less than seven days old. For premature babies, medical advice should be sought in each case.

Changes in cabin air pressure may cause distress to infants, which can be alleviated by feeding or giving a pacifier to stimulate swallowing.

Infants are more susceptible to dehydration than older children and adults. Adequate fluid intake should be maintained before and during the flight. Extra fluid (water or diluted juice) should be provided periodically during long flights.

*Pregnant Women*

Commercial flights are normally safe for mother and fetus. However, air travel is not recommended in the last month of pregnancy or until seven days after delivery. Most airlines restrict acceptance of pregnant women. The common guidelines for uncomplicated pregnancy are:

- For single pregnancies, long-distance flying until the 36th week.

- For multiple pregnancies, long-distance flying until the 32nd week.

A letter from a doctor or midwife confirming good health, normal pregnancy, and expected date of delivery should be carried after the 28th week of pregnancy. Medical clearance is required by some airlines for pregnant women if delivery is expected less than four weeks after the departure date or if any complications in delivery may be expected.

*Pre-Existing Illness*

People with diseases such as cancer, cardiovascular disorders, chronic respiratory disease, epilepsy, severe anaemia or unstable diabetes mellitus, and those who are taking immunosuppressive medication, are on renal dialysis, or whose fitness to travel is in doubt for any other reason should consult their doctor before deciding to travel by air. Medical clearance should be sought from the airline in case of doubt.

All medication for use during the journey and at the destination should be kept in the hand luggage and readily accessible at all times.

Flying is generally safe for passengers with pacemakers. Unipolar-lead pacing systems may be susceptible to electronic interference during flight and guidance on the effect of airport security screening devices should be obtained. Bipolar-lead pacing systems are not affected. However, hand-held security devices may interfere with implanted automatic defibrillators and travelers with these may find it useful to carry a physician's letter specifying this hazard.

*Smokers*

Smoking is banned on aircraft, except by a very few airlines. Smokers who regularly smoke heavily may experience stress and discomfort, particularly during long flights. Heavy smokers may benefit from medical advice before undertaking long-distance air travel. Nicotine-replacement patches or chewing-gum containing nicotine may be helpful and the use of a mild tranquillizer may be considered.

*Travelers with Disabilities*

A physical disability is not usually a contraindication for travel. Passengers who are unable to look after their own needs during the flight (including use of the toilet and transfer from wheelchair to seat and vice versa) will need to be accompanied by a competent escort. Travelers confined to wheelchairs should be advised not to dehydrate themselves deliberately before travel (as a means of avoiding use of toilets during flights).

Airlines have regulations on conditions of travel for passengers with disabilities. Disabled passengers should contact the airline in advance for guidance.

## Tuberculosis Risk on Aircraft

The CDC has been involved in a series of epidemiologic investigations related to the possibility of transmission of tuberculosis (TB) on airlines. The most recent investigation, published in the March 3, 1995 issue of the *Morbidity and Mortality Weekly Report* (*MMWR*), concluded that TB bacteria were transmitted from an infectious passenger with active TB to four other passengers during an eight and a half hour domestic airline flight.

While an earlier CDC study found that *Mycobacterium tuberculosis* was transmitted from an infectious flight attendant to other crew members who had spent significant time together, this incident is the first time that transmission of the bacteria from one passenger to another has been found. None of the passengers thought to be infected with TB during the flight has active disease. The risk of transmission on a commercial aircraft is low. There is no reason to suspect that the risk of transmission of TB on aircraft is greater than in any other confined space including other forms of public transportation if the duration is the same.

In the flight situation studied, transmission occurred because those in close proximity to the passenger with active infectious TB inhaled tiny infectious droplets produced when the infectious passenger coughed. The CDC did not study the air filtration systems in the aircraft. However, according to the airplane manufacturers, planes that recirculate air have HEPA (high-efficiency particulate air) filters in their air handling systems. HEPA filters are able to filter out TB bacteria from the air and are recommended by CDC for use in hospitals to protect persons from TB. Also, according to the Department of Transportation, the number of air exchanges per hour in airplanes exceeds the number recommended for hospital isolation rooms which are used to isolate persons with infectious TB.

To prevent possible exposure to TB aboard aircraft, CDC recommends that persons known to have infectious TB should travel by private transportation rather than commercial carrier, if travel is required. If an airline becomes aware that someone with active infectious TB has flown on a flight longer than eight hours, CDC suggests that the airline notify crew and passengers who may have worked or been seated near to the passenger with infectious TB. Anyone who is concerned about possible infection with TB should consult his/her primary health care provider or local health department and have a TB skin test.

TB is a treatable and preventable disease. Once infected, a person's body may harbor TB organisms for years, or for life, without progressing to active TB disease. In certain cases of infection, preventive treatment is recommended to prevent infection from progressing to disease.

In 1994, there were 24,361 cases of TB reported to the CDC, a 3.7% decrease from the year before. However, there was a 20% increase in the number of TB cases reported from 1985 to 1992 after a thirty year decline. The resurgence of TB was due in part to the lack of public health attention and resources directed toward this infectious disease that many believed to be on the way to elimination. This latest study regarding TB is a reminder of the importance of a sound national and international public health system for surveillance and control of infectious diseases.

## Guidelines for the Management of Airline Passengers Exposed to Meningococcal Disease

The Centers for Disease Control and Prevention receives reports of approximately 12 cases of confirmed meningococcal disease per year in which the index patient was likely contagious aboard an international conveyance. Most of these reports are received within days of transit; rarely is the diagnosis made in transit. Because of concerns about the possibility of secondary transmission to other passengers and crew, CDC is frequently asked to provide guidance on the need for antimicrobial chemoprophylaxis in these settings.

The public health decision to offer antimicrobial chemoprophylaxis should be based on an assessment of the risk of transmission in conjunction with the difficulty in identifying and notifying those passengers and the potential severity of illness. There are no documented instances of secondary disease among passengers, but, similar to household contacts, passengers who are seated next to a passenger with meningococcal disease for a prolonged flight may be at higher risk of developing meningococcal disease.

There is a need for more systematic collection of data on the risk of transmission to passenger contacts in order to provide a better basis for public health recommendations.

### Recomendations

CDC, in conjunction with the Council of State and Territorial Epidemiologists, recommends the following:

1. Household members traveling with the index patient as well as persons traveling with the index patient who have prolonged close contact (for example, roommates, members of the same sports team) should be identified and the need for antimicrobial chemoprophylaxis evaluated.

2. The health department from the state where the patient resides should be contacted promptly to facilitate antimicrobial

90

chemoprophylaxis of household members, day care center contacts, and other possible close contacts.

3. Antimicrobial chemoprophylaxis should be considered for:

- Passengers who have had direct contact with respiratory secretions from the index patient;
- Passengers seated directly next to the index patient on prolonged flights (more than eight hours).

4. CDC and state health departments should enhance surveillance for secondary cases associated with airline travel because identification of such cases would alter these recommendations. To facilitate this, state and local health departments should consider asking for recent travel history, including flight information, for all persons with meningococcal disease. The form for reporting meningitis cases to CDC should add an item on recent airline travel (within 10–14 days of onset) that includes details on flight (airline, date, time, locations). CDC should track this information to facilitate the identification of cases that may involve passengers who were on the same flight and became ill within 14 days of disembarkation.

5. Airlines should be responsible for maintaining a passenger manifest to aid in identification of passengers at risk for secondary infections. CDC should work with airlines to identify the location of potentially exposed passengers. With the assistance of the airline, CDC should identify the states where these passengers reside and contact the appropriate state and local health officials. The state or local health department will then contact passengers as necessary.

## *Background and Justification*

*Transmission of* Neisseria Meningitidis

*Neisseria meningitidis* is the leading cause of bacterial meningitis in children and young adults in the United States, with an estimated 2,600 cases each year and a case-fatality rate of 13%. *N. meningitidis* is spread through direct contact with the respiratory secretions of a patient with meningococcal disease, and antimicrobial chemoprophylaxis of persons in close contact with the index patient is the primary means for prevention of endemic meningococcal disease in the United States. Close contacts who have been identified to be at high risk of secondary disease include a) household members, b) day care center contacts, and c) anyone directly exposed to the patients' oral secretions (for example, through kissing, mouth-to-mouth resuscitation, endotracheal intubation, or endotracheal tube management). The attack rate for household contacts exposed to patients who have sporadic meningococcal disease has been estimated to be four cases per 1,000 persons exposed, which is 500–800 times greater than for the general population. Therefore, when a sporadic case of meningococcal disease occurs, the first priority for prevention of additional cases is identification of these close contacts to recommend antimicrobial chemoprophylaxis. Because the rate of secondary disease for close contacts is highest during the first few days after onset of disease in the primary patient, antimicrobial chemoprophylaxis should be administered as soon as possible (ideally within 24 hours after the case is identified). Conversely, antimicrobial chemoprophylaxis administered more than 14 days after onset of illness in the index case-patient is probably of limited value.

### Transmission of Infectious Diseases on Airplanes

At least seven investigations have examined possible transmission of *Mycobacterium tuberculosis* on airplanes (Tuberculosis and Air Travel: Guidelines for Prevention and Control. World Health Organization, 1998). One of these investigations documented transmission of *M. tuberculosis* from a symptomatic index passenger to six passengers with no other risk factors, sitting in the same section of a commercial aircraft during a long flight (more than eight hours) (*N. Engl. J. Med.* 1996, 334: 933–8).

### Rationale for Guidelines

The assessment of risk to passengers and flight crew members should be guided by two principles: the flight duration and the seating proximity to the index patient. For flights more than eight hours, passengers who are seated directly next to the index patient are more likely to be directly exposed to the patient's oral secretions and are therefore probably at higher risk than those seated farther from the index patient. In the absence of data regarding elevated risk among other passengers, antimicrobial chemoprophylaxis should be considered for those passengers seated directly next to the index patient. Given the increased frequency of ground delays prior to takeoff and after landing, one needs to count the total time and not just the air transit time; the more than eight-hour time period should include the total time from when the passengers are seated for takeoff until they disembark.

# Chapter 12

# *Discrimination on Airlines*

## *Air Travel Civil Rights Problems: Where to File Complaints*

This chapter provides contact information to help members of the public who feel they have been the subject of discriminatory action or treatment at airports file complaints with the appropriate agency in the federal government. Since the horrific attacks that occurred on September 11th, much effort has been expended by various agencies within the federal government to prevent intentional harm to our critical air transportation system. In securing our national air transportation system, we have also taken steps to ensure that all persons are provided equal protection of the laws and that no person is subject to unlawful discrimination when traveling in the Nation.

While we expect security personnel and law enforcement officials at airports to be in full compliance with the civil rights laws, we realize that, on occasion, individuals may believe they have been subjected

This chapter includes "Air Travel Civil Rights Problems: Where to File Complaints" U.S. Department of Transportation, available online at http://airconsumer.ost.dot.gov/DiscrimComplaintsContacts.htm, last updated on October 2, 2002; and "Answers to Frequently Asked Questions Concerning the Air Travel of People Who Are Or May Appear to Be of Arab, Middle Eastern or South Asian Descent and/or Muslim or Sikh," a Fact Sheet issued on November 19, 2001 by the Office of the Assistant General Counsel for Aviation Enforcement and Proceedings and its Aviation Consumer Protection Division, available online at http://www.faa.gov/acr/DOTAT-RNO.doc.

to unlawful discrimination. We also realize that with various types of security personnel and law enforcement officials at the airports, there is increased confusion regarding the appropriate place to file discrimination complaints. The Department of Transportation's Office of Aviation Enforcement and Proceedings has prepared this information sheet to assist consumers determine with whom to file a discrimination complaint and how to do so.

Complaints alleging discriminatory treatment by air carrier personnel (for example, pilots, flight attendants, gate agents or check in counter personnel) should be directed to the Department of Transportation's Aviation Consumer Protection Division. This office provides complaint forms for consumers to download and print on its website at http://airconsumer.ost.dot.gov/problems.htm. The Aviation Consumer Protection Division accepts complaints via e-mail to airconsumer@ost.dot.gov or via mail to the following address:

### Aviation Consumer Protection Division
Department of Transportation
400 7th Street, SW, Room 4107
Washington, DC 20590

Complaints alleging discriminatory treatment by Federal security screeners (for example, personnel screening and searching passengers and carry-on baggage at airport security checkpoints) should be directed to the Department of Transportation's Transportation Security Administration. The Transportation Security Administration accepts complaints via mail to the following address:

### Transportation Security Administration (TA-1)
Department of Transportation
400 Seventh St., SW
Washington, DC 20590

Complaints alleging discriminatory treatment by airport personnel (for example, airport police) should be directed to the Federal Aviation Administration's Office of Civil Rights. The Federal Aviation Administration's Office of Civil Rights accepts complaints via mail to the following address:

### Federal Aviation Administration
Office of Civil Rights
800 Independence Ave., SW., Room 1030
Washington, DC 20591

Complaints alleging discriminatory treatment by members of the National Guard should be directed to the National Guard Bureau's Equal Employment Office. The National Guard Bureau's Equal Employment Office accepts complaints via mail to the following address:

### *National Guard Bureau—EO*
Mr. Felon Page, Director
EEO Division
Jefferson Plaza 1, Room 2400
1411 Jefferson Davis Highway
Arlington, VA 22202-3231

Complaints alleging discriminatory treatment by Federal Bureau of Investigation (FBI) personnel should be directed to the Department of Justice's Office of the Inspector General and/or the Federal Bureau of Investigation's Office of Professional Responsibility. The Office of the Inspector General accepts complaints via e-mail to oig.hotline@usdoj.gov, via phone at (800) 869-4499 or via fax to (202) 616-9881 as well as via mail. The mailing addresses for these offices are:

### *Office of the Inspector General*
Department of Justice
950 Pennsylvania Ave., NW, Suite 4706
Washington, DC 20530

### *Office of Professional Responsibility*
Federal Bureau of Investigation
Department of Justice
935 Pennsylvania Ave., NW
Washington, DC 20535

Complaints alleging discriminatory treatment by Immigration and Naturalization Service (INS) personnel of the Department of Justice, including Border Patrol personnel, should be directed to the Department of Justice's Office of the Inspector General and/or the Immigration and Naturalization Service's Office of Internal Audit. The Office of the Inspector General accepts complaints via e-mail to oig.hotline@usdoj.gov, via phone at (800) 869-4499 or via fax to (202) 616-9881 as well as via mail. The mailing addresses for these offices are:

### *Office of the Inspector General*
Department of Justice
950 Pennsylvania Ave., NW, Suite 4706
Washington, DC 20530

**Office of Internal Audit**
Immigration and Naturalization Service
Department of Justice
425 I Street, NW, Room 3260
Washington, DC 20536

Complaints alleging discriminatory treatment by Customs Service officials should be directed to the Department of Treasury's Office of Internal Affairs. The Department of Treasury's Office of Internal Affairs accepts complaints via phone at 202-927-1016 or (877)-422-2557 (24 hours/day), via fax to 202-927-4607 or via mail to the following address:

**Department of Treasury**
Office of Internal Affairs
Customs Service
P.O. Box 14475
1200 Pennsylvania Avenue, NW
Washington, DC 20044

## Answers to Frequently Asked Questions Concerning the Air Travel of People Who Are Or May Appear to Be of Arab, Middle Eastern, or South Asian Descent and/or Muslim or Sikh

Since the terrorist hijackings and tragic events of September 11, the Federal Aviation Administration (FAA) has issued directives to strengthen security measures at airline checkpoints, passenger screening locations, and boarding gates. As the Department of Transportation (Department or DOT) works to strengthen transportation security in the aftermath of the horrific attacks that occurred on September 11, DOT is also continuing its efforts to ensure that those new security requirements preserve and respect the civil rights of individuals and protect them from unlawful discrimination. The Department is committed to ensuring that all persons are provided equal protection of the laws and that no person is subject to unlawful discrimination when traveling in the Nation. Various Federal statutes prohibit unlawful discrimination against air travelers because of their race, color, religion, ethnicity, or national origin.

The terrorist attacks of September 11, 2001, have raised concerns about intimidation, harassment and bias directed at individuals who are, or are perceived to be, of Arab, Middle Eastern, or South Asian descent and/or Muslim or Sikh. This chapter provides information about how the strengthened security requirements better secure our air transportation system and still fully comply with the civil rights laws by providing examples of the types of actions that airline or airport personnel may and may not take when checking in and screening passengers. The examples listed below are not all-inclusive and are simply meant to provide answers to frequently asked questions since September 11 concerning the air travel of people who are or may appear to be of Arab, Middle Eastern or South Asian descent and/or Muslim or Sikh.

### Question: What New DOT/FAA Security Restrictions on Carry-on Items Should I Be Aware of before I Fly on a Commercial Airliner?

- In addition to other weapons, knives of any length, composition or description, including Carpinus, are prohibited beyond the screener checkpoints. Knives may be placed in checked luggage.

### Question: What Are My Rights When I Fly on a Commercial Airliner?

- Individuals who may appear to be of Arab, Middle Eastern or South Asian descent and/or Muslim or Sikh have the right to be treated with the same respect as persons of other ethnicities and religions, and all persons should be treated in a polite, respectful and friendly manner.

- Persons or their property may not be subjected to inspection, search and/or detention solely because the persons appear to be Arab, Middle Eastern, Asian, and/or Muslim or Sikh; or solely because they speak Arabic, Farsi, or another foreign language; or solely because they speak with an accent that may lead another person to believe they are Arab, Middle Eastern, Asian, and/or Muslim or Sikh.

- Individuals may not be selected for additional screening based solely on appearance or mode of dress that is associated with a particular national origin or religion. For example, selecting a woman for additional screening solely because her hair is covered or she is wearing a veil, as some Muslim women do, is unlawful discrimination. Selecting a man for additional screening solely because he is wearing a long beard or hair covering, as some Muslim men do, is unlawful discrimination. Likewise, selecting a man for additional screening solely because he is wearing a turban, as some Sikh men and women do, is unlawful discrimination.

- Persons and their property may not be denied boarding or removed from an aircraft solely because the person appears to be Arab, Middle Eastern, Asian, and/or Muslim or Sikh; or solely because they speak Arabic, Farsi, or another foreign language; or solely because they speak with an accent that may lead airline or airport personnel to believe they are Arab, Middle Eastern, Asian, and/or Muslim or Sikh.

### *Question: What Can I Expect as I Go through the Security Screening Process at the Airport?*

- During the check-in process, names of passengers may be compared to an FBI watch list to ensure the safety of the traveling public.

- Knives found during the security screening of persons and their carry-on luggage will be confiscated and a ground security officer and/or law enforcement coordinator may be notified. Carpinus that are found during security screening will also be confiscated if not placed in checked luggage or removed from the airport by someone not entering the secure area.

- Some passengers will be selected for additional screening on a random basis when crossing the screener checkpoints. The additional screening often consists of the use of a hand held metal detector in conjunction with a pat-down search, and the search may become more thorough if the initial search indicates that a prohibited item may be concealed.

- Individuals who pass through a metal detector without setting off the device may be subjected to additional screening if the individual is properly selected on a truly random basis. Similarly, where a turbaned Sikh passes through a metal detector without setting off the device, the Sikh may be subjected to additional screening if the Sikh is properly selected on a truly random basis.

- Passengers who pass through a metal detector and set off the device will be subjected to additional screening through the use of a hand held metal detector if they wish to go beyond the screening checkpoint. Where a hand held metal detector is not available, the passengers will be subjected to a manual pat down as a means of ensuring that a prohibited item is not being carried. Similarly, where a turbaned Sikh passes through a metal detector and the device is set off, the screener should, where available, use a hand held metal detector around the turban to determine if there is a risk of a prohibited item being concealed.

- Passengers whose heads trigger the hand held metal detector will be subjected to a manual pat down including probing of the hair if they wish to go beyond the screener checkpoint. Similarly, where a turbaned Sikh triggers the hand held metal detector when it is near or over his or her head, then a manual pat down including probing of the turban and hair is necessary if the Sikh wishes to go beyond the screener checkpoint. Screening personnel must request permission to touch a person and his/her clothing, particularly the hair or turban of a Sikh, prior to doing so.

- In instances where a manual pat down indicates that a prohibited item may be concealed or the pat down is insufficient to make such a determination, then the passenger will be more thoroughly searched if he/she wishes to go beyond the screening checkpoint. Similarly, where a manual pat down of a turbaned Sikh's head indicates that the Sikh may be carrying a prohibited item in his/her hair or the pat down is not helpful in making such a determination, then the Sikh's turban must be searched, if the Sikh wishes to go beyond the screening checkpoint. Again, screening personnel must request permission to touch a person and his/her clothing, particularly the hair or turban of a Sikh, prior to doing so.

- If a search or inspection involving the removal of clothing is necessary for safety or security reasons, screeners should provide the person involved a choice of a public or private inspection. Private searches may be perceived to be overly intimidating while public searches may be viewed as humiliating or may violate an individual's religious tenants. For example, the removal of a Muslim woman's veil in public or in the presence of a man, not her husband, will violate her religious beliefs. Likewise, a Sikh's turban is a religious article of faith and a public search will likely create great embarrassment and fear for the Sikh. After a turban search in private, a Sikh should be provided a mirror to retie his or her turban.

- Passengers identified by the Computer Assisted Passenger Pre-screening System (CAMPS) as selectees, including those selected by a computer at random, will be subjected to additional screening at the boarding gate in addition to having their checked baggage being subject to additional security requirements. The CAMPS selection criteria have been reviewed by the Department of Justice to ensure that the methods of passenger selection are non-discriminatory and do not constitute impermissible profiling of passengers on the basis of their race, color, religion, ethnicity, or national origin. The additional screening will consist of a search of carry-on items and the search of the person through the use of a hand held metal detector in conjunction with a pat-down search. The search may become more intrusive if the initial search indicates that a prohibited item may be concealed.

## Question: How Do Screeners Determine When Additional Security Screening Is Appropriate?

- All available facts and circumstances must be taken into account in identifying persons or property that may be a safety or security risk. Although the screeners' actions could, at times, appear to be offensive to the person involved, screeners would continue to be justified in conducting additional questioning, inspections or searches, for safety or security reasons, in certain situations; for example: a person wearing a turban or head dress, while being searched at an airport security checkpoint, triggers the handheld metal detector when it is near his or her head; or a veiled woman shows photo identification to prove her identity but it is difficult to conclude that this woman is the same person as the woman in the photo without checking her face. When it is necessary to verify the identity of a veiled woman, whenever possible, her face should be checked by female safety or security personnel in private or only in the presence of other women so as not to violate her religious tenets.

- Airline and airport personnel must use the "but/for" test to help determine the justification for their actions. But for this person's perceived race, ethnic heritage or religious orientation, would I have subjected this individual to additional safety or security scrutiny? If the answer is "no," then the action may violate civil rights laws.

# Chapter 13

# *Safely Transporting Pets in Aircraft*

## Traveling with Your Pet

Dogs, cats, and most other warm-blooded animals transported in commerce are protected by the Animal Welfare Act (AWA). The U.S. Department of Agriculture's (USDA) Animal and Plant Health Inspection Service (APHIS) enforces this law. APHIS' shipping regulations help ensure that people who transport and handle animals covered under the AWA treat them humanely. Airlines and other shippers are affected by regulations established to protect the well-being of animals in transit.

### *Trip Preparation for Air Transportation*

Before taking a flight with your animal, have your veterinarian examine your pet to ensure that it is healthy enough to make the trip. Airlines and State health officials generally require health certificates for all animals transported by air. In most cases, health certificates must be issued by a licensed veterinarian who examined the animal within 10 days of transport. Ask your veterinarian to provide any required vaccinations or treatments. Administer tranquilizers only if specifically prescribed by your veterinarian and only in the prescribed dosage.

---

"Traveling with Your Pet," Animal and Plant Health Inspection Service, U.S. Department of Agriculture, Miscellaneous Publication No. 1536, issued August 1997, revised October 1998.

## *Trips Outside the Continental United States*

Hawaii, U.S. territories, and certain foreign governments have quarantine or health requirements for arriving pets. For information on Hawaii's requirements, contact your State Veterinarian's office. For U.S. territories and foreign countries, contact the appropriate embassy, governmental agency, or consulate at least four weeks in advance. You may also contact a full-service travel agency for assistance. Additional airline requirements also exist for international flights. These rules may require additional ventilation, labeling, and a shipper's certification.

Contact your airline for information about these requirements.

## *Bird Travel Abroad*

Bird owners who take their pets with them while traveling abroad are generally exempted from some of the USDA quarantine and foreign certification requirements for imported birds. This exception applies only to U.S.-origin birds and is permitted as long as the owner makes special arrangements in advance. If you wish to take your bird abroad, you must obtain all necessary documents from USDA and the Department of the Interior's U.S. Fish and Wildlife Service before departing the United States. Such preparation is especially critical for birds covered by the treaty known as the Convention on International Trade in Endangered Species. You should get a health certificate endorsed by a USDA-APHIS veterinarian. This endorsement is subject to a user fee. U.S.-origin birds may reenter the United States through any international airport that can be serviced by a USDA veterinary official. For more information on traveling abroad with your bird, contact:

*USDA-APHIS Veterinary Services*
4700 River Road, Unit 39
Riverdale, MD 20737-1231
Phone: (301) 734-5097

## *Airline Procedures*

No airline will guarantee acceptance of an animal it has not seen. Important considerations for acceptance of animals include the health and disposition of the animal, proper health certificates, and kennel markings and sizing. Airlines also require that, if wheels are installed as part of a kennel, they be removed or rendered inoperable prior to transport. This action prevents kennels from rolling, protecting both the animals and airline employees. USDA assigns airlines the final responsibility for determining the safety and compliance of the kennels they accept. Airlines generally transport animals in the cargo compartment of a plane. In doing so, the airlines advise the flight crew that animals are onboard the aircraft. Some airlines allow passengers to carry their pets in the cabin of a plane if the animals are capable of fitting under the passengers' seat. Carry-on pets are not protected under the AWA. Certain animals are accepted as baggage at passenger check-in locations, and others are accepted as cargo at the airlines' cargo facilities. For the specific requirements pertaining to your animal, make advance arrangements with the airline you are using. Airlines must ensure that they have facilities to handle animals at the airports of transfer and final destination. Airlines must comply with USDA-APHIS guidelines on allowable temperature limits for animal-holding areas. Finally, airlines are not required to carry live animals, and they reserve the right to refuse to carry an animal for any reason.

## *Pet Travel Requirements*

**Age:** Dogs and cats must be at least 8 weeks old and must have been weaned before traveling by air.

**Kennels:** Kennels must meet minimum standards for size, strength, sanitation, and ventilation.

- **Size and Strength:** Kennels must be enclosed and allow room for the animal to stand, sit, and lie in a natural position. They must be easy to open, strong enough to withstand the normal rigors of transportation, and free of objects that could injure the animal.

- **Sanitation:** Kennels must have a solid, leakproof floor that is covered with litter or absorbent lining. Wire or other ventilated sub-floors are generally allowed; pegboard flooring is prohibited. These requirements provide the maximum cleanliness for the animal in travel.

- **Ventilation:** Kennels must be well ventilated with openings that make up at least 14 percent of the total wall space. At least one-third of the openings must be located in the top half of the kennel. Kennels also must have rims to prevent ventilation openings from being blocked by other cargo. These rims, usually placed on the sides of the kennel, must provide at least three-quarters of an inch clearance.

- **Grips and Markings:** Kennels must have grips or handles for lifting to prevent cargo personnel from having to place their fingers inside the kennel and risk being bitten. Kennels also must be marked "live animals" or "wild animals" on the top and one side with directional arrows indicating proper position of the kennel. Lettering must be at least one inch high.

- **Animals per Kennel:** Each species must have its own kennel with the exception of compatible cats and dogs of similar size. Maximum numbers include two puppies or kittens under six months old and 20 pounds each and of similar size, 15 guinea pigs or rabbits, and 50 hamsters. Airlines may have more restrictive requirements, such as allowing only one adult animal per kennel. Be sure to check with the airline you are using.

### *Feeding and Watering while Traveling*

Instructions for feeding and watering the animal over a 24-hour period must be attached to the kennel. The 24-hour schedule will assist the airline in providing care for your animal in case it is diverted from its original destination. You as a pet owner or shipper are required to document that the animal was offered food and water within 4 hours of transport, and the documentation must include the time and date of feeding.

Food and water dishes must be securely attached and be accessible to caretakers without opening the kennel. Food and water must be provided to puppies and kittens every 12 hours if they are eight to 16 weeks old. Mature animals must be fed every 24 hours and given water every 12 hours.

### *Other Helpful Hints*

- As far in advance of the trip as possible, let your pet get to know the flight kennel. Veterinarians recommend leaving it open in the house with an old sock or other familiar object in it.

- At the time you make your trip reservations, advise the airline directly that you will have an animal with you. Be sure to reconfirm with the airline 24–48 hours before departure that you will be bringing your pet. Advance arrangements are not a guarantee that your animal will travel on a specific flight.

- Arrive at the airport with plenty of time to spare. If your animal is traveling as a carry-on pet or by the special expedited delivery service, check-in will usually be at the passenger terminal.

- If you are sending your pet through the cargo system, you will need to go to the airline cargo terminal, which is usually located in a separate part of the airport. Be sure to check with your airline for the acceptance cutoff time for your flight. Note that by regulation an animal may be presented for transport no more than four hours before flight time (six hours by special arrangement).

- Use direct flights whenever possible to avoid accidental transfers or delays.

- Travel on the same flight as your pet whenever possible.

- Remember that pug-nosed dogs, such as boxers and bulldogs, are more likely to experience breathing problems during transport. In the summer, choose early morning or late evening flights to avoid temperature extremes that may affect your pet. Avoid holiday traveling whenever possible.

- Carry a leash with you so that you may walk your pet before check-in and after arrival. Do not place the leash inside the kennel or attach it to the outside of the kennel.

- Do not take your pet out of its kennel inside the airport. In keeping with airport regulations and courtesy for other passengers, let your pet out only after you leave the terminal building.

- Outfit your pet with a sturdy collar and two identification tags. The tags should have both your permanent address and telephone number and an address and telephone number where you can be reached while traveling.

- Attach a label on the pet carrier with your permanent and travel addresses and telephone numbers.

- Make sure your pet's nails have been recently clipped to prevent them from hooking onto the carrier door or other openings.

- Carry a current photograph of your pet. If your pet is accidentally lost, having a current photograph will make the search easier.

- If you need to file a complaint regarding the care of your pet during transport, contact USDA-APHIS [United States Department of Agriculture, Animal and Plant Health Inspection Service].

## *If Your Pet Gets Lost*

If your pet should turn up missing during transport, immediately speak to airline personnel. Many airlines have computer tracking systems that can trace a pet transferred to an incorrect flight. Should there be no report of your animal, proceed with the following steps:

- Contact animal control agencies and humane societies in the local and surrounding areas. Check with them daily.

- Contact the APHIS Animal Care regional office closest to where your pet was lost.

- Provide descriptions and photographs to the airline, local animal control agencies, and humane societies. Help can also be sought from radio stations. Leave telephone numbers and addresses with all these people or businesses should you have to return home.

# Part Two

# Protecting Yourself during Crises and Emergencies while Traveling Abroad

# Chapter 14

# *U.S. Government Assistance Abroad*

## Chapter Contents

# Section 14.1

## *Overview: How the U.S. Government Helps in Crises Abroad*

This section includes "Crisis Abroad: What the State Department Does," Bureau of Consular Affairs, U.S. Department of State, available online at http://travel.state.gov/crisis_abroad.html, cited November 14, 2002, and "The Office of Overseas Citizens Services," Department of State Publication 10252, revised May 10, 2002.

### *Crisis Abroad: What the State Department Does*

What can the State Department's Bureau of Consular Affairs do for Americans caught in a disaster or a crisis abroad?

Earthquakes, hurricanes, political upheavals, acts of terrorism, and hijackings are only some of the events threatening the safety of Americans abroad. Each event is unique and poses its own special difficulties. However, for the State Department there are certain responsibilities and actions that apply in every disaster or crisis.

When a crisis occurs, the State Department sets up a task force or working group to bring together in one set of rooms all the people necessary to work on that event. Usually this Washington task force will be in touch by telephone 24 hours a day with our Ambassador and Foreign Service Officers at the embassy in the country affected.

In a task force, the immediate job of the State Department's Bureau of Consular Affairs is to respond to the thousands of concerned relatives and friends who begin to telephone the State Department immediately after the news of a disaster is broadcast.

Relatives want information on the welfare of their family members and on the disaster. The State Department relies for hard information on its embassies and consulates abroad. Often these installations are also affected by the disaster and lack electricity, phone lines, gasoline, etc. Nevertheless, foreign service officers work hard to get information back to Washington as quickly as possible. This is rarely as quickly as the press is able to relay information. Foreign Service Officers cannot speculate; their information must be accurate. Often this means getting important information from the local government, which may or may not be immediately responsive.

### Welfare and Whereabouts

As concerned relatives call in, officers of the Bureau of Consular Affairs collect the names of the Americans possibly involved in the disaster and pass them to the embassy and consulates. Officers at post attempt to locate these Americans in order to report on their welfare. The officers work with local authorities and, depending on the circumstances, may personally search hotels, airports, hospitals, or even prisons. As they try to get the information, their first priority is Americans dead or injured.

### Death

When an American dies abroad, the Bureau of Consular Affairs must locate and inform the next-of-kin. Sometimes discovering the next-of-kin is difficult. If the American's name is known, the Bureau's Office of Passport Services will search for his or her passport application. However, the information there may not be current.

The Bureau of Consular Affairs provides guidance to grieving family members on how to make arrangements for local burial or return of the remains to the U.S. The disposition of remains is affected by local laws, customs, and facilities which are often vastly different from those in the U.S. The Bureau of Consular Affairs relays the family's instructions and necessary private funds to cover the costs involved to the embassy or consulate. The Department of State has no funds to assist in the return of remains or ashes of American citizens who die abroad. Upon completion of all formalities, the consular officer abroad prepares an official Foreign Service Report of Death, based upon the local death certificate, and sends it to the next-of-kin or legal representative for use in U.S. courts to settle estate matters.

A U.S. consular officer overseas has statutory responsibility for the personal estate of an American who dies abroad if the deceased has no legal representative in the country where the death occurred. The consular officer takes possession of personal effects, such as convertible assets, apparel, jewelry, personal documents and papers. The officer prepares an inventory and then carries out instructions from members of the deceased's family concerning the effects. A final statement of the account is then sent to the next-of-kin. The Diplomatic

Pouch cannot be used to ship personal items, including valuables, but legal documents and correspondence relating to the estate can be transmitted by pouch. In Washington, the Bureau of Consular Affairs gives next-of-kin guidance on procedures to follow in preparing Letters Testamentary, Letters of Administration, and Affidavits of Next-of-Kin as acceptable evidence of legal claim of an estate.

### Injury

In the case of an injured American, the embassy or consulate abroad notifies the task force which notifies family members in the U.S. The Bureau of Consular Affairs can assist in sending private funds to the injured American; frequently it collects information on the individual's prior medical history and forwards it to the embassy or consulate. When necessary, the State Department assists in arranging the return of the injured American to the U.S. commercially, with appropriate medical escort, via commercial air ambulance or, occasionally, by U.S. Air Force medical evacuation aircraft. The use of Air Force facilities for a medical evacuation is authorized only under certain stringent conditions, and when commercial evacuation is not possible. The full expense must be borne by the injured American or his family.

### Evacuation

Sometimes commercial transportation entering and leaving a country is disrupted during a political upheaval or natural disaster. If this happens, and if it appears unsafe for Americans to remain, the embassy and consulates will work with the task force in Washington to charter special airflights and ground transportation to help Americans to depart. The U.S. Government cannot order Americans to leave a foreign country. It can only advise and try to assist those who wish to leave.

### Privacy Act

The provisions of the Privacy Act are designed to protect the privacy and rights of Americans, but occasionally they complicate our efforts to assist citizens abroad. As a rule, consular officers may not reveal information regarding an individual Americans location, welfare, intentions, or problems to anyone, including family members and Congressional representatives, without the expressed consent of that individual. Although sympathetic to the distress this can cause concerned families, consular officers must comply with the provisions of the Privacy Act.

# The Office of Overseas Citizens Services

## When You Need Help: Overseas Citizens Services

Overseas Citizens Services (OCS) in the State Department's Bureau of Consular Affairs is responsible for the welfare and whereabouts of U.S. citizens traveling and residing abroad. OCS has three offices: American Citizens Services and Crisis Management, the Office of Children's Issues and the Office of Policy Review and Interagency Liaison.

### American Citizens Services and Crisis Management (ACS)

American Citizens Services and Crisis Management corresponds organizationally to American Citizens Services offices set up at U.S. embassies and consulates throughout the world. ACS has five geographical divisions with case officers who assist in all matters involving protective services for Americans abroad, including arrests, death cases, financial or medical emergencies, and welfare and whereabouts inquiries. The office also issues Travel Warnings, Public Announcements and Consular Information Sheets and provides guidance on nationality and citizenship determination, document issuance, judicial and notarial services, estates and property claims, third-country representation, and disaster assistance.

*Arrests*

Over 2,500 Americans are arrested abroad annually. More than 30% of these arrests are drug related. Over 70% of drug related arrests involve marijuana or cocaine.

The rights an American enjoys in this country do not travel abroad. Each country is sovereign and its laws apply to everyone who enters regardless of nationality. The U.S. government cannot get Americans released from foreign jails. However, a U.S. consul will insist on prompt access to an arrested American, provide a list of attorneys, and provide information on the host countrys legal system, offer to contact the arrested Americans family or friends, visit on a regular basis, protest mistreatment, monitor jail conditions, provide dietary supplements, if needed, and keep the State Department informed.

ACS is the point of contact in the U.S. for family members and others who are concerned about a U.S. citizen arrested abroad.

## Deaths

Approximately 6,000 Americans die outside of the U.S. each year. The majority of these are long-term residents of a foreign country. ACS assists with the return of remains for approximately 2,000 Americans annually.

When an American dies abroad, a consular officer notifies the next of kin about options and costs for disposition of remains. Costs for preparing and returning a body to the U.S. are high and are the responsibility of the family. Often local laws and procedures make returning a body to the U.S. for burial a lengthy process.

## Financial Assistance

If destitute, Americans can turn to a U.S. consular officer abroad for help. ACS will help by contacting the destitute person's family, friends, or business associates to raise private funds. It will help transmit these funds to destitute Americans.

ACS transfers approximately 3 million dollars a year in private emergency funds. It can approve small government loans to destitute Americans abroad until private funds arrive.

ACS also approves repatriation loans to pay for destitute Americans' direct return to the U.S. Each year over $500,000 are loaned to destitute Americans.

## Medical Assistance

ACS works with U.S. consuls abroad to assist Americans who become physically or mentally ill while traveling. ACS locates family members, guardians, and friends in the U.S., assists in transmitting private funds, and, when necessary, assists in arranging the return of ill or injured Americans to the U.S. by commercial carrier.

## Welfare and Whereabouts of U.S. Citizens

ACS receives approximately 12,000 inquiries a year concerning the welfare or whereabouts of an American abroad. Many inquiries are from worried relatives who have not heard from the traveler. Others are attempts to notify the traveler about a family crisis at home.

Most welfare/whereabouts inquiries are successfully resolved. However, occasionally, a person is truly missing. It is the responsibility of local authorities to investigate and U.S. consuls abroad will work to ensure their continued interest in cases involving Americans. Unfortunately, as in the U.S., sometimes missing persons are never found.

### Consular Information Program

ACS issues fact sheets on every country in the world called Consular Information Sheets (CIS). The CIS contains information on entry requirements, crime and security conditions, areas of instability and other details relevant to travel in a particular country.

The Office also issues Travel Warnings. Travel Warnings are issued when the State Department recommends deferral of travel by Americans to a country because of civil unrest, dangerous conditions, terrorist activity and/or because the U.S. has no diplomatic relations with the country and cannot assist an American in distress.

Consular Information Sheets and Travel Warnings may be heard anytime, by dialing the Office of Overseas Citizens Services travelers' hotline at 202-647-5225 from a touchtone phone. They are also available via Consular Affairs' automated fax system at 202-647-3000, or at any of the 13 regional passport agencies, at U.S. embassies and consulates abroad, and through the airline computer reservation systems, or, by sending a self-addressed, stamped business size envelope to the Office of Overseas Citizens Services, Bureau of Consular Affairs, Room 4811, U.S. Department of State, Washington, DC 20520-4818.

If you have a personal computer and Internet access, you obtain them and other consular handouts and publications through the Consular Affairs web site at http://travel.state.gov.

### Disaster Assistance

ACS coordinates the Bureau's activities and efforts relating to international crises or emergency situations involving the welfare and safety of large numbers of Americans residing or traveling in a crisis area. Such crises can include plane crashes, hijackings, natural disasters, civil disorders, and political unrest.

## Children's Issues (CI)

The Office of Children's Issues (CI) formulates, develops, and coordinates policies and programs, and provides direction to foreign service posts on international parental child abduction and international adoptions. It also fulfills U.S. treaty obligations relating to the abduction of children.

*International Adoptions*

CI coordinates policy and provides information on international adoption to the potential parents. In 1994, over 8,000 foreign born children where adopted by U.S. citizens. The Department of State cannot intervene on behalf of an individual in foreign courts because adoption is a private legal matter within the judicial sovereignty of the country where the child resides. This office can, however, offer general information and assistance regarding the adoption process in over 60 countries.

*International Parental Child Abductions*

In recent years, the Bureau of Consular Affairs has taken action in thousands of cases of international parental child abduction. The Bureau also provides information in response to thousands of additional inquiries pertaining to international child abduction, enforcement of visitation rights and abduction prevention techniques. CI works closely with parents, attorneys, other government agencies, and private organizations in the U.S. to prevent international abductions.

The Hague Convention provides for the return of a child to his or her habitual place of residence if the child has been wrongfully removed or retained. CI has been designated by Congress as the Central Authority to administer the Hague Convention in the United States.

## Policy Review and Interagency Liaison (PRI)

The Office of Policy Review and Interagency Liaison (PRI) provides guidance concerning the administration and enforcement of laws on U.S. citizenship, and on the documentation of Americans traveling and residing abroad. The Office also provides advice on matters involving treaties and agreements, legislative matters, including implementation of new laws, conducts reconsiderations of acquisition and loss of U.S. citizenship in complex cases abroad, and administers the overseas federal benefits program.

*Consular Conventions and Treaties*

PRI works closely with other offices in the State Department in the negotiation of consular conventions and treaties, including prisoner transfer treaties.

116

As a result of these prisoner transfer treaties, many U.S. citizens convicted of crimes and incarcerated abroad have returned to the U.S. to complete their sentences.

### Federal Benefits

Over a half-million people receive monthly federal benefits payments outside the U.S. In many countries, the monthly benefits checks are mailed or pouched to the consular post and then distributed through the local postal service. In other countries, the checks are mailed directly into the beneficiaries foreign bank accounts. Consular officers assist in the processing of individual benefits claims and problems; investigate claims on behalf of the agency concerned; and perform other tasks requested by the agencies or needed by the beneficiaries or survivors.

### Legislation

PRI is involved with legislation affecting U.S. citizens abroad. The Office participates in hearings and provides testimony to Congress on proposed legislation, particularly legislation relating to the citizenship and welfare of U.S. citizens. They also interpret laws and regulations pertaining to citizens consular services, including the administration of the Immigration and Nationality Act.

### Privacy Act

PRI responds to inquires under the Privacy Act. The provisions of the Privacy Act are designed to protect the privacy and rights of Americans but occasionally complicate efforts to assist U.S. citizens abroad. As a general rule, consular officers may not reveal information regarding an individual Americans location, welfare, intentions, or problems to anyone, including family members and Congressional representatives, without the expressed consent of that individual. In all potential cases, consular officers explain Privacy Act restrictions and requirements so that all individuals involved in a case understand the Privacy Act's constraints.

## Hours of Operation

OCS is open Monday–Friday, 8:15 a.m. to 5:00 p.m. Eastern time. The OCS toll-free hotline at 1-888-407-4747 is available from 8:00 a.m. to 8:00 p.m. Eastern time, Monday–Friday, except U.S. federal holidays.

Callers who are unable to use toll-free numbers, such as those calling from overseas, may obtain information and assistance during these hours by calling 317-472-2328.

For after-hours emergencies, Sundays and holidays, please call 202-647-4000 and request the OCS duty officer.

# Section 14.2

# *Emergency Financial Assistance Abroad*

This section includes "Emergency Financial Assistance for U.S. Citizens Abroad," U.S. Department of State, available online at http://travel.state.gov/finance_assist.html, cited November 14, 2002, and "Sending Money to Overseas Citizens Services," U.S. Department of State, June 1, 2002.

**Disclaimer:** The information in this chapter is provided for general information only and may not be totally applicable in a particular case. Questions involving interpretation of specific U.S. or foreign laws should be addressed to appropriate legal counsel.

### *What Services Does the Department of State Provide to Assist U.S. Citizens Abroad Who Need Temporary Financial Assistance because They Are Destitute?*

Overseas Citizens Services, Office of American Citizen Services and Crisis Management in the U.S. Department of State, can assist U.S. citizens who are temporarily destitute abroad due to robbery or other unforeseen circumstances. If you find yourself in this situation, there are a number of alternatives available.

- **Contacting Home:** When U.S. citizens are stranded in another country, they may communicate with the American Citizen Services unit in the Consular Section of the nearest U.S. embassy or consulate for assistance in contacting their family, friends, or employer in the United States for financial help.

- **Wiring Money Directly:** You or your family, friends or associates may be able to contact Western Union or a similar commercial service which have offices in many foreign countries to wire money directly to the U.S. citizen abroad. It will be necessary for the person receiving the money to present proof of identity such as a passport.

- **Your Credit Card Company:** Another alternative is to contact your credit card company which may be able to advance you funds temporarily. If your credit card was lost or stolen, report this immediately to your credit card company. They may also be able to verify your credit card directly to your hotel or airline to enable you to checkout of your hotel, obtain replacement airline tickets, or other emergency services. It may be necessary for a person receiving funds and a new credit card to present proof of identity such as a passport. You may wish to confer with your credit card company before you travel abroad to find out what alternatives are available to you.

- **Bank to Bank Transfers:** It may also be possible to transfer funds directly from a bank in the United States to a bank in the foreign country where the U.S. citizen can receive the funds. Many foreign banks require that the U.S. citizen establish a foreign bank account to use this service. Bank to bank transfers can take several days to accomplish.

- **Send Money through the U.S. Department of State:** Family or friends may send funds to you through the U.S. embassy or consulate using the Department of State Overseas Citizens Services (OCS) Trust process: Learn About Sending Money Overseas to U.S. Citizen in an Emergency. A fee of $30.00 is charged for setting up and maintaining a trust account for one year or less to transfer funds to or for the benefit of an American in need in a foreign country. See the U.S. Department of State Schedule of Fees, 22 Code of Federal Regulations (CFR) 22.1, item No. 66. For additional information, contact the U.S. Department of State, Office of American Citizen Services and Crisis Management at 202-647-5225.

### If Family or Friends Are Unable to Provide Financial Assistance, Are There Other Services Available?

U.S. citizens destitute abroad in need of help should contact the nearest U.S. embassy or consulate or the U.S. Department of State, Overseas Citizens Services, Office of American Citizen Services and Crisis Management for information about other assistance available to eligible persons.

*If You Have a U.S. Citizen Relative or Friend Abroad in Need of Emergency Financial Assistance, Who Do You Contact at the Department of State for Help?*

Contact the Office of American Citizens Services and Crisis Management or the Consular Section (American Citizen Services Unit) at the nearest U.S. embassy or consulate. This information is listed in your U.S. passport.

## Sending Money to Overseas Citizens Services

The following are instructions for sending money to a U.S. citizen in an emergency financial situation abroad. When you use this service, a Department of State trust account is established in the recipient's name in order to forward funds overseas. There is a $30 processing fee. We do not accept personal checks. Your money order or cashier's check must be made payable to the Department of State. Upon receipt, we send a telegram to the appropriate U.S. Embassy or Consulate abroad authorizing next workday disbursement. The recipient must contact the Embassy or Consulate to arrange receipt. The forwarding of funds will be delayed if you fail to provide the recipient's name and overseas location. Funds are normally disbursed in the foreign country's currency and not in U.S. dollars.

- **Western Union:** If you have a major credit card, you may telephone Western Union at 1-800-325-6000 or 4176. Otherwise, tell your local Western Union agent that you wish to purchase a money order for the desired amount plus $30 (our fee) and made payable to the Department of State. A message with your name, address, and telephone number, as well as the name and overseas location of the recipient, must accompany the money order. Western Union charges a fee based on the amount sent. The money order and message are sent to: Overseas Citizens Services (OCS), Department of State, Washington, DC 20520. Funds are normally received electronically in OCS within several hours. We have a Western Union checkwriter in our office and an officer is available to receive funds during office hours. The U.S. embassy or consulate which is to disburse the funds will be notified and authorized to pay out the funds. However, it is important to understand that the funds are disbursed only during normal office hours, not during weekends or local holidays when the embassy or consulate is closed.

- **Bankwire:** It may take one to three days to process a bankwire transaction. If you choose this option, tell your bank that you want to wire the desired amount plus $42 to Bank of America, Department of State Branch, 2201 C St. NW, Washington, DC 20520 at 202-624-4750 via ABA Number: 114000653; Account Number: 7476363838; Account Name: PUPID State Department; Special Instructions: OCS/Trust for benefit of (recipient's name), US Embassy/Consulate (city, country); and include your name and telephone number. The wire instructions must include the recipient's full name and overseas location. Bank of America notifies our office when funds are received. The $42 fee includes our $30 fee and Bank of America's $12 wire fee.

- **Overnight Mail:** Obtain cashiers check or money order for the desired amount plus $30 (our fee), made payable to the Department of State. Attach a letter with your name, address, and telephone number, as well as the name and location of the overseas recipient. Mail to: Overseas Citizens Services, CA/OCS, Room 4811, Department of State, 2201 C St. NW, Washington, D.C. 20520. Delivery of overnight mail to CA/OCS may take two to three days.

- **Regular Mail:** Regular mail can take three to four weeks to reach CA/OCS due to on-going irradiation procedures. We strongly discourage this method for emergency use.

# Section 14.3

# *Locating Family and Friends Abroad in Emergency Situations*

"Consular Welfare/Whereabouts Services for U.S. Citizens Abroad," U.S. Department of State, available online at http://travel.state.gov/ wwflyer.html, cited November 14, 2002.

## *What Embassies and Consulates Can Do*

U.S. embassies and consulates help to locate U.S. citizens overseas when relatives or friends are concerned about their welfare or need to notify them of emergencies at home. The Department of State and U.S. embassies and consulates abroad handle over 200,000 welfare and whereabouts inquiries a year.

## *Privacy Act Issues*

The provisions of the Privacy Act require that U.S. citizens over the age of 18 must provide a written Privacy Act waiver before we can release information about them to third parties. This means that if the U.S. citizen you are looking for does not sign a Privacy Act waiver and agree to the release of information about his or her whereabouts, the U.S. Department of State and U.S. embassies and consulates abroad cannot release that information to you absent the applicability of one of the Act's conditions of disclosure. See the Department of State Prefatory Statement of Routine Uses Regarding Release of Records Under the Privacy Act. If there is no Privacy Act Waiver, we can simply confirm whether or not we were able to contact the individual, but cannot provide other information.

## *How to Request a Welfare/Whereabouts Check*

Welfare whereabouts requests may be directed to the appropriate office in the U.S. Department of State, Directorate of Overseas Citizens Services (CA/OCS).

For missing and sick adults, emergency family messages, and child abuse, neglect, abandonment or exploitation cases, and child welfare in cases not/not involving parental child abduction or custody disputes, contact of the Office of American Citizens Services at 202-647-5225/5226.

For a Child Custody/Parental Child Abduction Case of a U.S. citizen under the age of 18, phone or fax the Office of Children's Issues, (CA/OCS/CI), U.S. Department of State, 2201 C Street, NW, Washington, DC 20520-4818; Telefax: 202-312-9743; Phone: 888-407-4747 (outside the U.S. call 1-317-472-2328). If you make the request by phone, you will be asked to follow up with a written request via fax.

## *Or Contact the U.S. Embassy or Consulate*

It is also possible to contact the American Citizens Services Section of the nearest U.S. embassy or consulate directly. Telephone and fax numbers for U.S. embassies and consulates are available via our automated fax service by dialing 202-647-3000 from the phone on your fax machine.

### *What Information to Have Available before You Call*

In order to assist us in locating the U.S. citizen abroad, it is helpful to have the following information available:

- Caller's full name, address, phone number and relationship.
- Name of the Person abroad.
- Date and place of birth of the person abroad.
- Passport number (if known).
- Last known address and phone number; itinerary.
- Reason for their travel/residence abroad (business, tourism, etc.).
- Date of last contact.
- Other points of contact abroad (friends, business associates, hotel, etc.).
- If ill, where hospitalized and, if relevant to current hospitalization, the name and phone number of attending physician in the U.S.
- You may also be asked to provide a photo of the missing person.
- It may also be useful for you to contact credit card companies, telephone companies, etc. to try to determine if the missing

individual's accounts have been used recently and where those transactions occurred.

### For Emergency Family Messages Also Include

- Nature of the emergency.

- What you want the person told about the emergency.

- Name, address and telephone number and relationship of person you wish subject to call after the emergency family message is relayed to them by the U.S. embassy or consulate.

### How Will the U.S. Embassy or Consulate Try to Locate the Individual and Obtain Information about the Individual's Welfare and Whereabouts?

Consular officers will use a variety of methods to locate and confirm the welfare of the missing person, including, but not limited to:

- Using the information you provide to try to locate the person.

- Checking with local immigration and police officials if possible.

- Checking local hotels, youth hostels and other places where foreigners (U.S. citizens) are known to stay or visit.

- Checking local hospitals, jails, and, if appropriate, local morgues. (Note: In countries where a consular treaty is in force, local authorities have certain obligations to inform the nearest U.S. embassy or consulate of the arrest, injury, hospitalization, or death of a U.S. citizen.)

### Limitations on Consular Authority

- Consular authority to conduct welfare/whereabouts checks regarding U.S. citizens abroad is based on tradition, and is codified in large part in Articles 5, 36 and 37 of the Vienna Convention on Consular Relations and comparable provisions in bilateral Consular treaties. 22 Code of Federal Regulations (CFR) 71.1 and 71.6 provide that consular duties include protection of U.S. citizens abroad. The welfare whereabouts function of consular officers is described in detail in 7 Foreign Affairs Manual (FAM) 100.

- We cannot compel a U.S. citizen to speak to the consular officer, or to permit the consular officer to visit.

- We cannot compel a U.S. citizen to return to the United States. (An exception to this would be where the formal extradition of a fugitive, which is accomplished with the cooperation of foreign authorities pursuant to specific treaty obligations.)

- As noted above, we cannot release information about an individual without the individual's consent pursuant to the Privacy Act, with certain specific exceptions specified in the Privacy Act such as law enforcement requests, and where the subject's health and safety is in question.

### Runaways, Abandoned U.S. Citizen Minors, and Victims of Child Abuse or Other Crimes

- In the case of a runaway minor in a foreign country, consular officers cannot compel the return of the minor to the United States, but we try to facilitate a solution.

- We can and do work with local authorities in foreign countries to attempt to ensure the protection of U.S. citizen minors abroad.

- For young children, it is usually a relatively straightforward matter of coordinating with foreign authorities, family in the United States, and if necessary, our colleagues at the U.S. Department of Health and Human Services, the International Social Service (which works in cooperation with HHS to provide and coordinate these services for U.S. repatriates), and appropriate officials in U.S. states to arrange for the repatriation and resettlement of the U.S. citizen minor.

- For runaway teens who do not want to come home, particularly for teens over age 16, the level of assistance available from the foreign authorities varies from country to country, based on foreign laws regarding the age of consent and age of majority.

- For victims of child abuse or other crimes, we also coordinate with state child advocacy centers and our colleagues in the U.S. Department of Justice Office for Victims of Crime, and state victims of crime programs.

### Child Custody Disputes/Parental Abduction

- The recovery of a child who is the subject of a custody dispute or is the victim of parental child abduction must be done in accordance with local laws in the foreign country.

- If the parents cannot reach mutual agreement about custody of or access to their children, legal action in the foreign country may be necessary. Foreign countries may not recognize or enforce a U.S. custody order. For further information, see the Department of State, Bureau of Consular Affairs, Parental Child Abduction Internet feature. Lists of attorneys prepared by U.S. embassies and consulates abroad are also available on our home page or on request from our Office of American Citizen Services and Crisis Management at 202-647-5225.

- A consular officer cannot visit a child without permission from the child's parent, guardian or other custodian in the foreign country. If permission is refused and there is evidence of possible child abuse or neglect, the consular officer will request assistance from the appropriate local authorities. Evidence of child abuse or neglect would include, but not be limited to, police reports, medical reports, social services reports, etc.

- Consular officers at U.S. Embassies and Consulates abroad have no legal authority to obtain physical custody of abducted children and return them to a requesting parent.

- The consular officer cannot assist a parent to regain physical custody of a child by force or deception.

- The consular officer cannot provide legal advice, but can provide a list of attorneys in the foreign country.

- A consular officer is not a social worker and is not able to conduct a professional home study or similar analysis of the child's circumstances. For information about professional intercountry social work services see International Social Service (ISS) United States of America Branch.

- The consular officer will report observations made during the welfare whereabouts visit to the U.S. Department of State. This is simply a recitation of what the consular officer saw during the visit. While both parents may request to see the consular officer's report, the report is not subject to the editing by the parent(s), although parental disagreement with the report may be noted. The results of the consular welfare whereabouts visit are provided to parents upon request in the form of a letter. Official Department of State communications are not generally released except under the procedures explained below. Please note that these reports are not released to parents whose parental rights vis-à-vis the child have been legally terminated.

- The Privacy Act prohibits release of information about a U.S. citizen or Lawful Permanent Resident Alien to a third party absent a written waiver and the applicability of one of the Act's conditions of disclosure. Requests for copies of U.S. Department of State records may be made according to the Freedom of Information Act. 22 CFR 172 provides particulars regarding requests for consular records or testimony for use in a court in the United States.

# Section 14.4

# *Death while Traveling*

This section includes "Estates of Deceased U.S. Citizens," U.S. Department of State, September 1997, available online at travel.state.gov/estates.html, "Consular Report of a Death of a U.S. Citizen Abroad," U.S. Department of State, available online at http://travel.state.gov/deathrep.html, cited November 14, 2002, and "Death Overseas," Centers for Disease Control and Prevention, available online at http://www.cdc.gov/travel/other/death-overseas.htm, last reviewed February 25, 2002.

## *Estates of Deceased U.S. Citizens*

The authority and responsibilities of a U.S. consular officer concerning the personal estate of a citizen who dies abroad or who resided abroad at the time of death are based on U.S. laws, treaties, and international practice, subject to local (foreign) law (22 Code of Federal Regulations (C.F.R.) 72.16-72.55; 22 United States Code (U.S.C.) 4195–4197).

### *Notification of Next of Kin*

When a U.S. citizen dies abroad, and no legal representative is present in the country at the time of death, the consular officer usually notifies the decedent's next of kin by official telegram relayed through the Department of State in Washington, DC On the basis of instructions received from the legal representative or other qualified party, the consular officer arranges for the disposition of the remains.

### *Provisional Conservator of the Estate*

The consular officer also acts as provisional conservator of the decedent's personal effects, after receiving them from police officials, hospital authorities, tour managers, or other persons who have had temporary custody of the effects.

The consular officer usually takes physical possession of convertible assets, luggage, wearing apparel, jewelry, articles of sentimental value, non-negotiable instruments, personal documents, and other miscellaneous effects. The consular officer has no authority to withdraw funds from bank accounts in foreign countries or to obtain the face value of traveler's checks.

If the personal effects are not located within a reasonable distance from the Foreign Service post, the consular officer will request the temporary custodian of the effects to send them to the post at the expense of the estate or of the legal representative. The U.S. Government has no independent authority to pay for any expenses incurred relating to the effects of a deceased private citizen.

Large, bulky articles found in residences are seldom taken into actual possession by the consular officer. However, reasonable steps are taken to ensure that the effects are adequately safeguarded until arrangements for disposition can be made by the legal representative.

The responsibilities of a consular officer as provisional conservator include taking possession of, inventorying, and appraising personal effects, paying local debts such as hospital and hotel bills from funds available in the estate or from funds received from the legal representative, and delivering effects to the person entitled to receive them.

A legal representative, as relates to the personal estate of a deceased person, may be:

1. An executor appointed in testate proceedings;

2. An administrator appointed in intestate proceedings;

3. An agent of the executor or administrator, qualifying by power of attorney;

4. A surviving spouse;

5. A child of legal age;

6. A parent;

7. A sibling; or

8. Next of kin.

### *Entitlement to Receive Personal Estate*

The consular officer does not establish the ownership of nor entitlement to the personal estate of the person(s) who will receive it in the absence of presentation of proof of entitlement by the potential legal claimant. Depending on the value of the estate and whether there is a disagreement among claimants, the consular officer may require that a document issued under the seal and signature of a court official be submitted to establish a claimant's proof of entitlement to receive the effects. Satisfactory proof may take the form of "Letters Testamentary," which are generally issued by a U.S. court when a person has left a valid will, or "Letters of Administration," which are issued by a U.S. court when a person dies without a will or leaves no valid will. In most cases, when the monetary value of the personal estate is small, an affidavit of surviving spouse or next of kin, is sufficient to effect the release of the personal estate.

### *Shipment of Personal Effects*

After the personal effects have been inventoried and documentary proof of entitlement has been furnished, the consular officer requests instructions from the claimant regarding shipment of the effects. Because of the high costs of shipment, many persons instruct the consular officer to ship only items of commercial and sentimental value and to donate the remaining effects to a local charity or to dispose of them in another manner. In some instances a forwarding company in the foreign country must be selected by a legal claimant to ship the effects to a designated address. It is the responsibility of the forwarding company to obtain the necessary customs clearance from the country of departure. Additional customs clearance required by the United States at the port of entry is the responsibility of the person receiving the effects.

### *Questions*

For additional information, you may contact the Office of American Citizens Services at 202-647-5225 or 5226; fax: 202-647-2835.

## Consular Report of Death of a U.S. Citizen Abroad

### Foreign Death Certificate

Foreign death certificates are issued by the local registrar of deaths or similar local authority. The certificates are written in the language of the foreign country and prepared in accordance with the laws of the foreign country. Although authenticated copies of the foreign death certificate can be obtained, since the documents are written in the language of the foreign country they are sometimes unacceptable in the United States for insurance and estate purposes. In the United States, a "Report of Death of an American Citizen Abroad" issued by the U.S. consular officer is generally used in lieu of a foreign death certificate as proof of death.

### Report of Death of a U.S. Citizen Abroad

The consular "Report of Death of an American Citizen Abroad" is a report that provides the essential facts concerning the death of a U.S. citizen, disposition of remains, and custody of the personal effects of a deceased citizen. This form is generally used in legal proceedings in the United States in lieu of the foreign death certificate. The Report of Death is based on the foreign death certificate, and cannot be completed until the foreign death certificate has been issued. This can sometimes take from four to six weeks or longer after the date of the death, depending on how long it takes local authorities to complete the local form. U.S. embassies and consulates work with local authorities to see that this time is as short as possible.

### Copies of the Report of Death

U.S. consular officer will send the family up to 20 certified copies of the Report of Death at the time the initial report is issued. These are provided at no fee. Additional copies can be obtained subsequently by contacting the Department of State, Passport Services, Correspondence Branch, 1111 19th Street, NW, Suite 510, Washington, DC 20522-1705, 202-955-0307. Submit a signed, written request including all pertinent facts along with requester's return address and telephone number. Effective June 1, 2002, there is a $30 fee for a certified copy of Reports of Death, and a $20 fee for each additional copy provided at the same time. See Federal Register, May 16, 2002, Volume 67, Number 95, Rules and Regulations, Page 34831-34838; 22 Code of Federal Regulations (CFR) 22.1, Item 43 (a) and 43(f). Fees are payable to the Department of State. See also the Department of State, Consular Affairs home page on the Internet at http://travel.state.gov/ under "Passport Services" for further information about obtaining copies of Reports of Death.

### Legal Authority

U.S. insurance companies and other agencies sometimes inquire regarding the authority for issuance of Reports of Death. See 22 U.S. Code 4196; 22 Code of Federal Regulations 72.1.

### Additional Information

For additional information concerning Reports of Death, contact the appropriate geographic division of the Office of American Citizens Services and Crisis Management, Department of State, 2201 C Street NW, Room 4817 N.S., Washington, DC 20520, tel: 202-647-5225 or 202-647-5226.

## Death Overseas: Importation or Exportation of Human Remains

There are no federal restrictions on the importation of human remains, unless the cause of death was one of the following communicable diseases: cholera or suspected cholera, diphtheria, infectious tuberculosis, plague, suspected smallpox, yellow fever, or suspected viral hemorrhagic fevers (Lassa, Marburg, Ebola, Congo-Crimean, or others not yet isolated or named). If the death was the result of one of these diseases, the remains must be cremated or properly embalmed; placed in a hermetically sealed casket; and be accompanied by a death certificate, translated into English, that states the cause of death. The local mortician handling the remains following their importation will be subject to the regulations of the state and local health authorities for interstate and intrastate shipment.

The United States has no requirements for the exportation of human remains; however, travelers should be advised that the requirements of the country of destination must be met. Travelers should also be advised that information regarding these requirements may be obtained from the appropriate embassy or local consulate general.

# Chapter 15

# *Security from Terrorism while Traveling*

## *Chapter Contents*

# Section 15.1

# *How to Respond to and Prepare for Bombs and Bomb Threats*

"Fact Sheet: Terrorism," Federal Emergency Management Agency, available online at http://www.fema.gov/hazards/terrorism/terrorf.shtm, last updated September 27, 2002.

## *Before*

Learn about the nature of terrorism.

- Terrorists look for visible targets where they can avoid detection before or after an attack such as international airports, large cities, major international events, resorts, and high-profile landmarks.

Learn about the different types of terrorist weapons including explosives, kidnappings, hijackings, arson, and shootings.

Prepare to deal with a terrorist incident by adapting many of the same techniques used to prepare for other crises.

- Be alert and aware of the surrounding area. The very nature of terrorism suggests that there may be little or no warning.

- Take precautions when traveling. Be aware of conspicuous or unusual behavior. Do not accept packages from strangers. Do not leave luggage unattended.

- Learn where emergency exits are located. Think ahead about how to evacuate a building, subway or congested public area in a hurry. Learn where staircases are located.

- Notice your immediate surroundings. Be aware of heavy or breakable objects that could move, fall or break in an explosion.

### *Preparing for a Building Explosion*

The use of explosives by terrorists can result in collapsed buildings and fires. People who live or work in a multi-level building can do the following:

- Review emergency evacuation procedures. Know where fire exits are located.

- Keep fire extinguishers in working order. Know where they are located, and how to use them.

- Learn first aid. Contact the local chapter of the American Red Cross for additional information.

- Keep the following items in a designated place on each floor of the building:

  - Portable, battery-operated radio and extra batteries.

  - Several flashlights and extra batteries.

  - First aid kit and manual.

  - Several hard hats.

  - Fluorescent tape to rope off dangerous areas.

### Bomb Threats

If you receive a bomb threat, get as much information from the caller as possible. Keep the caller on the line and record everything that is said. Notify the police and the building management.

After you've been notified of a bomb threat, do not touch any suspicious packages. Clear the area around the suspicious package and notify the police immediately. In evacuating a building, avoid standing in front of windows or other potentially hazardous areas. Do not restrict sidewalk or streets to be used by emergency officials.

## During

In a building explosion, get out of the building as quickly and calmly as possible.

If items are falling off of bookshelves or from the ceiling, get under a sturdy table or desk.

If there is a fire:

- Stay low to the floor and exit the building as quickly as possible.

- Cover nose and mouth with a wet cloth.

- When approaching a closed door, use the palm of your hand and forearm to feel the lower, middle and upper parts of the door. If it is not hot, brace yourself against the door and open it slowly.

If it is hot to the touch, do not open the door—seek an alternate escape route.

- Heavy smoke and poisonous gases collect first along the ceiling. Stay below the smoke at all times.

## After

If you are trapped in debris.

- Use a flashlight.

- Stay in your area so that you don't kick up dust. Cover your mouth with a handkerchief or clothing.

- Tap on a pipe or wall so that rescuers can hear where you are. Use a whistle if one is available. Shout only as a last resort—shouting can cause a person to inhale dangerous amounts of dust.

### Assisting Victims

- Untrained persons should not attempt to rescue people who are inside a collapsed building. Wait for emergency personnel to arrive.

### Chemical Agents

Chemical agents are poisonous gases, liquids or solids that have toxic effects on people, animals or plants. Most chemical agents cause serious injuries or death.

Severity of injuries depends on the type and amount of the chemical agent used, and the duration of exposure.

Were a chemical agent attack to occur, authorities would instruct citizens to either seek shelter where they are and seal the premises or evacuate immediately. Exposure to chemical agents can be fatal. Leaving the shelter to rescue or assist victims can be a deadly decision. There is no assistance that the untrained can offer that would likely be of any value to the victims of chemical agents.

# Section 15.2

# *How to Respond to and Prepare for Biological and Chemical Threats*

This section includes "Fact Sheet: Chemical and Biological Agents," U.S. Department of State, October 2001, and "Responding to a Biological or Chemical Threat: A Practical Guide," Bureau of Diplomatic Security, U.S. Department of State, cited November 14, 2002.

## *Chemical and Biological Agents*

Some general information on chemical-biological agents (CBA) follows:

1. Biological agents can be dispersed by an aerosol spray which must be inhaled. However, these agents can also be used to contaminate food, water and other products. Attention to basic food hygiene when traveling abroad is very important.

2. Some chemical agents may be volatile—evaporating rapidly to form clouds of agent. Others may be persistent. These agents may act directly on the skin, lungs, eyes, respiratory tract or be absorbed through your skin and lungs causing injury. Choking and nerve agents damage the soft tissue in these organs.

3. When properly used, appropriate masks are effective protection to prevent the inhalation of either biological or chemical agents; however this assumes an adequate warning. Gas masks alone do not protect against agents that act through skin absorption. Those who wish to acquire protective equipment for personal use should contact commercial vendors.

4. There is an incubation period after exposure to biological agents. It is essential that you seek appropriate care for illnesses acquired while traveling abroad to assure prompt diagnosis and treatment.

5. One of the biological agents is the spore-forming bacterium that causes Anthrax, an acute infectious disease. It should be

noted, however, that effective dispersal of the Anthrax bacteria is difficult.

- Anthrax is treatable if that treatment is initiated promptly after exposure. The post-exposure treatment consists of certain antibiotics administered in combination with the vaccine.

- An anthrax vaccine that confers protective immunity does exist, but is not readily available to private parties. Efficacy and safety of use of this vaccine for persons under 18 or over 65 and pregnant women have not been determined.

- The anthrax vaccine is produced exclusively by Bioport under contract to the Department of Defense. Virtually all vaccine produced in the United States is under Defense Department contract primarily for military use and a small number of other official government uses.

For additional information, please consult your health care provider or local health authority.

## Responding to a Biological or Chemical Threat

This section provides a broad over view of the chemical and biological terrorist threat and, drawing on the lessons learned from the few chemical and biological incidents to date, suggests some basic means of detection, defense, and decontamination. The intention is not to alarm people but to enable people to recognize and properly react to a chemical or biological situation in the even they encounter one.

In 1995, the Aum Shinrikyo, a Japanese religious cult, launched a large-scale chemical attack on the Tokyo subway system. The attack focused on four stations using Sarin gas, a potent chemical warfare nerve agent. Twelve people were killed but the attack fell far short of the apparent objective to inflict thousands of casualties. Subsequent investigation by authorities revealed that the cult had previously conducted several unsuccessful attacks against a variety of targets using other chemical agents and the biological agents botulism toxin and anthrax.

Since 1997, religious organizations, health clinics, and Government agencies in Indiana, Kentucky, Tennessee, California, Hawaii, and the

District of Columbia, among other states, have received threatening letters purporting to contain the biological agent anthrax. While none of the letters were found to contain anthrax, they caused considerable fear and disruption where received.

Disturbing as they are, these incidents serve to illustrate a potentially new type of terrorist threat of concern to law enforcement and emergency planning officials throughout the U.S. Government. The State Department and its Diplomatic Security Service share that concern and have taken, and will continue to take, appropriate steps to meet the potential consequences of this threat.

Aside from their common lethality, there is no "one size fits all" when it comes to describing the types and effects of possible chemical or biological agents. Chemical agents are generally liquids, often aerosolized, and most have immediate effects or are delayed for a few hours. Many chemical agents have a unique odor and color. Biological agents differ in that the effects are delayed, often for days. The effects of toxins, such as botulinum toxin, occur typically in less than a day. Living biological agents, such as anthrax or plague, generally take 2–5 days for symptoms to appear. Biological agents have no odor or color and can be in either liquid or powder form. There are many different potential chemical and biological agents that a terrorist could use as a weapon, but we can make the following broad generalizations:

- Although food or water contamination or absorption through the skin are possible attack routes, most experts agree that inhalation of chemical or biological agents is the most likely and effective means. Protection of breathing airways is therefore the single most important factor in a situation where chemical or biological agents may be present.

- Many likely agents are heavier than air and would tend to stay close to the ground. This dictates an upward safehaven strategy.

- Basic decontamination procedures are generally the same no matter what the agent. Thorough scrubbing with large amounts of warm soapy water or a mixture of 10 parts water to 1 part bleach (10:1) will greatly reduce the possibility of absorbing an agent through the skin.

- If water is not available, talcum powder or flour are also excellent means of decontamination of liquid agents. Sprinkle the flour or powder liberally over the affected skin area, wait 30 seconds, and brush off with a rag or gauze pad. (Note: The powder absorbs the agent so it must be brushed off thoroughly. If available, rubber gloves should be used when carrying out this procedure.)

• Generally, chemical agents tend to present an immediately noticeable effect, whereas many biological agents will take days before symptoms appear. In either case, medical attention should be sought immediately, even if exposure is thought to be limited.

• Most chemical and biological agents that present an inhalation hazard will break down fairly rapidly when exposed to the sun, diluted with water, or dissipated in high winds.

• No matter what the agent or its concentration, evacuation from the area of attack is always advisable unless you are properly equipped with an appropriate breathing device and protective clothing or have access to collective protection.

## *Warning Signs of an Attack or Incident*

A chemical or biological attack or incident won't always be immediately apparent given the fact that many agents are odorless and colorless and some cause no immediately noticeable effects or symptoms. Be alert to the possible presence of agent. Indicators of such an attack include:

• Droplets of oily film on surfaces.

• Unusual dead or dying animals in the area.

• Unusual liquid sprays or vapors.

• Unexplained odors (smell of bitter almonds, peach kernels, newly mown hay, or green grass).

• Unusual or unauthorized spraying in the area.

• Victims displaying symptoms of nausea, difficulty breathing, convulsions, disorientation, or patterns of illness inconsistent with natural disease.

• Low-lying clouds or fog unrelated to weather; clouds of dust; or suspended, possibly colored, particles.

• People dressed unusually (long-sleeved shirts or overcoats in the summertime) or wearing breathing protection particularly in areas where large numbers of people tend to congregate, such as subways or stadiums.

## *What to Do in Case of Attack*

Protection of breathing airways is the single most important thing a person can do in the event of a chemical or biological incident or attack. In most cases, absent a handy gas mask, the only sure way to protect an airway is to put distance between you and the source of the agent. While evacuating the area, cover your mouth and nose with a handkerchief, coat sleeve, or any piece of cloth to provide some moderate means of protection. Other basic steps one can take to avoid or mitigate exposure to chemical or biological agents include:

- Stay alert for attack warning signs. Early detection enhances survival.

- Move upwind from the source of the attack.

- If evacuation from the immediate area is impossible, move indoors (if outside) and upward to an interior room on a higher floor. Remember many agents are heavier than air and will tend to stay close to the ground.

- Once indoors, close all windows and exterior doors and shut down air conditioning or heating systems to prevent circulation of air.

- Cover your mouth and nose. If gas masks are not available, use a surgical mask or a handkerchief. An improvised mask can be made by soaking a clean cloth in a solution of one tablespoon of baking soda in a cup of water. While this is not highly effective, it may provide some protection. Cover bare arms and legs and make sure any cuts or abrasions are covered or bandaged.

- If splashed with an agent, immediately wash it off using copious amounts of warm soapy water or a diluted 10:1 bleach solution.

- Letters from unknown sources should first be screened by security personnel. If opened, letters allegedly containing anthrax or another toxin should be handled carefully. Note if there was a puff of dust or particles from the envelope when it was opened and be sure to report that when assistance arrives. Carefully place such a letter and its envelope in a sealed plastic pouch. Thoroughly wash face and hands with warm soapy water before calling for assistance.

141

- If circumstances dictate, plan and prepare a chemical/biological safehaven in your residence using guidelines listed below.

  - At the office, familiarize yourself in advance with established emergency procedures and equipment.

  - If in a car, shut off outside air intake vents and roll up windows if no gas has entered the vehicle. Late model cars may provide some protection from toxic agents.

  - In any case of suspected exposure to chemical or biological agents, no matter what the origin, medical assistance should be sought as soon as possible, even if no symptoms are immediately evident.

### Preparing a Safehaven

In some remote but possible scenarios (such as the incident in Bhopal, India) an entire city or neighborhood could become endangered by lethal gas. If possible, you may want to plan and prepare a sealed chemical/biological safehaven at your residence as follows:

*Choosing a Safehaven Room*

- Select an inner room on an upstairs floor with the least number of windows and doors.

- Choose a large room with access to a bathroom and preferably with a telephone.

- Avoid choosing rooms with window or wall air conditioners; they are more difficult to seal.

*Sealing a Room*

- Close all windows, doors, and shutters.

- Seal all cracks around window and door frames with wide tape.

- Cover windows and exterior doors with plastic sheets (6 mil minimum) and seal with pressure-sensitive adhesive tape. (This provides a second barrier should the window break or leak).

- Seal all openings in windows and doors (including keyholes) and any cracks with cotton wool or wet rags and duct tape. A water-soaked cloth should be used to seal gaps under doors.

- Shut down all window and central air and heating units.

142

*Suggested Safehaven Equipment*

- Protective equipment—biological/chemical rated gas masks, if available; waterproof clothing including long-sleeved shirts, long pants, raincoats, boots, and rubber gloves.

- Food and water—a three-day supply.

- Emergency equipment—flashlights, battery-operated radio, extra batteries, can or bottle opener, knife and scissors, first aid kit, fire extinguisher, etc.

- Miscellaneous items—prescription medicines and eyeglasses, fan, extra blankets, passports and other important papers, television set, toys, books, and games.

Chapter 16

# Information for Travelers about Arrests in Foreign Countries

## Chapter Contents

145

# Section 16.1

## *Understanding and Obeying Local Laws*

Excerpted with permission from, "Legalities and Coping with Emergencies" http://www.studyabroad.com/handbook/legal_iss.html and "Safety and Security" http://www.studyabroad.com/handbook/safety.html, sections of the *StudyAboad.com Handbook* by Bill Hoffa. © 2000 Educational Directories Unlimited, Inc. For additional information, visit www.studyabroad.com.

While you are visiting another country you are subject to the laws of that country. Legal protection taken for granted in the United States is left behind when you leave the U.S. American embassies and consulates are very limited in the assistance they can provide: the names of competent attorneys and doctors, but not any financial assistance in paying for legal or medical services. Nor can they intervene on your behalf in the administration of justice as seen from the point of view of the host country.

Bail provisions as we know them in the United States are rare in many other countries and pretrial detention without bail is not uncommon. Prison conditions in developing or fundamentalist countries may often be deplorable, in comparison to conditions in the United States. The principle of "innocent until proven guilty" is not necessarily a tenet of legal systems abroad. The best advice is of course to know the laws and obey them scrupulously. If you get in trouble, seek local legal assistance as quickly as possible.

## *Drugs*

Avoid any possible involvement with drugs. Drug laws of course vary from country to country, but in many cases they are extremely severe, regardless of whether the drug in your possession is for personal use or for sale to others. Bail is not granted for drug-trafficking cases in most countries. Pretrial detention, often in solitary confinement, can last for months. Many countries do not provide a jury trial, and in many cases you need not even be present at your trial.

Most prison and law enforcement officials abroad will probably not speak English, the significance of which you may not fully appreciate until you are confined and feeling helpless, in very hard conditions. The average jail sentence in drug cases worldwide is about seven years. In at least four countries (Iran, Algeria, Malaysia, and Turkey) the death penalty can be imposed for conviction on some drug charges.

Do not wrongly assume that buying or carrying small amounts of drugs cannot result in their arrest. In reality, Americans have been jailed abroad for possessing as little as three grams (about one-tenth of an ounce) of marijuana.

## Crime, Violence, and Terrorism

Most countries in the world have less street crime and personal violence than is potentially present in urban and suburban America. Indeed, in many countries U.S. students report when they return that they had never felt safer in their lives. This does not mean that there is no crime and that your safety is assured—because of, or in spite of, the fact that you carry a U.S. passport in a perhaps statistically more peaceful local environment.

The simple fact of being a foreigner and not knowing quite what is and isn't safe behavior increases the possibility that you can be victimized by petty crime, such as fraud, robbery, theft, or even physical attack. Further, in certain places and at certain times, it is very possible to get caught in the midst of forms of political strife which may not be directed at you personally or even at you as an American, but nevertheless can be very dangerous.

With regard to the threat of terrorism, in those few sites where even remote danger might occasionally exist, program directors work with local police and U.S. consular personnel and local university officials in setting up whatever practical security measures are deemed prudent. In such places, you will be briefed during orientation programs and reminded at any times of heightened political tension about being security conscious in your daily activities. Terrorism is a twentieth-century reality and is not likely to diminish significantly. To succumb to the threat by reacting in fear may well be the objective that terrorists seek to achieve. Nevertheless, there are certain rather obvious precautions that American students abroad can take.

## Common Sense Precautions

- Do your homework, listen, and heed the counsel you are given.

- Keep a low profile and try not to make yourself conspicuous by dress, speech, or behavior, in ways that might identify you as a target.

- Do not draw attention to yourself either through expensive dress, personal accessories (cameras, radios, sunglasses, etc.) or careless behavior.

- Avoid crowds, protest groups, or other potentially volatile situations, as well as restaurants and entertainment places where Americans are known to congregate. Keep abreast of local news. Read local newspapers, magazines, etc. and speak with local officials to learn about any potential civil unrest. If there should be any political unrest, do not get involved.

- Be wary of unexpected packages and stay clear of unattended luggage or parcels in airports, train stations, or other areas of uncontrolled public access.

- Report to the responsible authority any suspicious persons loitering around residence or instructional facilities, or following you; keep your residence area locked; use common sense in divulging information to strangers about your study program and your fellow students.

- If you travel to countries beyond your program site and expect to be there for more than a week, register upon arrival at the U.S. consulate or embassy having jurisdiction over the location.

- Make sure the resident director, host family, or foreign university official who is assigned the responsibility for your welfare always knows where and how to contact you in an emergency and your schedule and itinerary of you are traveling, even if only overnight.

- Develop with your family a plan for regular telephone or e-mail contact, so that in times of heightened political tension, you will be able to communicate with your parents directly about your safety.

- The U.S. government monitors the political conditions in every country around the world. For current information, advisories, or warnings contact the State Department in Washington DC (202-647-4000) or the local U.S. embassy or consulate where you are.

- Be aware of local health conditions abroad: especially if you are traveling to remote areas, you should be aware of any public health service recommendations or advisories. For current health conditions abroad contact local officials, contact the country desk at the State Department (202-647-4000), or the Centers for Disease Control (404-639-3311).

- Know local laws: laws and systems of justice are not universal Do not assume that just because it is legal in the United States, that it is legal abroad.

- Use banks to exchange your money: do not exchange your money on the black market, on the street. Do not carry on your person more money than you need for the day. Carry your credit cards, etc. in a very safe place.

- Do not impair your judgment due to excessive consumption of alcohol, and do not fall under the influence of drugs.

- Female travelers are sometimes more likely to encounter harassment, but uncomfortable situations can usually be avoided by taking the following precautions: Dress conservatively. While short skirts and tank tops may be comfortable, they may also encourage unwanted attention. Avoid walking along late at night or in questionable neighborhoods. Do not agree to meet a person whom you do not know in a non-public place, be aware that some men from other countries tend to mistake the friendliness of American women for romantic interest.

## *In Case of Emergency*

### *American Embassies and Consulates*

Should you encounter serious social, political, health, or economic problems, the American Embassies and/or Consulates can offer some, but limited, assistance. They can provide the following services:

- List of local attorneys and physicians;

- Contact next of kin in the event of emergency or serious illness;

- Contact friends or relatives on your behalf to request funds or guidance;

- Provide assistance during civil unrest or natural disaster;

- Replace a lost or stolen passport.

They cannot, however, provide the services of a travel agency, give or lend money, cash personal checks, arrange free medical service or legal advice, provide bail or get you out of jail, act as couriers or interpreters, search for missing luggage, or settle disputes with local authorities. Remember that their primary occupation abroad is to help fulfill the diplomatic mission of the United States government; they are not there to play nursemaid to American travelers.

## Section 16.2

## *What to Do If Arrested*

Excerpted from the "Counterintelligence Awareness Guide" http://www.nnsi.doe.gov/C/Courses/CI_Awareness_Guide/Home.htm, produced by the Counterintelligence Training Academy, Nonproliferation and National Security Institute, Department of Energy, cited November 2002.

Foreign police and intelligence agencies can detain persons for many reasons, or for no reason other than suspicion or curiosity. In some countries where security organizations have sweeping powers to detain persons believed to be a threat to national security, virtually any government document or official statistic falls under the definition of "state secret." American standards of what is "open information" do not apply in many foreign countries.

If arrested, follow these guidelines.

- Ask to contact the nearest American embassy or consulate. As a citizen of another country, you have this right; but that does not mean that your hosts will allow you to exercise that right. If you are refused or just ignored, continue to make the request periodically until they accede and let you contact the embassy or consulate.

- Stay calm, maintain your dignity and do not do anything to provoke the arresting officer(s).

150

- Do not admit anything or volunteer any information.

- Do not sign anything. Often, part of the detention procedure is to ask or tell the detainee to sign a written report. Decline politely until such time as the document is examined by an attorney or an embassy/consulate representative.

- Do not accept anyone on face value. When the embassy or consulate representative arrives, request some identification before discussing your situation.

- Do not fall for the ruse of helping the ones who are detaining you in return for your release. They can be very imaginative in their proposals on how you can be of assistance to them. Do not sell yourself out by agreeing to anything. If they will not take no for an answer, do not make a firm commitment or sign anything. Tell them that you will think it over and let them know. Once out of their hands, contact the American embassy or consulate for protection and assistance in getting out of the country.

## Section 16.3

# *How the U.S. Government Can Help If You Are Arrested Abroad*

This section includes "Assistance to U.S. Citizens Arrested Abroad," U.S. Department of State, Document No. CA/OCS/ACS/EA., September 1997 and "Prisoner Transfer Treaties," U.S. Department of State, an undated document produced by the U.S. Department of State, available online at http://travel.state.gov/transfer.html, cited November 2002.

### *Assistance to U.S. Citizens Arrested Abroad*

The following is a summary of services that U.S. consular officers provide to U.S. citizens arrested abroad. Since conditions vary from country to country, the precise nature of services may vary likewise, depending on individual circumstances in a particular case.

151

## Summary

One of the most essential tasks of the Department of State and of U.S. embassies and consulates abroad is to provide assistance to U.S. citizens incarcerated abroad. The State Department is committed to ensuring fair and humane treatment for American citizens imprisoned overseas. We stand ready to assist incarcerated citizens and their families within the limits of our authority, in accordance with international law. We can and do monitor conditions in foreign prisons and immediately protest allegations of abuse against American prisoners. We work with prison officials to ensure treatment consistent with internationally recognized standards of human rights and to ensure that Americans are afforded due process under local laws.

## Background

While in a foreign country, a U.S. citizen is subject to that country's laws and regulations, which sometimes differ significantly from those in the United States and may not afford the protections available to the individual under U.S. law. Penalties for breaking the law can be more severe than in the United States for similar offenses. Persons violating the law, even unknowingly, may be expelled, fined, arrested, or imprisoned. Penalties for possession, use, or trafficking in illegal drugs are strict, and convicted offenders can expect jail sentences and fines. If arrested abroad, a citizen must go through the foreign legal process for being charged or indicted, prosecuted, possibly convicted and sentenced, and for any appeals process. Within this framework, U.S. consular officers provide a wide variety of services to U.S. citizens arrested abroad and their families.

## Consular Access to Prisoners

Article 36(a) of the Vienna Convention on Consular Relations of 1963, 21 USED 77, TAIS 6820, 596 UNIT 261, a multilateral treaty to which many, but not all, countries are party provides that consular officers shall be free to communicate with their nationals and to have access to them. However, Article 36(b) provides that the foreign authorities shall inform the consular officer or the arrest of a national "without delay" (no time frame specified), if the national requests such notification. Bilateral consular conventions between the United States and individual countries are more specific, requiring notification, regardless of whether the arrested person requests it, and generally specifying the time period in which such notification is to be made. When there is no treaty in force, notification and access are based on comity and largely dependent on whether the two countries have diplomatic relations.

## *Consular Services*

Consular officers abroad provide a wide variety of services to U.S. citizens incarcerated abroad. Specific services vary depending on local laws and regulations, the level of local services available in the country in question, and the circumstances of the individual prisoner. The frequency of U.S. consular visits to citizens arrested abroad may likewise vary, depending upon circumstances consular services include:

*Upon Initial Notification of Arrest*

- Visiting the prisoner as soon as possible after notification of the arrest.

- Providing a list of local attorneys to assist the prisoner obtain legal representation.

- Providing information about judicial procedures in the foreign country.

- Notifying family and/or friends, if authorized by the prisoner.

- Obtaining a Privacy Act consent.

- Relaying requests to family and friends for money or other aid.

*On-Going Support to Incarcerated Americans*

- Providing regular consular visits to the prisoner and reporting on those visits to the Department of State.

- Providing loans to qualified destitute prisoners through the Emergency Medical/Dietary Assistance (EDDA) program.

- Arranging dietary supplements (vitamins/minerals) to qualified prisoners.

- Arranging for medical and dental care if not provided by prison, to be paid for from prisoner's funds, funds provided by family or funds loaned to the prisoner by the U.S. Government under the EDDA program for destitute Americans incarcerated abroad under the conditions specified at 22 Code of Federal Regulations (CFR) 71.10.

- Arranging for examinations by an independent physician if needed.

- Arranging special family visits, subject to local law.

- Protesting mistreatment or abuse to the appropriate authorities.

- Attending the trial, if the embassy/consulate believes that discrimination on the basis of U.S. nationality might occur or if specifically requested by the prisoner or family, if possible.

- Providing information about procedures to applications for pardons or prisoner transfer treaties, if applicable.

*Discretionary Support Provided as Needed*

- Providing reading materials subject to local laws and regulations.

- Arranging with American community to provide holiday meals.

- Providing personal amenities such as stamps, toiletries, stationary, if permitted by prison authorities, from prisoner's or family's private funds.

- Assisting in finding ways to expedite prisoners' mail.

- Inquiring about the possibility of prison employment.

- Assisting in arranging correspondence courses.

- Arranging for American community volunteer visits to prisoners.

*A Consular Officer Cannot*

- Demand the immediate release of a U.S. citizen arrested abroad or otherwise cause the citizen to be released.

- Represent a U.S. citizen at trial, give legal advice or pay legal fees and/or fines with U.S. Government funds.

### Additional Information

Lists of foreign attorneys and country-specific information sheets regarding arrests abroad are available from the Department of State, Office of American Citizens Services or directly from U.S. embassies and consulates abroad. Contact information is available in the Additional Help and Information section of this *Sourcebook*.

## *Prisoner Transfer Treaties*

**DISCLAIMER:** The information in this section is provided for general information only and may not be totally applicable in a particular case. Questions involving interpretation of foreign law should be addressed to a foreign attorney.

### *Is It Possible for a Person Convicted of a Crime in One Country to Be Transferred to His/Her Home Country Where He/She Will Serve the Remainder of His/Her Sentence?*

Yes. Under U.S. law (18 United States Code [U.S.C.] §§ 4100-4115) foreign nationals convicted of a crime in the United States, and United States citizens or nationals convicted of a crime in a foreign country, may apply for a prisoner transfer to their home country if a treaty providing for such transfer is in force between the United States and the foreign country involved.

### *What Countries Does the United States Have Prisoner Transfer Treaties with at Present?*

The United States has 12 bilateral prisoner transfer treaties in force in Bolivia, Canada, France, Hong Kong S.A.R., Marshall Islands, Mexico, Micronesia, Palau, Panama, Peru, Thailand and Turkey.

In addition, the United States is a party to two multilateral prisoner transfer treaties.

1. The Council of Europe Convention on the Transfer of Sentenced Persons (or COE Convention). (Europeans countries refer to it as the Strasbourg Convention.) The COE Convention is in force in the following countries: Albania, Andorra, Armenia, Austria, Azerbaijan, Bahamas, Belgium, Bulgaria, Canada, Chile, Costa Rica, Croatia, Cyprus, Czech Republic, Denmark, Estonia, Finland, France, Georgia, Germany, Greece, Hungary, Iceland, Ireland, Israel, Italy, Latvia, Liechtenstein, Lithuania, Luxembourg, Macedonia (Former Yugoslav Republic of), Malta, the Netherlands (including Netherlands Antilles and Aruba), Nicaragua, Norway (including Bovid Island, Peter I's Island and Queen Maud Land), Panama, Poland, Portugal, Romania, Slovak Republic, Slovenia, Spain, Sweden, Switzerland, Tonga, Trinidad and

Tobago, Turkey, Ukraine, the United Kingdom (including Anguilla, British Indian Ocean Territory, British Virgin Islands, Cayman Islands, Duce and Oana Islands, Falkland Islands, Gibraltar, Henderson, Isle Of Man, Montserrat, Pitcairn, St. Helena and Dependencies and the Sovereign Base Areas of Excretory and Dhekelia on the Island of Cyprus), Yugoslavia and the United States.

2. The Inter-American Convention on Serving Criminal Sentences Abroad (or OAS Convention). The U.S. signed the OAS multilateral prisoner transfer treaty on January 10, 1995. The treaty was submitted to the U.S. Senate for advice and consent to ratification September 30, 1996. On September 27, 2000, the Senate Foreign Relations Committee approved the OAS Prisoner Transfer Treaty. The Treaty was approved by the U.S. Senate on October 18, 2000. The President signed the instruments of accession, and on May 25, 2001 at 11:30 a.m., the U.S. deposited the instruments of accession with the OAS. The Convention entered into force for the U.S. on June 24, 2001.

The OAS Convention is in force in the following countries: Brazil, Canada, Chile, Costa Rica, Mexico, Nicaragua, Panama, the United States and Venezuela.

### How Can Other Countries Enter into a Treaty Relationship with the United States to Permit Prisoner Transfer?

In recent years, it has been the posture of the United States to encourage countries which have approached us to consider acceding to a multilateral convention rather than initiating the lengthy and costly process of negotiating, signing, and ratifying new bilateral treaties. This is an area where a multilateral approach, as exemplified by the Council of Europe Convention, has proven effective in offering an existing mechanism which new states can join, as well as standardizing transfer procedures for current members.

### What U.S. Law Governs the Transfer of Prisoners to and from Foreign Countries?

The United States has enacted legislation implementing all prisoner transfer treaties. See 18 U.S.C. §§ 4100 et seq. See also 28 CFR 2.62.

## Who Must Authorize the Transfer of the Prisoner?

The consent of the U.S. Government, the foreign government and the prisoner is required for each transfer. If the person was convicted of a crime by a state in the United States, and is serving a sentence in a state facility, consent of the state is also required. The decision to transfer a prisoner is a discretionary decision to be made by each country.

## Who Is Eligible to Apply for Transfer?

A prisoner may apply for transfer to a country of which he is a citizen or national in accordance with the provisions of the governing treaty. However, a prisoner is not eligible for transfer until the judgment and sentence in his case is final; that is, when no appeals or collateral attacks are pending. Some prisoner transfer treaties require that fines imposed as part of the criminal sentence be paid prior to transfer. Depending on the provisions of the governing treaty, prisoners who are convicted of certain types of crimes (such as military offenses and political offenses) or who have less than a specified amount of time remaining on their sentences (normally six months or a year, depending on the treaty involved), are not eligible for transfer.

## How Does a Prisoner Apply for Transfer?

The transfer process for a U.S. citizen incarcerated abroad usually begins with the prisoner notifying the U.S. embassy that he/she wishes to be transferred under the treaty. Thereafter, the U.S. Department of Justice, in its discretion, determines whether a prisoner can transfer to the United States, pursuant to internal Guidelines for Evaluation of Prisoner Transfer Applications. If the U.S. Department of Justice concurs, the U.S. embassy will contact the foreign ministry. The U.S. embassy will also assist the prisoner in transmitting the necessary paperwork to the appropriate government authorities, normally the respective Attorney Generals' offices. Should the prisoner's request for transfer be approved by both governments, a consent verification hearing (CVH) will be held, and arrangements will be made between the two governments for the prisoner's transfer to be effected at a time mutually agreeable to the governments.

## What Documentation Is Required to Apply for a Transfer?

Documents required for prisoner transfer applications vary depending on the treaty and the laws or procedures of the country in which a prisoner is incarcerated. United States citizens or nationals incarcerated abroad should contact U.S. consular authorities at the U.S. embassy or consulate, who will assist inmates in obtaining the necessary documents and completing any required forms.

Foreign nationals incarcerated in the United States should consult prison authorities about their interest in transfer. In the case of foreign nationals in federal prisons, prison authorities will arrange for submission of the necessary documents to the United States Department of Justice, which serves as the Central Authority for international prisoner transfer. Documentation provided to the Department of Justice generally includes:

- Form or letter signed by prisoner indicating interest in transfer.
- Birth certificate or passport.
- Judgment or sentence.
- Pre-sentence report.
- Fingerprints and photograph.
- Sentence calculation.
- Prison progress report (security level, disciplinary reports, prison jobs, program participation, psychological evaluation, current medical condition).
- Immigration status.
- Family and residence information.

### What Happens Once a Transfer Request Has Been Approved by the United States and the Foreign Country?

Arrangements are made to conduct a consent verification hearing for the prisoner.

### What Is a Consent Verification Hearing?

United States law (18 U.S.C. § 4108) requires that a prisoner transferring into or out of the United States give his/her consent before being transferred. This is done at a hearing called a consent verification hearing (CVH). For prisoners transferring from foreign countries to the United States the CVH is normally conducted by a United States magistrate judge in the foreign country prior to the transfer date. This hearing may occur anywhere from a day or two before transfer to as much as two months before transfer. Some countries are sensitive to the idea of a United States magistrate conducting a CVH in the host country. If this poses a serious problem, another U.S. official, such as a consular officer, can be commissioned to act as the hearing officer. Prisoners seeking transfer to the United States have the right to consult an attorney, at their expense, if they wish. If they cannot afford an attorney, they may request that they be represented by a United States Public Defender. If they make such a request, the U.S. Public Defender will be appointed and will travel to the foreign country to discuss with the prisoner the effects of transferring. If the prisoner still wishes to transfer, he/she would then appear before the hearing officer at the CVH and give his/her consent to the transfer. Special arrangements are made for handling cases involving minors or the mentally ill (18 U.S.C. § 4102(8) and (9)).

### *After the Consent of a Prisoner Seeking Transfer to the United States Has Been Verified, How Is the Physical Transfer of that Prisoner Back to the United States Accomplished?*

Officials of the Federal Bureau of Prisons travel to the foreign country to escort the prisoner to the United States. The transferee returns to the United States in the custody of these officials and is placed in a federal prison. Because of security concerns, information about specific dates and timing of a transfer are not provided to the prisoner, family or other persons until the actual transfer has occurred as a matter of security policy of the Federal Bureau of Prisons.

### *Once a U.S. Citizen Has Been Transferred to the United States, How Is His/Her Foreign Sentence Administered?*

At the outset it is important to recognize that a transferred prisoner has no right to appeal, modify, set aside, or otherwise challenge his/her foreign conviction in a United States court or administrative agency after being transferred back to the United States. (18 U.S.C. § 3244(1)) Such authority remains with the courts in the sentencing country. However, the United States must execute the sentence imposed by the foreign country. To do so it must go through a careful analysis to determine how a comparable crime would be punished in the United States and then determine a release date for such an offense. The responsibility for determining the release date, as well as any period of supervised release and conditions that will apply, has been given to the United States Parole Commission, an administrative agency within the United States Department of Justice. See 18 U.S.C. § 4106A (for offenses committed on or after November 1, 1987); 18 U.S.C. § 4106 (for offenses committed before November 1, 1987).

The process for determining the release date for the transferred prisoner begins shortly after the prisoner enters the United States. Following the prisoner's return to the United States, the Federal Bureau of Prisons designates an appropriate federal institution for service of the sentence after considering a number of factors, including the nature of the offense, the sentence imposed, prior history of the prisoner, and the prisoner's home area. Next, a United States probation officer, who is located near the institution in which the prisoner is incarcerated, reviews the documents submitted by the sentencing country which describe the offense committed by the prisoner. After reviewing these materials, the probation officer interviews the prisoner and prepares a post-sentence report. The Parole Commission then schedules a special transferee hearing. Prior to this hearing, the transferred prisoner is provided with an opportunity to be represented by counsel.

At the hearing, the Parole Commission is presented with information and arguments regarding the appropriate period of imprisonment. Following the hearing, the Parole Commission deliberates and determines the date on which the prisoner will be released on supervised release. It also determines the length of the supervised release period and the conditions of supervised release. While on supervised release, the prisoner is supervised in the community for a specified period of time by a probation officer. An offender on supervised release must abide by certain terms and conditions. A violation of the conditions of supervised release could result in the revocation of the supervised release and a return to prison.

In determining an appropriate release date and the length of the supervised release period, the Parole Commission considers many factors, including the nature of the offense, whether the prisoner has accepted responsibility for his actions, and the sentence that would be applied for a comparable federal offense under the United States Sentencing Guidelines. It is important to stress that, in determining a suitable release date from the foreign sentence, the Parole Commission cannot overturn the prisoner's conviction, reduce or modify the original sentence, or make findings of fact that are inconsistent with the findings of the foreign court. Although the release date determined by the Parole Commission may sometimes be less than the duration of the sentence imposed by the foreign country, it can never be greater than the foreign sentence. 18 U.S.C. § 4106A(b)(1)(C). A transferred prisoner who is dissatisfied with the decision of the Parole Commission may appeal the decision to the United States Court of Appeals.

The Federal Bureau of Prisons will compute the sentence. The prisoner will receive credit for all the time spent in custody from the day of arrest. Additionally, the release date set by the Parole Commission may be reduced by any foreign labor and good time credits earned prior to the transfer. The prisoner will also received good time credits earned in the United States. 18 U.S.C. § 4105. (A transferred prisoner, like all regular federal prisoners, is expected to abide by prison rules and, if he fails to do so, he/she risks losing good conduct time credits.)

After a prisoner is released from the custody of the Bureau of Prisons, a probation officer, usually from the prisoner's home district, will be responsible for supervising the prisoner during any period of supervised release that has been imposed. During this period the offender must report regularly to the probation officer and must abide by all of the conditions that have been imposed in connection with the term of supervised release. Failure to do so could result in a United States court revoking the supervised release and returning the offender to prison to serve the remainder of the sentence.

Additional questions regarding this subject should be directed to the United States parole Commission. For additional information see the United States Parole Commission website at http://www.usdoj.gov/uspc.

### Are U.S. Military Personnel Governed by Prisoner Transfer Treaties?

Yes. 10 U.S.C. § 955 provides that prisoner transfer treaties do apply to U.S. military personnel.

# Section 16.4

# *Avoiding Drug Arrests Abroad*

This section includes "Travel Warnings on Drugs Abroad," United States Department of State, Bureau of Consular Affairs, February 2000, and "Medications/Drugs," by the U.S. Customs and Border Protection, located at http://www.customs.gov/xp/cgov/travel/alerts/medication_drugs.xml, cited November 2002.

## *Travel Warning on Drugs Abroad*

### *Hard Facts*

Each year, 2,500 Americans are arrested overseas. One third of the arrests are on drug-related charges. Many of those arrested assumed as U.S. citizens that they could not be arrested. From Asia to Africa, Europe to South America, U.S. citizens are finding out the hard way that drug possession or trafficking equals jail in foreign countries.

There is very little that anyone can do to help you if you are caught with drugs.

It is your responsibility to know what the drug laws are in a foreign country before you go, because "I didn't know it was illegal" will not get you out of jail.

In recent years, there has been an increase in the number of women arrested abroad. The rise is a result of women who serve as drug couriers or "mules" in the belief they can make quick money and have a vacation without getting caught. Instead of a short vacation, they get a lengthy stay or life sentence in a foreign jail.

A number of the Americans arrested abroad on drug charges in 1994 possessed marijuana. Many of these possessed one ounce or less of the substance. The risk of being put in jail for just one marijuana cigarette is not worth it.

If you are purchasing prescription medications in quantities larger than that considered necessary for personal use, you could be arrested on suspicion of drug trafficking.

Once you're arrested, the American consular officer cannot get you out!

You may say "it couldn't happen to me" but the fact is that it could happen to you if you find yourself saying one of the following:

*"I'm an American citizen and no foreign government can put me in their jail."*

*"If I only buy or carry a small amount, it won't be a problem."*

If you are arrested on a drug charge it is important that you know what your government can and cannot do for you.

### The U.S. Consular Officer Can

- Visit you in jail after being notified of your arrest.

- Give you a list of local attorneys (The U.S. Government cannot assume responsibility for the professional ability or integrity of these individuals or recommend a particular attorney.)

- Notify your family and/or friends and relay requests for money or other aid—but only with your authorization.

- Intercede with local authorities to make sure that your rights under local law are fully observed and that you are treated humanely, according to internationally accepted standards.

- Protest mistreatment or abuse to the appropriate authorities.

### The U.S. Consular Officer Cannot

- Demand your immediate release or get you out of jail or the country.

- Represent you at trial or give legal counsel.

- Pay legal fees and/or fines with U.S. Government funds.

If you are caught buying, selling, carrying or using drugs (from hashish to heroin, marijuana to mescaline, cocaine to quaaludes, to designer drugs like ecstacy) it could mean:

- **Interrogation and Delays Before Trial:** including mistreatment and solitary confinement for up to one year under very primitive conditions.

- **Lengthy Trials:** conducted in a foreign language, with delays and postponements.

163

- **Weeks, Months or Life in Prison:** some places include hard labor, heavy fines, and/or lashings, if found guilty.

- **The Death Penalty:** in a growing number of countries (for example, Malaysia, Pakistan and Turkey).

Although drug laws vary from country to country, it is important to realize before you make the mistake of getting involved with drugs that foreign countries do not react lightly to drug offenders. In some countries, anyone who is caught with even a very small quantity for personal use may be tried and receive the same sentence as the large-scale trafficker.

## *Don't Let Your Trip Abroad Become a Nightmare*

This information has been provided to inform you before it is too late. So think first!

- A number of countries, including the Bahamas, the Dominican Republic, Jamaica, Mexico and the Philippines, have enacted more stringent drug laws which impose mandatory jail sentences for individuals convicted of possessing even small amounts of marijuana or cocaine for personal use.

- Once you leave the United States, you are not covered by U.S. laws and constitutional rights.

- Bail is not granted in many countries when drugs are involved.

- The burden of proof in many countries is on the accused to prove his/her innocence.

- In some countries, evidence obtained illegally by local authorities may be admissible in court.

- Few countries offer drug offenders jury trials or even require the prisoner's presence at his/her trial.

- Many countries have mandatory prison sentences of seven years or life, without the possibility of parole for drug violations.

## *Remember*

- If someone offers you a free trip and some quick and easy money just for bringing back a suitcase.... Say No!

- Don't carry a package for anyone, no matter how small it might seem.

- The police and customs officials have a right to search your luggage for drugs. If they find drugs in your suitcase, you will suffer the consequences.

- You could go to jail for years and years with no possibility of parole, early release or transfer back to the U.S.

- Don't make a jail sentence part of your trip abroad.

## Importation of Prescription Medication/Drugs

### Consumer Alert

The U.S. Customs Service enforces Federal laws and regulations, including those of the Drug Enforcement Administration (DEA) and the Food and Drug Administration (FDA).

A new bill was recently passed by Congress that amends a portion of the Controlled Substances Act (21 United States Code [U.S.C] 956(a)). This amendment allows a United States resident to import up to 50 dosage units of a controlled medication without a valid prescription at an international land border. These medications must be declared upon arrival, be for your own personal use and in their original container. However, travelers should be aware that drug products which are not approved by the U.S. Food and Drug Administration may not be acceptable for such importation. FDA warns that such drugs are often of unknown quality and discourages buying drugs sold in foreign countries. Please go to http://www.fda.gov/ora/import/purchasing_medications.htm for further information.

The United States Federal Food, Drug, and Cosmetic Act (21 U.S.C. sections 331(d), and 355(a)), which is administered by FDA, prohibits the interstate shipment (which includes importation) of unapproved new drugs. Unapproved new drugs are any drugs, including foreign-made versions of U.S. approved drugs, that have not received FDA approval to demonstrate they meet the federal requirements for safety and effectiveness. It is the importer's obligation to demonstrate to FDA that any drugs offered for importation have been approved by FDA.

FDA has developed guidance entitled "Coverage of Personal Importations" which sets forth that agency's enforcement priorities with respect to the personal importation of unapproved new drugs by individuals for their personal use. The guidance identifies circumstances in which FDA may consider exercising enforcement discretion and refrain from taking legal action against illegally imported drugs. Those circumstances are as follows:

1.   The intended use (of the drug) is unapproved and for a serious condition for which effective treatment may not be available domestically either through commercial or clinical means;

2.   There is no known commercialization or promotion to persons residing in the U.S. by those involved in the distribution of the product at issue;

3.   The product is considered not to represent an unreasonable risk;

4.   The individual seeking to import the product affirms in writing that it is for the patient's own use (generally not more than a 3-month supply) and provides the name and address of the doctor licensed in the U.S. responsible for his or her treatment with the product, or provides evidence that the product is for the continuation of a treatment begun in a foreign country.

FDA's guidance is not, however, a license for individuals to import unapproved (and therefore illegal) drugs for personal use into the U.S. Even if all of the factors noted in the guidance are present, the drugs remain illegal and FDA may decide that such drugs should be refused entry or seized. The guidance represents FDA's current thinking regarding the issues of personal importation and is intended only to provide operating guidance for FDA personnel. The guidance does not create any legally enforceable rights for the public; nor does it operate to bind FDA or the public.

To avoid travel delays and to prevent possible harm from taking unsafe or ineffective medications, residents and visitors upon arrival to or departure from the U.S. should keep in mind the following precautions:

- Do not assume that medications which are legal in foreign countries are also approved for use in the United States. These products may be illegal and may include addictive and dangerous substances;

- Be aware that the labeled uses (conditions for which the product is represented to be effective) for a product purchased outside the U.S. may not be approved in the United States;

- It can be dangerous to take some medications without medical supervision. The reason why some medications are limited to prescription use in the United States is that either they are unsafe without medical supervision or a medical diagnosis is required to ensure that the medication is appropriate for your condition;

- Avoid purchasing any drug products that they do not approve for sale in the U.S. (including foreign-manufactured versions of U.S. approved drugs). FDA cannot assure that these products conform to the manufacturing and quality assurance procedures mandated by U.S. laws and regulations and, therefore, these products may be unsafe. In addition, such products are illegal in the U.S. and, therefore, may be subject to entry refusal;

- Some medications which may appear to be U.S. approved drug products may in fact be counterfeit versions of such products. (The term "counterfeit drug" is defined as "a drug which, or the container or labeling of which, without authorization, bears the trademark, trade name, or other identifying mark, imprint, or device, or any likeness thereof, of a drug manufacturer, processor, packer, or distributor other than the person or persons who in fact manufactured, processed, packed, or distributed such drug and which thereby falsely purports or is represented to be the product of, or to have been packed or distributed by, such other drug manufacturer, processor, packer, or distributor." See 21 U.S.C. 321(g)(2));

- In the event you develop complications from using a medication which require medical attention, your treatment could be delayed or made more difficult unless there is sufficient information available about the product, such as the generic name of the product, dosage form and strength, and how often you need to take the product.

- Possession of certain medications without a prescription from a physician licensed in the United States may violate Federal, State, and/or local laws;

- It is important to have medications in the originally dispensed container;

- FDA's personal importation guidance provides that when bringing unapproved drugs into the U.S. for use in treating serious or life threatening illness, such products should be used under the care and supervision of a U.S. licensed physician. It is advisable to make available for examination by U.S. Customs Inspectors

167

or other appropriate government authorities appropriate documentation of such monitoring;

- It is against the law not to properly declare imported medications to U.S. Customs.

- When the type of drug, the quantity, or the combination of various drugs arouse suspicions, U.S. Customs Inspectors will ordinarily contact the nearest FDA or DEA office for advice and will then make a final determination about whether to release or detain the article. (See 19 U.S.C. 1499).

In addition to federal requirements, individual states may have additional requirements covering prescription (Rx) or controlled medications. Travelers should check with state authorities, where they reside or are traveling, to verify that a particular prescription does in fact comply with state regulations. In many areas, the local police department and pharmacies can provide additional information.

# Chapter 17

# *Preparing for Crises and Emergencies in Adventure Travel Abroad*

## Before You Leave

By doing your homework before you leave, you minimize the chances of something going wrong. Take the time to learn about your destination and what you are about to do. Most of all, before you undertake a trip that will test you mentally and physically, make sure you know yourself. Is this what you want to do? Is this something you are capable of doing?

To find out about local conditions before you leave, consult reports which provide information on safety and security conditions, health issues, and entry and visa requirements of your destinations.

## Your Trip Is Unique... and So Are You

When choosing an adventure trip or excursion, there are many things to consider. Under-estimating the risks or having too much confidence in your own abilities can lead to trouble, especially in extreme conditions or at unusual destinations.

Even though others are doing it, the risk for you may be different. Research your destination and be aware of the dangers. Conditions may vary from month to month.

---

From "Out on a Limb: Advice for the Adventure Traveller," published by the Department of Foreign Affairs and International Trade, Ottawa, ON, Canada. June 2001.

In 1998, a young couple from Newfoundland went on a surfing holiday to a popular beach in Indonesia. On the second day of the vacation, the woman watched helplessly as her boyfriend disappeared into the ocean. He was unfamiliar with local conditions and had underestimated the strong currents and undertow. His body was recovered four days later.

Two high school students and an adult guardian were drowned during a field trip along the rocky coast of California. A freak wave hit and the 45-year-old woman was pulled into the water. The two students died in a failed rescue attempt.

### *"It's Safe Because I'll Have a Tour Guide."*

Having a guide doesn't eliminate risk. There are many situations that guides cannot control.

A young, physically fit woman went on a guided rafting expedition in Nepal. On her way back to base camp, she and three others, including her guide, were crossing a small river. The current swept her down the river to her death. Her body was never found.

### *"It's Safe Because I'll Be Part of a Group."*

Traveling with a group doesn't eliminate risk, either. Never yield to others the responsibility for your own safety. Carefully research the company you plan to travel with. Speak to others who have already made the trip. Is the company responsible enough to reject clients who do not meet established preconditions?

A woman from Toronto signed on for a nature tour in Latin America. She became tired and told the guide she was going to stop for a rest and wait for the group to return. The group returned as arranged, but she wasn't there. She was never found despite extensive searching.

## Take Precautions

1. Know what to expect on your trip. Enquire about the accommodations and food. Find out about the group size and about the gender, age and ability level of fellow travelers. Some companies offer adventure tours geared to families or to specific groups based on age, gender or physical ability.

2. Assess the skills as well as the physical and mental stamina that will be required of you for the trip. Carefully evaluate

your level of preparedness. Consult your physician and provide details about what you plan to do. Respect your personal capabilities. Your body will already be under stress from time and climate changes, unfamiliar food and a different environment. If needed, upgrade your skills. If that is not possible, don't go.

3.  Talk to people who have similar interests and similar physical abilities to your own, and who have experience with this kind of travel.

4.  Choose a company experienced in the type of adventure travel you're interested in and research their track record. Such companies should:

    - Provide rating systems indicating the difficulty level and the risks.

    - Employ good risk management practices.

    - Give a good cancellation policy.

    - Offer guides who speak the local language and are trained in first aid.

5.  Use appropriately certified guides and instructors, if certifying bodies exist, such as PADI (Professional Association of Diving Instructors [www.padi.com]) or DAN (Divers Alert Network [www.diversalertnetwork.org]), for scuba diving.

6.  Find out if your destination is dangerous in either physical or political terms. In many countries there is political instability, police and judicial corruption, an ongoing war, insurgencies or sporadic unrest. Tourists can be lucrative targets for kidnappers. A wilderness expedition in such an environment is risky and foolhardy.

7.  Detail what equipment and clothing you'll need. Take a medical kit, toiletries, and enough money to get you through an emergency. And remember that the longer you're going to be on your feet, the heavier your bag will become.

8.  Buy comprehensive health, travel and life insurance. Many insurance policies do not cover activities that involve risk such as scuba diving, skydiving or even snorkeling. Always carry evidence of your insurance with you.

## Supplemental Health Insurance

Do not rely on your health plan to cover the costs if you get sick or are injured while you are abroad. At best, your health plan will cover only a portion of the bill.

It is your responsibility to obtain and understand the terms of your supplementary insurance policies.

Some credit cards offer health and travel insurance. Do not assume the card alone provides adequate coverage.

## Getting Medical Advice

Before you leave, get advice on health issues at your destination. It is strongly recommended that you obtain an individual risk assessment by your doctor or a travel medicine specialist prior to traveling. Based on your health risks, the need for vaccinations or other special precautions can be determined.

Chapter 18

# *Preparing for Natural Disasters while Traveling*

## *Chapter Contents*

# Section 18.1

## *Earthquakes*

"What Should I Do?" Federal Emergency Management Agency, available online at http://www.fema.gov/hazards/earthquakes/ equakes.shtm, last updated October 8, 2002.

### *Before the Earthquake Strikes*

If you are at risk from earthquakes:

- Pick "safe places" in each room of your home. A safe place could be under a sturdy table or desk or against an interior wall away from windows, bookcases, or tall furniture that could fall on you. The shorter the distance to move to safety, the less likely you will be injured. Injury statistics show that people moving as little as 10 feet during an earthquake's shaking are most likely to be injured. Also pick safe places, in your office, school and other buildings you are frequently in.

- Practice drop, cover, and hold-on in each safe place. Drop under a sturdy desk or table and hold on to one leg of the table or desk. Protect your eyes by keeping your head down. Practice these actions so that they become an automatic response. When an earthquake or other disaster occurs, many people hesitate, trying to remember what they are supposed to do. Responding quickly and automatically may help protect you from injury.

- Practice drop, cover, and hold-on at least twice a year. Frequent practice will help reinforce safe behavior.

- Wait in your safe place until the shaking stops, then check to see if you are hurt. You will be better able to help others if you take care of yourself first, then check the people around you. Move carefully and watch out for things that have fallen or broken, creating hazards. Be ready for additional earthquakes called "aftershocks."

- Be on the lookout for fires. Fire is the most common earthquake-related hazard, due to broken gas lines, damaged electrical lines or appliances, and previously contained fires or sparks being released.

- If you must leave a building after the shaking stops, use the stairs, not the elevator. Earthquakes can cause fire alarms and fire sprinklers to go off. You will not be certain whether there is a real threat of fire. As a precaution, use the stairs.

- If you're outside in an earthquake, stay outside. Move away from buildings, trees, streetlights, and power lines. Crouch down and cover your head. Many injuries occur within 10 feet of the entrance to buildings. Bricks, roofing, and other materials can fall from buildings, injuring persons nearby. Trees, streetlights, and power lines may also fall, causing damage or injury.

- Inform guests, babysitters, and caregivers of your plan. Everyone in your home should know what to do if an earthquake occurs. Assure yourself that others will respond properly even if you are not at home during the earthquake.

- Get training. Take a first aid class from your local Red Cross chapter. Get training on how to use a fire extinguisher from your local fire department. Keep your training current. Training will help you to keep calm and know what to do when an earthquake occurs.

- Discuss earthquakes with your family. Everyone should know what to do in case all family members are not together. Discussing earthquakes ahead of time helps reduce fear and anxiety and lets everyone know how to respond.

- Talk with your insurance agent. Different areas have different requirements for earthquake protection. Study locations of active faults, and if you are at risk, consider purchasing earthquake insurance.

## During an Earthquake

- Drop, cover, and hold on! Move only a few steps to a nearby safe place. It is very dangerous to try to leave a building during an earthquake because objects can fall on you. Many fatalities occur when people run outside of buildings, only to be killed by falling debris from collapsing walls. In U.S. buildings, you are safer to stay where you are.

- If you are in bed, hold on and stay there, protecting your head with a pillow. You are less likely to be injured staying where you are. Broken glass on the floor has caused injury to those who have rolled to the floor or tried to get to doorways.

- If you are outdoors, find a clear spot away from buildings, trees, streetlights, and power lines. Drop to the ground and stay there until the shaking stops. Injuries can occur from falling trees, street-lights and power lines, or building debris.

- If you are in a vehicle, pull over to a clear location, stop and stay there with your seatbelt fastened until the shaking has stopped. Trees, power lines, poles, street signs, and other over-head items may fall during earthquakes. Stopping will help reduce your risk, and a hard-topped vehicle will help protect you from flying or falling objects. Once the shaking has stopped, proceed with caution. Avoid bridges or ramps that might have been damaged by the quake.

- Stay indoors until the shaking stops and you're sure it's safe to exit. More injuries happen when people move during the shaking of an earthquake. After the shaking has stopped, if you go outside, move quickly away from the building to prevent injury from falling debris.

- Stay away from windows. Windows can shatter with such force that you can be injured several feet away.

- In a high-rise building, expect the fire alarms and sprinklers to go off during a quake. Earthquakes frequently cause fire alarm and fire sprinkler systems to go off even if there is no fire. Check for and extinguish small fires, and, if exiting, use the stairs.

- If you are in a coastal area, move to higher ground. Tsunamis are often created by earthquakes.

- If you are in a mountainous area or near unstable slopes or cliffs, be alert for falling rocks and other debris that could be loosened by the earthquake. Landslides commonly happen after earthquakes. (See the "Landslide" section for more information.)

## After the Earthquake

- Check yourself for injuries. Often people tend to others without checking their own injuries. You will be better able to care for others if you are not injured or if you have received first aid for your injuries.

- Protect yourself from further danger by putting on long pants, a long-sleeved shirt, sturdy shoes, and work gloves. This will protect your from further injury by broken objects.

- After you have taken care of yourself, help injured or trapped persons. If you have it in your area, call 9-1-1, then give first aid when appropriate. Don't try to move seriously injured people unless they are in immediate danger of further injury.

- Look for and extinguish small fires. Eliminate fire hazards. Putting out small fires quickly, using available resources, will prevent them from spreading. Fire is the most common hazard following earthquakes. Fires followed the San Francisco earthquake of 1906 for three days, creating more damage than the earthquake.

- Leave the gas on at the main valve, unless you smell gas or think it's leaking. It may be weeks or months before professionals can turn gas back on using the correct procedures. Explosions have caused injury and death when homeowners have improperly turned their gas back on by themselves.

- Clean up spilled medicines, bleaches, gasoline, or other flammable liquids immediately and carefully. Avoid the hazard of a chemical emergency.

- Open closet and cabinet doors cautiously. Contents may have shifted during the shaking of an earthquake and could fall, creating further damage or injury.

- Inspect your home for damage. Get everyone out if your home is unsafe. Aftershocks following earthquakes can cause further damage to unstable buildings. If your home has experienced damage, get out before aftershocks happen.

- Help neighbors who may require special assistance. Elderly people and people with disabilities may require additional assistance. People who care for them or who have large families may need additional assistance in emergency situations.

- Listen to a portable, battery-operated radio (or television) for updated emergency information and instructions. If the electricity is out, this may be your main source of information. Local radio and local officials provide the most appropriate advice for your particular situation.

- Expect aftershocks. Each time you feel one, drop, cover, and hold on! Aftershocks frequently occur minutes, days, weeks, and even months following an earthquake.

- Watch out for fallen power lines or broken gas lines, and stay out of damaged areas. Hazards caused by earthquakes are often difficult to see, and you could be easily injured.

- Stay out of damaged buildings. If you are away from home, return only when authorities say it is safe. Damaged buildings may be destroyed by aftershocks following the main quake.

- Use battery-powered lanterns or flashlights to inspect your home. Kerosene lanterns, torches, candles, and matches may tip over or ignite flammable inside.

- Inspect the entire length of chimneys carefully for damage. Unnoticed damage could lead to fire or injury from falling debris during an aftershock. Cracks in chimneys can be the cause of a fire years later.

- Take pictures of the damage, both to the house and its contents, for insurance claims.

- Avoid smoking inside buildings. Smoking in confined areas can cause fires.

- When entering buildings, use extreme caution. Building damage may have occurred where you least expect it. Carefully watch every step you take.

  - Examine walls, floor, doors, staircases, and windows to make sure that the building is not in danger of collapsing.

  - Check for gas leaks. If you smell gas or hear a blowing or hissing noise, open a window and quickly leave the building. Turn off the gas, using the outside main valve if you can, and call the gas company from a neighbor's home. If you turn off the gas for any reason, it must be turned back on by a professional.

  - Look for electrical system damage. If you see sparks or broken or frayed wires, or if you smell burning insulation, turn off the electricity at the main fuse box or circuit breaker. If you have to step in water to get to the fuse box or circuit breaker, call an electrician first for advice.

- Check for sewage and water line damage. If you suspect sewage lines are damaged, avoid using the toilets and call a plumber. If water pipes are damaged, contact the water company and avoid using water from the tap. You can obtain safe water from undamaged water heaters or by melting ice cubes.

- Watch for loose plaster, drywall, and ceilings that could fall.

- Use the telephone only to report life-threatening emergencies. Telephone lines are frequently overwhelmed in disaster situations. They need to be clear for emergency calls to get through.

- Watch animals closely. Leash dogs and place them in a fenced yard. The behavior of pets may change dramatically after an earthquake. Normally quiet and friendly cats and dogs may become aggressive or defensive.

# Section 18.2

# *Floods and Flash Floods*

This chapter contains material excerpted from "Backgrounder: Floods and Flash Floods," Federal Emergency Management Agency, 2002, http://www.fema.gov/hazards/floods/flood.shtm, and "Fact Sheet: Floods and Flash Floods," Federal Emergency Management Agency, 2002, http://www.fema.gov/hazards/floods/floodf.shtm.

## *What Is a Flood?*

Floods are the most common and widespread of all natural disasters—except fire. Most communities in the United States can experience some kind of flooding after spring rains, heavy thunderstorms, or winter snow thaws. Floods can be slow, or fast rising but generally develop over a period of days.

Dam failures are potentially the worst flood events. A dam failure is usually the result of neglect, poor design, or structural damage caused by a major event such as an earthquake. When a dam fails, a gigantic quantity of water is suddenly let loose downstream, destroying anything in its path.

## *What Is a Flash Flood?*

Flash floods usually result from intense storms dropping large amounts of rain within a brief period. Flash floods occur with little or no warning and can reach full peak in only a few minutes.

## *Before, during and after*

Nobody can stop a flood. But if you are faced with one, there are actions you can take to protect your family and keep your property losses to a minimum.

### *Before a Flood*

What is your flood risk? Your community officials or local emergency management office are your best resources to learn about the history of flooding for your region. Ask whether your property is in the flood plain and if it is above or below the flood stage water level. Have disaster supplies on hand.

- Flashlights and extra batteries.
- Portable, battery-operated radio and extra batteries tuned to a local station, and follow emergency instructions.
- First aid kit and manual.
- Emergency food and bottled water.
- Non-electric can opener.
- Essential medicines.
- Cash and credit cards.
- Sturdy shoes.

If you are in a frequently flooded area, take preventative measures and stockpile emergency building materials:

- Plywood, plastic sheeting, lumber, nails, hammer and saw, pry bar, shovels, and sandbags.
- Have check valves installed in building sewer traps to prevent flood waters from backing up in sewer drains.
- As a last resort, use large corks or stoppers to plug showers, tubs, or basins.

Plan and practice an evacuation route.

- Learn flood-warning signs and your community's alert signals.
- Contact your local emergency management office or local American Red Cross chapter for a copy of the community flood evacuation plan.
- This plan should include information on the safest routes to shelters. Individuals living in flash flood areas should have several alternative routes.
- Request information on preparing for floods and flash floods.
- Develop an emergency communication plan.
- In case family members are separated from one another during floods or flash floods, have a plan for getting back together.

- Ask an out-of-state relative or friend to serve as the "family contact." After a disaster, it's often easier to call long distance. Make sure everyone in the family knows the name, address, and phone number of the contact person.

- Make sure that all family members know how to respond after a flood or flash flood.

- Teach all family members how and when to turn off gas, electricity, and water.

- Teach children how and when to call 9-1-1, police, fire department, and which radio station to tune to for emergency information.

- Be prepared to evacuate.

*If Time Permits, Here Are Other Steps That You Can Take before the Flood Waters Come*

- Turn off all utilities at the main power switch and close the main gas valve if evacuation appears necessary.

- Move valuables, such as papers, furs, jewelry, and clothing to upper floors or higher elevations.

- Fill bathtubs, sinks and plastic soda bottles with clean water. Sanitize the sinks and tubs first by using bleach. Rinse, then fill with clean water.

- Bring outdoor possessions, such as lawn furniture, grills and trash cans inside, or tie them down securely.

### Once the Flood Arrives

- Don't drive through a flooded area. If you come upon a flooded road, turn around and go another way. More people drown in their cars than anywhere else.

- If your car stalls, abandon it immediately and climb to higher ground. Many deaths have resulted from attempts to move stalled vehicles.

- Don't walk through flooded areas. As little as six inches of moving water can knock you off your feet.

- Stay away from downed power fines and electrical wires. Electrocution is another major source of deaths in floods. Electric current passes easily through water.

- Look out for animals—especially snakes. Animals lose their homes in floods, too. They may seek shelter in yours.

- If the waters start to rise inside your house before you have evacuated, retreat to the second floor, the attic, and if necessary, the roof.

- Take dry clothing, a flashlight and a portable radio with you. Then, wait for help.

- Don't try to swim to safety; wait for rescuers to come to you.

- If outdoors, climb to high ground and stay there.

### _After the Flood_

- Flood dangers do not end when the water begins to recede. Listen to a radio or television and don't return home until authorities indicate it is safe to do so.

- Remember to help your neighbors who may require special assistance—infants, elderly people, and people with disabilities.

- If your home, apartment or business has suffered damage, call the insurance company or agent who handles your flood insurance policy right away to file a claim.

- Before entering a building, inspect foundations for cracks or other damage. Don't go in if there is any chance of the building collapsing.

- Upon entering the building, don't use matches, cigarette lighters or any other open flames, since gas may be trapped inside. Instead, use a flashlight to light your way.

- Keep power off until an electrician has inspected your system for safety.

- Flood waters pick up sewage and chemicals from roads, farms and factories. If your home has been flooded, protect your family's health by cleaning up your house right away. Throw out foods and medicines that may have met flood water.

- Until local authorities proclaim your water supply to be safe, boil water for drinking and food preparation vigorously for five minutes before using.

- Be careful walking around. After a flood, steps and floors are often slippery with mud and covered with debris, including nails and broken glass.

*Inspecting Utilities in a Damaged Home*

Check for gas leaks—if you smell gas or hear blowing or hissing noise, open a window and quickly leave the building. Turn off the gas at the outside main valve if you can and call the gas company from a neighbor's home. If you turn off the gas for any reason, it must be turned back on by a professional.

Look for electrical system damage—if you see sparks or broken or frayed wires, or if you smell hot insulation, turn off the electricity at the main fuse box or circuit breaker. If you have to step in water to get to the fuse box or circuit breaker, call an electrician for advice.

Check for sewage and water line damage—if you suspect sewage lines are damaged avoid using the toilets and call a plumber. If water pipes are damaged, contact the water company and avoid the water from the tap. You can obtain safe water by melting ice cubes.

## Emergency Information

1.  Flood waters can be extremely dangerous. The force of six inches of swiftly moving water can knock people off their feet. The best protection during a flood is to leave the area and go to shelter on higher ground.

2.  Flash flood waters move at very fast speeds and can roll boulders, tear out trees, destroy buildings, and obliterate bridges. Walls of water can reach heights of 10 to 20 feet and generally are accompanied by a deadly cargo of debris. The best response to any signs of flash flooding is to move immediately and quickly to higher ground.

3.  Cars can be easily be swept away in just 2 feet of moving water. If flood waters rise around a car, it should be abandoned. Passengers should climb to higher ground.

## Danger Zones

Floods and flash floods occur within all 50 states. Communities particularly at risk are those located in low-lying areas, near water, or downstream from a dam.

# Section 18.3

## *Hurricanes*

This section contains "Hurricane Backgrounder," Federal Emergency Management Agency, available online at http://www.fema.gov/hazards/ hurricanes/hurfacts.shtm, last updated September 27, 2002, and "What Should I Do?" Federal Emergency Management Agency, available online at http://www.fema.gov/hazards/hurricanes/whatshouldido.shtm, last updated September 27, 2002.

## *Hurricane Backgrounder*

### *What Is a Hurricane?*

A hurricane is a tropical storm with winds that have reached a constant speed of 74 miles per hour or more. Hurricane winds blow in a large spiral around a relative calm center known as the "eye." The "eye" is generally 20 to 30 miles wide, and the storm may extend outward 400 miles. As a hurricane approaches, the skies will begin to darken and winds will grow in strength. As a hurricane nears land, it can bring torrential rains, high winds, and storm surges. A single hurricane can last for more than two weeks over open waters and can run a path across the entire length of the eastern seaboard. August and September are peak months during the hurricane season that lasts from June 1 through November 30.

The center, or eye, of a hurricane is relatively calm. The most violent activity takes place in the area immediately around the eye, called the eyeball. At the top of the eyeball (about 50,000 feet), most of the air is propelled outward, increasing the air's upward motion. Some of the air, however, moves inward and sinks into the eye, creating a cloud-free area.

Tropical cyclones are classified as follows:

**Tropical Depression**—An organized system of clouds and thunderstorms with a defined circulation and maximum sustained winds of 38 mph (33 knots) or less.

**Tropical Storm**—An organized system of strong thunderstorms with a defined circulation and maximum sustained winds of 39 to 73 mph (34–63 knots).

**Hurricane**—An intense tropical weather system with a well-defined circulation and maximum sustained winds of 74 mph (64 knots) or higher. Hurricanes are called "typhoons" in the western Pacific, while similar storms in the Indian Ocean are called "cyclones."

Hurricanes form in the Atlantic Ocean, Gulf of Mexico, Indian Ocean, Caribbean Sea and Pacific Ocean. Hurricane winds in the Northern Hemisphere circulate in a counterclockwise motion around the hurricane's center or "eye," while hurricane winds in the Southern Hemisphere circulate clockwise. Natural phenomena, which affect a storm, include temperature of the water, the Gulf Stream, and steering wind currents. Powered by heat from the sea, they are steered by the easterly trade winds and the temperate westerlies as well as by their own ferocious energy. Around their core, winds grow with great velocity, generating violent seas. Moving ashore, they sweep the ocean inward while spawning tornadoes and producing torrential rains and floods.

In the eastern Pacific, hurricanes begin forming by mid-May, while in the Atlantic, Caribbean, and Gulf of Mexico, hurricane development starts in June. For the United States, the peak hurricane threat exists from mid-August to late October although the official hurricane season extends through November. Over other parts of the world, such as the western Pacific, hurricanes can occur year-round. Areas in the United States vulnerable to hurricanes include the Atlantic and Gulf coasts from Texas to Maine, the territories in the Caribbean, and tropical areas of the western Pacific, including Hawaii, Guam, American Samoa, and Saipan.

### Hurricane Threats

The 74 to 160 mile per hour winds of a hurricane can extend inland for hundreds of miles. Hurricanes can spawn tornadoes, which add to the destructiveness of the storm. Floods and flash floods generated by torrential rains also cause damage and loss of life. Following a hurricane, inland streams and rivers can flood and trigger landslides. Even more dangerous than the high winds of a hurricane is the storm surge—a dome of ocean water that can be 20 feet at its peak and 50 to 100 miles wide. The surge can devastate coastal communities as it sweeps ashore. Nine out of 10 hurricane fatalities are attributable to the storm surge.

#### Rainfall and Flooding

Heavy rains and ocean waters brought ashore by strong winds can cause flooding in excess of 50 cm (20 in) over a 24 hour period. The run-off systems in many cities are unable to handle such an increase in water because of the gentle topography in many of the coastal areas where hurricanes occur. Hurricanes are capable of producing copious amounts of flash flooding rainfall. During landfall, a hurricane rainfall of 10 to 15 inches or more is common. If the storm is large and moving slowly—less than 10 mph—the rainfall amounts from a well-organized storm are likely to be even more excessive. To get a generic estimate of the rainfall amount (in inches) that can be expected, divide the storm's forward motion by 100, for example, forward speed/100 = estimated inches of rain.

The heaviest rain usually occurs along the coastline, but sometimes there is a secondary maximum further inland. This heavy rain usually occurs slightly to the right of the cyclone track and usually occurs between 6 hours before and 6 hours after landfall. The amount of rain depends on the size of the cyclone, the forward speed of the cyclone and whether it interacts with a cold front. Interaction with a cold front will not only produce more tornadoes but more rainfall as well.

*Storm Surge*

Storm surge is an abnormal increase in the ocean's level, sometimes in excess of several meters high and miles wide. Storm surges can come ashore up to five hours before the storm and destroy low-elevation coastal areas. It is especially damaging when the storm surge occurs during high tide and consequently is often responsible for most hurricane-related deaths. Storm surge is a large dome of water often 50 to 100 miles wide that sweeps across the coastline near where a hurricane makes landfall. Storm surge can range from 4 to 6 feet for a minimal hurricane to greater than 20 feet for the stronger ones. The surge of high water topped by waves is devastating. The stronger the hurricane and the shallower the offshore water, the higher the surge will be. Along the immediate coast, storm surge is the greatest threat to life and property, even more so than the high winds.

- Over 6000 people were killed in the Galveston Hurricane of 1900, most by storm surge.

- Hurricane Camille produced a 25-foot storm surge in Mississippi.

- Hurricane Hugo in 1989 generated a 20-foot storm tide in South Carolina.

*Tornadoes*

Hurricanes also produce tornadoes, which add to the hurricane's destructive power. Typically, the more intense a hurricane is, the greater the tornado threat. When a hurricane brings its winds inland, the fast-moving air hits terrain and structures, causing a frictional convergence which enhances lifting. Frictional convergence may be at least a contributing factor to tornado formation in hurricanes. The greatest concentration of tornadoes occurs in the right front quadrant of the hurricane. A number of theories exist about their origin, but in the case of Hurricane Andrew, severe damage was inflicted by small spin-up vortices that developed in regions of strong wind-shear found in the hurricane's the eye wall. The strong damaging winds of the hurricane frequently cover the smaller tornado paths, making the separation of their damaging effects very difficult.

*Tropical Cyclone Spawned Tornadoes Facts*

- 10% of deaths in the United States are associated with hurricanes are a result of tornadoes.

- Most tornadoes occur within 24 hours after hurricane landfall. The exception is when there is interaction with a cold front after landfall. Then more tornadoes will occur two or three days after landfall, well inland.

- Most tornadoes occur within 150 miles of the coastline.

- More tornadoes occur during the morning and afternoon rather than evening or night due to the need for a tornado to have a heat source.

- The Gulf of Mexico hurricanes produce more tornadoes than Atlantic storms.

- The majority of tornadoes occur within 30 miles of the center of the cyclone, but there is a secondary maximum further away in the outer rain bands (100–150 miles away from the center).

- Tornado winds can reach up to 300 mph at a forward speed of 60 mph and are usually 100–300 yards wide.

## What Should I Do?

### During a Hurricane Watch

(A hurricane watch is issued when there is a threat of hurricane conditions within 24–36 hours.)

- Listen to a battery-operated radio or television for hurricane progress reports.

- Check emergency supplies.

- Fuel car.

- Bring in outdoor objects such as lawn furniture, toys, and garden tools and anchor objects that cannot be brought inside.

- Secure buildings by closing and boarding up windows and remove outside antennas.

- Turn refrigerator and freezer to coldest settings. Open only when absolutely necessary and close quickly.

- Store drinking water in clean bathtubs, jugs, bottles, and cooking utensils.

- Store valuables and personal papers in a waterproof container on the highest level of your home.

- Review evacuation plan.

- Moor boat securely or move it to a designated safe place. Use rope or chain to secure boat to trailer. Use tiedowns to anchor trailer to the ground or house.

## *During a Hurricane Warning*

(A hurricane warning is issued when hurricane conditions [winds of 74 miles per hour or greater, or dangerously high water and rough seas] are expected in 24 hours or less.)

- Listen constantly to a battery-operated radio or television for official instructions.

- If in a mobile home, check tiedowns and evacuate immediately.

- Avoid elevators.

- If at home.
  - Stay inside, away from windows, skylights, and glass doors.
  - Keep a supply of flashlights and extra batteries handy. Avoid open flames, such as candles and kerosene lamps, as a source of light.
  - If power is lost, turn off major appliances to reduce power "surge" when electricity is restored.

- If officials indicate evacuation is necessary.
  - Leave as soon as possible. Avoid flooded roads and watch for washed-out bridges.

- Secure your home by unplugging appliances and turning off electricity and the main water valve.

- Tell someone outside of the storm area where you are going.

- If time permits, and you live in an identified surge zone, elevate furniture to protect it from flooding or better yet, move it to a higher floor.

- Take pre-assembled emergency supplies, warm protective clothing, blankets and sleeping bags to shelter.

- Lock up home and leave.

### After the Storm

- Stay tuned to local radio for information.

- Help injured or trapped persons.

- Give first aid where appropriate.

- Do not move seriously injured persons unless they are in immediate danger of further injury, call for help.

- Return home only after authorities advise that it is safe to do so.

- Avoid loose or dangling power lines and report them immediately to the power company, police, or fire department.

- Enter your home with caution. Beware of snakes, insects, and animals driven to higher ground by flood water.

- Open windows and doors to ventilate and dry your home.

- Check refrigerated foods for spoilage.

- Take pictures of the damage, both to the house and its contents for insurance claims.

- Drive only if absolutely necessary and avoid flooded roads and washed-out bridges.

- Use telephone only for emergency calls.

- Inspecting utilities in a damaged home.
    - Check for gas leaks—if you smell gas or hear blowing or hissing noise, open a window and quickly leave the building. Turn off the gas at the outside main valve if you can and call the gas company from a neighbor's home. If you

turn off the gas for any reason, it must be turned back on by a professional.

- Look for electrical system damage—if you see sparks or broken or frayed wires, or if you smell hot insulation, turn off the electricity at the main fuse box or circuit breaker. If you have to step in water to get to the fuse box or circuit breaker, call an electrician first for advice.

- Check for sewage and water lines damage—if you suspect sewage lines are damaged avoid using the toilets and call a plumber. If water pipes are damaged, contact the water company and avoid the water from the tap. You can obtain safe water by melting ice cubes.

# Section 18.4

# *Landslides*

From: Talking about Disaster: Guide for Standard Messages. Produced by the National Disaster Education Coalition, Washington, DC, 1999.

## *Why Talk about Landslides?*

Landslides are a serious geologic hazard common to almost every state in the United States. It is estimated that nationally they cause up to $2 billion in damages and from 25 to 50 deaths annually. Globally, landslides cause billions of dollars in damage and thousands of deaths and injuries each year. Individuals can take steps to reduce their personal risk. Know about the hazard potential where you live, take steps to reduce your risk, and practice preparedness plans.

## *What Are Landslides and Debris Flows, and What Causes Them?*

Some landslides move slowly and cause damage gradually, whereas others move so rapidly that they can destroy property and take lives suddenly and unexpectedly. Gravity is the force driving landslide movement. Factors that allow the force of gravity to overcome the resistance of earth material to landslide movement include: saturation by water, steepening of slopes by erosion or construction, alternate freezing or thawing, earthquake shaking, and volcanic eruptions.

Landslides are typically associated with periods of heavy rainfall or rapid snow melt and tend to worsen the effects of flooding that often accompanies these events. In areas burned by forest and brush fires, a lower threshold of precipitation may initiate landslides.

Debris flows, sometimes referred to as mudslides, mudflows, lahars, or debris avalanches, are common types of fast-moving landslides. These flows generally occur during periods of intense rainfall or rapid snow melt. They usually start on steep hillsides as shallow landslides that liquefy and accelerate to speeds that are typically about 10 miles per hour, but can exceed 35 miles per hour. The consistency of debris flows ranges from watery mud to thick, rocky mud that can carry large items such as boulders, trees, and cars. Debris flows from many different sources can combine in channels, and their destructive power may be greatly increased. They continue flowing down hills and through channels, growing in volume with the addition of water, sand, mud, boulders, trees, and other materials. When the flows reach flatter ground, the debris spreads over a broad area, sometimes accumulating in thick deposits that can wreak havoc in developed areas.

Among the most destructive types of debris flows are those that accompany volcanic eruptions. A spectacular example in the United States was a massive debris flow resulting from the 1980 eruptions of Mount St. Helens, Washington. Areas near the bases of many volcanoes in the Cascade Mountain Range of California, Oregon, and Washington are at risk from the same types of flows during future volcanic eruptions.

Wildfires can also lead to destructive debris-flow activity. In July 1994, a severe wildfire swept Storm King Mountain, west of Glenwood Springs, Colorado, denuding the slopes of vegetation. Heavy rains on the mountain in September resulted in numerous debris flows, one of which blocked Interstate 70 and threatened to dam the Colorado River.

Learn whether landslides or debris flows have occurred in your area by contacting local officials, state geological surveys or departments of natural resources, and university departments of geology.

## Awareness Information

Areas that are generally prone to landslide hazards include existing old landslides; the bases of steep slopes; the bases of drainage channels; and developed hillsides where leach-field septic systems are used.

Areas that are typically considered safe from landslides include areas that have not moved in the past; relatively flat-lying areas away from sudden changes in slope; and areas at the top or along ridges, set back from the tops of slopes.

Learn what to watch for prior to major landsliding. Look for patterns of storm-water drainage on slopes near your home, noting especially the places where runoff water converges, increasing flow over soil-covered slopes. Check hillsides around your home for any signs of land movement, such as small landslides or debris flows or progressively tilting trees.

## If You Are at Risk from Landslides

- Develop an evacuation plan. You should know where to go if you have to leave. Trying to make plans at the last minute can be upsetting and create confusion.

- Discuss landslides and debris flow with your family. Everyone should know what to do in case all family members are not together. Discussing disaster ahead of time helps reduce fear and lets everyone know how to respond during a landslide or debris flow.

## What to Do before Intense Storms

- Become familiar with the land around you. Learn whether landslides and debris flows have occurred in your area by contacting local officials, state geological surveys or departments of natural resources, and university departments of geology. Knowing the land can help you assess your risk for danger.

- Watch the patterns of storm-water drainage on slopes near your home, and especially the places where runoff water converges, increasing flow over soil-covered slopes. Watch the hillsides around your home for any signs of land movement, such as small landslides or debris flows, or progressively tilting trees. Watching small changes could alert you to the potential of a greater landslide threat.

## What to Do during Intense Storms

- Stay alert and awake. Many debris-flow fatalities occur when people are sleeping. Listen to portable, battery-powered radio or television for warnings of intense rainfall. Be aware that intense, short bursts of rain may be particularly dangerous, especially after longer periods of heavy rainfall and damp weather.

- If you are in areas susceptible to landslides and debris flows, consider leaving if it is safe to do so. Remember that driving during an intense storm can be hazardous. If you remain at home, move to a second story if possible. Staying out of the path of a landslide or debris flow saves lives.

- Listen for any unusual sounds that might indicate moving debris, such as trees cracking or boulders knocking together. A trickle of flowing or falling mud or debris may precede larger landslides. Moving debris can flow quickly and sometimes without warning.

- If you are near a stream or channel, be alert for any sudden increase or decrease in water flow and for a change from clear to muddy water. Such changes may indicate landslide activity upstream, so be prepared to move quickly. Don't delay! Save yourself, not your belongings.

- Be especially alert when driving. Embankments along roadsides are particularly susceptible to landslides. Watch the road for collapsed pavement, mud, fallen rocks, and other indications of possible debris flows.

## What to Do If You Suspect Imminent Landslide Danger

- Contact your local fire, police, or public works department. Local officials are the best persons able to assess potential danger.

- Inform affected neighbors. Your neighbors may not be aware of potential hazards. Advising them of a potential threat may help save lives. Help neighbors who may need assistance to evacuate.

- Evacuate. Getting out of the path of a landslide or debris flow is your best protection.

## What to Do during a Landside

- Quickly move out of the path of the landslide or debris flow. Moving away from the path of the flow to a stable area will reduce your risk.

- If escape is not possible, curl into a tight ball and protect your head. A tight ball will provide the best protection for your body.

## *What to Do after a Landslide*

- Stay away from the slide area. There may be danger of additional slides.

- Check for injured and trapped persons near the slide, without entering the direct slide area. Direct rescuers to their locations.

- Help a neighbor who may require special assistance—infants, elderly people, and people with disabilities. Elderly people and people with disabilities may require additional assistance. People who care for them or who have large families may need additional assistance in emergency situations.

- Listen to local radio or television stations for the latest emergency information.

- Watch for flooding, which may occur after a landslide or debris flow. Floods sometimes follow landslides and debris flows because they may both be started by the same event.

- Look for and report broken utility lines to appropriate authorities. Reporting potential hazards will get the utilities turned off as quickly as possible, preventing further hazard and injury.

- Check the building foundation, chimney, and surrounding land for damage. Damage to foundations, chimneys, or surrounding land may help you assess the safety of the area.

- Replant damaged ground as soon as possible since erosion caused by loss of ground cover can lead to flash flooding.

- Seek the advice of a geotechnical expert for evaluating landslide hazards or designing corrective techniques to reduce landslide risk. A professional will be able to advise you of the best ways to prevent or reduce landslide risk, without creating further hazard.

# Section 18.5

# *Tornadoes*

This section includes "Tornado: A Prevention Guide to Promote Your Personal Health and Safety," Centers for Disease Control and Prevention, available online at http://www.cdc.gov/nceh/emergency/tornado/default. htm, last reviewed June 22, 2002, and "Fact Sheet: Tornadoes," Federal Emergency Management Agency, available online at http://www.fema.gov/ hazards/tornadoes/tornadof.shtm, last updated 2002.

## *Tornado: A Prevention Guide to Promote Your Personal Health and Safety*

Knowing what to do when you see a tornado, or when you hear a tornado warning, can help protect you and your family. During a tornado, people face hazards from extremely high winds and risk being struck by flying and falling objects. After a tornado, the wreckage left behind poses additional injury risks. Although nothing can be done to prevent tornadoes, there are actions you can take for your health and safety. This section provides information to help you to watch for tornadoes, to plan ahead to reduce hazards, and to avoid injuries during and after the storm.

Although tornadoes are occasionally reported in other parts of the world, most occur in the United States east of the Rocky Mountains during the spring and summer. However, tornadoes can occur in any state at any time of the year. Nationally, an average of 800 tornadoes are sighted each year, causing about 80 deaths and more than 1,500 injuries.

### *Tornado Basics*

A tornado is a violent whirlwind—a rotating funnel of air that extends from a cloud to the ground. Tornadoes can travel for many miles at speeds of 250 miles per hour or more. These storms change direction without warning, randomly destroying homes and power lines, uprooting trees, and even hurling large objects—such as automobiles—over long distances.

Tornadoes usually accompany severe thunderstorms. Occasionally, tornadoes occur during tropical storms or hurricanes. The path of damage left behind by a tornado averages 9 miles long by 200 yards wide, but a severe tornado can damage an area up to 50 miles long and a mile wide.

Tornadoes that occur over oceans and lakes are called waterspouts. Because they rotate less vigorously and affect less-populated areas, waterspouts are usually not as destructive as tornadoes; however, waterspouts can move inland and become tornadoes. Waterspouts are more common in the Southeast, particularly along the Gulf Coast, but can form over any body of warm water.

The most destructive force in a tornado is the updraft in the funnel. As this unstable air moves upward at high speed, it can suction up houses and trees and move them hundreds of feet.

### *How Tornadoes Are Formed*

When unseasonably warm humid air collides with a cold front, intense thunderstorm clouds form and tornadoes may develop.

As warm air rises within the storm clouds, cooler air rushes in from the sides, creating a whirling wind that draws surrounding air toward its center.

An area of strong rotation develops, two to six miles wide. Next to appear is a dark, low cloud base called a rotating wall cloud.

Moments later, as rotation becomes even stronger, a funnel develops.

## *Tornado Safety Tips*

When a tornado is coming, you have only a short amount of time to make life-or-death decisions. Advance planning and quick response are the keys to surviving a tornado.

### *Before*

- Conduct tornado drills each tornado season.

- Designate an area in the home as a shelter, and practice having everyone in the family go there in response to a tornado threat.

- Discuss with family members the difference between a "tornado watch" and a "tornado warning."

- Contact your local emergency management office or American Red Cross chapter for more information on tornadoes.

*Have Disaster Supplies on Hand*

- Flashlight and extra batteries.
- Portable, battery-operated radio and extra batteries.
- First aid kit and manual.
- Emergency food and water.
- Non-electric can opener.
- Essential medicines.
- Cash and credit cards.
- Sturdy shoes.

*Develop an Emergency Communication Plan*

In case family members are separated from one another during a tornado (a real possibility during the day when adults are at work and children are at school), have a plan for getting back together.

Ask an out-of-state relative or friend to serve as the "family contact." After a disaster, it's often easier to call long distance. Make sure everyone in the family knows the name, address, and phone number of the contact person.

*Tornado Watches and Warnings*

A tornado watch is issued by the National Weather Service when tornadoes are possible in your area. Remain alert for approaching storms. This is time to remind family members where the safest places within your home are located, and listen to the radio or television for further developments.

A tornado warning is issued when a tornado has been sighted or indicated by weather radar.

*Tornado Danger Signs*

Learn these tornado danger signs:

- An approaching cloud of debris can mark the location of a tornado even if a funnel is not visible.
- Before a tornado hits, the wind may die down and the air may become very still.
- Tornadoes generally occur near the trailing edge of a thunderstorm. It is not uncommon to see clear, sunlit skies behind a tornado.

## During

If at home:

- Go at once to a windowless, interior room; storm cellar; basement; or lowest level of the building.
- If there is no basement, go to an inner hallway or a smaller inner room without windows, such as a bathroom or closet.
- Get away from the windows.
- Go to the center of the room. Stay away from corners because they tend to attract debris.
- Get under a piece of sturdy furniture such as a workbench or heavy table or desk and hold on to it.
- Use arms to protect head and neck.
- If in a mobile home, get out and find shelter elsewhere.

If at work or school:

- Go to the basement or to an inside hallway at the lowest level.
- Avoid places with wide-span roofs such as auditoriums, cafeterias, large hallways, or shopping malls.
- Get under a piece of sturdy furniture such as a workbench or heavy table or desk and hold on to it.
- Use arms to protect head and neck.

If outdoors:

- If possible, get inside a building.
- If shelter is not available or there is no time to get indoors, lie in a ditch or low-lying area or crouch near a strong building. Be aware of the potential for flooding.
- Use arms to protect head and neck.

If in a car:

- Never try to outdrive a tornado in a car or truck. Tornadoes can change direction quickly and can lift up a car or truck and toss it through the air.
- Get out of the car immediately and take shelter in a nearby building.

- If there is no time to get indoors, get out of the car and lie in a ditch or low-lying area away from the vehicle. Be aware of the potential for flooding.

## After

- Help injured or trapped persons.

- Give first aid when appropriate.

- Don't try to move the seriously injured unless they are in immediate danger of further injury.

- Call for help.

- Turn on radio or television to get the latest emergency information.

- Stay out of damaged buildings. Return home only when authorities say it is safe.

- Use the telephone only for emergency calls.

- Clean up spilled medicines, bleaches, or gasoline or other flammable liquids immediately.

- Leave the buildings if you smell gas or chemical fumes.

- Take pictures of the damage—both to the house and its contents—for insurance purposes.

Remember to help your neighbors who may require special assistance—infants, the elderly, and people with disabilities.

## Inspecting Utilities in a Damaged Home

Check for gas leaks—if you smell gas or hear a blowing or hissing noise, open a window and quickly leave the building. Turn off the gas at the outside main valve if you can and call the gas company from a neighbor's home. If you turn off the gas for any reason, it must be turned back on by a professional.

Look for electrical system damage—if you see sparks or broken or frayed wires, or if you smell hot insulation, turn off the electricity at the main fuse box or circuit breaker. If you have to step in water to get to the fuse box or circuit breaker, call an electrician first for advice.

Check for sewage and water lines damage—if you suspect sewage lines are damaged, avoid using toilets and call a plumber. If water pipes are damaged, contact the water company and avoid using water from the tap. You can obtain safe water by melting ice cubes.

### Fujita-Pearson Tornado Scale

- **F-0:** 40–72 mph, chimney damage, tree branches broken.

- **F-1:** 73–112 mph, mobile homes pushed off foundation or overturned.

- **F-2:** 113–157 mph, considerable damage, mobile homes demolished, trees uprooted.

- **F-3:** 158–205 mph, roofs and walls torn down, trains overturned, cars thrown.

- **F-4:** 207–260 mph, well-constructed walls leveled.

- **F-5:** 261–318 mph, homes lifted off foundation and carried considerable distances, autos thrown as far as 100 meters.

# Section 18.6

# *Tsunamis*

From: Talking about Disaster: Guide for Standard Messages. Produced by the National Disaster Education Coalition, Washington, DC, 1999.

## *Why Talk about Tsunamis?*

Twenty-four tsunamis have caused damage in the United States and its territories during the last 204 years. Just since 1946, six tsunamis have killed more than 350 people and caused a half billion dollars of property damage in Hawaii, Alaska, and the West Coast. As a tsunami nears the coastline, it may rise to several feet or, in rare cases, tens of feet, and can cause great loss of life and property damage when it comes ashore. Tsunamis can travel upstream in coastal estuaries and rivers, with damaging waves extending farther inland than the immediate coast. A tsunami can occur during any season of the year and at any time, day or night.

## *What Are Tsunamis, and What Causes Them?*

Tsunamis are ocean waves produced by earthquakes or underwater landslides. The word is Japanese and means "harbor wave," because of the devastating effects these waves have had on low-lying Japanese coastal communities. Tsunamis are often incorrectly referred to as tidal waves, but a tsunami is actually a series of waves that can travel at speeds averaging 450 (and up to 600) miles per hour in the open ocean. In the open ocean, tsunamis would not be felt by ships because the wavelength would be hundreds of miles long, with an amplitude of only a few feet. This would also make them unnoticeable from the air. As the waves approach the coast, their speed decreases and their amplitude increases. Unusual wave heights have been known to be over 100 feet high. However, waves that are 10 to 20 feet high can be very destructive and cause many deaths or injuries.

Tsunamis are most often generated by earthquake-induced movement of the ocean floor. Landslides, volcanic eruptions, and even meteorites can also generate a tsunami. If a major earthquake is felt, a tsunami could reach the beach in a few minutes, even before a warning is issued. Areas at greatest risk are less than 25 feet above sea level and within one mile of the shoreline. Most deaths caused by a tsunami are because of drowning. Associated risks include flooding, contamination of drinking water, fires from ruptured tanks or gas lines, and the loss of vital community infrastructure (police, fire, and medical facilities).

From an initial tsunami generating source area, waves travel outward in all directions much like the ripples caused by throwing a rock into a pond. As these waves approach coastal areas, the time between successive wave crests varies from 5 to 90 minutes. The first wave is usually not the largest in the series of waves, nor is it the most significant. Furthermore, one coastal community may experience no damaging waves while another, not that far away, may experience destructive deadly waves. Depending on a number of factors, some low-lying areas could experience severe inland inundation of water and debris of more than 1,000 feet.

Learn whether tsunamis have occurred in your area by contacting your local emergency management office, National Weather Service office, or American Red Cross chapter. If you are in a tsunami risk area, learn how to protect yourself, your family, and your property.

## Awareness Information

The West Coast/Alaska Tsunami Warning Center (WC/ATWC) is responsible for tsunami warnings for California, Oregon, Washington, British Columbia, and Alaska.

The Pacific Tsunami Warning Center (PTWC) is responsible for providing warnings to international authorities, Hawaii, and U.S. territories within the Pacific basin. The two Tsunami Warning Centers coordinate the information being disseminated.

All tsunamis are potentially dangerous, even though they may not damage every coastline they strike. Damaging tsunamis are very rare. Our coastlines are vulnerable, but tsunamis are infrequent. Understand the hazard and learn how to protect yourself, but don't let the threat of tsunamis ruin your enjoyment of the beach.

The WC/ATWC and PTWC may issue the following bulletins:

- Warning: A tsunami was or may have been generated, which could cause damage; therefore, people in the warned area are strongly advised to evacuate.

- Watch: A tsunami was or may have been generated, but is at least two hours travel time to the area in watch status. Local officials should prepare for possible evacuation if their area is upgraded to a warning.

- Advisory: An earthquake has occurred in the Pacific basin, which might generate a tsunami. WC/ATWC and PTWC will issue hourly bulletins advising of the situation.

- Information: A message with information about an earthquake that is not expected to generate a tsunami. Usually only one bulletin is issued.

Be familiar with the tsunami warning signs. A strong earthquake lasting 20 seconds or more near the coast may generate a tsunami. A noticeable rapid rise or fall in coastal waters is also a sign that a tsunami is approaching.

Tsunamis most frequently come onshore as a rapidly rising turbulent surge of water choked with debris. They are not V-shaped or rolling waves, and are not "surfable."

## Plan for a Tsunami

Develop a family disaster plan. Tsunami-specific planning should include the following:

- Find out if you are in tsunami hazard areas. Know the height of your street above sea level and the distance of your street from the coast or other high-risk waters. Evacuation orders may be based on these numbers.

- If you are visiting an area at risk from tsunamis, check with the hotel, motel, or campground operators for tsunami evacuation information and how you would be warned. It is important to know designated escape routes before a warning is issued.

If you are at risk from tsunamis, do the following:

- Plan an evacuation route from your home, school, workplace, or any other place you'll be where tsunamis present a risk. If possible, pick an area 100 feet above sea level or go up to two miles inland, away from the coastline. If you can't get this high or far, go as high as you can. Every foot inland or upwards may make a difference. You should be able to reach your safe location on foot within 15 minutes. After a disaster, roads may become impassable or blocked. Be prepared to evacuate by foot if necessary. Footpaths normally lead uphill and inland, while many roads parallel coastlines. Follow posted tsunami evacuation routes; these will lead to safety. Local emergency management officials can help advise you as to the best route to safety and likely shelter locations.

- Practice your evacuation route. Familiarity may save your life. Be able to follow your escape route at night and during inclement weather. Practicing your plan makes the appropriate response more of a reaction, requiring less thinking during an actual emergency situation.

- Use a National Oceanic and Atmospheric Administration (NOAA) Weather Radio with a tone-alert feature to keep you informed of local watches and warnings. The tone alert feature will warn you of potential danger even if you are not currently listening to local radio or television stations.

- Discuss tsunamis with your family. Everyone should know what to do in case all family members are not together. Discussing tsunamis ahead of time will help reduce fear and anxiety, and let everyone know how to respond. Review flood safety and preparedness measures with your family.

## What to Do If You Feel a Strong Coastal Earthquake

If you feel an earthquake that lasts 20 seconds or longer when you are on the coast:

- Drop, cover, and hold on. You should first protect yourself from the earthquake.

- When the shaking stops, gather your family members and evacuate quickly. Leave everything else behind. A tsunami may be coming within minutes. Move quickly to higher ground away from the coast.

- Be careful to avoid downed power lines and stay away from buildings and bridges from which heavy objects might fall during an aftershock.

## What to Do When a Tsunami Watch Is Issued

- Listen to a NOAA Weather Radio, Coast Guard emergency frequency station, or other reliable source for updated emergency information. As the energy of a tsunami is transferred through open water, it is not detectable. Seismic action may be the only advance warning before the tsunami approaches the coastline.

- Locate family members and review evacuation plans. Make sure everyone knows there is a potential threat and the best way to safer ground.

- If you have special evacuation needs (small children, elderly people, or persons with disabilities), consider early evacuation. Evacuation may take longer, allow extra time.

- If time permits, secure unanchored objects around your home or business. Tsunami waves can sweep away loose objects. Securing these items or moving them inside will reduce potential loss or damage.

- Be ready to evacuate. Being prepared will help you to move more quickly if a tsunami warning is issued.

## What to Do When a Tsunami Warning Is Issued

- Listen to a NOAA Weather Radio, Coast Guard emergency frequency station, or other reliable source for updated emergency information. Authorities will issue a warning only if they believe there is a real threat from tsunami.

- Follow instructions issued by local authorities. Recommended evacuation routes may be different from the one you use, or you may be advised to climb higher.

- If you are in a tsunami risk area, do the following:

    - If you hear an official tsunami warning or detect signs of a tsunami, evacuate at once. A tsunami warning is issued when authorities are certain that a tsunami threat exists, and there may be little time to get out.

    - Take your disaster supplies kit. Having supplies will make you more comfortable during the evacuation.

    - Get to higher ground as far inland as possible. Officials cannot reliably predict either the height or local effects of tsunamis. Watching a tsunami from the beach or cliffs could put you in grave danger. If you can see the wave, you are too close to escape it.

Return home only after local officials tell you it is safe. A tsunami is a series of waves that may continue for hours. Do not assume that after one wave the danger is over. The next wave may be larger than the first one.

## *What to Do after a Tsunami*

- Continue listening to a NOAA Weather Radio, Coast Guard emergency frequency station, or other reliable source for emergency information. The tsunami may have damaged roads, bridges, or other places that may be unsafe.

- Help injured or trapped persons. Give first aid where appropriate. Call for help. Do not move seriously injured persons unless they are in immediate danger of further injury.

- Help a neighbor who may require special assistance—infants, elderly people, and people with disabilities. Elderly people and people with disabilities may require additional assistance. People who care for them or who have large families may need additional assistance in emergency situations.

- Use the telephone only for emergency calls. Telephone lines are frequently overwhelmed in disaster situations. They need to be clear for emergency calls to get through.

- Stay out of the building if waters remain around it. Tsunami waters, like flood waters, can undermine foundations, causing buildings to sink, floors to crack, or walls to collapse.

- When re-entering buildings or homes, use extreme caution. Tsunami-driven flood waters may have damaged buildings where you least expect it. Carefully watch every step you take.

  - Wear sturdy shoes. The most common injury following a disaster is cut feet.

  - Use battery-powered lanterns or flashlights when examining buildings. Battery-powered lighting is the safest and easiest, preventing fire hazard for the user, occupants, and building.

  - Examine walls, floors, doors, staircases, and windows to make sure that the building is not in danger of collapsing.

  - Inspect foundations for cracks or other damage. Cracks and damage to a foundation can render a building uninhabitable.

- Look for fire hazards. There may be broken or leaking gas lines, flooded electrical circuits, or submerged furnaces or electrical appliances. Flammable or explosive materials may come from upstream. Fire is the most frequent hazard following floods.

- Check for gas leaks. If you smell gas or hear a blowing or hissing noise, open a window and quickly leave the building. Turn off the gas using the outside main valve if you can, and call the gas company from a neighbor's home. If you turn off the gas for any reason, it must be turned back on by a professional.

- Look for electrical system damage. If you see sparks or broken or frayed wires, or if you smell burning insulation, turn off the electricity at the main fuse box or circuit breaker. If you have to step in water to get to the fuse box or circuit breaker, call an electrician first for advice. Electrical equipment should be checked and dried before being returned to service.

- Check for sewage and water line damage. If you suspect sewage lines are damaged, avoid using the toilets and call a plumber. If water pipes are damaged, contact the water company and avoid using water from the tap. You can obtain safe water from undamaged water heaters or by melting ice cubes.

- Use tap water if local health officials advise it is safe.

- Watch out for animals, especially poisonous snakes, that may have come into buildings with the water. Use a stick to poke through debris. Tsunami flood waters flush snakes and animals out of their homes.

- Watch for loose plaster, drywall, and ceilings that could fall.

- Take pictures of the damage, both of the building and its contents, for insurance claims.

- Open the windows and doors to help dry the building.

- Shovel mud while it is still moist to give walls and floors an opportunity to dry.

- Check food supplies. Any food that has come in contact with flood waters may be contaminated and should be thrown out.

# Section 18.7

## *Volcanoes*

"Volcanoes," U.S. Geological Survey, United States
Department of the Interior, 1998.

Explosive volcanoes blast hot solid and molten rock fragments and gases into the air. As a result, ashflows can occur on all sides of a volcano and ash can fall hundreds of miles downwind. Dangerous mudflows and floods can occur in valleys leading away from volcanoes. If you are near a known volcano, active or dormant, be prepared to follow instructions from your local emergency officials.

### *Before*

Learn about your community warning systems and emergency plans.

Be prepared for the hazards that can accompany volcanoes:

- Mudflows and flash floods.
- Landslides and rockfalls.
- Earthquakes.
- Ashfall and acid rain.
- Tsunamis.

Make evacuation plans. If you live in a known volcanic hazard area, plan a route out and have a backup route in mind.

Develop an emergency communication plan. In case family members are separated from one another during a volcanic eruption (a real possibility during the day when adults are at work and children are at school), have a plan for getting back together. Ask an out-of-state relative or friend to serve as the "family contact," because after a disaster, it's often easier to call long distance. Make sure everyone knows the name, address, and phone number of the contact person.

Have disaster supplies on hand:

- Flashlight and extra batteries.

- First aid kit and manual.
- Emergency food and water.
- Non-electric can opener.
- Essential medicines.
- Dust mask.
- Sturdy shoes.

Get a pair of goggles and a throw-away breathing mask for each member of the household in case of ashfall.

## During

- Follow the evacuation order issued by authorities.
- Avoid areas downwind and river valleys downstream of the volcano.

If caught indoors:

- Close all windows, doors, and dampers.
- Put all machinery inside a garage or barn.

If trapped outdoors:

- Seek shelter indoors.
- If caught in a rockfall, roll into a ball to protect your head.
- If caught near a stream, be aware of mudflows. Move up slope, especially if you hear the roar of a mudflow.

Protect yourself during ashfall:

- Wear long-sleeved shirts and long pants.
- Use goggles to protect your eyes.
- Use a dust mask or hold a damp cloth over your face to help breathing.
- Keep car or truck engines off.

Stay out of the area defined as a restricted zone by government officials. Effects of a volcanic eruption can be experienced many miles from a volcano. Mudflows and flash flooding, wildland fires, and even deadly hot ashflow can reach you even if you cannot see the volcano during an eruption. Avoid river valleys and low lying areas. Trying to watch an erupting volcano up close is a deadly idea.

Listen to a battery-operated radio or television for the latest emergency information.

## After

If possible, stay away from volcanic ashfall areas.

When outside:

- Cover your mouth and nose. Volcanic ash can irritate your respiratory system.
- Wear goggles to protect your eyes.
- Keep skin covered to avoid irritation from contact with ash.

Clear roofs of ashfall. Ashfall is very heavy and can cause buildings to collapse. Exercise great caution when working on a roof.

Avoid driving in heavy ashfall. Driving will stir up more ash that can clog engines and stall vehicles.

If you have a respiratory ailment, avoid contact with any amount of ash. Stay indoors until local health officials advise it is safe to go outside.

Remember to help your neighbors who may require special assistance—infants, elderly people, and people with disabilities.

## Evacuation

Although it may seem safe to stay at home and wait out an eruption, if you are in a hazardous zone, doing so could be very dangerous. Stay safe. Follow authorities' instructions and put your disaster plan into action.

## Mudflows

Mudflows are powerful "rivers" of mud that can move 20 to 40 mph. Hot ash or lava from a volcanic eruption can rapidly melt snow and ice at the summit of a volcano. The melt water quickly mixes with falling ash, with soil cover on lower slopes, and with debris in its path. This turbulent mixture is dangerous in stream channels and can travel more than 50 miles away from a volcano. Also intense rainfall can erode fresh volcanic deposits to form large mudflows. If you see the water level of a stream begin to rise, quickly move to high ground. If a mudflow is approaching or passes a bridge, stay away from the bridge.

# Part Three

# Protecting Your Health during International Travel

# Chapter 19

# *General Health Tips for International Travel*

## *General*

The risk of becoming ill while traveling abroad may depend on three important factors:

1.  Making adequate pre-departure preparations.

2.  Knowing what health and safety risks are involved where you are.

3.  Following sound medical counsel.

In addition, you should know that living away from the cultural environment you are used to can sometimes cause a degree of mental and emotional stress—which, in turn, can trigger physiological consequences. The impact of studying abroad on personal relationships, on counseling sessions (if you are in therapy), and on your general health (if you are on medication of any kind) is something you need to consider as you prepare for your sojourn abroad.

In most developed countries and regions, such as Australia, New Zealand, Japan, and Western Europe, health risks may be no greater than comparable risks while traveling in the United States. On the other

---

Excerpted with permission from, "Health and Nutrition," http://www.study abroad.com/handbook/health.html, a section of the *StudyAboad.com Handbook* by Bill Hoffa. © 2000 Educational Directories Unlimited, Inc. For additional information, visit www.studyabroad.com.

hand, in the countries of Africa, Asia, South and Central America, the South Pacific, Middle and Far East, living conditions and standards of sanitation and hygiene can vary greatly, depending on where you are. Some cities in these areas provide safer and healthier environments than outlying rural areas. But the opposite can also be true. The key to survival and good health is, beyond everything else, in knowing what to expect.

Wherever you go, if your travel is limited primarily to tourist areas, there is understandably less risk of exposure to food or water of questionable quality, and thus the risk of disease remains narrow. You may travel to cities off the usual tourist routes or live in small villages or rural areas for extended periods of time. In doing so, you of course enrich your education, but you may also run a greater risk of acquiring infectious diseases through exposure to water and food of uncertain quality.

### Some Not-Too-Uncommon Diseases

Diarrhea is a common affliction that usually strikes a couple of days after arrival in a new area of the world and seldom lasts longer than about five days. Diarrhea is nature's way of ridding the body of noxious agents; intestinal motility serves as the normal cleansing mechanism of the intestine. The most important way of coping with this disorder is to maintain adequate fluid intake to prevent dehydration. Most cases of diarrhea are self-limited and require only simple replacement of fluids and salts lost in diarrhea stools. Fluids that are readily available, such as canned fruit juices, hot tea, or carbonated drinks, may be used. Your physician may be able to prescribe medication to take along for relief of the symptoms. However, it is strongly recommended that you consult a physician rather than attempt self-medication if your diarrhea condition is severe or does not resolve itself within several days, if there is blood and/or mucus in the stool, if fever occurs with shaking chills, or if there is persistent diarrhea with dehydration.

Tetanus, commonly known as "lockjaw," is an infection of the nervous tissue produced by a contaminated wound or injury. Severe muscle spasms are produced, and if left untreated, tetanus can be fatal. Cleanliness (lots of soap and water to remove contamination of a wound or injury) is one of the most effective weapons to prevent this kind of infection. Tetanus immunization is available, often in combination with the diphtheria vaccine. Tetanus boosters are recommended every ten years after the initial series of three injections administered one month apart.

216

Hepatitis A (Infectious Hepatitis) is most prevalent in North Africa, the Middle East, and the Caribbean. However, it is possible to contract the disease anywhere (including in the United States) that living conditions are crowded and unsanitary. Hepatitis A is transmitted orally through the ingestion of contaminated food or water; clams, oysters, and other shellfish, especially if eaten raw, are common sources of the disease in contaminated areas. A variety of symptoms are associated with the disease, including fever, loss of appetite, nausea, abdominal pain, and yellowing of the eyes.

Malaria, which is transmitted by the female Anopheline mosquito, is common to parts of the Caribbean, Latin America, Africa, the Middle East, and Asia. Anti-malaria medication is available and is required for those who will be participating in a program in Africa. Instructions on taking the medication must be followed carefully to insure adequate protection; you must usually begin taking the medication prior to your departure, during the entirety of your visit, and for two or three weeks after return to the United States. (The organisms that cause the disease do not invade the red blood cells until about a week or so after the bite of the mosquito.)

### Other Infectious Diseases

Certain viral, bacterial, and parasitic infections acquired abroad may not result in any immediately illness. Some diseases (such as malaria) may not produce symptoms for as long as six months to a year after a traveler returns. Should you become ill even well after returning to the United States, you should not hesitate to inform your physician of your travel outside the United States within the 12 months preceding onset of the illness. Knowledge of the possibility of exposure to certain diseases abroad will help the physician arrive at a correct diagnosis.

## Food and Water

In areas where chlorinated tap water is not available, or where hygiene and sanitation are poor (most of Western Europe is excluded from this category), travelers should be advised that only the following may be safe to drink:

1.  Beverages, such as tea and coffee, made with boiled water.

2.  Canned or bottled carbonated beverages, including carbonated bottled water and soft drinks.

3.  Beer and wine: Where water may be contaminated, ice (or containers for drinking) can also be considered contaminated, and it is generally safer to drink directly from the can or bottle of a beverage than from a questionable container. Wet cans or bottles should be dried before being opened, and surfaces that come into direct contact with the mouth should first be wiped clean. If no source of safe drinking water is available, for example, verifiably safe bottled-water, tap water that is uncomfortably hot to touch may be safe, once it has cooled and put in a thoroughly cleaned container; it can also be used for brushing teeth as well as for drinking.

4.  Fresh Fruit and Vegetables: In areas of the world where hygiene and sanitation are known to be poor, to avoid illness, fresh food should always be selected with care. You should avoid unpasteurized milk and milk products, such as cheese, and eat only fruit that you have peeled yourself. Since the sources of the organisms causing travelers' diarrhea are usually contaminated food or water, precautionary measures are particularly helpful in preventing most serious intestinal infections. However, even when persons follow these general guidelines for prevention, they may still develop diarrhea. You may prepare your own fruit juice from fresh fruit. Iced drinks and non-carbonated bottled fluids made from water of uncertain quality should be avoided.

5.  Street-food: Many developing (and developed) countries offer an abundance of food sold from stands along the road. It is advisable to avoid such food unless and until you have ample evidence from reliable local sources that it is safe for visitors to eat. Note: many locals may have no trouble with such food or drink, but this is often because they have developed over time bodily immunities against its possible impurities, which is not the case for visitors. You will be tempted, but be careful.

6.  Restaurants: It is difficult to generalize about the quality of restaurant food in the U.S., and even more so to do this about all the varieties of restaurant food you are likely to encounter overseas. General principles obviously apply: establishments which cater to outsiders and/or are in the expensive price ranges, are almost always going to offer safe and nutritious food, while those at the other end of the economic spectrum and serve locals may or may not. Assuming that there are no

such restaurants or you are on a limited budget, and also that you would like to sample local foods and eating styles, the best advice is to seek sound advice from reputable travel guides or, even better, from your program director or on-site hosts.

## Prescriptions

Should you currently be under the care of a physician or require regular medication or injections (for example, insulin or allergy shots), be sure to check with your personal physician for any advice or recommendations concerning your welfare while abroad. It is a good idea to notify the on-site coordinator of any special needs you may have.

If you need medications regularly, take an adequate supply with you. Do not buy medications "over the counter" while you are overseas unless you are familiar with the product: "Over the counter" drugs abroad are not regulated by the U.S. Food and Drug Administration.

If you have diabetes, are allergic to penicillin, or have any physical condition that may require emergency care, carry some kind of identification—a tag, bracelet, or card—on your person at all times indicating the specific nature of the problem and spelling out clearly what must or must not be done should you be unable to communicate this information yourself (for example, in case of unconsciousness).

Prescription medicines should be accompanied by a letter from your physician. This letter should include a description of the problem, the dosage of prescribed medications to assist medical authorities during an emergency, and the generic name(s) of medicine listed.

Any special health needs or medical conditions should be noted on medical history forms you are advised to travel with you. If you are required to take a medicine containing habit-forming or narcotic drugs you should carry a doctor's certificate attesting to that fact. It is also advisable to keep all medicines in their original and labeled containers. To avoid potential problems and because laws may vary from country to country, if you need to carry such medicines you should consult the embassies of the countries you will visit before departing the U.S. (from the Bureau of Public Affairs, Department of State, March 1986).

## Insurance

Be sure that you have adequate health insurance and understand your family and/or institutional policy, especially what is and isn't or may not be covered outside the U.S.A. Make sure you know how this system works, meaning how bills are paid, in the case of a medical emergency, and also routine treatments.

Personal liability insurance against injury or damage caused by or resulting from your acts or omissions during enrollment in any program is highly recommended.

Should you require medical attention abroad, it may be necessary for you to have sufficient cash on hand to make payment at the time of treatment since the foreign physician and/or hospital may not be able to process medical bills through an American insurance company. In such cases, be sure to obtain a receipt to submit with your insurance claim for reimbursement upon return to the U.S. It might also be helpful to carry a few blank claim forms with you in case you should need them while abroad.

## Immunizations

At the present time, no immunizations are required for entry to or return from Australia, Western Europe, Japan, Israel, or the Commonwealth of Independent States (Russia). This, of course, can change periodically, depending on the prevailing health conditions, so it is always a good idea to check on the latest status just prior to your departure. This is especially important if your post-program travel plans include visits to countries other than the aforementioned. Information on immunizations can also be found via the World Wide Web.

Protection against cholera and yellow fever are recommended for those going to certain parts of Africa, along with medicine for protection against malaria. Remember that to be effective, these anti-malaria drugs must be taken regularly and in strict accordance with the doctor's instructions. Even though you may be limiting your travel to western Europe, you may still wish to discuss with your personal physician the advisability of receiving certain basic immunizations, like tetanus and typhoid fever. Since you will probably be doing a lot of knocking around overseas, it will be easy to suffer a few minor cuts and abrasions on occasion; it is always a good idea to have protection against tetanus just in case such a wound might become contaminated.

## Medical Care Abroad

In order to provide appropriate physicians and local medical authorities abroad with sufficient information to respond promptly and effectively to situations which require medical attention, many programs ask you to complete a medical history form, at the time of acceptance.

During weekend or post-program travel, you may find yourself in a variety of unfamiliar and possibly remote locations. If you are not fluent in the language of the host country, of course try to seek out an English-speaking doctor if you need medical attention: when it comes to health matters, you will not want to take any chances on a breakdown in communications. American embassies and consulates, many large travel agencies (for example, Thomas Cook) and a number of the larger hotels abroad will have lists of English-speaking physicians. Some agencies have also been established to assure travelers needing medical care (for example, with a pre-existing medical problem) a reasonable, preset fee with reputable physicians fluent in English.

If you have a pre-existing medical condition or simply are concerned about health facilities while you are overseas, you must take steps to find out about health care in each countries in which you expect to spend any time.

## AIDS

Everything you already know about what AIDS is and how it is contracted is as deadly true overseas as it is at home. Knowing this and taking all advised precautions is the only way to protect yourself. AIDS is considerably less an epidemic in some countries than in the U.S., and considerably more in others. Whatever the situation in the country you are going to, you are not more likely to contract AIDS there than here—If you act sensibly and refrain from unprotected sex and other behaviors and habits with carry the risk of infection. As The World Health Organization states: "AIDS is not spread by daily and routine activities such as sitting next to someone or shaking hands, or working with people. Nor is it spread by insects or insect bites. AIDS is not spread by swimming pools, public transportation, food, cups, glasses, plates, toilets, water, air, touching or hugging, coughing or sneezing." This is as biologically true abroad as it is in your hometown.

However, since you will not know your environment overseas as well as you do at home, or might not be able to control it to the same degree, there are some things you should be concerned about in advance, to prepare yourself for all eventualities.

### Knowing Your HIV Status

When traveling abroad, be aware that some countries may require HIV antibody tests, a test for antibodies to the human immune-deficiency virus (HIV) that causes AIDS. You should also know that some countries may not have the resources to adequately screen blood or provide sterile needles.

Living overseas in certain areas may present greater risks to those who test positive for the HIV virus. Some overseas locations have limited medical facilities that cannot monitor the progress of such infections. Therefore, if you believe you may be infected, knowing your HIV status will help when planning your trip.

### If the Country You Are Going to Requires an HIV Antibody Test

Some countries now require incoming foreigners, including students, to take the HIV antibody test. Usually this is required for long term stays. Check to see if the country you are going to requires HIV-testing. You may need a "doctor's certificate" showing the results of an HIV antibody test. Consulates in Washington DC and/or New York City carry information on HIV testing as well. If you decide you want to be tested, do so only at a center that offers pre- and post-test counseling. There are many institutions whose primary focus is AIDS counseling. Allow yourself two weeks for the testing process. Finally, consider getting tested twice-first anonymously (which allows you the privacy to decide what you want to do if the result is positive), then again for a doctor's certificate, if needed.

### Overseas Blood Transfusions and Blood Products and HIV Screening

While many countries such as the United States, Australia, Canada, Japan, and the western European countries have mandatory screening of donated blood for the AIDS virus, not all do. You should find out before you go from your campus resources, from your local Red Cross and/or western embassies about safe sources of blood overseas. In some locales, ascertaining the availability of HIV-screened blood and blood products may be difficult. Because of obvious uncertainties, consider these precautions: If you are injured or ill while abroad, avoid or postpone any blood transfusion unless it is absolutely necessary. If you do need blood, try to ensure that screened blood is used.

Regardless of the blood screening practices abroad, always try to reduce the risk of serious injury which may require blood transfusions by taking everyday precautions. If you are sexually active, always use a latex condom. Take a supply with you as conditions, manufacturing and storage of condoms in other countries may be questionable. Take good care of yourself while traveling! Don't wear yourself down, watch out for excessive exposure to heat, drink plenty of fluids to avoid dehydration, and get plenty of sleep!

### Overseas Injections and AIDS

Here in the United States, we may take for granted disposable equipment such as needles and syringes. Be advised that some foreign countries will reuse even disposable equipment. In some countries, if injection is required, you can buy needles and syringes and bring them to the hospital for you own use. Avoid injections unless absolutely necessary. If injections are required, make sure the needles and syringes come straight from a package or have been sterilized with chemicals or by boiling for twenty minutes. When in doubt, ask to see how the equipment has been sterilized.

Caution regarding instrument sterilization applies to all instruments that pierce the skin, including tattooing, acupuncture, ear piercing and dental work.

The Center for Disease Control recommends that "Diabetics or other persons who require routine or frequent injections should carry a supply of syringes and needles sufficient to last their stay abroad." It is not uncommon to bring needles for your own use. However, be aware that carrying needles and syringes without a prescription may be illegal in some countries. Take a note from your doctor if you do need to carry needles and syringes. Some countries have needles and syringes for sale. Do not use or allow the use of contaminated, unsterilized syringes or needles for any injections, for example, illicit drugs, tattooing, acupuncture, or for medical/dental procedures.

# Chapter 20

# Medical Emergencies during Travel Abroad

## If Medical Care Is Needed Abroad

If an American citizen becomes seriously ill or is injured abroad, a U.S. consular officer can assist in locating appropriate medical services and informing family or friends. If necessary, a consular officer can also assist in the transfer of funds from the United States. However, payment of hospital and other expenses is the responsibility of the traveler.

Protection against potentially hazardous drugs is nonexistent in some countries, increasing the risk of adverse reactions. Do not buy medications "over the counter" unless you are familiar with the product.

Before going abroad, learn what medical services your health insurance will cover overseas. If your health insurance policy provides coverage outside the United States, remember to carry both your insurance policy identity card, as proof of such insurance, and a claim form. Although some health insurance companies will pay "customary and reasonable" hospital costs abroad, very few will pay for medical evacuation to the United States. Medical evacuation can easily cost $10,000 or more, depending on the location and medical condition.

"Illness Abroad," excerpted from *Health Information for International Travel, 2001-2002*, produced by the Centers for Disease Control and Prevention (CDC), available online at http://www.cdc.gov/travel/other/illness-abroad.htm.

## World Health Organization (WHO) Blood Transfusion Guidelines for International Travelers

There is a growing public awareness of the AIDS (acquired immunodeficiency syndrome) epidemic and a resulting concern about acquiring the AIDS virus through blood transfusion. Systematic screening of blood donations is not yet feasible in all developing countries. Persons planning international travels have requested to have their own blood or blood from their home country available to them in case of urgent need. These requests raise logistic, technical, and ethical issues that are not easy to resolve. Ultimately, the safety of blood for such persons will depend on the quality of blood transfusion services in the host country. The strengthening of these services is of the highest priority. While efforts are being made to achieve this end, other approaches are also needed.

### *Basic Principles*

1. Unexpected, emergency blood transfusion is rarely required. It is needed only in situations of massive hemorrhage such as severe trauma, gynecologic and obstetric emergency, or gastrointestinal bleeding.

2. In many cases, resuscitation can be achieved by use of colloid or crystalloid plasma expanders instead of blood.

3. Blood transfusion is not free of risk, even in the best of conditions. In most developing countries, the risk is increased by limited technical resources for screening blood donors for HIV (human immunodeficiency virus) infection and other diseases transmissible by blood.

4. The international shipment of blood for transfusion is practical only when handled by agreement between two responsible organizations, such as national blood transfusion services. This mechanism is not useful for emergency needs of individual patients and should not be attempted by private individuals or organizations not operating recognized blood programs.

### *Therefore*

1. There are no medical indications for travelers to take blood with them from their home country.

2. The limited storage period of blood and the need for special equipment negate the feasibility of independent blood banking for individual travelers or small groups.

3. Blood should be transfused only when absolutely indicated. This applies even more forcefully in those countries where screening of blood for transmissible diseases is not yet widely performed.

### Proposed Options

1. When urgent resuscitation is necessary, the use of plasma expanders rather than blood should always be considered.

2. In case of emergency need for blood, use of plasma expanders and urgent evacuation home may be the actions of choice.

3. When blood transfusion cannot be avoided, the attending physician should make every effort to ensure that the blood has been screened for transmissible diseases, including HIV.

4. International travelers should

   • take active steps to minimize the risk of injury, such as avoiding night driving, employing safe driving practices, and wearing seatbelts whenever possible;

   • establish a plan for dealing with medical emergencies;

   • support the development within countries of safe and adequate blood supplies.

This information is taken from the WHO publication "World Health Organization Global Programme on AIDS: Blood Transfusion Guidelines for International Travelers."

## Death Overseas

### Importation or Exportation of Human Remains

There are no federal restrictions on the importation of human remains unless the death was the result of one of the following communicable diseases: cholera or suspected cholera, diphtheria, infectious tuberculosis, plague, suspected smallpox, yellow fever, suspected viral hemorrhagic fevers (Lassa, Marburg, Ebola, Congo-Crimean, and others not yet isolated or named). If the death was the result of one of these diseases, the remains must be cremated or properly embalmed, placed in a hermetically sealed casket, and be accompanied by a death certificate, translated into English, that states the cause of death. Following importation, the local mortician will be subject to the regulations of the state and local health authorities for interstate or intrastate shipment.

The United States has no requirements for the exportation of human remains; however, the requirements of the country of destination must be met. Information regarding these requirements may be obtained from the appropriate embassy or local consulate general.

## The Post-Travel Period

Some diseases may not manifest themselves immediately. If travelers become ill after they return home, they should tell their physician where they have traveled.

Most persons who acquire viral, bacterial, or parasitic infections abroad become ill within six weeks after returning from international travel. However, some diseases may not manifest themselves immediately; for example, malaria may not cause symptoms for as long as six months to a year after the traveler returns to the United States. It is recommended that a traveler always advise a physician of the countries visited within the 12 months preceding onset of illness.

Knowledge of such travel and the possibility the patient may be ill with a disease the physician rarely encounters will help the physician arrive at a correct diagnosis.

# Chapter 21

# Infectious Diseases of Risk to Travelers Abroad

## Chapter Contents

# Section 21.1

# *Overview*

"Infections Diseases of Potential Risk for Travelers," is excerpted from *International Travel and Health,* © 2002 World Health Organization. Reprinted with permission.

Depending on the travel destination, travelers may be exposed to a number of infectious diseases; exposure depends on the presence of infectious agents in the area to be visited. The risk of becoming infected will vary according to the purpose of the trip and the itinerary within the area, the standards of accommodation, hygiene and sanitation, as well as the behavior of the traveler. In some instances, disease can be prevented by vaccination, but there are some infectious diseases, including some of the most important and most dangerous, for which no vaccines exist.

General precautions can greatly reduce the risk of exposure to infectious agents and should always be taken for visits to any destination where there is a significant risk of exposure. These precautions should be taken regardless of whether any vaccinations or medication have been administered.

## *Modes of Transmission and General Precautions*

The modes of transmission for different infectious diseases and the corresponding general precautions are outlined in the following paragraphs.

### *Foodborne and Waterborne Diseases*

Food and waterborne diseases are transmitted by consumption of contaminated food and drink. The risk of infection is reduced by taking hygienic precautions with all food, drink and drinking water consumed when traveling and by avoiding direct contact with polluted recreational waters. Examples of diseases transmitted by food and water are hepatitis A, typhoid fever and cholera.

230

*Vector-Borne Diseases*

A number of particularly serious infections are transmitted by insects and other vectors such as ticks. The risk of infection can be reduced by taking precautions to avoid insect bites and contact with other vectors in places where infection is likely to be present. Examples of vector-borne diseases are malaria, yellow fever, dengue and tick-borne encephalitis.

*Zoonoses (Diseases Transmitted from Animals)*

Zoonoses include many infections that can be transmitted to humans through animal bites or contact with contaminated body fluids or feces from animals, or by consumption of foods of animal origin, particularly meat and milk products. The risk of infection can be reduced by avoiding close contact with any animals—including wild, captive and domestic animals—in places where infection is likely to be present. Particular care should be taken to prevent children from approaching and handling animals. Examples of zoonoses are rabies, brucellosis, leptospirosis and certain viral hemorrhagic fevers.

*Sexually Transmitted Diseases*

Sexually transmitted diseases are passed from person to person through unsafe sexual practices. The risk of infection can be reduced by avoiding casual and unprotected sexual intercourse, and by use of condoms. Examples of sexually transmitted diseases are hepatitis B, HIV/AIDS and syphilis.

*Bloodborne Diseases*

Bloodborne diseases are transmitted by direct contact with infected blood or other body fluids. The risk of infection can be reduced by avoiding direct contact with blood and body fluids, by avoiding the use of potentially contaminated needles and syringes for injection or any other medical or cosmetic procedure that penetrates the skin (including acupuncture, piercing and tattooing), and by avoiding transfusion of unsafe blood. Examples of bloodborne diseases are hepatitis B and C, HIV/AIDS and malaria.

*Airborne Diseases*

Airborne diseases are transmitted from person to person by aerosol and droplets from the nose and mouth. The risk of infection can

be reduced by avoiding close contact with people in crowded and enclosed places. Examples of airborne diseases are influenza, meningococcal disease and tuberculosis.

*Diseases Transmitted from Soil*

Soil-transmitted diseases include those caused by dormant forms
(spores) of infectious agents, which can cause infection by contact with
broken skin (minor cuts, scratches, etc.). The risk of infection can be
reduced by protecting the skin from direct contact with soil in places
where soil-transmitted infections are likely to be present. Examples
of bacterial diseases transmitted from soil are anthrax and tetanus.
Certain intestinal parasitic infections, such as ascariasis and trichu-
riasis, are transmitted via soil and infection may result from consumption of soil-contaminated vegetables.

# Section 21.2

# *Cholera*

"Cholera," excerpted from *Health Information for International Travel,
2001–2002,* a brochure produced by the Centers for Disease Control and
Prevention (CDC), available online at http://www.cdc.gov/travel/diseases/
cholera.htm. 2002.

Cholera is an acute intestinal infection caused by toxigenic *Vibrio
cholerae* O-group 1 or O-group 139. The infection is often mild and
self-limited or subclinical. People with severe cases respond dramatically to simple fluid—and electrolyte—replacement therapy. Infection
is acquired primarily by ingesting contaminated water or food; person-to-person transmission is rare.

## *Occurrence*

Since 1961, *V. cholerae* has spread from Indonesia through most
of Asia into eastern Europe and Africa, and from North Africa to the
Iberian Peninsula. In 1991, an extensive epidemic began in Peru and
spread to neighboring countries in the Western Hemisphere. In 1999,

nearly 255,000 cases from 61 countries were reported to the World Health Organization.

## Risk for Travelers

People who follow usual tourist itineraries and who observe food safety recommendations while in countries reporting cholera have virtually no risk. Risk increases for those who drink untreated water or ingest poorly cooked or raw seafood in endemic areas.

## Preventive Measures

### Vaccine

The risk of cholera to U.S. travelers is so low that vaccination is of questionable benefit. At the present time, the manufacture and sale of the only licensed cholera vaccine in the United States (by Wyeth Ayerst) has been discontinued. It has not been recommended for travelers because of the brief and incomplete immunity it offers.

Two recently developed vaccines for cholera are licensed and available in other countries (Dukoral® from Biotec AB, and Mutacol® from Berna). Both vaccines appear to provide a somewhat better immunity and have fewer side effects than the previously available vaccine. However, neither of these two vaccines is recommended for travelers nor are they available in the United States. Further information on these vaccines can be obtained from the manufacturers at: Active Biotec AB (publ), http://www.activebiotech.com; and Mutacol®, Berna, http://www.berna.org.

Currently, no country or territory requires vaccination as a condition for entry. Local authorities, however, may continue to require documentation of vaccination against cholera. In such cases, a single dose of either oral vaccine is sufficient to satisfy local requirements, or a medical waiver may be given.

### Other

Travelers to cholera-affected areas should be advised to avoid eating high-risk foods, especially fish and shellfish. Food that is cooked and served hot, fruits and vegetables peeled by the traveler personally, and beverages and ice that are made from boiled or chlorinated water or that are carbonated are usually safe.

# Section 21.3

# *Hepatitis A and E*

"Hepatitis, Viral, Type A," and "Hepatitis, Viral, Type E," excerpted from *Health Information for International Travel, 2001–2002,* a brochure produced by the Centers for Disease Control and Prevention (CDC), available online at http://www.cdc.gov/travel/diseases/hav.htm, and http://www. cdc.gov/travel/diseases/hev.htm. 2002.

## *Hepatitis, Viral, Type A*

Hepatitis A is an enterically transmitted viral disease that causes fever, malaise, anorexia, nausea, and abdominal discomfort, followed within a few days by jaundice. The disease ranges in clinical severity from no symptoms to a mild illness lasting 1 to 2 weeks to a severely disabling disease lasting several months. In developing countries, hepatitis A virus (HAV) is usually acquired during childhood, most frequently as an asymptomatic or mild infection. Transmission can occur by direct person-to-person contact; through exposure to contaminated water, ice, or shellfish harvested from sewage-contaminated water; or from fruits, vegetables, or other foods that are eaten uncooked, and which can become contaminated during harvesting or subsequent handling.

### *Occurrence*

HAV is highly endemic throughout the developing world, but, in general, of low endemicity in developed countries (within developed countries there might be pockets of increased endemicity).

### *Risk for Travelers*

The risk of acquiring HAV infection for U.S. residents traveling abroad varies with living conditions, length of stay, and the incidence of HAV in the area visited. HAV is the most common vaccine-preventable disease in travelers and HAV vaccine or immune globulin (IG), or both, is recommended for all susceptible people traveling to or working in countries with an intermediate or a high endemicity of infection. Travelers to North America (except Mexico), Japan, Australia, New Zealand, and developed countries in Europe are at no greater risk of infection than in the United States. For travelers to developing countries, risk of infection increases with duration of travel and is highest for those who live in or visit rural areas, trek in back country areas, or frequently eat or drink in settings of poor sanitation. Nevertheless, many cases of travel-related HAV occur in travelers to developing countries with standard tourist itineraries, accommodations, and food consumption behaviors.

*Preventive Measures*

*Vaccine:* Two HAV vaccines are currently licensed in the United States: Havrix® (manufactured by GlaxoSmithKline) and Vaqta® (manufactured by Merck & Co., Inc). Both vaccines are made of inactivated virus adsorbed to aluminum hydroxide as an adjuvant. Havrix® is prepared with 2-phenoxyethanol as a preservative, while Vaqta® is formulated without a preservative. The vaccine should be administered by intramuscular injection in the deltoid muscle. Travelers younger than 2 years of age should receive a single dose of IG (0.02 mL/kg) because neither vaccine is licensed for infants. Travelers who are allergic to a vaccine component or otherwise elect not to receive vaccine should receive a single dose of IG (0.02 mL/kg), which provides effective protection against HAV for up to 3 months. For anyone traveling for longer than 3 months, an IG dose of 0.06 mL/kg should be given, and must be repeated if the duration of travel is longer than 5 months. (See Table 21.1 for approximate IG dosages.)

Although vaccination of an immune traveler is not contraindicated and does not increase the risk of adverse effects, screening for total antibodies to HAV (anti-HAV) before travel can be useful to determine susceptibility and eliminate unnecessary vaccination or IG prophylaxis of immune travelers. Such serologic screening for susceptibility might be indicated for adult travelers who are likely to have had prior HAV infection if the cost of screening (laboratory and office visit) is less than the cost of vaccination or IG prophylaxis and if testing will not interfere with subsequent receipt of vaccine or IG. Such travelers can include those older than 40 years of age and those born in parts of the world with intermediate or high endemicity. Postvaccination testing for serologic response is not indicated.

*Adverse Reactions:* Among those 19 years of age or older, the most frequently reported side effects occurring within 3 days following a dose of Havrix® were soreness at the injection site (56%), headache (14%), and malaise (7%). In clinical studies among those 18 years of age or younger, the most frequently reported side effects were soreness at the injection site (15%), feeding problems (8%), headache (4%), and injection-site induration (4%). Among those 19 years of age or older, the most frequent side effects occurring within 5 days following vaccination with Vaqta® were tenderness (53%), pain (51%), warmth at the injection site (17.3%), and headache (16.1%). Among those 18 years of age or younger, the most common side effects reported were pain (19%), tenderness (17%), and warmth at the injection site (9%).

Postlicensure reports, without regard to causality, of serious events received by the vaccine manufacturers have included (but might not have been limited to) anaphylaxis, Guillain-Barré syndrome, brachial plexus neuropathy, transverse myelitis, multiple sclerosis, encephalopathy, and erythema multiforme. Most of these events have occurred among adults, and many have occurred among people receiving other vaccines concurrently. For serious adverse events for which background incidence data were known, the rates for vaccine recipients were not higher than would be expected for an unvaccinated population.

*Immune Globulin:* Immune globulin for intramuscular administration prepared in the United States has few side effects (primarily soreness at the injection site) and has never been shown to transmit infectious agents (hepatitis B virus [HBV], hepatitis C virus [HCV], or human immunodeficiency virus [HIV]). Since December 1994, all IG products commercially available in the United States have had to

**Table 21.1.** Immune Globulin for Protection against Viral Hepatitis A

| Length of Stay | Body Weight in Pounds | Body Weight in Kilograms | Dose Volume* | Comments |
|---|---|---|---|---|
| Less than 3 months | Less than 50 | Less than 23 | 0.5 Milliliters | Dose |
| | 50 to 100 | 23 to 45 | 1.0 milliliters | volume |
| | More than 100 | More than 45 | 2.0 milliliters | depends |
| | | | | on body |
| 3 to 5 Months | Less than 22 | Less than 10 | 0.5 milliliters | weight |
| | 22 to 49 | 10 to 22 | 1.0 milliliters | and |
| | 50 to 100 | 23 to 45 | 2.5 milliliters | length |
| | More than 100 | More than 45 | 5.0 milliliters | of stay |

*For intramuscular injection.

undergo a viral inactivation procedure or be negative for HCV ribonucleic acid (RNA) before release.

*Precautions and Contraindications:* Neither vaccine should be administered to travelers with a history of hypersensitivity to alum and Havrix® should not be administered to travelers with a history of hypersensitivity reactions to the preservative 2-phenoxyethanol. Because the vaccine is inactivated, no special precautions need to be taken for vaccination of immunocompromised travelers.

*Pregnancy:* The safety of HAV vaccine for pregnant women has not been determined. However, because HAV vaccine is produced from inactivated HAV, the theoretical risk to either the pregnant woman or the developing fetus is thought to be very low. The risk of vaccination should be weighed against the risk of HAV in women travelers who might be at high risk for exposure to HAV. Pregnancy is not a contraindication to using immune globulin.

*Other:* HAV is inactivated by boiling or cooking food and beverage items to 85° Celsius (185° Fahrenheit) for at least one minute. Foods and beverages heated to this temperature and for this length of time cannot serve as vehicles for disease unless contaminated after heating. Adequate chlorination of water as recommended in the United States will inactivate HAV. Travelers should be advised that, to minimize their risk of HAV and other enteric diseases in developing countries, they should avoid potentially contaminated water or food. Travelers should also be advised to avoid drinking beverages (with or without ice) of unknown purity, and eating uncooked shellfish and uncooked fruits or vegetables that are not peeled or prepared by the traveler personally.

### Hepatitis, Viral, Type E

Hepatitis E is an enterically transmitted viral disease that can be distinguished from other forms of acute viral hepatitis only by using specific serological testing, the availability of which is limited at this time. Disease occurs primarily in adults. A low (0.5% to 4.0%) case fatality rate is associated with hepatitis E in the general population, but among pregnant women mortality has ranged from 17% to 33%; the highest rates of fulminant hepatitis and death have occurred during the third trimester. No chronic infection after initial hepatitis E infection has been documented.

Hepatitis E virus (HEV) is transmitted by the fecal-oral route. HEV occurs both in epidemic and sporadic forms and is associated primarily with the ingestion of fecally contaminated drinking water. The potential for HEV transmission from contaminated food is still under investigation, and there is no evidence of transmission by percutaneous or sexual exposures.

*Occurrence*

Epidemics and sporadic cases of HEV have been reported from areas of Asia (Afghanistan, Bangladesh, Burma (Myanmar), China, India, Indonesia, Kazakhstan, Kyrgyzstan, Malaysia, Mongolia, Nepal, Pakistan, Tajikistan, Turkmenistan, and Uzbekistan), Mexico, the Middle East, northern Africa, and sub-Saharan Africa. Outbreaks have not been recognized in Europe, the United States, Australia, or South America. Several imported cases of HEV have been identified in American travelers and two cases have been identified in patients with no history of international travel; studies are in progress to determine if HEV is an endemic disease in the United States.

*Risk for Travelers*

Travelers to developing countries where HEV occurs can be at risk of acquiring this disease through contaminated water.

*Preventive Measures*

There is no vaccine to prevent HEV. Immune globulin (IG) prepared from plasma collected in HEV endemic areas has not been effective in preventing clinical disease during HEV outbreaks. IG prepared from plasma collected from parts of the world where HEV is not an endemic disease is unlikely to be effective. The best prevention of infection is to avoid potentially contaminated water (and food), as with hepatitis A and other enteric infections.

# Section 21.4

# *Malaria*

"Malaria," excerpted from *Health Information for International Travel, 2001–2002,* a brochure produced by the Centers for Disease Control and Prevention (CDC), available online at http://www.cdc.gov/travel/diseases/malaria/index.htm. 2002.

Malaria in humans is caused by one of four protozoan species of the genus *Plasmodium*: *P. falciparum, P. vivax, P. ovale,* or *P. malariae.* All are transmitted by the bite of an infected female Anopheles mosquito. Occasionally, transmission occurs by blood transfusion or congenitally from mother to fetus. The disease is characterized by fever and influenza-like symptoms, including chills, headache, myalgias, and malaise; these symptoms can occur at intervals. Malaria can be associated with anemia and jaundice, and *P. falciparum* infections can cause kidney failure, coma, and death. However, deaths from malaria are preventable.

## *Occurrence*

Malaria is a major international public health problem, causing 300 to 500 million infections worldwide and several million deaths annually. Information on malaria risk in specific countries is derived from various sources, including the World Health Organization. The information presented in this chapter was accurate at the time of publication; however, factors that can vary from year to year, such as local weather conditions, mosquito vector density, and prevalence of infection, can have a marked effect on local malaria transmission patterns.

## *Risk for Travelers*

Malaria transmission occurs in large areas of Central and South America, Hispaniola, sub-Saharan Africa, the Indian subcontinent, Southeast Asia, the Middle East, and Oceania. The estimated risk of a traveler's acquiring malaria varies markedly from area to area. This variability is a function of the intensity of transmission within the

239

various regions and of the itinerary and time and type of travel. From 1985 through 1998, 3,555 cases of *P. falciparum* among U.S. civilians were reported to the Centers for Disease Control and Prevention (CDC). Of these, 3,007 (84%) were acquired in sub-Saharan Africa; 236 (7%) in Asia; 206 (6%) in the Caribbean and Central or South America; and 106 (3%) in other parts of the world. During this period, there were 47 fatal malaria infections among U.S. civilians; 46 (98%) caused by *P. falciparum*, of which 36 (78%) were acquired in sub-Saharan Africa.

Thus, most imported *P. falciparum* malaria among American travelers was acquired in Africa south of the Sahara, even though only 508,000 U.S. residents traveled to countries in that region in 1998. In contrast, 25 million U.S. residents traveled from the United States that year to other countries with malaria (including 18 million travelers to Mexico). This disparity in the risk of acquiring malaria reflects the fact that the predominant species of malaria transmitted in sub-Saharan Africa is *P. falciparum*, that malaria transmission is generally higher in Africa than in other parts of the world, and that malaria is often transmitted in urban areas as well as rural areas in sub-Saharan Africa. In contrast, malaria transmission in general is lower in Asia and South America, a larger proportion of the malaria is *P. vivax*, and most urban areas do not have malaria transmission.

Estimating the risk of infection for different categories of travelers is difficult and can be significantly different even for people who travel or reside temporarily in the same general areas within a country. For example, travelers staying in air-conditioned hotels might be at lower risk than backpackers or adventure travelers. Similarly, long-term residents living in screened and air-conditioned housing are less likely to be exposed than are people living without such amenities, such as Peace Corps volunteers.

### Preventive Measures

No vaccine is currently available. However, all travelers to malarious areas of the world should be advised to use an appropriate drug regimen and personal protection measures to prevent malaria; however, travelers should be informed that, regardless of methods employed, malaria still can be contracted. Malaria symptoms can develop as early as 6 days after initial exposure in a malaria-endemic area and as late as several months after departure from a malarious area, after chemoprophylaxis has been terminated. Travelers should be advised that malaria can be treated effectively early in the course of the disease, but that delay of appropriate therapy can have serious or even fatal consequences. Travelers who have symptoms of malaria should be advised to seek prompt medical evaluation, including thick and thin blood smears, as soon as possible.

The resistance of *P. falciparum* to chloroquine has been confirmed in all areas with *P. falciparum* malaria except the Dominican Republic, Haiti, Central America west of the former Panama Canal Zone, Egypt, and some countries in the Middle East. In addition, resistance to both chloroquine and Fansidar® is widespread in Thailand; Burma (Myanmar); Cambodia; the Amazon River basin area of South America; and, increasingly, parts of east Africa. Resistance to mefloquine has been confirmed on the borders of Thailand with Burma (Myanmar) and Cambodia, in the western provinces of Cambodia, and in the eastern states of Burma (Myanmar).

### Personal Protection Measures

Because of the nocturnal feeding habits of Anopheles mosquitoes, malaria transmission occurs primarily between dusk and dawn. Travelers should be advised to take protective measures to reduce contact with mosquitoes, especially during these hours. Such measures include remaining in well-screened areas, using mosquito nets, and wearing clothes that cover most of the body. Additionally, travelers should be advised to purchase insect repellent before travel for use on exposed skin. The most effective repellents contain N, N-diethylmetatoluamide (DEET), an ingredient in many commercially available insect repellents. The actual concentration of DEET varies among repellents and can be as high as 95%. Repellents with DEET concentrations of 30% to 35% are quite effective, and the effects should last for about 4 hours. Long-acting DEET products are now commercially available. Rarely, children exposed to DEET have had toxic encephalopathy. Travelers should be advised that the possibility of adverse reactions to DEET will be minimized if they take the following precautions: (1) apply repellent sparingly and only to exposed skin or clothing; (2) avoid applying high-concentration products to the skin; (3) avoid inhaling or ingesting repellents or getting them in the eyes; (4) avoid applying repellents to portions of children's hands that are likely to have contact with the eyes or mouth; (5) never use repellents on wounds or irritated skin; and (6) wash repellent-treated skin after coming indoors. If a reaction to insect repellent is suspected, travelers should be advised to wash treated skin and seek medical attention.

Travelers who will not be staying in well-screened or air-conditioned rooms should be advised to use a pyrethroid-containing flying-insect spray in living and sleeping areas during evening and nighttime hours. In addition, they should take additional precautions, including sleeping under mosquito netting (that is, bed nets). Permethrin (Permanone®) may be sprayed on clothing and bed nets for additional protection against mosquitoes. Bed nets are more effective if they are treated with permethrin or deltamethrin insecticides. In the United States, permethrin spray or liquid can be used, or bed nets may be purchased that have already been impregnated. Permethrin or deltamethrin liquid may also be purchased overseas for the treatment of bed nets.

## Checklist for Travelers to Malarious Areas

The following is a checklist of key issues to be considered in advising travelers.

- Travelers should be informed about the risk of malaria infection and the presence of drug-resistant *Plasmodium falciparum* malaria in their areas of destination.

- Travelers should be advised how to protect themselves against mosquito bites.

- Travelers should be advised to start chemoprophylaxis before travel, and to use prophylaxis continuously while in malaria-endemic areas and for 4 weeks (chloroquine, mefloquine, and doxycycline) or 7 days (Malarone™) after leaving such areas.

- Travelers should be questioned about drug allergies and other contraindications for use of drugs to prevent malaria.

- Travelers should be advised which drug to use for chemoprophylaxis and, if appropriate, whether Fansidar® or Malarone™ should be carried for presumptive self-treatment.

- Travelers should be informed that any antimalarial drug can cause side effects and, if these side effects are serious, that medical help should be sought promptly and use of the drug discontinued.

- Travelers should be warned that they could acquire malaria even if they use malaria chemoprophylaxis.

In case of illness, travelers should be:

- Informed that symptoms of malaria can be mild, and that they should suspect malaria if they experience fever or other symptoms such as persistent headaches, muscular aching and weakness, vomiting, or diarrhea.

- Informed that malaria can be fatal if treatment is delayed. Medical help should be sought promptly if malaria is suspected, and a blood sample should be taken and examined for malaria parasites on one or more occasions.

- Reminded that self-treatment should be taken only if prompt medical care is not available and that medical advice should still be sought as soon as possible after self-treatment.

Pregnant women and young children require special attention because of the potential effects of malaria illness and their inability to use some drugs (for example, doxycycline).

### *Chemoprophylaxis*

In choosing an appropriate chemoprophylactic regimen before travel, the traveler and his or her health care provider should consider several factors. The travel itinerary should be reviewed in detail and compared with the information on areas of risk within a given country to determine whether the traveler will actually be at risk of acquiring malaria. Whether the traveler will be at risk of acquiring drug-resistant *P. falciparum* malaria should also be determined. In addition, it should be established whether the traveler has previously experienced an allergic or other reaction to one of the antimalarial drugs of choice and whether medical care will be readily accessible during travel.

Malaria chemoprophylaxis with mefloquine or chloroquine should begin 1 to 2 weeks before travel to malarious areas (except for doxycycline or Malarone™, which can begin 1 to 2 days before travel). This allows for antimalarial drug to be in the blood prior to exposure, as well as for any potential side effects to be evaluated and treated before the traveler's departure.

Chemoprophylaxis should continue during travel in the malarious areas and after leaving the malarious areas (4 weeks after travel for chloroquine, mefloquine, and doxycycline, and 7 days after travel for Malarone™). Drugs with longer half-lives (that are taken weekly) offer the advantage that they might have a wider margin of error if the traveler is late with a dose than drugs with short half-lives (that are taken daily). For example, if a traveler is 1 to 2 days late with a weekly drug, prophylactic blood levels can remain adequate; if they are 1 to 2 days late with a daily drug, protective blood levels are less likely to be maintained.

### *Travel to Areas without Chloroquine-Resistant* P. Falciparum

For travel to areas of risk where chloroquine-resistant *P. falciparum* has NOT been reported, once-a-week use of chloroquine alone should be recommended. Chloroquine is usually well tolerated. The few people who experience uncomfortable side effects might tolerate the drug better by taking it with meals or in divided twice-a-week doses. As an alternative, the related compound hydroxychloroquine might be better tolerated. Chloroquine prophylaxis should begin 1 to 2 weeks before travel to malarious areas. It should be continued weekly during travel in malarious areas and for 4 weeks after a traveler leaves such areas.

### *Travel to Areas with Chloroquine-Resistant* P. Falciparum

For travel to areas of risk where chloroquine-resistant *P. falciparum* exists, options include the following drugs.

**Mefloquine (Lariam®):** Mefloquine is usually well tolerated, but precautions should be observed. Mefloquine prophylaxis should begin 1 to 2 weeks before travel to malarious areas. It should be continued weekly during travel in malarious areas and for 4 weeks after a traveler leaves such areas. Mefloquine can be used for long-term prophylaxis.
Note: In some foreign countries, a fixed combination of mefloquine and Fansidar® is marketed under the name Fansimef®. Fansimef® should not be confused with mefloquine, and it is not recommended for prophylaxis of malaria because of the potential for severe adverse reactions associated with prophylactic use of Fansidar®.

**Doxycycline:** Doxycycline is as efficacious as mefloquine for travel to most malarious areas. It can be used by travelers to areas with mefloquine-resistant strains of *P. falciparum* (the borders of Thailand with Burma [Myanmar] and Cambodia, western Cambodia, and eastern Burma). Travelers who use doxycycline should be cautioned about possible side effects. Doxycycline prophylaxis should begin 1 to 2 days before travel to malarious areas. It should be continued daily during travel in malarious areas and for 4 weeks after the traveler leaves such areas.

**Malarone™:** Malarone™ has shown good prophylactic efficacy for prevention of *P. falciparum* malaria, including those infections acquired in areas with chloroquine-resistant strains. Recent data have demonstrated its efficacy in people without antimalarial immunity (that is, in populations whose members are similar to travelers from nonmalarious areas who travel to malarious areas, including people who formerly lived in malarious countries but who now live in nonmalarious countries), in addition to preexisting information on its good prophylactic efficacy in semi-immune people (that is, people living in malarious areas for extended periods of time). It is now one of three options (the others are mefloquine or doxycycline) for prevention of malaria when traveling to areas with chloroquine-resistant *P. falciparum* malaria. The adult dosing regimen for prophylaxis with Malarone™ is one adult tablet daily starting 1 to 2 days before travel, taken daily during travel, and continuing daily for 7 days after leaving the malarious area.

Of note, CDC no longer lists chloroquine/proguanil as an option for travel to areas with chloroquine-resistant *P. falciparum*.

### Chemoprophylaxis for Infants, Children, and Adolescents

Infants, children, and adolescents of any age can contract malaria. Consequently, the indications for prophylaxis are identical to those described for adults. Chloroquine is the drug of choice for children traveling to areas without chloroquine-resistant *P. falciparum*. Data suggest that mefloquine is also well tolerated by young children (<15 kilograms [kg] [<33 pounds (lbs)]). Mefloquine is an option for use in children when travel to areas with chloroquine-resistant *P. falciparum* is unavoidable. Doxycycline is contraindicated in infants and children younger than 8 years of age. Infants and children who cannot take mefloquine or doxycycline can be given Malarone™ for prophylaxis. At this time, no data are available on the safety and efficacy of Malarone™ for prevention of malaria in children weighing <11 kg (<25 lbs), although studies are in progress.

Mefloquine and chloroquine phosphate are manufactured in the United States in tablet form only and have a very bitter taste. Pediatric doses should be calculated carefully according to body weight. Pharmacists can pulverize tablets and prepare gelatin capsules with calculated pediatric doses. Mixing the powder in food or drink can facilitate the administration of antimalarial drugs to infants and children. Chloroquine in suspension is widely available overseas. Physicians should calculate the dose and volume to be administered based on body weight, because the concentration of chloroquine base varies in different suspensions. Malarone™ is available in pediatric tablet form.

Overdose of antimalarial drugs can be fatal medication should be stored in childproof containers out of the reach of infants and children.

## Chemoprophylaxis during Pregnancy

Malaria infection in pregnant women can be more severe than in nonpregnant women. Malaria can increase the risk of adverse pregnancy outcomes, including prematurity, abortion, and stillbirth. For these reasons and because no chemoprophylactic regimen is completely effective, women who are pregnant or likely to become pregnant should be advised to avoid travel to areas with malaria transmission if possible.

**Chloroquine:** Women traveling to areas where drug-resistant *P. falciparum* has not been reported may take chloroquine prophylaxis. Chloroquine has not been found to have any harmful effects on the fetus when used in the recommended doses for malaria prophylaxis; therefore, pregnancy is not a contraindication for malaria prophylaxis with chloroquine or hydroxychloroquine.

**Mefloquine:** A review of mefloquine use in pregnancy from clinical trials and reports of inadvertent use of mefloquine during pregnancy suggests that its use during the second and third trimesters of pregnancy is not associated with adverse fetal or pregnancy outcomes. Limited data suggest it is also safe to use during the first trimester. Consequently, mefloquine may be considered for prophylaxis in women who are pregnant or likely to become so, when exposure to chloroquine-resistant *P. falciparum* is unavoidable.

**Doxycycline:** Doxycycline is contraindicated for malaria prophylaxis during pregnancy and lactation. Adverse effects of tetracyclines on the fetus include discoloration and dysplasia of the teeth and inhibition of bone growth. During pregnancy, tetracyclines are indicated only to treat life-threatening infections from multidrug-resistant *P. falciparum*.

**Primaquine:** Primaquine should not be used during pregnancy because the drug can be passed transplacentally to a glucose-6-phosphate dehydrogenase (G6PD)-deficient fetus and cause hemolytic anemia in utero. Whenever radical cure or terminal prophylaxis with primaquine is indicated during pregnancy, chloroquine should be given once a week until delivery, at which time primaquine may be given.

**Malarone™:** There are insufficient data regarding the use of Malarone™ during pregnancy. Therefore, Malarone™ is not currently recommended for pregnant women unless the potential benefit outweighs the potential risk to the fetus (for example, for a pregnant women who has acquired *P. falciparum* malaria in an area of multidrug-resistant strains and who cannot tolerate other treatment options).

### Prophylaxis while Breast-Feeding

Data are available for some antimalarial agents on the amount of drug secreted in breast milk of lactating women. Very small amounts of chloroquine and mefloquine are secreted in the breast milk of lactating women. The amount of drug transferred is not thought to be harmful to a nursing infant. Because the quantity of antimalarials transferred in breast milk is insufficient to provide adequate protection against malaria, infants who require chemoprophylaxis should receive the recommended dosages of antimalarials. No information is available on the amount of primaquine that enters human breast milk; the infant should be tested for G6PD deficiency before primaquine is given to a woman who is breast-feeding. Sulfonamides do enter human breast milk and should not be given to infants younger than 2 months of age. However, in most cases, the potential benefit to the woman when Fansidar® is used for treatment of malaria would outweigh any theoretical risks to an infant.

It is not known whether atovaquone is excreted in human milk. Proguanil is excreted in human milk in small quantities. Based on experience with other antimalarial drugs, the quantity of drug transferred in breast milk is likely insufficient to provide adequate protection against malaria for the infant. Because data are not yet available on the safety and efficacy of Malarone™ in infants weighing less than 11 kg (25 lbs), it should not be given to a woman who breast feeds an infant who weighs less than 11 kg (25 lbs) unless the potential benefit to the woman outweighs the potential risk for the infant (for example, for a lactating woman who has acquired

*P. falciparum* malaria in an area of multidrug-resistant strains and who cannot tolerate other treatment options).

### Self-Treatment

CDC recommends the use of malaria prophylaxis for travel to malarious areas. Travelers who elect not to take prophylaxis and plan to treat themselves only if they experience symptoms or who require or choose regimens that do not have optimal efficacy (for example, use of chloroquine for travel to areas with chloroquine-resistant *P. falciparum*) should be provided with a treatment dose of one of the antimalarials recommended for presumptive self-treatment should it be needed.

Presumptive self-treatment is recommended for travelers with illness suspected to be malaria who cannot reach medical care within 24 hours. These travelers should be advised to take presumptive self-treatment promptly if they have a febrile illness during their travel and if professional medical care is not available within 24 hours; however, they should be advised that this self-treatment of a possible malarial infection should be only a temporary measure and that prompt medical evaluation is imperative.

### Drugs Recommended for Presumptive Self-Treatment

**Fansidar®:** To date, sulfadoxine-pyrimethamine (SP) (Fansidar®) has been the drug recommended by CDC for presumptive self-treatment for travelers not allergic to sulfa drugs and remains a recommended drug for self-treatment for travelers to areas without SP resistance.

**Malarone™:** Malarone™ is now another option for presumptive self-treatment for travelers not taking Malarone™ for prophylaxis. Malarone™ is the drug of choice for presumptive self-treatment for travelers to areas with SP resistance, which includes the Amazon River basin of South America, Southeast Asia, and some countries in eastern and southern Africa (specifically, Kenya, Malawi, Mozambique, South Africa, Tanzania, and Uganda). Travelers on Malarone™ prophylaxis who take presumptive self-treatment should be advised to use Fansidar® if they are traveling to an area without Fansidar® resistance. If traveling to an area with Fansidar® resistance, travelers should be advised to consult a health care provider prior to travel; CDC can provide consultation in these cases.

## *Drugs Not Recommended for Presumptive Self-Treatment*

**Mefloquine:** Mefloquine should not be used for self-treatment because of the frequency of serious side effects (for example, hallucinations and seizures) that have been associated with the high doses of mefloquine used for treatment of malaria.

**Halofantrine:** Halofantrine (Halfan®) is not recommended for self-treatment of malaria because of potentially serious electrocardiogram changes that have been documented following treatment doses.

**Table 21.2.** Presumptive Treatment of Malaria

*Drug*
 Sulfadoxine-pyrimethamine (SP) (Fansidar®).
 Self-treatment drug to be used if professional medical care is not available within 24 hours. Medical care should be sought immediately after treatment.

*Adult Dose*
 3 tablets (75 mg pyrimethamine and 1,500 mg sulfadoxine), orally as a single dose.

*Pediatric Dose*
 5 to 10 kg: 1/2 tablet      11 to 20 kg: 1 tablet
 21 to 30 kg: 1 1/2 tablets   31 to 45 kg: 2 tablets
 46 or more kg: 3 tablets

*Comments*
 Contraindicated in people with sulfa allergy. Resistance to SP occurs in Amazon River basin, Southeast Asia, and parts of east Africa; Malarone™ is preferred in these areas.

*Drug*
 Atovaquone/proguanil (Malarone™).

*Adult Dose*
 4 tablets (each tablet contains 1,000 mg atovaquone and 400 mg proguanil) orally as a single daily dose for 3 consecutive days.

*Pediatric Dose*
 Daily dose to be taken for 3 consecutive days using adult strength tablets:
 11 to 20 kg: 1 tablet       21 to 30 kg: 2 tablets
 31 to 40 kg: 3 tablets      41 kg or more: 4 tablets

*Comments*
 Not recommended for self-treatment in people on Malarone(tm) prophylaxis.

Abbreviations: mg—milligram; kg—kilogram.
Kilogram = 2.2 pounds.

In many of these reports, halofantrine was administered in the presence of other antimalarial drugs (for example, mefloquine). The safety of halofantrine for self-treatment of travelers on mefloquine prophylaxis has not been established and, because halofantrine is widely available overseas, health care providers might choose to caution travelers to avoid the use of halofantrine if they are taking mefloquine.

### Prevention of Relapses of P. Vivax and P. Ovale: Primaquine

P. vivax and P. ovale parasites can persist in the liver and cause relapses for as long as 4 years after routine chemoprophylaxis is discontinued. Travelers to malarious areas should be alerted to this risk and, if they develop malaria symptoms after leaving a malarious area, they should be advised to report their travel history and the possibility of malaria to a physician as soon as possible. Primaquine decreases the risk of relapses by acting against the liver stages of P. vivax or P. ovale. Primaquine is administered after the traveler has left a malaria-endemic area, usually during or following the last 2 weeks of prophylaxis.

Because most malarious areas of the world (except Haiti and the Dominican Republic) have at least one species of relapsing malaria, travelers to these areas have some risk of acquiring either P. vivax or P. ovale, although the actual risk for an individual traveler is difficult to define. Terminal prophylaxis with primaquine for prevention of relapses is generally indicated only for people who have had prolonged exposure in malaria-endemic areas (for example, missionaries and Peace Corps volunteers). Most people can tolerate the standard regimen of primaquine, with the exception of individuals deficient in G6PD.

### Adverse Reactions and Contraindications

Following is a discussion of the frequent or serious side effects of recommended antimalarials.

**Chloroquine and Hydroxychloroquine:** Chloroquine and hydroxychloroquine rarely cause serious adverse reactions when taken at prophylactic doses for malaria. Minor side effects that can occur include gastrointestinal disturbance, headache, dizziness, blurred vision, and pruritus, but generally these effects do not require that the drug be discontinued. High doses of chloroquine, such as those used to treat rheumatoid arthritis, have been associated with retinopathy, but this serious side effect has not been associated with routine weekly malaria prophylaxis. Chloroquine and related compounds have been reported to exacerbate psoriasis. Chloroquine can interfere with the antibody response to human diploid cell rabies vaccine when the vaccine is administered intradermally.

**Mefloquine:** Mefloquine is generally well tolerated when used for chemoprophylaxis. It has rarely been associated with serious adverse reactions (for example, psychoses or seizures) at prophylactic doses; these reactions are more frequent with the higher doses used in treatment. Minor side effects observed with prophylactic doses, such as gastrointestinal disturbance, insomnia, and dizziness, tend to be transient and self-limited.

Mefloquine is contraindicated for use by travelers with a known hypersensitivity to mefloquine and is not recommended for use by travelers with a history of seizures or severe psychiatric disorders. A review of available data suggests that mefloquine may be used in people concurrently on beta blockers, if they have no underlying arrhythmia. However, mefloquine is not recommended for people with cardiac conduction abnormalities.

**Doxycycline:** Doxycycline can cause photosensitivity, usually manifested as an exaggerated sunburn reaction. The risk of such a reaction can be minimized by avoiding prolonged, direct exposure to the sun and by using sunscreens that absorb long-wave ultraviolet (UVA) radiation. In addition, doxycycline use is associated with an increased frequency of *Candida vaginitis*.

Gastrointestinal side effects (nausea or vomiting) may be minimized by taking the drug with a meal. To reduce the risk of esophagitis, travelers should be advised not to take doxycycline before going to bed. Doxycycline is contraindicated in pregnancy and in infants and children younger than 8 years of age.

**Malarone™:** The most common adverse effects reported in people using Malarone™ for prophylaxis or treatment were abdominal pain, nausea, vomiting, and headache.

**Fansidar®:** Adverse reactions reported in people taking sulfonamides included nausea, vomiting, and headache. Travelers should be advised not to use Fansidar® for prophylaxis because of the risk for severe cutaneous adverse reactions. Fansidar® is contraindicated in people with a history of sulfonamide intolerance and in infants younger than 2 months of age.

**Primaquine:** Primaquine can cause severe hemolysis in G6PD-deficient individuals. Before primaquine is used, G6PD deficiency should be ruled out by appropriate laboratory testing.

### *Malaria Hotline*

Detailed recommendations for the prevention of malaria are available from CDC 24 hours a day from the voice information service (1-888-232-3228) or the fax information service (1-888-232-3299), or on the Internet at http://www.cdc.gov/travel.

## Section 21.5

# *Mad Cow Disease*

"Bovine Spongiform Encephalopathy and New Variant Creutzfeldt-Jakob Disease," excerpted from *Health Information for International Travel, 2001–2002,* a brochure produced by the Centers for Disease Control and Prevention (CDC), available online at http://www.cdc.gov/travel/madcow.htm. 2002.

Since 1996, evidence has been increasing for a causal relationship between ongoing outbreaks in Europe of a disease in cattle called bovine spongiform encephalopathy (BSE, or mad cow disease) and a disease in humans called new variant Cruetzfeldt-Jakob disease (nvCJD). Both disorders are invariably fatal brain diseases with unusually long incubation periods measured in years, and are caused by an unconventional transmissible agent (a prion). Although there is strong evidence that the agent responsible for these human cases was the same agent responsible for the BSE outbreaks in cattle, the specific foods that might be associated with the transmission of the agent from cattle to humans are unknown. However, bioassays have identified the presence of the BSE agent in the brain, spinal cord, retina, dorsal root ganglia (nervous tissue located near the backbone), distal ileum, and bone marrow of cattle experimentally infected with this agent by the oral route.

In addition to cattle, sheep are susceptible to experimental infection with the BSE agent by the oral route. Thus, in countries where flocks of sheep and goats might have been exposed to the BSE agent through contaminated feed, a theoretical risk exists that these animals might have developed infections caused by the BSE agent and that these infections are being maintained in the flocks, even in the absence of continued exposure to contaminated feed (for example, through maternal transmission). In December 1999, the World Health Organization published a report encouraging countries to conduct risk assessments related to BSE in populations of sheep and goats. In August 2000, survey data of sheep farms in the United Kingdom were reported to have shown no rise in BSE-like illnesses in sheep that could be related to the BSE outbreaks in cattle. Currently, cattle remain the only known food animal species with disease caused by the BSE agent.

## *Occurrence*

From 1986 through August 2000, less than 99% of the cases of BSE reported were from the United Kingdom, but endemic cases of BSE were also reported in other European countries, including Belgium, Denmark, France, Liechtenstein, Luxembourg, Netherlands, Portugal, Ireland, and Switzerland. From 1995 through early August 2000, 79 human cases of nvCJD were reported in the United Kingdom, 3 in France, and 1 in Ireland. During that period, the reported rate of occurrence of these new cases increased. Based on data available in mid-2000, the proportion of the total number of BSE cases in Europe reported outside the United Kingdom rose to 6.7% in 1998 and to >10% in 1999, primarily reflecting the declining large outbreak of BSE in the United Kingdom and the sharp rise in the number of reported cases in Portugal. In July 2000, the European Union Scientific Steering Committee (SSC) on the geographic risk of BSE adopted a final opinion on the risk of BSE in the cattle populations of 23 different countries. The United Kingdom and Portugal were the only ones classified as countries where BSE was confirmed in domestic cattle at a higher level (over 100 cases per 1 million adult cattle in the 12-month period ended June 15, 2000).

Despite the absence of reported endemic cases of BSE in Germany, Italy, and Spain, the SSC concluded that it was likely that cattle were infected in those three countries and classified their geographic risk of BSE as similar to that of the countries where BSE had been confirmed (but at a level below 100 cases per 1 million adult cattle). Because no data were available from Greece, the SSC reported that it was prudent to assume that the geographic BSE risk there was at a high level. The reports of the final opinion of the SSC and its BSE risk assessments of individual countries are available on the European Union Commission on Food Safety and Animal Welfare Internet website, http://europa.eu.int/comm/food/index_en.html (search for BSE-risk assessment). In addition, the numbers of reported cases, by country, are available on the Internet website of the Office International des Epizooties, at http://www.oie.int/eng/info/en_esb.htm. These numbers should be interpreted with caution because of differences in the intensity of surveillance over time and by country. Information is being generated rapidly on BSE issues. Updated sources should be consulted.

### Risk to Travelers

The current risk of acquiring nvCJD from eating beef (muscle meat) and beef products produced from cattle in Europe cannot be precisely determined, and this risk in specific countries might not reflect the fact that cattle products from one country might be distributed and consumed in others. Nevertheless, in the United Kingdom, this current risk appears to be extremely small, perhaps about 1 case per 10 billion servings. In the other countries of Europe, this current risk, if it exists at all, would not likely be any higher than that in the United Kingdom, except possibly in Portugal. In the 12-month period ending June 15, 2000, Portugal had about half the reported incidence of BSE cases per 1 million adult cattle as that reported in the United Kingdom; however, Portugal has less experience with implementing the BSE-related public health control measures.

### Preventive Measures

Public health control measures, such as BSE surveillance, the culling of sick animals, or banning specified risk materials (SRMs), or a combination of these, have been instituted in Europe to prevent potentially BSE-infected tissues from entering the human food chain. The most stringent of these control measures have been applied in the United Kingdom and appear to have been highly effective. In June 2000, the European Union Commission on Food Safety and Animal Welfare adopted a decision requiring all member states to remove SRMs from animal feed and human food chains as of October 1, 2000; such bans had already been instituted in most member states.

To reduce the possible current risk of acquiring nvCJD from food, travelers to Europe should be advised to consider either (1) avoiding beef and beef products altogether or (2) selecting beef or beef products, such as solid pieces of muscle meat (versus brains or beef products such as burgers and sausages), that might have a reduced opportunity for contamination with tissues that might harbor the BSE agent. Milk and milk products from cows are not believed to pose any risk for transmitting the BSE agent.

# Section 21.6

# *Yellow Fever*

"Yellow Fever," excerpted from *Health Information for International Travel, 2001–2002,* a brochure produced by the Centers for Disease Control and Prevention (CDC), available online at http://www.cdc.gov/travel/diseases/yellowfever.htm. 2002.

Yellow fever is a mosquito-borne viral disease. Illness varies in severity from a flu-like syndrome to severe hepatitis and hemorrhagic fever.

## *Occurrence*

The disease occurs only in sub-Saharan Africa (where it is endemic) and tropical South America. In Africa, a variety of vectors are responsible for the disease and it is in Africa where the majority of the cases are reported. The case fatality rate is approximately 23%, and infants and children are at greatest risk for infection. In South America, cases occur most frequently in young men who have an occupational exposure to the vector in forested or transitional areas of Bolivia, Brazil, Colombia, Ecuador, and Peru. The case fatality rate is approximately 65%.

## *Risk for Travelers*

Although yellow fever has rarely occurred in travelers, fatal cases of yellow fever have occurred in some unvaccinated travelers visiting rural areas within the yellow fever endemic zone.

## *Vaccine*

Yellow fever is preventable by a safe, effective vaccine. International regulations require proof of vaccination for travel to and from certain countries. For purposes of international travel, vaccines produced by different manufacturers worldwide must be approved by the World Health Organization and administered at an approved yellow fever vaccination center. State and territorial health departments have authority to designate nonfederal vaccination centers; these can be identified by contacting state or local health departments. (The Centers for Disease Control and Prevention [CDC] does not maintain a list of the designated centers.) Vaccines should receive an international certificate of vaccination completed, signed, and validated with the center's stamp where the vaccine was given.

A number of countries require a certificate from travelers arriving from infected areas or from countries with infected areas. Some countries in Africa require evidence of vaccination from all entering travelers; others may waive the requirements for travelers coming from noninfected areas and staying in the country less than 2 weeks.

Vaccination is also recommended for travel outside the urban areas of countries that do not officially report the disease, but which lie in the yellow fever endemic zone. It should be noted that the actual areas of yellow fever virus activity can extend beyond the officially reported infected zones.

Some countries require a traveler, even if only in transit, to have a valid international certificate of vaccination if he or she has been in any country either known or thought to harbor yellow fever virus. Such requirements may be strictly enforced, particularly for people traveling from Africa or South America to Asia. Travelers with a specific contraindication to yellow fever vaccine should be advised to obtain a waiver before traveling to countries requiring vaccination.

### *Adverse Reactions*

Reactions to yellow fever vaccine are generally mild. From 2% to 5% of vaccinees have mild headaches, myalgia, low-grade fevers, or other minor symptoms 5 to 10 days after vaccination. Fewer than 0.2% of vaccinees find it necessary to curtail regular activities. Immediate hypersensitivity reactions, characterized by rash, urticaria, or asthma, or a combination of these, are extremely uncommon (incidence less than 1 case per 1,000,000 vaccinees) and occur principally in people with histories of egg allergy.

*Precautions and Contraindications*

**Age:** The risk of adverse reactions appears to be age related. Infants younger than 4 months of age are more susceptible to serious adverse reactions (encephalitis) than older infants and children and should not be immunized. Immunization should be delayed until an infant is at least 9 months of age.

A recent analysis of adverse events passively reported to the Vaccine Adverse Event Reporting System (VAERS) during the period 1990 through 1998 suggests that people 65 years of age or older might be at increased risk for a variety of systemic adverse events following vaccination compared with people 25 through 44 years of age. Among civilians administered an estimated 1.5 million doses of yellow fever vaccine during this 9-year period, there were four cases (63, 67, 76, and 79 years of age) of severe illness with fever and multisystem viscerotropic manifestations characteristic of vaccine-induced yellow fever. In Brazil, during an ongoing mass vaccination campaign in which 34 million doses of Brazilian-manufactured yellow fever vaccine (a different vaccine strain than that used in the United States) have been administered since 1998, two similar cases (although 5 and 22 years of age) have recently been reported. Additional studies are now underway to better define the cause and risk factors for these rare, but significant, adverse events associated with two different yellow fever vaccines.

Yellow fever remains an important cause of illness and death in sub-Saharan Africa. In South America, the number of reported cases of yellow fever has increased dramatically and the potential yellow fever transmission zone has expanded to urban areas with large populations of susceptible humans and the *Aedes aegyptii* vector mosquito, thus threatening to reestablish the urban cycle of yellow fever transmission. For the first time in decades, unvaccinated U.S. travelers to South America have contracted fatal yellow fever. Consequently, despite the reported adverse events, which are exceedingly rare, yellow fever vaccination in endemic areas and of travelers should generally be encouraged as an important prevention strategy. Elderly travelers should be encouraged to discuss with their physicians the risks and benefits of vaccination in the context of the destination-specific risk for exposure to yellow fever.

**Pregnancy:** A small study showed that yellow fever vaccine virus given in pregnancy can infect the developing fetus, but the potential risk of adverse events associated with congenital infection is unknown. Therefore, it is prudent to avoid vaccinating pregnant women and for nonimmunized pregnant women to postpone travel to transmission areas until after delivery. If the travel itinerary of a pregnant woman does not present a substantial risk of exposure and immunization is contemplated solely to comply with an international travel requirement, then the traveler should be advised to obtain a waiver letter from her physician. Pregnant women who must travel to areas with active, ongoing transmission should be vaccinated. It is believed that under these circumstances, the small theoretical risk for mother and fetus from vaccination is far outweighed by the risk of yellow fever infection.

**Immunosuppression:** Infection with yellow fever virus poses a theoretical risk to travelers with immunosuppression in association with acquired immunodeficiency syndrome (AIDS) or other manifestations of human immunodeficiency virus (HIV) infection, leukemia, lymphoma, or generalized malignancy; or with the administration of corticosteroids, alkylating drugs, antimetabolites, or radiation. There are no anecdotal reports or systematically collected data, however, linking an immunosuppressed state with adverse events in a yellow fever vaccine recipient. The decision to immunize immunocompromised travelers with yellow fever vaccine should be based on a physician's evaluation of the traveler's state of immunosuppression weighed against the risk of exposure to the virus. If travel to a yellow fever-infected zone is necessary and immunization is contraindicated, a traveler should be advised of the risk, instructed in methods to avoid bites of vector mosquitoes, and supplied a vaccination waiver letter by his or her physician. Anecdotal experience suggests that low-dose (10 milligrams of prednisone or equivalent daily) or short-term (less than 2 weeks) corticosteroid therapy, or intra-articular, bursal, or tendon injections with corticosteroid do not pose a risk to recipients of yellow fever vaccine. Travelers with asymptomatic HIV infections who cannot avoid potential exposure to yellow fever virus should be offered the choice of immunization. If vaccinated, they should be monitored for possible adverse effects. Because immunization for these travelers might be less effective than for uninfected travelers, the neutralizing antibody response should be measured following vaccination prior to travel. Physicians should consult the applicable state health department or CDC, Fort Collins, Colorado, 1-970-221-6400, for more information.

Family members or close contacts of immunosuppressed travelers, who themselves have no contraindications, may receive yellow fever vaccine.

**Hypersensitivity:** Live yellow fever vaccine is produced in chick embryos and should not be given to travelers clearly hypersensitive to eggs; generally, people who are able to eat eggs or egg products may receive the vaccine. If vaccination of a person with a questionable history of egg hypersensitivity is considered essential because of a high risk of exposure, an intradermal test dose may be administered under close medical supervision. Specific directions for skin testing are found in the package insert. In some instances, small test doses for vaccine administered intradermally have led to an antibody response.

If international travel regulations are the only reason to vaccinate a traveler hypersensitive to eggs, efforts should be made to obtain a waiver. A physician's letter clearly stating the contraindications to vaccination is acceptable to some governments. (Ideally, it should be written on letterhead stationary and bear the stamp used by health department and official immunization centers to validate the international certificate of vaccination.) Under these conditions, it is also useful for the traveler to obtain specific and authoritative advice from the embassy or consulate of the country or countries he or she plans to visit. Waivers of requirements obtained from embassies or consulates should be documented by appropriate letters and retained for presentation with the international certificate of vaccination.

**Simultaneous Administration of Other Vaccines and Drugs:** Studies have shown that the seroimmune response to yellow fever vaccine is not inhibited by administration of certain other vaccines concurrently or at various intervals of a few days to one month. Measles and bacille Calmette-Guerin (BCG) have been administered in combination with yellow fever vaccines without interference. Additionally, the severity of reactions to vaccination has not been amplified by concurrent administration of yellow fever and measles vaccines. Hepatitis B and yellow fever vaccines may be given concurrently. If live virus vaccines are not given concurrently, 4 weeks should be allowed to elapse between sequential vaccinations.

There are no data on possible interference between yellow fever and typhoid, rabies, or Japanese encephalitis vaccines.

A prospective study of people given yellow fever vaccine and 5 milliliters of commercially available immune globulin revealed no alteration of the immunologic response to yellow fever vaccine when compared with controls. Although chloroquine inhibits replication of yellow fever virus in vitro, it does not adversely affect antibody responses to yellow fever vaccine in people receiving the drug as antimalarial prophylaxis.

## Other

In addition to vaccination, travelers should be advised to take precautions against exposure to mosquitoes when traveling in areas with yellow fever transmission. Yellow fever is rarely transmitted in urban areas, except during an epidemic. Travelers to rural areas of Africa and South America, however, might be exposed sporadically to mosquitoes transmitting yellow fever and other mosquito-borne diseases. Mosquitoes that transmit urban yellow fever generally feed during the day, both indoors and outdoors. Staying in air-conditioned or well-screened quarters and wearing long-sleeved shirts and long pants will help to prevent mosquito bites. Insect repellents containing N, N-diethylmetatoluamide (DEET) should be used on exposed skin only. Permethrin-containing repellents should be applied to clothing. Travelers to rural areas should bring mosquito nets and aerosol insecticides or mosquito coils.

## Section 21.7

## *Traveler's Diarrhea*

"Travelers' Diarrhea," excerpted from *Health Information for International Travel, 2001–2002,* a brochure produced by the Centers for Disease Control and Prevention (CDC), available online at http://www.cdc.gov/travel/diarrhea.htm. 2002.

Travelers' diarrhea (TD) is a syndrome characterized by a twofold or greater increase in the frequency of unformed bowel movements. Commonly associated symptoms include abdominal cramps, nausea, bloating, urgency, fever, and malaise. Episodes of TD usually begin abruptly, occur during travel or soon after returning home, and are generally self-limited. The most important determinant of risk is the destination of the traveler. Attack rates of 20% to 50% are commonly reported. High-risk destinations include most of the developing countries of Latin America, Africa, the Middle East, and Asia. Intermediate-risk destinations include most of the southern European countries and a few Caribbean islands. Low-risk destinations include Canada, northern Europe, Australia, New Zealand, the United States, and some of the Caribbean islands.

TD is slightly more common in young adults than in older people. The reasons for this difference are unclear, but could include a lack of acquired immunity, more adventurous travel styles, and different eating habits. Attack rates are similar in men and women. The onset of TD is usually within the first week of travel, but can occur at any time during the visit and even after returning home.

TD is acquired through ingestion of fecally contaminated food or water, or both. Both cooked and uncooked foods might be implicated if they have been improperly handled. Especially risky foods include raw or undercooked meat and seafood and raw fruits and vegetables. Tap water, ice, and unpasteurized milk and dairy products can be associated with increased risk of TD; safe beverages include bottled carbonated beverages (especially flavored beverages), beer, wine, hot coffee or tea, or water boiled and appropriately treated with iodine or chlorine.

The place food is prepared appears to be an important variable, with private homes, restaurants, and street vendors listed in order of increasing risk.

TD typically results in four to five loose or watery stools per day. The median duration of diarrhea is 3 to 4 days. Approximately 10% of the cases persist longer than 1 week, approximately 2% longer than 1 month, and <1% longer than 3 months. Persistent diarrhea is, thus, quite uncommon and can differ considerably from acute TD with respect to etiology and risk factors. Approximately 15% of ill people experience vomiting, and 2% to 10% have diarrhea accompanied by fever or bloody stools, or both. Travelers can experience more than one episode of TD during a single trip. Rarely is TD life threatening.

### *Etiology*

Infectious agents are the primary cause of TD. Travelers from developed countries to developing countries frequently experience a rapid, dramatic change in the type of organisms in their gastrointestinal tract. These new organisms often include potential enteric pathogens. Those who develop diarrhea have ingested an inoculum of virulent organisms sufficiently large to overcome individual defense mechanisms, resulting in symptoms.

#### *Enteric Bacterial Pathogens*

Enterotoxigenic *Escherichia coli* (ETEC) are among the most common causative agents of TD in all countries where surveys have been conducted. ETEC produce a watery diarrhea associated with cramps and a low-grade or no fever.

Salmonella gastroenteritis is a well-known disease that occurs throughout the world. In developed nations, this large group of organisms is the most common cause of outbreaks of food-associated diarrhea. In developing countries, the proportion of cases of TD caused by nontyphoidal *salmonellae* varies, but is not high. *Salmonellae* also can cause dysentery characterized by small-volume stools containing bloody mucus.

*Shigellae* are well known as the cause of bacillary dysentery. The *shigellae* are the cause of TD in up to 20% of travelers to developing countries.

*Campylobacter jejuni* is a common cause of diarrhea throughout the world; it is responsible for a small percentage of the reported cases of TD, some with bloody diarrhea. Additional studies are needed to determine how frequently it causes TD.

*Vibrio parahaemolyticus* is associated with ingestion of raw or poorly cooked seafood and has caused TD in passengers on Caribbean cruise ships and in people traveling in Asia. How frequently it causes disease in other areas of the world is unknown.

Less common bacterial pathogens include other diarrheagenic *E. coli, Yersinia enterocolitica, Vibrio cholerae* O1 and O139, non-O1 *V. cholerae, Vibrio fluvialis,* and possibly *Aeromonas hydrophila* and *Plesiomonas shigelloides.*

*Viral Enteric Pathogens—Rotaviruses and Norwalk-Like Virus*

Along with the newly acquired bacteria, the traveler can also acquire many viruses. In six studies, for example, as much as 36% of diarrheal illnesses in travelers (median 22%) was associated with rotaviruses in the stools. However, a comparable number of asymptomatic travelers also had rotaviruses, and up to 50% of symptomatic people with rotavirus infections also had nonviral pathogens. Approximately 10% to 15% of travelers develop serologic evidence of infection with Norwalk-like viruses. The roles of adenoviruses, astroviruses, coronaviruses, enteroviruses, or other viral agents in causing TD are even less clear. Although viruses are commonly acquired by travelers, they do not appear to be frequent causes of TD in adults.

*Parasitic Enteric Pathogens*

While less commonly implicated as the cause of TD than bacteria, enteric protozoa are recognized etiologic agents of TD. In the small number of studies that have included appropriate testing for these parasites in travelers or expatriates in developing countries, a variable proportion of TD has been attributed to *Giardia intestinalis* (0% to 12%), *Entamoeba histolytica* (0% to 5%), *Cryptosporidium parvum* (2% to 5%), and *Cyclospora cayetanensis* (1% to 11%). The likelihood of a parasitic etiology is higher when diarrheal illness is prolonged. *E. histolytica* should be considered when the patient has dysentery or invasive diarrhea (bloody stools). Specific diagnostic testing is required to identify *E. histolytica*, *C. parvum*, and *C. cayetanensis*. *Dientamoeba fragilis*, *Isospora belli*, *Balantidium coli*, and *Strongyloides stercoralis* can cause occasional cases of TD. While not common causes of TD, these parasites should be considered in persistent, unexplained cases.

*Unknown Causes*

No data have been presented to support noninfectious causes of TD, such as changes in diet, jet lag, altitude, and fatigue. Existing evidence indicates that in all but a few instances, such as drug-induced or preexisting gastrointestinal disorders, an infectious agent or agents can cause diarrhea in travelers. However, even with the application of the best existing methods for detecting bacteria, viruses, and parasites, 20% to 50% of cases of TD remain without recognized etiologies.

## Prevention

There are four possible approaches to prevention of TD: (1) instruction regarding food and beverage consumption, (2) immunization, (3) use of nonantimicrobial medications, and (4) use of prophylactic antimicrobial drugs. Data indicate that meticulous attention to food and beverage consumption, as mentioned previously, can decrease the likelihood of developing TD. Most travelers, however, encounter difficulty in observing the requisite dietary restrictions.

No available vaccines and none that are expected to be available in the next 3 years are effective against TD. Several nonantimicrobial agents have been advocated for prevention of TD. Available controlled studies indicate that prophylactic use of difenoxine, the active metabolite of diphenoxylate (Lomotil®), actually increases the incidence of TD, in addition to producing other undesirable side effects. Antiperistaltic agents (for example, Lomotil® and Imodium® are not effective in preventing TD. No data support the prophylactic use of activated charcoal.

Bismuth subsalicylate, taken as the active ingredient of Pepto-Bismol® (2 ounces four times a day, or two tablets four times a day), has decreased the incidence of diarrhea by about 60% in several placebo-controlled studies. Side effects include temporary blackening of the tongue and stools; occasional nausea and constipation; and, rarely, tinnitus. Available data are not sufficient to exclude a risk to the traveler from the use of such large doses of bismuth subsalicylate for a period of more than 3 weeks. Bismuth subsalicylate should be avoided by travelers with aspirin allergy, renal insufficiency, and gout, and by those who are taking anticoagulants, probenecid, or methotrexate. In travelers already taking aspirin or related salicylates for arthritis, large concurrent doses of bismuth subsalicylate can produce toxic serum concentrations of salicylate. Caution should be used in giving bismuth subsalicylate to children and adolescents with chickenpox or influenza because of a potential risk of Reye's syndrome. Bismuth subsalicylate has not been approved for infants and children younger than 3 years of age. Bismuth subsalicylate appears to be an effective prophylactic agent for TD, but is not recommended for prophylaxis of TD for periods of more than 3 weeks. Further studies of the efficacy and side effects of lower dose regimens are needed.

Controlled data are available on the prophylactic value of several other nonantimicrobial drugs. Enterovioform® and related halogenated hydroxyquinoline derivatives (for example, clioquinol, iodoquinol, Mexaform®, and Intestopan® are not helpful in preventing TD, can have serious neurologic side effects, and should never be used for prophylaxis of TD.

Controlled studies have indicated that a variety of antibiotics, including doxycycline, trimethoprim/sulfamethoxazole (TMP/SMX), trimethoprim alone, and the fluoroquinolone agents ciprofloxacin and norfloxacin, when taken prophylactically have been 52% to 95% effective in preventing TD in several areas of the developing world. The effectiveness of these agents, however, depends on the antibiotic resistance patterns of the pathogenic bacteria in each area of travel, and such information is seldom available. Resistance to fluoroquinolones is the least common, but this is changing as use of these agents increases worldwide.

Although effective in preventing some bacterial causes of diarrhea, antibiotics have no effect on the acquisition of various viral and parasitic diseases. Prophylactic antibiotics can give travelers a false sense of security about the risk associated with consuming certain local foods and beverages.

The benefits of widespread prophylactic use of doxycyline, fluroquinolones, TMP/SMX, or TMP alone in several million travelers must be weighed against the potential drawbacks. The known risks include allergic and other side effects (such as common skin rashes, photo-sensitivity of the skin, blood disorders, Stevens-Johnson syndrome, and staining of the teeth in children), as well as other infections that might be induced by antimicrobial therapy (such as antibiotic-associated colitis, Candida vaginitis, and Salmonella enteritis). Because of the uncertain risk involved in the widespread administration of these antimicrobial agents, their prophylactic use is not recommended. Although it seems reasonable to use prophylactic antibiotics in certain high-risk groups, such as travelers with immunosuppression or immunodeficiency, no data directly support this practice. There is little evidence that other disease entities are worsened sufficiently by an episode of TD to risk the rare undesirable side effects of prophylactic antimicrobial drugs. Therefore, prophylactic antimicrobial agents are not recommended for travelers. Instead, available data support the recommendation that travelers be instructed in sensible dietary practices as a prophylactic measure. This recommendation is justified by the excellent results of early treatment of TD as outlined in the following section. Some travelers might wish to consult with their physicians and might elect to use prophylactic antimicrobial agents for travel under special circumstances, once the risks and benefits are clearly understood.

## *Treatment*

Travelers with TD have two major complaints for which they desire relief—abdominal cramps and diarrhea. Many agents have been proposed to control these symptoms, but few have been demonstrated to be effective in rigorous clinical trials.

### *Nonspecific Agents*

A variety of adsorbents have been used in treating diarrhea. For example, activated charcoal has been found to be ineffective in the treatment of diarrhea. Kaolin and pectin have been widely used for diarrhea. While the combination appears to give the stools more consistency, it has not been shown to decrease cramps and frequency of stools or to shorten the course of infectious diarrhea. *Lactobacillus* preparations and yogurt have also been advocated, but no evidence supports use of these treatments for TD.

Bismuth subsalicylate preparation (1 ounce of liquid or two 262.5-milligram [mg] tablets every 30 minutes for eight doses) decreased the frequency of stools and shortened the duration of illness in several placebo-controlled studies. Treatment was limited to 48 hours at most, with no more than eight doses in a 24-hour period. There is concern about taking large amounts of bismuth and salicylate without supervision, especially for people who might be intolerant of salicylates, who have renal insufficiency, or who take salicylates for other reasons.

## Antimotility Agents

Antimotility agents are widely used in treating diarrhea of all types. Natural opiates (paregoric, tincture of opium, and codeine) have long been used to control diarrhea and cramps. Synthetic agents, such as diphenoxylate and loperamide, come in convenient dosage forms and provide prompt symptomatic but temporary relief of uncomplicated TD. However, they should not be used by people with high fever or with blood in the stools. Use of these drugs should be discontinued if symptoms persist beyond 48 hours. Diphenoxylate and loperamide should not be used in infants younger than 2 years of age.

## Antimicrobial Treatment

Travelers who develop diarrhea with three or more loose stools in an 8-hour period, especially if associated with nausea, vomiting, abdominal cramps, fever, or blood in the stools, might benefit from antimicrobial treatment. A typical 3- to 5-day illness can often be shortened to 1 to 1 1/2 days by effective antimicrobial agents. The effectiveness of antibiotic therapy will depend on the etiologic agent and its antibiotic sensitivity. The antibiotic regimen most likely to be effective is ciprofloxacin (500 mg) taken twice a day. Other fluroquinolones, such as norfloxacin, ofloxacin, or levofloxacin might be equally as effective. Fewer side effects and less widespread antibiotic resistance has been reported with the fluoroquinolones than with TMP/SMX. Three days of treatment is recommended, although 2 or fewer days might be sufficient. Nausea and vomiting without diarrhea should not be treated with antimicrobial drugs.

Travelers should be advised to consult a physician rather than attempt self-medication if the diarrhea is severe or does not resolve within several days; if there is blood or mucus, or both, in the stools; if fever occurs with shaking chills; or if there is dehydration with persistent diarrhea.

## Oral Fluids

Most cases of diarrhea are self-limited and require only simple replacement of fluids and salts lost in diarrheal stools. This is best achieved by use of an oral rehydration solution such as World Health

Organization oral rehydration salts (ORS) solution (Table 21.3). This solution is appropriate for treating as well as preventing dehydration. Travelers should be advised that ORS packets are available at stores or pharmacies in almost all developing countries. ORS is prepared by adding one packet to boiled or treated water. Packet instructions should be checked carefully to ensure that the salts are added to the correct volume of water. ORS solution should be consumed or discarded within 12 hours if held at room temperature or 24 hours if kept refrigerated.

Travelers should be advised to avoid iced drinks and noncarbonated bottled fluids made from water of uncertain quality. Dairy products aggravate diarrhea in some people and travelers with diarrhea should be advised to avoid them.

### *Infants with Diarrhea*

Infants 2 years of age or younger are at high risk of acquiring TD. The greatest risk to the infant with diarrhea is dehydration (Table 21.4). Travelers should be advised that dehydration is best prevented by use of the WHO ORS solution in addition to the infant's usual food. ORS packets are available at stores or pharmacies in almost all developing countries. ORS is prepared by adding one packet to boiled or treated water. Travelers should be advised to check packet instructions carefully to ensure that the salts are added to the correct volume of water. ORS solution should be consumed or discarded within 12 hours if held at room temperature, or 24 hours if kept refrigerated. A dehydrated child will drink ORS avidly; travelers should be advised to give it to the child as long as the dehydration persists. An infant who vomits the ORS will usually keep it down if it is offered by spoon in frequent small sips. Breast-fed infants should continue nursing on demand. For bottle-fed infants, full-strength, lactose-free or lactose-reduced formulas should be administered. Older infants and children receiving semi-solid or solid foods should continue to receive their usual diet during the illness. Recommended foods include starches, cereals, yogurt, fruits, and vegetables. Immediate medical attention is required for the infant with diarrhea who develops signs of moderate to severe dehydration (Table 21.4), bloody diarrhea, >39° Celsius (>102° Fahrenheit) fever, or persistent vomiting. While medical attention is being obtained, the infant should be offered ORS.

### *Precautions for Children and Pregnant Women*

Although infants and children do not make up a large proportion of travelers to high-risk areas, some children do accompany their families.

Teenagers should follow the advice given to adults, with possible adjustments of doses of medication. Physicians should be aware of the risks of tetracyclines for infants and children younger than 8 years of age. Few data are available about the usage of antidiarrheal drugs in infants and children. Drugs should be prescribed with caution for pregnant women and nursing mothers.

**Table 21.3.** Composition of World Health Organization (WHO) Oral Rehydration Solution (ORS) for Diarrheal Illness

| Ingredient | Amount |
|---|---|
| Sodium chloride | 3.5 grams per liter |
| Potassium chloride | 1.5 grams per liter |
| Glucose | 20.0 grams per liter |
| Trisodium citrate* | 2.9 grams per liter |

*An earlier formulation that used sodium bicarbonate 2.5 grams per liter had a shorter shelf-life, but was physiologically equivalent and may still be produced in some countries.

**Table 21.4.** Assessment of Dehydration Levels in Infants

| Signs | Severity: | | |
|---|---|---|---|
| | *Mild* | *Moderate* | *Severe* |
| General condition | Thirsty, restless, agitated | Thirsty, restless, irritable | Withdrawn, somnolent, or comatose |
| Pulse | Normal | Rapid, weak | Rapid, weak |
| Anterior fontanelle | Normal | Sunken | Very sunken |
| Eyes | Normal | Sunken | Very sunken |
| Tears | Present | Absent | Absent |
| Urine | Normal | Reduced, concentrated | None for several hours |
| Weight loss | 4% to 5% | 6% to 9% | 10% or more |

# Section 21.8

# *HIV and Travel*

"Acquired Immunodeficiency Syndrome (AIDS)," and "General information Regarding Human Immunodeficiency Virus and Travel," excerpted from *Health Information for International Travel, 2001–2002,* a brochure produced by the Centers for Disease Control and Prevention (CDC). Available online at http://www.cdc.gov/travel/hivaids.htm and http://www.cdc .gov/travel/hivtrav.htm, 2002; and "Human Immunodeficiency Virus (HIV) Testing Requirements for Entry into Foreign Countries," from the U.S. Department of State, February 2002. Available online at http://travel. state.gov/HIVtestingreqs.html.

## *Acquired Immunodeficiency Syndrome (AIDS)*

AIDS is a serious disease, first recognized as a distinct syndrome in 1981. This syndrome represents the late clinical state of infection with the human immunodeficiency virus (HIV), resulting in progressive damage to the immune system and in life-threatening infectious and noninfectious complications.

### *Occurrence*

AIDS and HIV infection occur worldwide. Comprehensive surveillance systems are lacking in many countries, so the true number of cases is likely to be far greater than the numbers officially reported, particularly from developing nations. The Joint United Nations Program on HIV/ AIDS (UNAIDS) estimates that 34.3 million people are HIV-infected worldwide. Because HIV infection and AIDS are globally distributed, the risk to international travelers is determined less by their geographic destination than by their sexual and drug-using behaviors.

### *Risk for Travelers*

The risk of HIV infection for international travelers is generally low. Factors to consider when assessing risk include the extent of direct contact with blood or secretions and of sexual contact with potentially infected people. In addition, the blood supply in developing countries might not be adequately screened.

*Preventive Measures*

No vaccine is available to prevent infection with HIV. Travelers should be advised that HIV infection is preventable. HIV is transmitted through sexual intercourse and needle- or syringe-sharing; by medical use of blood, blood components, or organ or tissue transplantation; and perinatally from an infected woman to her infant. HIV is not transmitted through casual contact; air, food, or water routes; contact with inanimate objects; or mosquitoes or other arthropod vectors. The use of any public conveyance (for example, an airplane, an automobile, a boat, a bus, or a train) by people with AIDS or HIV infection does not pose a risk of infection for the crew members or other travelers.

Travelers should be advised that they are at risk if they:

- Have sexual intercourse (heterosexual or homosexual) with an infected person.

- Use or allow the use of contaminated, unsterilized syringes or needles for any injections or other skin-piercing procedures, including acupuncture, use of illicit drugs, steroid or vitamin injections, medical or dental procedures, ear or body piercing, or tattooing.

- Use infected blood, blood components, or clotting factor concentrates. HIV infection by this route is rare in those countries or cities where donated blood and plasma are screened for HIV antibody.

Travelers should be advised to avoid sexual encounters with people who are infected with HIV or whose HIV infection status is unknown. This includes avoiding sexual activity with intravenous drug users and people with multiple sexual partners, such as male or female sex workers. Condoms, when used consistently and correctly, prevent transmission of HIV. Travelers who engage in vaginal, anal, or oral-genital intercourse with anyone who is infected with HIV or whose infection status is unknown should use a latex condom. For those who are sensitive to latex, polyurethane or other plastic condoms are available. (Travelers should be advised to look for the words "for the prevention of disease" on the condom packaging.)

In many countries, needle sharing by intravenous drug users is a major source of HIV transmission and other infections, such as hepatitis B (HBV) and hepatitis C (HCV). Travelers should be advised not to use drugs intravenously or share needles for any purpose.

270

In the United States, Australia, New Zealand, Canada, Japan, and western European countries, the risk of transfusion-associated HIV infection has been virtually eliminated through required testing of all donated blood for antibody to HIV. In the United States, donations of blood and plasma must be screened for HIV-1 and HIV-2 antibodies and HIV-1 p24 antigen.

If produced in the United States according to U.S. Food and Drug Administration-approved procedures, immune globulin preparations (such as those used for the prevention of hepatitis A (HAV) and HBV) and HBV vaccines undergo processes that are known to inactivate HIV; therefore, these products should be used as indicated. Less developed nations might not have a formal program for testing blood or biological products for antibody to HIV. In those countries, travelers should (when medically prudent) avoid use of unscreened blood-clotting factor concentrates or those of uncertain purity. If transfusion is necessary, the blood should be tested, if at all possible, for HIV antibody by appropriately trained laboratory technicians using a reliable test.

Needles used to draw blood or administer injections should be sterile, preferably single use and disposable, and prepackaged in a sealed container. Travelers with insulin-dependent diabetes or hemophilia, or who require routine or frequent injections should be advised to carry a supply of syringes, needles, and disinfectant swabs (for example, alcohol wipes) sufficient to last their entire stay abroad.

International travelers should be advised that some countries serologically screen incoming travelers (primarily those planning extended visits, such as for work or study) and deny entry to people with AIDS and those whose test results indicate infection with HIV. People intending to visit a country for a substantial period or to work or study abroad should be informed of the policies and requirements of the particular country. This information is usually available from the consular officials of the individual nations.

Further information is available from 1-800-342-AIDS, toll free from the United States or its territories (for Spanish-speaking callers, 1-800-344-SIDA, or for hearing-impaired callers with teletype equipment, 1-800-AIDS-TTY).

## General Information Regarding Human Immunodeficiency Virus and Travel

Acquired immunodeficiency syndrome (AIDS), caused by the human immunodeficiency virus (HIV), has a very long and variable incubation period, generally lasting for many years. Some people infected with HIV have remained asymptomatic for more than a decade. Currently, there is no vaccine to protect against infection with HIV. Although there is no cure for AIDS, treatments and prophylaxis for many opportunistic diseases associated with AIDS are available.

International travelers should be advised that some countries serologically screen incoming travelers (primarily those with extended visits, such as for work or study) and deny entry to people with AIDS and those whose test results indicate infection with HIV. Moreover, travelers carrying antiretroviral medication might be denied entry to some countries. People who intend to visit a country for a substantial period or to work or study abroad should be informed of the policies and requirements of the particular country. This information is usually available from the consular officials of the individual nations.

## Specific Precautions for HIV-Infected Travelers

Health care providers should advise HIV-infected travelers of the following:

• Travel, particularly to developing countries, can carry significant risks for exposure to opportunistic pathogens for HIV-infected travelers, especially those who are severely immunosuppressed. Consultation with a health care provider or with experts in travel medicine will help in planning itineraries.

• During travel to developing countries, HIV-infected travelers are at even higher risk for food and waterborne diseases than they are in the United States. Food and beverages—in particular, raw fruits and vegetables, raw or undercooked seafood or meat, tap water, ice made with tap water, unpasteurized milk and dairy products, and food and beverages purchased from street vendors—might be contaminated. Food and beverages that are generally safe include steaming hot foods, fruits that are peeled by the traveler personally, bottled (carbonated) beverages, hot coffee or tea, beer, wine, or water brought to a rolling boil for one minute. When local sources of water must be used and boiling is not practical, certain portable water filtration units, when used in conjunction with chlorine or iodine, can increase the safety of water. Some units are available that offer the effects of iodine treatment with filtration in the same unit.

• Waterborne infections can also result from swallowing water during recreational water activities. To reduce the risk of cryptosporidiosis and giardiasis, travelers should be advised to avoid swallowing water during swimming and to avoid swimming in water that might be contaminated (for example, with sewage or animal waste).

- Prophylactic antimicrobial agents against travelers' diarrhea are not recommended routinely for HIV-infected travelers to developing countries. These agents have adverse effects and can promote the emergence of drug-resistant organisms. However, several studies have shown that prophylactic antimicrobials can reduce the risk of diarrhea in travelers, though none has involved an HIV-infected population. In selected circumstances (for example, a brief period of travel to an area where the risk of infection is very high), after weighing the potential risks and benefits, the health care provider and traveler might decide that prophylactic antibiotics are warranted.

For travelers to whom prophylaxis is offered, fluoroquinolones such as ciprofloxacin (500 milligrams [mg] taken once a day), can be considered. Trimethoprim-sulfamethoxazole (TMP-SMX) (one double-strength tablet daily) has also been shown to be effective as a prophylactic agent against travelers' diarrhea, but drug resistance is now common in tropical areas. Travelers already taking TMP-SMX for prophylaxis against *Pneumocystis carinii* pneumonia (PCP) might receive some protection against travelers' diarrhea. Health care providers of HIV-infected travelers who are not already taking TMP-SMX should carefully consider prescribing this agent solely for diarrhea prophylaxis because of high rates of adverse reactions and anticipated future need for the agent (for example, for PCP treatment and prophylaxis).

- All HIV-infected travelers to developing countries should be advised to carry an antimicrobial agent (for example, ciprofloxacin, 500 mg twice a day for 3 to 7 days) with them to be taken as empirical therapy should diarrhea develop. Alternative antibiotics (for example, TMP-SMX) for empirical therapy for infants, children, adolescents, and pregnant women should be discussed. Travelers should be advised to consult a physician if the diarrhea is severe and does not respond to empirical therapy, if there is blood in the stool, if fever occurs with shaking chills, or if there is dehydration. Antiperistaltic agents (for example, diphenoxylate [Lomotil] and loperamide [Imodium]) are used to relieve the symptoms of diarrhea; however, they should not be used by travelers with high fever or with blood in the stool;

these drugs should be discontinued if symptoms persist beyond 48 hours. These drugs are not recommended for HIV-positive infants, children, or adolescents.

- Travelers should be advised about other preventive measures appropriate for anticipated exposures, such as malaria chemo-prophylaxis, protection against arthropod vectors, immune globulin, and vaccination. Travelers should avoid direct skin contact with soil and sand (for example, by wearing shoes and protective clothing, and using towels on beaches) in areas where fecal contamination of soil is likely.

- In general, live virus vaccines should be avoided. An exception is measles vaccine, which is recommended for nonimmune travelers. However, measles vaccine is not recommended for travelers who are severely immunocompromised; immune globulin should be considered for measles-susceptible, severely immunosuppressed travelers who are anticipating travel to measles endemic countries. Travelers at risk for exposure to typhoid fever should be given the inactivated parenteral typhoid vaccine, instead of the live, attenuated oral typhoid vaccine. Yellow fever vaccine is a live virus vaccine with uncertain safety and efficacy in those who are HIV infected. Travelers with asymptomatic HIV infection who cannot avoid potential exposure to yellow fever should be offered the choice of vaccination. If travel to a yellow fever-infected zone is necessary and immunization is not performed, travelers should be advised of the risk, instructed in methods to avoid bites of vector mosquitoes, and provided a vaccination waiver letter.

- In general, killed vaccines (for example, diphtheria-tetanus, hepatitis A, rabies, and Japanese encephalitis vaccines) should be used for HIV-infected travelers, just as they would be used for non-HIV-infected travelers. Preparation for travel should include a review and updating of routine vaccinations, including diphtheria-tetanus in adults and routine immunizations for infants, children, and adolescents.

- Health care providers should identify other area-specific risks and instruct travelers in ways to reduce the risk of infection. Geographically focal infections that pose high risk to HIV-infected travelers include: *visceral leishmaniasis* and several fungal infections (for example, *Penicillium marneffei, coccidioidomycosis*, and *histoplasmosis*). Many tropical and developing areas of the world have high rates of tuberculosis.

### Vaccine Recommendations for Travelers with Altered Immunocompetence, including HIV

Killed or inactivated vaccines do not represent a danger to immunocompromised travelers and generally should be administered as recommended for healthy travelers. However, the immune response to these vaccines might be suboptimal.

Virus replication after administration of live, attenuated virus vaccines can be enhanced and prolonged in travelers with immunodeficiency diseases and in those with a suppressed capacity for immune response, as occurs with HIV disease; leukemia; lymphoma; generalized malignancy; or therapy with corticosteroids, alkylating agents, antimetabolites, or radiation. Severe complications have been reported following vaccination with live, attenuated virus vaccines (for example, measles and polio) and with live bacterial vaccines (for example, Bacille Calmette-Guerin [BCG]) in patients with HIV disease, leukemia, and lymphoma or other people with suppressed capacity for immune response. In general, travelers with such conditions should not be given live organism vaccines.

Evidence based on case reports has linked measles vaccine virus infection to subsequent death in six severely immunosuppressed persons. For this reason, travelers who are severely immunosuppressed for any reason should not be given measles, mumps, and rubella (MMR) combined vaccine. Healthy, susceptible close contacts of severely immunosuppressed travelers may be vaccinated. MMR and other measles-containing vaccines are not recommended for HIV-infected travelers with evidence of severe immunosuppression (for example, travelers with a very low CD+4 T-lymphocyte count), primarily because of the report of a case of measles *pneumonitis* in a measles vaccinee who had an advanced case of AIDS. Refer to the 1998 Advisory Committee on Immunization Practices (ACIP) statement on MMR for additional details on vaccination of travelers with symptomatic HIV infection.

Measles disease can be severe in people with HIV infection. MMR vaccine is recommended for all asymptomatic HIV-infected travelers and should be considered for symptomatic travelers who are not severely immunosuppressed. Asymptomatic infants, children, and adolescents do not need to be evaluated and tested for HIV infection before MMR or other measles-containing vaccines are administered. A theoretical risk of an increase (probably transient) in HIV viral load following MMR vaccination exists because such an effect has been observed with other vaccines. The clinical significance of such an increase is not known.

In general, travelers receiving large daily doses of corticosteroids (>2 milligrams per kilogram [mg/kg] per day or >20 mg per day of prednisone) for 14 days or more should not receive MMR vaccine because of concern about vaccine safety. MMR and its component vaccines should be avoided for at least one month after cessation of high-dose therapy. Travelers receiving low-dose or short-course (fewer than 14 days) therapy; alternate-day treatment; maintenance physiologic doses; or topical, aerosol, intra-articular, bursal, or tendon injections may be vaccinated. Although travelers receiving high doses of systemic corticosteroids daily or on alternate days during an interval of less than 14 days generally can receive MMR or its component vaccines immediately after cessation of treatment, some experts prefer waiting until 2 weeks after completion of therapy.

Travelers receiving cancer chemotherapy or radiation who have not received chemotherapy for at least 3 months may receive MMR or its component vaccines.

Travelers with leukemia in remission whose chemotherapy has been terminated for at least 3 months and transplant recipients who are beyond the period of immunosuppression may receive live virus vaccines. Most experts agree that steroid therapy usually does not contraindicate administration of live virus vaccine when it is short term; low to moderate dose (less than 2 weeks); long-term, alternate-day treatment with short-acting steroids; maintenance physiologic doses (replacement therapy); or administered topically (that is, to the skin or eyes) by aerosol or by intra-articular, bursal, or tendon injection.

Infants and children infected with HIV should receive, on schedule, all the routinely recommended inactivated vaccines (that is, acellular pertussis [DTaP], *Haemophilus influenzae* type B [Hib], and hepatitis B vaccines) whether or not they are symptomatic. Inactivated poliovirus vaccine (IPV) is the polio vaccine of choice for HIV-infected asymptomatic and symptomatic travelers and their household members and other close contacts. Pneumococcal vaccine is recommended for anyone 6 months of age or older with HIV infection. Because influenza can result in serious illness and complications, vaccination against influenza is a prudent precaution in HIV-infected travelers. Varicella vaccine may be considered for asymptomatic HIV-infected travelers with CD4+ percentages >25% (CDC Class 1; that is, no evidence of suppression).

Because oral poliovirus vaccine (OPV) is no longer available, IPV should be used to immunize HIV-infected travelers and their household contacts.

## Safety of Vaccines for Human Immunodeficiency Virus-Infected People

Scientists have reviewed the safety and efficacy of vaccines (such as those for measles, yellow fever, influenza, or pneumococcal pneumonia) in people with HIV infection or AIDS. No increased incidence of adverse reactions to inactivated vaccines has been noted in these people. However, administration of live organism vaccines can carry increased risks of adverse reactions. In addition, the likelihood of successful immune response is reduced in some HIV-infected people (depending on the degree of immunodeficiency). On the other hand, because of their immuno-deficiency, many HIV-infected people are at increased risk for complications of vaccine-preventable diseases. Thus, the risk-benefit balance usually favors administration of vaccines to HIV-infected people, especially inactivated vaccines. Administration of vaccines should be backed up by behaviors to prevent infections (for example, avoiding mosquito bites in yellow fever areas and avoiding exposure to people with measles or chickenpox).

## Human Immunodeficiency Virus (HIV) Testing Requirements for Entry into Foreign Countries

An increasing number of countries require that foreigners be tested for Human Immunodeficiency Virus (HIV) prior to entry. It is usually required as part of a medical exam for long-term visitors (i.e., students and workers). The following list of country requirements is based on information available as of February 2002 and is subject to change. Before traveling abroad, check with the embassy of the country to be visited to learn about entry requirements and specifically whether AIDS testing is a requirement. If the list indicates U.S. test results are acceptable and the word "Yes" appears with an asterisk beside it (Yes*) in a particular country, prospective travelers should inquire at the embassy of that country for details (i.e., which laboratories in the United States may perform tests and where to have results certified and authenticated) before departing the United States.

**Table 21.5.** HIV Testing Requirements (continued on pp. 278–281)

| Country | Test Required for | U.S. Test Accepted? |
|---|---|---|
| Aruba | Intending immigrants | No* |

**Table 21.5.** HIV Testing Requirements (continued from previous page)

| Country | Test Required for | U.S. Test Accepted? |
|---------|-------------------|---------------------|
| Australia | All applicants for permanent residence over age 15 (All other applicants who require medical examinations are tested if it is indicated on clinical grounds.) | Yes* |
| Bahrain | Individuals employed in jobs involving food handling, and patient or child care. | No |
| Belarus | All persons staying longer than 3 months. | Yes |
| Belize | All persons applying for residency permits. | No |
| Brunei | All persons applying for work permits. | No |
| Bulgaria | All intending immigrants (and may be required for foreigners staying longer than 1 month for purposes of study or work.) | Yes* |
| Canada | Any foreigner suspected of being HIV positive (HIV testing is not mandatory for entry.) | Yes* |
| Central African Republic | Anyone seeking residence, work and student permits must submit to a medical exam (which includes an HIV test). | Yes |
| China, People's Republic of | Foreigners planning to stay for more than 6 months (Testing is not required for entry or residency in Hong Kong or Macau.) | Yes* |
| Colombia | Anyone suspected of being HIV positive (HIV positive persons are not admitted without a waiver from a Colombian consulate in the U.S.) | No* |
| Cuba | Anyone staying over 90 days, excluding diplomats. | Yes* |
| Cyprus | All foreigners working or studying are tested after entry. | N/A |
| Dominican Republic | Foreigners planning to reside, study or work. | No |
| Egypt | Foreigners applying for study, training or work permits (spouses of applicants are exempt.) | Yes* |
| El Salvador | Anyone age 15 and older applying for temporary and permanent residency | No |
| Georgia | All foreigners staying longer than 1 month. | Yes, if issued 30 days before arrival* |

**Table 21.5.** HIV Testing Requirements (continued from previous page)

| Country | Test Required for | U.S. Test Accepted? |
|---|---|---|
| Greece | Prostitutes (as defined by Greek law.) | Yes* |
| Hungary | Anyone staying over 1 year, and all intending immigrants (some employers may require workers to be tested.) | Yes* |
| India | All students over 18, anyone between the ages of 18 and 70 with a visa valid for 1 year or more, and anyone extending a stay to a year or more, excluding accredited journalists and those working in foreign missions. | Test must be taken within 30 days of arrival* |
| Iraq | All foreigners (except diplomats, Muslim pilgrims transiting through Iraq, children under 14 who do not suffer from hemophilia, men over 60 and women over 50 years of age) will be tested upon entry and are required to pay a $50 (U.S.) fee for the test (Persons possessing a current medical certificate confirming that they do not suffer from AIDS may also be exempt from being tested.) | Yes* |
| Jordan | Anyone staying longer than 3 months | No |
| Kazakstan | All visitors staying more then 1 month must present a certificate of an HIV test within 10 days of their arrival. | Yes, if issued 30 days before arrival* |
| Korea, Republic of | Foreigners working as entertainers staying over 90 days. | Yes |
| Kuwait | Those seeking to obtain a residence permit. | No |
| Kyrgyzstan | All foreigners, excluding diplomats, staying more than one month. | Yes |
| Latvia | Anyone seeking a residency permit. | Yes |
| Lebanon | Those planning to reside or work (Universities may require testing of foreign students). | No* |
| Libya | Those seeking residency permits, excluding official visitors. | Yes |
| Lithuania | Applicants for permanent residence permits. | Yes* |
| Malaysia | Foreigners seeking work permits as unskilled laborers. | Yes* |
| Marshall Islands, Republic of the | Temporary visitors staying more than 30 days, and applicants for residence and work permits. | Yes* |

**Table 21.5.** HIV Testing Requirements (continued from previous page)

| Country | Test Required for | U.S. Test Accepted? |
|---|---|---|
| Mauritius | Foreigners planning to work or seek permanent residence (testing performed upon arrival in Mauritius.) | No |
| Micronesia, (Federated States of) | Anyone applying for a permit needs to obtain a medical clearance, which may include an HIV test. | Yes |
| Moldova | Anyone staying more than 3 months. | Yes* |
| Montserrat | University students and applicants for work and residency. | Yes* |
| Oman | Those newly-employed by private sector companies and upon renewal of work permit. | No |
| Panama | Women intending to work in prostitution and anyone who adjusts visa status once in Panama. | No* |
| Papua New Guinea | Applicants seeking work or residency visas and their dependents. | Yes |
| Paraguay | Applicants seeking temporary or permanent residency status. | Yes* |
| Qatar | Applicants seeking work or residency visas and visitors staying more than 1 month. | No |
| Russia | All foreign visitors staying longer than 3 months. | Yes* |
| Saudi Arabia | Applicants for residency/work permits. | Yes* |
| St. Vincent | Applicants seeking temporary and permanent residency visas. | Yes |
| St. Kitts and Nevis | Students, intending immigrants and anyone seeking employment. | Yes* |
| Seychelles | Foreigners planning to work must under go a medical exam, which includes an HIV test, upon arrival. | No |
| Singapore | Workers who earn less than $1,250 per month and applicants for permanent resident status (except spouses and children of Singapore citizens.) | No |
| Slovak Republic | Applicants for long term or permanent residency visas. | No* |
| South Africa | All mine workers (irrespective of their positions.) | Yes* |

**Table 21.5.** HIV Testing Requirements (continued from previous page)

| Country | Test Required for | U.S. Test Accepted? |
|---------|-------------------|---------------------|
| Spain | Anyone seeking residence, work and student permits must submit to a medical exam (which may include an AIDS test.) | Yes* |
| Syria | All foreigners (ages 15 to 60 years) staying more than 15 days. | Yes* |
| Taiwan | Applicants for residency and work permits (Testing is also required for anyone staying over 90 days.) | No* |
| Tajikistan | Anyone staying more than 90 days (pending legislation). | Yes* |
| Turkmenistan | All foreigners staying longer than 3 months. | No* |
| Turks and Caicos | Foreign workers (HIV testing is part of the medical exam that is required for work permits.) | No |
| United Arab Emirates | Applicants for work or residence permits except those under age 18. | No, testing performed upon arrival. |
| Ukraine | Anyone staying longer than 3 months. | Yes, if issued 30 days before arrival* |
| United Kingdom | Anyone who does not appear to be in good health may be required to undergo a medical exam (including an HIV test) prior to being granted or denied entry. | No* |
| Uzbekistan | Anyone staying more than 15 days (Long-term visitors must renew HIV certificate after the first 3 months in Uzbekistan and annually thereafter.) | Yes* |
| Yemen | Applicants seeking permanent residence including work or study (students over age 16), all foreigners staying longer than 1 month, and foreign spouses of Yemeni nationals (excludes experts, teachers, and foreign missions who are required to work in Yemen.) | No |

# Section 21.9

# *Sexually Transmitted Diseases*

"Sexually Transmitted Diseases (STDs)," excerpted from *Health In-formation for International Travel, 2001–2002,* a brochure produced by the Centers for Disease Control and Prevention (CDC). 2002.

Sexually transmitted diseases (STDs) are the infections and result-ing clinical syndromes caused by more than 25 infectious organisms transmitted through sexual activity. Serious sequelae include pelvic inflammatory disease, infertility, stillbirths and neonatal infections, genital cancers, and (in the case of human immunodeficiency virus [HIV] and tertiary syphilis) death.

## *Occurrence*

Acquired immunodeficiency syndrome (AIDS) has become a global health problem, and the prevalence of IIIV infection in many populations continues to escalate. Also of concern are the antibiotic-resistant STD agents, particularly penicillin-, tetracycline-, and quinolone-resistant strains of *Neisseria gonorrhoeae.*

## *Risk for Travelers*

International travelers are at risk of contracting STDs, including HIV, if they have sex with partners who have these diseases. Travel-ers should be aware that the risk of STDs is high in some parts of the world.

## *Preventive Measures*

*Vaccine*

Hepatitis B is the only STD for which a vaccine is available.

*Other*

To avoid acquiring STDs, travelers should be advised not to have sexual contact with people who might be infected. People most likely to be infected are those with numerous sex partners. In many places, people who make themselves available for sex with travelers are likely to be people, such as commercial sex workers, with many partners. In addition, injecting drug users are at high risk of being infected with HIV, regardless of the number of their sex partners.

Travelers who wish to absolutely protect themselves from acquiring an STD should be advised to refrain from sexual contact. If, however, they choose not to do this, travelers should be advised that they can reduce their risk of acquiring infection by consistently and correctly using a latex condom during sexual contact, whether vaginal, oral, or anal, as well as using a vaginal spermicide. If lubricants are used during sex, only water-based lubricants (for example, K-Y Jelly® or glycerin) should be used with latex condoms, because oil-based lubricants (for example, petroleum jelly, shortening, mineral oil, or massage oils) can weaken latex condoms.

Any traveler who might have been exposed to an STD and who develops either a vaginal or urethral discharge, an unexplained rash or genital lesion, or genital or pelvic pain should be advised to cease sexual activity and promptly seek competent medical care. Because STDs are often asymptomatic, especially in women, travelers who believe that they might have been exposed to an STD should be advised to consult a physician regarding the advisability of screening for STDs.

# Section 21.10

# *Influenza on Cruise Ships and Land-Based Tours*

"Influenza," excerpted from *Health Information for International Travel, 2001–2002*, a brochure produced by the Centers for Disease Control and Prevention (CDC). Available online at http://www.cdc.gov/travel/diseases/ influenza.htm. 2002.

Influenzas A and B are the major types of influenza viruses that cause human respiratory disease. Influenza A viruses are further classified into subtypes on the basis of two surface antigens: hemagglutinin (H) and neuraminidase (N). Although both influenza A and B viruses undergo continual antigenic change (that is, antigenic drift), influenza B viruses undergo antigenic change more slowly and are not divided into subtypes. Since 1977, influenza A (H1N1 and H3N2) viruses and influenza B viruses have been in global circulation.

## *Occurrence*

Epidemics of influenza generally occur during the winter months on an annual or near annual basis and are responsible for an average of approximately 20,000 deaths in the United States each year. Influenza virus infections cause disease in all age groups. Rates of infection are highest among infants, children, and adolescents, but rates of serious morbidity and mortality are highest among people 50 years of age or older and people of any age who have medical conditions that place them at high risk for complications from influenza. Influenza viruses also can cause global epidemics of disease, known as pandemics, during which rates of morbidity and mortality from influenza-related complications can increase dramatically.

## *Risk for Travelers*

The risk for exposure to influenza during international travel varies depending on the time of year and destination. In the tropics, influenza

284

can occur throughout the year, while most activity occurs from April through September in the temperate regions of the Southern Hemisphere. In temperate climates, travelers can also be exposed to influenza during the summer, especially when traveling as part of large tourist groups with travelers from areas of the world where influenza viruses are circulating. Travelers at high risk for complications of influenza should be advised to consider receiving influenza vaccine before travel if (1) influenza vaccine was not received during the preceding fall or winter, (2) travel is planned to the tropics, (3) travel is planned with large groups of tourists at any time of year, or (4) travel is planned to the Southern Hemisphere from April through September. Travelers at high risk who received the previous season's vaccine before travel should be revaccinated in the fall or winter with the current vaccine.

Because influenza vaccine might not be available during the summer in North America, travelers 50 years of age or older and others at high risk for influenza-related complications who plan summer travel might be advised to consult with their physicians to discuss the symptoms and risks of influenza before embarking on their travel.

### *Preventive Measures*

*Vaccine*

In the United States, the main option for reducing the impact of influenza is immunoprophylaxis with inactivated (that is, killed-virus) vaccine. In addition, the use of influenza-specific antiviral drugs for chemoprophylaxis or therapy of influenza are important adjuncts to vaccine. Annual vaccination of people at high risk for complications before the influenza season is the most effective measure for reducing the impact. Vaccine is recommended for all travelers, and particularly for the following groups who are at risk for complications from influenza:

- People 50 years of age or older. (In 2000, the 50- through 64-years-of-age group was added to those recommended for annual vaccination because a substantial proportion of them have a medical condition that places them at increased risk of influenza-related complications.)

- Residents of nursing homes and other chronic-care facilities that house people of any age who have chronic medical conditions.

- Anyone 6 months of age or older who has chronic disorders of the pulmonary or cardiovascular systems, including asthma.

- Anyone 6 months of age or older who has required regular medical follow-up or hospitalization during the preceding year because of chronic metabolic diseases (including diabetes mellitus), renal dysfunction, hemoglobinopathies, or immunosuppression (including immunosuppression caused by medications, human immunodeficiency virus [HIV], or acquired immunodeficiency syndrome [AIDS]).

- Anyone 6 months to 18 years of age who is receiving long-term aspirin therapy and, therefore, might be at risk for developing Reye's syndrome after influenza.

- Women who will be in the second or third trimester of pregnancy during the influenza season.

*Dosing, Route, and Timing of Vaccination*

Even when current influenza vaccine contains one or more of the antigens administered in previous years, annual vaccination with the current vaccine is necessary because immunity declines during the year after vaccination. Dosage recommendations differ according to age group. Two doses administered at least one month apart may be required for satisfactory antibody responses among previously unvaccinated infants and children younger than 9 years of age. The second dose should be administered before December, if possible. In adults, studies have indicated little or no improvement in antibody response when a second dose is administered during the same season.

The intramuscular route is recommended for influenza vaccine. Infants and young children should be vaccinated in the anterolateral aspect of the thigh; all other vaccine recipients should be vaccinated in the deltoid muscle.

*Composition of the Vaccine*

Influenza vaccine contains three strains of inactivated influenza viruses. These viruses are updated annually and are representative of viruses likely to circulate in the upcoming season. Because the vaccine is grown in hen eggs, the vaccine might contain small amounts of egg protein. Influenza vaccine distributed in the United States might also contain thimerosal, a mercury-containing preservative. Manufacturing processes differ by manufacturer and the package insert should be consulted regarding the use of other compounds to inactivate the viruses or limit bacterial contamination.

### *Adverse Reactions*

Inactivated influenza vaccine contains noninfectious viruses and cannot cause influenza. Respiratory disease after vaccination represents coincidental illness unrelated to influenza vaccination.

**Local Reactions:** The most frequent side effect of vaccination is soreness at the vaccination site that lasts up to 2 days. These local reactions generally are mild and rarely interfere with the ability to conduct usual daily activities.

**Systemic Reactions:** Fever, malaise, myalgia, and other systemic symptoms can occur following vaccination and most often affect people who have had no previous exposure to the influenza virus antigens in the vaccine (for example, young children). These reactions begin 6 to 12 hours after vaccination and can persist for 1 to 2 days.

Immediate—presumably allergic—reactions (for example, hives, angioedema, allergic asthma, and systemic anaphylaxis) rarely occur after influenza vaccination. These reactions probably result from hypersensitivity to some vaccine component; most reactions likely are caused by residual egg protein and occur among people who have severe egg allergy. People who have developed hives, have had swelling of the lips or tongue, or have experienced acute respiratory distress or collapse after eating eggs should be advised to consult a physician for appropriate evaluation to help determine if vaccine should be administered. People who have documented immunoglobulin E (IgE)-mediated hypersensitivity to eggs—including those who have had occupational asthma or other allergic responses due to exposure to egg protein—might also be at increased risk for reactions from influenza vaccine, and similar consultation should be advised. Protocols have been published for safely administering influenza vaccine to people with egg allergies.

**Guillain-Barré Syndrome (GBS):** Investigations to date suggest that there is no large increase in GBS associated with influenza vaccines (other than the swine flu vaccine) and that if influenza vaccine does pose a risk it is probably quite small—on the order of 1 to 2 episodes per million people vaccinated. There are case reports of GBS following influenza, but no epidemiologic studies documenting such an association.

*Precautions and Contraindications*

The target groups for influenza and pneumococcal vaccination overlap considerably. For travelers at high risk who have not previously been vaccinated with pneumococcal vaccine, health care providers should strongly consider administering pneumococcal and influenza vaccines concurrently. Both vaccines can be administered at the same time at different sites without increasing side effects. However, influenza vaccine is administered each year, while pneumococcal vaccine is not. Infants and children at high risk for influenza-related complications can receive influenza vaccine at the same time they receive other routine vaccinations.

**Pregnancy:** Because currently available influenza vaccine is an inactivated vaccine, many experts consider influenza vaccination safe during any stage of pregnancy. A study of influenza vaccination of more than 2,000 pregnant women demonstrated no adverse fetal effects associated with influenza vaccine. However, more data are needed. Some experts prefer to administer influenza vaccine during the second trimester to avoid a coincidental association with spontaneous abortion, which is common in the first trimester, and because exposures to vaccines have traditionally been avoided during this time. Influenza vaccine does not affect the safety of mothers who are breast-feeding or their infants. Breast-feeding does not adversely affect immune response and is not a contraindication for vaccination.

**People Infected with Human Immunodeficiency Virus (HIV):** Limited information exists regarding the frequency and severity of influenza illness or the benefits of influenza vaccination among HIV-infected people. Influenza vaccine has produced protective influenza antibody titers and has been shown to prevent influenza in HIV-infected people who have minimal AIDS-related symptoms and high CD4+ T-lymphocyte cell counts. However, in people who have advanced HIV disease and low CD4+ T-lymphocyte cell counts, influenza vaccine might not induce protective antibody titers; a second dose of vaccine does not improve the immune response in these people. Deterioration of CD4+ T-lymphocyte cell counts and progression of HIV disease have not been demonstrated among HIV-infected people who receive the vaccine. The effect of antiretroviral therapy on potential increases in HIV ribonucleic acid (RNA) levels following either natural influenza infection or influenza vaccine is unknown. Because influenza can result in serious illness and complications and because influenza vaccination can result in the production of protective antibody titers, vaccination will benefit many HIV-infected people, including HIV-infected pregnant women.

## Other

Antiviral drugs for influenza are an important adjunct to influenza vaccine for the control and prevention of influenza. The four currently licensed U.S. agents are amantadine, rimantadine, zanamivir, and oseltamivir. Amantadine and rimantadine have specific activity against influenza A viruses but not influenza B viruses. Both are approved by the U.S. Food and Drug Administration for the treatment and prophylaxis of influenza A virus infections. Zanamivir and oseltamivir have activity against both influenzas A and B. Both drugs are currently approved for treatment, though only oseltamivir has been approved for prophylaxis. These four drugs differ in terms of dosing, approved age groups for use, side effects, and cost. The package inserts should be consulted for more information.

## Section 21.11

# *Tropical Diseases*

© 1997 American Society of Tropical Medicine and Hygiene. Reprinted with permission. Available online at http://www.astmh.org/q&a/tropdise. html. Despite the age of this document, readers seeking information on tropical diseases will find this information useful.

Some of the organisms that cause tropical diseases are bacteria and viruses, terms that may be familiar to most people since these types of organisms cause illness common in the U.S. Less well known are those more complex organisms commonly referred to as parasites. All of these types of agents may be referred to generically as pathogens—meaning any organisms that cause disease.

In the temperate climate zones, many familiar viral and bacterial diseases are spread directly from person to person, by airborne routes of transmission or by sexual contact. In the tropics, respiratory diseases (such as measles, respiratory syncytial virus, tuberculosis) and sexually transmitted diseases are also of great importance. In addition, many diseases are spread by contaminated water and food sources, since clean water and sanitary conditions are often a luxury in developing countries. Alternatively, some tropical disease agents are transmitted by an intermediate carrier or vector. The insect or other invertebrate vector picks up the pathogen from an infected person or animal and transmits it to others in the process of feeding. Often, tropical disease agents must undergo important developmental changes within the vector before they complete their life cycle and once again become infective for man.

### Viruses

Viruses are minute infectious agents that generally consist only of genetic material covered by a protein shell. They only replicate within cells, which provide the synthetic machinery necessary to produce new virus particles.

*Arboviruses (ar'bow):* The term arboviruses is short for arthropod-borne viruses. Arthropods include many of the medically important bugs (mosquitoes, ticks, flies, etc.) that may transmit pathogens to humans. Arboviruses are of special relevance as tropical diseases.

*Dengue (deng'ee) fever,* caused by a mosquito-borne flavivirus, is found in tropical and subtropical regions of the Americas, Africa, Asia and Australia. In its acute form, dengue is characterized by flu-like symptoms including severe pain in the head, eyes, muscles and joints. Some patients, particularly infants and children, develop dengue hemorrhagic fever, a severe and sometimes fatal variation involving circulatory failure and shock. The incidence of both forms of dengue infection has recently been increasing, as expanding urbanization enlarges the regions inhabited by the Aedes mosquito vector. Mosquitoes capable of transmitting this disease are also found within the United States.

*Yellow fever* is another arboviral disease, characterized by fever, hemorrhage, and often fatal liver complications. It is limited to tropical South America and Africa, where it is sometimes epidemic in spite of the existence of a safe and effective vaccine. The potential for increased incidence of yellow fever appears to be growing with the expanding distribution of the vector Aedes mosquitoes.

*Rotavirus (row'ta):* Rotavirus causes watery diarrhea and vomiting, primarily in young children. These viruses are distributed worldwide and transmission is usually due to contact with infected individuals or fecally contaminated objects. The majority of infections are self-limiting, but infant mortality is higher in developing countries and is generally associated with severe dehydration. As with cholera, treatment consists of replacing lost fluids and electrolytes.

*AIDS:* The human immunodeficiency viruses (HIV) associated with the Acquired Immunodeficiency Syndrome (AIDS) have become widespread in developing nations. By 1996, over 13 million adults were living with HIV in sub-Saharan Africa, representing about 60% of the global number of infected individuals. The spread of HIV in this region has been exacerbated by recent crises, such as natural disasters and armed conflict, with resulting mass population movements. The number of infected individuals in Asia is also rapidly rising; it is currently estimated that over 5 million people are living with HIV/AIDS in South and Southeast Asia. The progressive erosion of the immune system suffered by HIV-infected individuals renders them more susceptible to other infections. Often these secondary (or opportunistic) infections are atypical or more severe than they would appear in an immunocompetent person. Since different diseases are prominent in tropical regions, patterns of the HIV-associated infections may diverge significantly from those seen in the developed nations. Moreover, it is thought that being infected with one or more tropical diseases may affect the course of AIDS upon subsequent HIV infection.

*Ebola (ee-bow'lah):* Ebola virus causes fever, severe headache, backache, vomiting, diarrhea, and severe hemorrhaging. The method by which Ebola is transmitted in nature, and what animal is its natural host, remains unclear. In recent outbreaks such as those that have occurred in Zaire, Sudan and Gabon, man's initial contact with the virus has clearly been accidental. When humans acquire the infection, however, it spreads rapidly to those in contact with body fluids from the patient and the mortality rate is very high.

*Marburg virus* is related to Ebola, but usually has a somewhat lower mortality rate.

*Lassa fever (lah'sah):* Lassa is another often fatal hemorrhagic fever virus. It is transmitted by rodents. Symptoms of Lassa fever include sharp backache and/or headache, sore throat, fever, rashes, dehydration, general swelling, skin hemorrhaging, irregular heart beat, and disorientation. Viruses causing several types of South American hemorrhagic fevers belong to the arenavirus family like Lassa, and are also carried by rodents.

## Bacteria

Bacteria (singular = bacterium) are more complex than viruses, containing genetic information and much of the equipment necessary to produce energy and replicate independently. Some bacteria, however, can only reproduce when growing inside a cell, from which they derive required nutrients.

*Cholera (kol' er-ah):* Cholera is a diarrheal disease caused by infection with *Vibrio cholerae*, a bacterium most often found in contaminated water and shellfish, which produces a toxin that upsets the biochemical balance of cells lining the intestine and makes them secrete copious amounts of water and electrolytes. Cholera is endemic in a number of tropical countries, and periodically major epidemics break out such as that affecting some 900,000 persons in South America between 1991 and 1993. Cholera is characterized by severe watery diarrhea which, if left untreated, can result in serious dehydration and death. Treatment consists of replacement of lost water, salts and sugar.

*Escherichia coli (esh-er-i'kee-a koh'lye):* *Escherichia coli* bacteria, more widely known as *E. coli*, can produce toxins similar to those of the cholera bacteria, causing illness ranging from traveler's diarrhea to persistent diarrhea with associated malnutrition. An extremely pathogenic form of these bacteria causes bloody diarrhea and kidney complications, such as recently observed in outbreaks in the U.S., Japan, and Scotland, which can be lethal—particularly in children and the elderly. This form, sometimes known as 0157:H7 or EHEC (enterohemorrhagic *E. coli*) is often associated with ingestion of undercooked meat, but has also been found in other foods, including unpasteurized milk and fruit juices.

*Tuberculosis (tu-ber-ku-loh'sis):* Caused primarily by the bacterium *Mycobacterium tuberculosis* (my-koh-bak-teer'ee-uhm), this is an infection that can last a lifetime, resulting in disease to virtually every organ in the body but primarily affecting the lungs. Tuberculosis occurs all over the world. Until recently, it was thought to be well controlled in the more developed countries; unfortunately, however, it is again on the increase due to its association as an opportunistic infection of AIDS and its prevalence in drug-abusers. Tuberculosis remains a major problem in the developing world, where conditions of poverty, poor nutrition and crowding contribute to its prevalence.

It has been estimated that 5 to 15% of infected individuals develop disease. Pulmonary tuberculosis is the most common manifestation worldwide, and is associated with fatigue, weight loss, coughing and difficulty in breathing. Several drugs are available, but drawbacks include the need for lengthy treatment and increasing development of drug resistance by the bacteria.

*Hansen's disease:* Hansen's disease, also known as leprosy, is caused by the bacterium, *Mycobacterium leprae*, which is related to the agent that causes tuberculosis. 3.7 million cases are officially registered, but the actual number of infected individuals is at least two to three times higher. The exact mechanism of transmission from person to person remains unknown, but likely involves contact with infected skin or nasal secretions. The bacteria grow mainly in tissue cells known as macrophages (literally big eaters, these cells are important components of the immune system) in the skin and in Schwann cells surrounding nerves. As in the case of some of the parasitic diseases, the body's reaction to the leprosy bacillus is responsible for disease. The clinical course of leprosy is extremely variable. Some infected individuals may remain without symptoms. In its worst form, bacterial growth is uncontrolled, leading to loss of sensation in the affected area which may predispose to trauma and consequent deformity. Presently, no methods for prevention exist. Treatment relies on long-term administration of antibiotics. Difficulties are encountered due to the development of drug resistance and the failure of patients to comply with treatment regimens.

## Parasites

Parasites are organisms that live within or on another organism, the host, at whose expense they obtain some advantage such as nourishment. This group of pathogens includes the protozoa (single-celled organisms more complex than bacteria) and the helminths (multicellular organisms commonly referred to as worms). Thus, parasites can range all the way from microscopic protozoa up to worms that reach three feet long. The environment in which parasites can live is spectacularly diverse: different types of protozoa may set up housekeeping in red blood cells, white blood cells (including those that are normally responsible for killing intruding microorganisms), muscle cells, brain cells, heart cells, liver cells and others, or they may live extracellularly in such sites as the blood, tissues or mucosal secretions. Incredibly, some types of worms may also live within cells, but for the most part they live extracellularly within the gut, the blood, the lymphatics, or tissues of the skin, eyes and elsewhere. As opposed to bacteria and viruses, many types of parasites undergo complex developmental transformations, involving growth within both mammalian and invertebrate hosts as well as both sexual and asexual types of reproduction, during their complicated life cycles.

*Malaria (mah-lair'ee-ah):* Over 300 million people develop clinical cases of malaria each year, and one to three million of them die. Many of these are children living in sub Saharan Africa. Almost half of the world's population lives in an area where they are at risk of contracting the disease. Malaria is caused by protozoa of genus *Plasmodium.* Each of the four species of malaria parasite that infect man causes a somewhat different form of the disease. Malaria caused by *P. falciparum* is the most dangerous form and accounts for the overwhelming majority of deaths. Unless appropriately treated, it can produce several life-threatening complications including kidney failure and coma.

The parasites are transmitted to humans by female anopheline mosquitoes. When the mosquito takes a blood meal on the host, she injects the parasites along with her saliva. The parasites develop first in liver cells and then infect red blood cells (erythrocytes), where they consume hemoglobin, the oxygen-carrying component of the blood. The parasites divide in the red cell, and at the completion of development the red cell ruptures releasing parasites that can infect many other erythrocytes. The typical symptoms of malaria, cycles of chills, fever and sweating, are experienced by patients at these times.

In 1955, the World Health Organization began an extensive campaign, using insecticides and drugs, to eradicate malaria. Despite a number of dramatic successes, the objective proved elusive. Mosquitoes not only modified their behavior to avoid coming into contact with insecticides, but actually developed resistance to these chemicals. Parasites also became resistant to the widely used drug chloroquine and other antimalarials. Mounting evidence shows that malaria is once again gaining the upper hand. Areas that have been free of malaria have been experiencing outbreaks, and the number of cases have been rising alarmingly in the Amazon and parts of Asia, especially

Southeast Asia. In Africa, malaria has been moving from rural areas to the cities.

At one time, malaria was a serious health problem in the U.S.; in 1914 more than 600,000 cases of malaria occurred here. Although improved public health led to a substantial decline in the following decades, minor resurgences have occurred as troops returned from both the Korean and Vietnam wars. In 1995, approximately 1200 cases of malaria were reported to the U.S. Centers for Disease Control and Prevention. Not all of these cases of imported (acquired outside the U.S.); several were recent infections acquired within the U.S. following the bite of indigenous mosquitoes. Recently, cases of locally transmitted malaria have been appearing in regions as diverse as California, Florida, New Jersey, New York, Texas and Michigan.

*Leishmaniasis (leesh-mah-nye'ah-sis):* Leishmaniasis is actually a group of diseases, caused by infection with protozoa belonging to the genus Leishmania. There are about 20 different species that are transmitted to man by the bite of infected female sandflies. In the mammalian host, the parasite is found within macrophages. These cells are usually responsible for destroying invading microorganisms, and the remarkable ability of leishmanial parasites to evade their antimicrobial mechanisms has attracted considerable scientific interest.

Like malaria, leishmaniasis is widely distributed over large portions of the tropical and subtropical areas of the world, including portions of southern Europe. Cases have been anecdotally reported in the Southwestern U. S. The World Health Organization reports 12 million infected individuals with 300 million people at risk in some 80 countries. Reservoir hosts, such as dogs and rodents, play an important role in the distribution of the infection. People contract leishmaniasis when their activities bring them into close association with sandflies; for example, workers in the forests of South America are frequently exposed.

Leishmaniasis takes many forms, depending on both host and parasite factors. Symptoms may range from self-healing skin ulcers to severe life threatening disease. Cutaneous leishmaniasis, known locally by various names such as Baghdad ulcer, Delhi boil or oriental sore, is manifested by skin lesions that usually resolve but may leave ugly scars. In some individuals, the disease spreads to the mucous membranes of the nose and mouth, resulting in hideous destruction of facial features. The most dangerous form is visceral leishmaniasis, where parasites invade the internal organs. This disease is commonly referred to as kala-azar, a Hindi term for black-sickness which describes the increased pigmentation of the skin. Symptoms include fever and weight loss. If left untreated, kala-azar invariably leads to death. Recent leishmaniasis epidemics in Sudan and India have highlighted the problem.

*Trypanosomiasis (tri-pan-o-so-mye'ah-sis):* The protozoa causing trypanosomiasis are closely related to leishmania parasites. In humans, different species of the genus *Trypanosoma* are responsible for diseases that are quite distinct in clinical outcome and in geographic distribution. The New World form, Chagas' disease or American trypanosomiasis, caused by *Trypanosoma cruzi*, affects about 18 million people living mostly in Latin America. The parasite is transmitted to man by blood-sucking reduviid bugs, also known as kissing bugs due to their predilection for feeding on the faces of their victims. Unlike malaria and leishmaniasis, the parasites are not injected during feeding; rather they are deposited by defecating bugs. The parasite enters the host through the eyes, nose or mouth, or through breaks in the skin. Symptoms may appear as acute disease shortly after infection or as chronic disease years later. Acute disease involves fever, swelling of the lymph nodes and, sometimes, inflammation of the heart muscle and of the brain. Although the acute stage may be fatal, especially in children, most infected individuals survive and enter a long symptom-less stage. One quarter or more will develop cardiac damage that may result in heart failure and sudden death; others may develop digestive disorders. *Trypanosoma cruzi* infection is not limited to humans and the presence of other infected mammals is sufficient to sustain the infection in nature. Control measures rely on limiting contact with infected bugs, because prophylaxis and drug treatment are not effective. Vector control methods involve insecticide spraying and eliminating the breeding grounds of the bugs.

The trypanosomes responsible for human disease in Africa, African trypanosomiasis or sleeping sickness, are different from those causing Chagas' disease. This disease affects some 25,000 people per year; however, epidemics involving many times that number are well-known. These parasites are very closely related to trypanosomes that produce veterinary disease and prevent development of ranch lands in Africa, thereby depriving people of an important source of food. These trypanosomes are transmitted to man by the bite of tsetse flies. Initial symptoms include fever, headache, dizziness and weakness. Later, parasites invade the central nervous system, causing neurological and psychological problems, including hallucinations, delusions and seizures. Untreated, the patient may become comatose and die.

A feature of parasite biology that has long intrigued scientists is the ability of these organisms to evade the immune response by a process known as antigenic variation. By means of a complex genetic mechanism, which is currently being unraveled, the parasite is able to repeatedly change the protein that covers its entire surface, thereby staying one step ahead of the ability of the host immune system to recognize and react to it. The inability of the host to recognize these new variants allows the parasite to survive for long periods of time.

*Schistosomiasis (shis-toh-soh-my'uh-sis):* This disease is caused by several species of flatworms of the genus *Schistosoma*. About 200 million people are infected, with three times that many at risk. An estimated 200,000 people (0.1% of those infected) die every year, but many more (about 10% of infected individuals) suffer chronic damage to vital organs including the liver and kidney.

Interestingly, while this parasite's life cycle also involves an invertebrate vector, it is not transmitted through the bite of an insect, but rather develops within freshwater snails. After exiting from the snail vector, schistosome larvae swim along until they contact a human host bathing or working in the water. They penetrate the skin, and subsequently migrate through the blood vessels until finally establishing residence in veins of the intestines or urinary bladder, depending on the parasite species. The adult male and female worms pair, mate and produce large numbers of eggs, some of which are excreted in either feces or urine and wind up in the water supply where they hatch and complete the cycle by infecting new snail hosts.

The adult worms do not cause the most common manifestations of the disease. Those eggs that are not excreted but instead become lodged in the body's tissues cause disease. In a process known as granuloma formation, masses of cells form around the eggs in an effort to destroy them; in so doing, however, these cells initiate a process of tissue scarring (fibrosis). In those forms of the disease involving the liver and intestines, this impedes blood circulation and can cause death due to rupture of distended blood vessels. In the form involving the bladder, the extensive scarring can result in obstruction of urinary outflow.

*Filariasis (fil-ah-rye'ah-sis):* Filarial diseases are rarely life threatening or acute; they are, however, extremely debilitating and disfiguring, and make affected individuals dependent on others or on limited health care resources. These roundworms are related to the dog heartworm, which is well known to pet lovers in the temperate zones. Transmitted to man by the bite of infected mosquitoes, filarial worms of the genera *Wuchereria* and *Brugia* cause lymphatic filariasis. One billion people live in areas where filariasis is found, and approximately 90 million people are estimated to have the disease. When the infected female mosquito feeds on humans, she injects larval stages of the parasite. These larvae migrate through the tissues, and develop into adults that take up residence in the lymphatic system. Disease results from extensive obstruction and damage to the lymphatic system. The end result is frequently a build up of lymph fluid in the limbs, and sometimes scrotal sac, which may cause the grotesque swelling known as elephantiasis, hanging groin and hydrocele. Male and female worms mate to produce millions of progeny called microfilaria, which end up in the blood and serve to transmit the parasite back to the insect vector.

The form of filariasis known as onchocerciasis or river blindness, caused by *Onchocerca volvulus*, is transmitted by a group of insects known as blackflies, which breed in fast moving rivers and streams. Some 90 million people are at risk in 36 countries, mostly in Africa and South America, and 18 million people are infected. The adult forms of *O. volvulus* live under the skin, forming visible nodules. Most of the symptoms of the disease result from the migration of the larval stages (microfilaria) into the skin and eyes. Reaction to these stages leads to intense itching and disfiguring dermatitis as well as damage to the eyes, including corneal scarring. Onchocerciasis is a frequent cause of blindness in the tropics, affecting well over 300,000 people. Disease control in West Africa has been brought about by the Onchocerciasis Control Programme, which coordinates the regular release of insecticides into the rivers and streams of 11 countries in this region. The program is designed to eliminate the larval stages of the blackfly vector. Ivermectin (Mectizan®), a drug originally developed for veterinary use, has proven to be an effective treatment. Merck, Sharp and Dohme, the manufacturers, have provided the compound free to all countries with endemic onchocerciasis.

### Enteric Protozoa

Two parasitic infections that have recently come to widespread public attention in the U.S. are *Cryptosporidium parvum* (krip-toh-spohrid'ee-uhm) and *Cyclospora cayetanensis* (sye-kloh-spoh'rah). These protozoan parasites cause persistent diarrhea, and are usually acquired by ingestion of contaminated water or food. Travelers to tropical countries may be at increased risk for acquiring these infections, but more and more cases are being recognized in countries such as the U.S. and Canada.

The first outbreak of cryptosporidiosis in a child-care center was observed in 1983. In 1993, an outbreak associated with contaminated drinking water occurred in Milwaukee, Wisconsin, that affected some 403,000 people. Cryptosporidiosis causes especially severe diarrhea in AIDS patients. It has been estimated that 10–15% of the chronic diarrhea and wasting observed in AIDS patients in the U.S. is due to this infection, while it may account for as much as 30–50% of severe diarrhea in AIDS patients in developing countries. There is still no adequate treatment of cryptosporidiosis.

Although probably discovered around the turn of the century, *Cyclospora cayatenensis* was actually characterized and named in the course of ongoing studies in Peru. Like cryptosporidiosis, our understanding of cyclospora infection has been influenced by the AIDS epidemic and subsequent improvements in diagnosis. It appears that globally, Cyclospora affects approximately equivalent numbers of immunocompetent and immunosuppressed individuals. The emergence of this parasite as a problem in developed countries became widely recognized in the summer of 1996, when over 1500 cases were reported from some 14 U.S. states and Canada as a result of eating contaminated berries.

Another water-borne protozoan, *Giardia lamblia* (gee-ar'dee-ah), which causes diarrheal disease, is also endemic in the U.S. It has become recognized as one of the most common causes of waterborne disease in humans in the U.S., and is also found throughout the world. Diarrhea, abdominal cramps, and nausea are the most common symptoms of giardiasis. These may lead to weight loss and dehydration. Persons at increased risk for giardiasis include child care workers, diaper-aged children who attend day-care centers, international travelers, and hikers or campers who drink untreated water from contaminated sources.

The protozoan *Entamoeba histolytica* (en-tah-mee'bah), which causes severe dysentery and liver disease, is estimated to kill up to 100,000 people annually. This parasite is found throughout the world, although it is especially problematic in underdeveloped tropical and subtropical regions. The main source of transmission is people who carry a chronic infection; feces infected with the cyst form of the parasite may contaminate fresh food or water.

### Other Protozoa

*Toxoplasma gondii* (toks-oh-plaz'mah) is a protozoan parasite common in the U.S. and other developed countries. It is estimated that more than 60 million people in the U.S. carry the toxoplasma parasite, which is transmitted in the feces of infected cats or can be acquired by eating undercooked meat. Ordinarily *T. gondii* infection is benign, because the immune system keeps the parasite from causing illness. In most cases, it can be mistaken for the flu, causing swollen lymph nodes or muscle aches. But it can cause serious neurological disorders in immunocompromised people, or in the fetus if first acquired by a mother during pregnancy.

*Trichomonas vaginalis* (trih-koh-moh'nas) a sexually transmitted protozoan parasite, which causes vaginal and urinary tract inflammation and, in women, has been associated with adverse outcomes of pregnancy.

### Other Helminth Parasites

It is estimated that at least one quarter of the world's population is infected with parasitic worms. Many people living in tropical regions, where famine and malnutrition already create health problems, are infected with more than one of these helminth parasites. These parasites further rob their human hosts of blood and nutrients; it is easy to understand how they can affect the physical and mental development of children and the ability of adults to work.

Hookworm infections occur mostly in tropical and subtropical climates. One type of hookworm, *Necator americanus* (neh-kay'tor), was widespread in the southeastern U.S. early in this century. Hookworm infection usually causes mild diarrhea or cramps. However, heavy infection with these bloodsucking intestinal roundworms can cause profound anemia, resulting in growth and mental retardation in children. People generally acquire hookworm infection by direct contact with contaminated soil, for example, by walking barefoot. When eggs passed in the feces reach the soil, they hatch and develop into infective larvae that can penetrate the skin. Children, because they play in dirt and often go barefoot, are at particularly high risk for infection.

Ascaris (as-kar'is) worms are found in temperate as well as tropical regions; indeed they are probably the most common parasite in the world. While the mortality rate is relatively low (estimated at 20,000 per year), ascaris infection can be debilitating, causing abdominal pain and lack of weight gain in children and sometimes resulting in intestinal obstruction. Other intestinal roundworms are also prevalent in the developing world. Trichuris (trik-u'ris) worms afflict approximately 750 million people, and can cause severe anemia, abdominal pain, nausea and weight loss. Strongyloides (stron-ji-loi'deez) worms infect around 80 million people, and cause abdominal pain, nausea and diarrhea.

Another type of helminth parasite, the tapeworm *Taenia solium* (te'ne-yah), also causes serious human disease. Pigs and humans are affected by this tapeworm. Generally, people acquire an active infection by eating undercooked pork containing the larval form of the parasite. The ingested larvae then develop into adult, egg-laying, worms in the person's intestine. Eggs pass out of the body in the feces, and are spread to the environment where they may be ingested by pigs, to continue this life cycle, or by other humans. When eggs are inadvertently eaten by people, the larvae may infect the central nervous system and brain, causing serious neurologic disorders, including seizures. This disease, called neurocysticercosis (nu-row-sis-te-sir-ko'sis) after the name of the larval stage, is a serious problem in rural parts of Latin America. It may be also be emerging in the U.S.

## Section 21.12

# *Countries with Areas Infected with Quarantinable Diseases*

"Summary of Health Information for International Travel," 2002 Centers for Disease Control and Prevention (CDC). Available online at http://www.cdc.gov/travel/blusheet.htm.

This section contains a summary of health information for international travel of countries with areas infected with quarantinable diseases according to the World Health Organization (WHO).

*NOTE:* No country requires cholera vaccination for direct travel from the United States, and no vaccinations are required to reenter the United States. This listing supplements information in Health Information for International Travel, 2001–2002 and should be used in conjunction with that document to determine required and recommended vaccinations.

**Table. 21.6.** Cholera-Infected Countries

This list represents those countries reporting cholera cases to WHO 14 days prior to October 25, 2002.

**Africa**
Angola
Benin
Burkina Faso
Burundi
Cameroon
Cape Verde
Central African Republic
Chad
Comoros
Congo
Côte d'Ivoire
Democratic Republic of Congo
Djibouti
Ghana
Guinea
Guinea-Bissau
Kenya
Liberia
Madagascar
Malawi
Mali
Mauritania
Mozambique
Niger
Nigeria
Rwanda
São Tomé & Príncipe
Senegal
Sierra Leone
Somalia
South Africa
Swaziland
Tanzania
Togo
Uganda
Zambia
Zimbabwe

**Central America**
El Salvador
Guatemala
Nicaragua

**South East Asia**
East Timor

**East Asia**
China
Republic of Korea

**Indian Subcontinent**
Afghanistan
Bhutan
India
Nepal

**Middle East**
Iran
Iraq

**South America**
Brazil
Ecuador
Peru
Venezuela

**Southeast Asia**
Cambodia
Laos
Myanmar
Philippines
Vietnam

**Table 21.7.** Yellow Fever-Infected Countries

### Africa

| Country | Region Within Country |
|---|---|
| Angola: | *Provinces*: Bengo and Luanda |
| Benin: | *Department:* Atakora, du Borgou |
| Burkina Faso: | Gaoua Region |
| Cameroon: | Northern Province |
| Côte d'Ivoire | Department de l'Ouest |
| Democratic Republic of Congo: | North of 10° South |
| Gabon: | Ogooue'-Ivindo Province |
| Gambia: | Upper River Division |
| Ghana: | Upper West Region, Upper East Region |
| Guinea: | Siguiri Region |
| Liberia: | *Counties*: Bassa County, Boma County, Bong County, Lofa County, Rivercess County, Sinoe County |
| Nigeria: | *States*: Anambra, Bauchi, Bendel, Benue, Cross River, Imo, Kaduna, Kano, Kwara, Lagos, Niger, Ogun, Ondo, Oyo, and Plateau. |
| Sierra Leone: | Kenema District |
| Senegal | Kolda, Diourbel, Fatick, Tambacounda, Ziguinchor, Louga, Thies, and Dakar |
| Sudan: | South of 12° North |

### South America

| Country | Region within Country |
|---|---|
| Bolivia: | *Departments*: Beni, Cochabamba, La Paz, and Santa Cruz |
| Brazil: | *States*: Acre, Amapá, Amazonas, Goiás, Maranhão, Mato Grosso, Mato Grosso do Sul, Pará, Rondonia, Roraima, and Tocantins, and certain areas of Bahia, Minas Gerais, Parana, Piaui, Rio Grande do Sul, São Paulo, Santa Catarina |
| Colombia: | *Departments*: Antioquia, Boyaca, Caqueta, Casanare, Cesar, Choco, Cundinamarca, Meta, Norte de Santander, Santander, and Vichada. *Intendencias*: Arauca, Cucuta, Guaviare, and Putumayo |
| Ecuador: | Provinces: Morona-Santiago, Napo, Pastaza, Sucumbios, and Zamora Chinchipe |
| French Guiana: | Saint Laurent-du-Moroni region |
| Peru: | *Departments:* Amazonas, Ancash, Ayacucho, Cusco, Huanuco, Junin, Loreto, Madre de Dios, Puno, Pasco, San Martin, and Ucayali |
| Venezuela: | Amazonas State, Bolivar State |

# Section 21.13

## *Diseases Which Manifest Post-Travel*

"The Post-Travel Period," excerpted from *Health Information for International Travel, 2001–2002,* a brochure produced by the Centers for Disease Control and Prevention (CDC). Available online at http://www.cdc.gov/travel/other/post-travel.htm. 2002.

Some diseases might not manifest themselves immediately. If travelers become ill after they return home, they should be advised to tell their physician where they have traveled.

Most travelers who acquire viral, bacterial, or parasitic infections abroad become ill within 6 weeks after returning from international travel. However, some diseases might not manifest themselves immediately; for example, malaria might not cause symptoms for as long as 6 months to a year after a traveler returns to the United States. The traveler should be advised to inform his or her physician of the countries visited within the 12 months preceding onset of illness. Knowledge of such travel and the possibility the traveler might be ill with a disease the physician rarely encounters will help the physician arrive at a correct diagnosis.

# Chapter 22

# *Health Risks from Food and Drink in Foreign Countries*

## *Risks from Food and Drink*

Contaminated food and drink are common sources for the introduction of infection into the body. Among the more common infections that travelers can acquire from contaminated food and drink are *Escherichia coli* infections, shigellosis or bacillary dysentery, giardiasis, cryptosporidiosis, and hepatitis A. Other less common infectious disease risks for travelers include typhoid fever and other salmonelloses, cholera, infections caused by rotavirus and Norwalk-like viruses, and a variety of protozoan and helminthic parasites (other than those that cause giardiasis and cryptosporidiosis). Many of the infectious diseases transmitted in food and water can also be acquired directly through the fecal-oral route.

## *Water*

Water that has been adequately chlorinated, using minimum recommended water treatment standards employed in the United States, will afford significant protection against viral and bacterial waterborne diseases. However, chlorine treatment alone, as used in the routine disinfection of water, might not kill some enteric viruses and the

This chapter contains "Risks from Food and Drink," excerpted from *Health Information for International Travel, 2001-2002*, produced by the Centers for Disease Control and Prevention (CDC), available online at http://www.cdc.gov/travel/food-drink-risks.htm. The chapter also contains *A Guide on Safe Food for Travellers*, Copyright © 1997 World Health Organization. Reprinted with permission.

parasitic organisms that cause giardiasis, amebiasis, and cryptosporidiosis. In areas where chlorinated tap water is not available or where hygiene and sanitation are poor, travelers should be advised that only the following might be safe to drink:

- Beverages, such as tea and coffee, made with boiled water.

- Canned or bottled carbonated beverages, including carbonated bottled water and soft drinks.

- Beer and wine.

Where water might be contaminated, travelers should be advised that ice should also be considered contaminated and should not be used in beverages. If ice has been in contact with containers used for drinking, travelers should be advised to thoroughly clean the containers, preferably with soap and hot water, after the ice has been discarded.

It is safer to drink a beverage directly from the can or bottle than from a questionable container. However, water on the outside of beverage cans or bottles might be contaminated also. Therefore, travelers should be advised to dry wet cans or bottles before they are opened, and to wipe clean surfaces with which the mouth will have direct contact. Where water might be contaminated, travelers should be advised to avoid brushing their teeth with tap water.

*Treatment of Water*

Travelers should be advised of the following methods for treating water to make it safe for drinking and other purposes.

**Boiling** is by far the most reliable method to make water of uncertain purity safe for drinking. Water should be brought to a vigorous rolling boil for 1 minute and allowed to cool to room temperature; ice should not be added. This procedure will kill bacterial and parasitic causes of diarrhea at all altitudes and viruses at low altitudes. To kill viruses at altitudes above 2,000 meters (6,562 feet), water should be boiled for 3 minutes or chemical disinfection should be used after the water has boiled for 1 minute. Adding a pinch of salt to each quart or pouring the water several times from one clean container to another will improve the taste.

**Chemical disinfection** with iodine is an alternative method of water treatment when it is not feasible to boil water. However, this method cannot be relied upon to kill *Cryptosporidium* unless the water is allowed to sit for 15 hours before it is drunk. Two well-tested methods for disinfection with iodine are the use of tincture of iodine (Table 22.1) and the use of tetraglycine hydroperiodide tablets (for example, Globaline®, Potable-Aqua®, or Coghlan's®). These tablets are available from pharmacies and sporting goods stores. The manufacturers' instructions should be followed. If water is cloudy, the number of tablets used should be doubled; if water is extremely cold (<5° Celsius [<41° Fahrenheit]), an attempt should be made to warm the water, and the recommended contact time should be increased to achieve reliable disinfection. Cloudy water should be strained through a clean cloth into a container to remove any sediment or floating matter, and then the water should be boiled or treated with iodine. Chlorine, in various forms, can also be used for chemical disinfection. However, its germicidal activity varies greatly with the pH, temperature, and organic content of the water to be purified and, therefore, it can produce less consistent levels of disinfection in many types of water. Chemically treated water is intended for short-term use only. If iodine-disinfected water is the only water available, it should be used for only a few weeks.

**Portable filters** currently on the market will provide various degrees of protection against microbes. Reverse-osmosis filters provide protection against viruses, bacteria, and protozoa, but they are expensive, are larger than most filters used by backpackers, and the small pores on this type of filter are rapidly plugged by muddy or cloudy water. In addition, the membranes in some filters can be damaged by chlorine in water. Microstrainer filters with pore sizes in the 0.1- to 0.3-micrometer range can remove bacteria and protozoa from drinking water, but they do not remove viruses. To kill viruses, travelers using microstrainer filters should be advised to disinfect the water with iodine or chlorine after filtration, as described previously. Filters with iodine-impregnated resins are most effective against bacteria, and the iodine will kill some viruses; however, the contact time with the iodine in the filter is too short to kill the protozoa *Cryptosporidium* and, in cold water, *Giardia*. Proper selection, operation, care, and maintenance of water filters is essential to producing safe water. The manufacturers' instructions should be followed. NSF International, an independent testing company, tests and certifies water filters for their ability to remove protozoa, but not for their ability to remove bacteria or viruses. Few published reports in the scientific literature have evaluated the efficacy of specific brands or models of filters against bacteria and viruses in water. Until such information becomes available, the Centers for Disease Control and Prevention (CDC) cannot identify which specific brands or models of filters are most likely to remove bacteria and viruses. A list of filters that have passed NSF tests for parasite removal can be obtained by calling 1-800-673-8010; by writing to NSF at 789 North Dixboro Road, P.O. Box 130140, Ann Arbor, Michigan 48113-0140; or online at http://www.nsf.org.

As a last resort, if no source of safe drinking water is available or can be obtained, tap water that is uncomfortably hot to touch might be safer than cold tap water; however, proper disinfection, filtering, or boiling is still advised.

**Table 22.1.** Treatment of Water with Tincture of Iodine

**Tincture of Iodine—2%**

| | Clear Water | Cold or Cloudy Water** |
|---|---|---|
| Drops* to be Added per Quart or Liter | 5 | 10 |

* 1 drop = 0.05 milliliter. Water must stand for a minimum of 30 minutes before it is safe to use.

** Very turbid or very cold water can require prolonged contact time; if possible, such water should be allowed to stand several hours prior to use. To ensure that *Cryptosporidium* is killed, water must stand for 15 hours before drinking.

*Note:* tincture of iodine can come from a medicine chest or first-aid kit.

## Food

To avoid illness, travelers should be advised to select food with care. All raw food is subject to contamination. Particularly in areas where hygiene and sanitation are inadequate, the traveler should be advised to avoid salads, uncooked vegetables, and unpasteurized milk and milk products such as cheese, and to eat only food that has been cooked and is still hot, or fruit that has been peeled by the traveler personally. Undercooked and raw meat, fish, and shellfish can carry various intestinal pathogens. Cooked food that has been allowed to stand for several hours at ambient temperature can provide a fertile medium for bacterial growth and should be thoroughly reheated before serving. Consumption of food and beverages obtained from street food vendors has been associated with an increased risk of illness. The easiest way to guarantee a safe food source for an infant younger than 6 months of age is to have the infant breast feed. If the infant has already been weaned from the breast, formula prepared from commercial powder and boiled water is the safest and most practical food.

Some species of fish and shellfish can contain poisonous biotoxins, even when well cooked. The most common type of biotoxin in fish is ciguatoxin. The flesh of the barracuda is the most toxic laden and should always be avoided. Red snapper, grouper, amberjack, sea bass, and a wide range of tropical reef fish contain the toxin at unpredictable times. The potential for ciguatera poisoning exists in all subtropical and tropical insular areas of the West Indies and the Pacific and Indian Oceans where the implicated fish species are eaten. Symptoms of ciguatera poisoning include gastroenteritis followed by neurologic problems such as dysesthesias; temperature reversal; weakness; and, rarely, hypotension. Scombroid is another common fish poisoning that occurs worldwide in tropical, as well as temperate, regions. Fish of the *Scombridae* family (for example, bluefin, yellowfin tuna, mackerel, and bonito), as well as some nonscombroid fish (for example, mahimahi, herring, amberjack, and bluefish) may contain high levels of histidine in their flesh. With improper refrigeration or preservation, histidine is converted to histamine, which can cause flushing, headache, nausea, vomiting, diarrhea, and urticaria.

Cholera cases have occurred among people who ate crab brought back from Latin America by travelers. Travelers should be advised not to bring perishable seafood with them when they return to the United States from high-risk areas.

## A Guide on Safe Food for Travelers

### How to Avoid Illnesses Caused by Unsafe Food and Drink and What to Do If You Get Diarrhea

When you travel, be it for pleasure, business or any other reason, contaminated food and drink are often a serious threat to health. In particular, diarrhea affects a great number of travelers. Physical pain and discomfort, along with the problem of finding suitable medical treatment, especially when there are language barriers, can spoil your entire stay away from home. This chapter gives some practical advice and basic hints on how to eat safely and what to do if you get diarrhea.

Observation of the advice given in this chapter is of particular importance for vulnerable groups, i.e. infants and children, the elderly, pregnant women and persons with impaired immune systems.

### Before Leaving Home

- Consult your physician for advice on the various diseases to which you may be exposed, and the need for vaccinations or other preventive measures.

- Make sure your medical kit contains Oral Rehydration Salts (ORS) and a water-disinfectant agent.

### Eating Safely

The following recommendations apply to all situations, from food vendors on the street to expensive hotel restaurants:

- Cooked food that has been held at room temperature for several hours constitutes one of the greatest risks of foodborne illness. Make sure your food has been thoroughly cooked and is still hot when served.

- Avoid any uncooked food, apart from fruits and vegetables that can be peeled or shelled. Avoid fruits with damaged skin. Remember the dictum "Cook it, peel it or leave it."

- Dishes containing raw or undercooked eggs, such as home-made mayonnaise, some sauces (e.g. hollandaise sauce) and some desserts (e.g. mousses) may be dangerous.

- Ice cream from unreliable sources is frequently contaminated and can cause illness. If in doubt, avoid it.

- In some countries, certain species of fish and shellfish may contain poisonous biotoxins even when they are well cooked. Local people can advise you about this.

- Unpasteurized milk should be boiled before consumption.

- When the safety of drinking-water is doubtful, have it boiled, or if this is not possible, disinfect it with a reliable, slow-release, disinfectant agent, that are generally available in pharmacies.

- Avoid ice unless you are sure that it is made from safe water.

- Beverages such as hot tea or coffee, wine, beer and carbonated soft drinks or fruit juices which are either bottled or otherwise packaged are usually safe to drink.

## What to Do If You Get Diarrhea

Most diarrheal attacks are self-limiting and clear up in a few days. The important thing is to avoid becoming dehydrated. As soon as diarrhea starts, drink more fluids, such as bottled, boiled or treated water, or weak tea. Fruit juice (diluted with safe water) or soup may also be taken. If diarrhea continues for more than one day, prepare and drink ORS solution and continue to eat normally (see Table 22.2).

Seek medical help if diarrhea lasts for more than 3 days and/or there are very frequent watery bowel movements, blood in the stools, repeated vomiting or fever.

- When there is no medical help available and there is blood in the stools, a course (5 days) of cotrimoxazole may be taken (see Table 22.3).

- Prophylactic use of antibiotics is not recommended. Antidiarrheals (e.g. loperamide) are not recommended but may be used, in addition to fluids, by adults only, for symptomatic relief. They should never be used for children.

- If there are other symptoms, seek medical advice.

If ORS are not available, mix 6 level teaspoons of sugar plus 1 level teaspoon of salt in one liter of safe water. Drink this as indicated above for ORS.

**Table 22.2.** Amounts of Fluid or ORS to Drink

| | |
|---|---|
| Children less than 2 years: | ¼–½ cup (50–100ml) after each loose stool |
| 2 years to 10 years: | ½–1 cup (100–200ml) after each loose stool |
| Older children and adults: | unlimited amount |

**Table 22.3.** Dosage for Cotrimoxazole (Trimethoprim, Sulfamethoxazole)

| | |
|---|---|
| For adults: | 160 mg of trimethoprim and 800 mg of sulfamethoxazole, twice a day, for 5 days |
| For children: | 5 mg of trimethoprim and 25 mg of sulfamethoxazole per kg of body weight, twice a day, for 5 days. |

# Chapter 23

# *Altitude Sickness, Heat and Cold, and Other Environmental Health Risks*

## *Environmental Effects*

International travelers can be subject to certain stresses that can lower resistance to disease, such as crowding; disruption of usual eating and drinking habits; and time changes, with jet lag contributing to a disturbed pattern of the sleep and wakefulness cycle. These conditions of stress can lead to nausea, indigestion, fatigue, or insomnia. Complete adaptation depends on the number of time zones crossed and can take a week or more.

Heat and cold can be directly or indirectly responsible for some diseases and can give rise to serious skin conditions. Dermatophytoses such as athlete's foot are often made worse by warm, humid conditions.

Excessive heat and humidity alone, or strenuous activity under those conditions, can lead to heat exhaustion from salt and water deficiency and to the more serious heat stroke or hyperthermia. Travelers who anticipate being exposed to excessive heat should be advised to increase consumption of nonalcoholic liquids and to be aware of signs of heat illness, such as headache; dizziness; and red, hot, and

---

Text in this chapter is excerpted from *Health Information for International Travel, 2001-2002*, produced by the Centers for Disease Control and Prevention (CDC) and includes, "Environmental Effects," available at http://www.cdc.gov/travel/other/enviro.htm; "Natural Disasters and Environmental Hazards," available at http://www.cdc.gov/travel/other/natural-diasters.htm; and "Altitude Illness," available at http://www.cdc.gov/travel/diseases/altitude.htm.

dry skin. The ultraviolet rays of the sun can cause severe and very debilitating sunburn in lighter skinned people. Wearing a wide-brimmed hat and using a sunscreen with a sun protection factor (SPF) of 15 or higher on exposed skin will reduce the likelihood of severe sunburn.

Excessive cold affects people who might be inadequately dressed or who remain outside for extended periods of time. Cold particularly affects the elderly and the young. Exposure to cold can lead to hypothermia and to frostbite of exposed parts of the body. Alcohol consumption can amplify the adverse effects of cold temperatures.

Breathing and swallowing dust when traveling on unpaved roads or in arid areas can be followed by nausea and malaise and can cause increased susceptibility to infections of the upper respiratory tract. The harmful effects of air pollution are difficult to avoid when visiting some cities; limiting strenuous activity and not smoking can help.

## Natural Disasters and Environmental Hazards

Natural disasters can contribute to the transmission of some diseases; however, unless the causative agent is in the environment, transmission cannot take place. Natural disasters often disrupt water supplies and sewage systems. Epidemic typhoid has been conspicuously absent following natural disasters in developing countries where typhoid is endemic. It takes several weeks for typhoid antibodies to develop, and even then immunization provides only moderate protection. Floods pose no additional risk of typhoid. In flood areas where the organism has been present, recent studies have identified outbreaks of leptospirosis.

Of greatest important in preventing enteric disease transmission when water and sewage systems have been disrupted is ensuring that water and food supplies are safe to consume. If contamination is suspected, water should be boiled and appropriately disinfected.

Contamination of rivers and lakes with chemical or organic or inorganic compounds (such as heavy metals or other toxins) can be harmful both to fish and to the humans who eat the fish or who swim or bathe in the water. Sufficient warning that such a hazard exists in a body of water is often difficult to provide.

Air pollution is widespread in large cities. Uncontrolled forest fires have been known to cause widespread pollution over vast expanses of the world. Health risks associated with these environmental occurrences have not been fully studied, and travelers with chronic pulmonary disease might be more susceptible to respiratory infection.

314

Any risk to short-term healthy travelers to such areas is probably small.

## Altitude Illness

Travelers whose itineraries will take them above an altitude of 1,829 to 2,438 meters (6,000 to 8,000 feet) should be aware of the risk of altitude illness. Travelers are exposed to higher altitudes in a number of ways: by mountain climbing or trekking in or to high-altitude destinations such as Cuzco, Peru (3,000 meters [11,000 feet]); La Paz, Bolivia (3,444 meters [11,300 feet]); or Lhasa, Tibet (3,749 meters [12,500 feet]). Travelers with underlying medical conditions, such as congestive heart failure or pulmonary insufficiency, should be advised to consult a doctor familiar with high-altitude illness before undertaking such travel. The risk of ischemic heart disease does not appear to be increased at high altitudes, but having a heart attack in a remote area increases the problems of obtaining appropriate treatment.

Travelers vary considerably in their susceptibility to altitude illness, and there are currently no screening tests that predict whether someone is at greater risk of getting altitude illness. Past experience is the most reliable guide; susceptibility to altitude illness appears to be genetic, and is not affected by training or physical fitness.

Altitude illness is divided into three syndromes: acute mountain sickness (AMS), high-altitude cerebral edema (HACE), and high-altitude pulmonary edema (HAPE). AMS is the most common presentation of altitude illness and, while it can occur at altitudes as low as 1,219 to 1,829 meters (4,000 to 6,000 feet), most often occurs in abrupt ascents to over 2,743 meters (9,000 feet). The symptoms resemble an alcohol hangover: headache; profound fatigue; loss of appetite; nausea; and, occasionally, vomiting. The onset of AMS is delayed, usually beginning at least 6 to 12 hours after arrival at a higher altitude.

HACE is considered a severe progression of AMS. In addition to the AMS symptoms, lethargy becomes profound, confusion can manifest, and ataxia will be demonstrated during the tandem gait test. The tandem gait test—having the traveler walk a straight line while placing the heel of the front foot against the toe of the rear foot—is the best test for determining whether HACE is present. A traveler who falls off the line while trying to do the tandem gait test has HACE by definition, and immediate descent is mandatory.

HAPE can occur by itself or in conjunction with HACE. The initial symptoms are increased breathlessness with exertion, and eventually increased breathlessness at rest. The diagnosis can usually be made when breathlessness fails to resolve after several minutes of rest. At this point, it is critical to descend to a lower altitude.

The main point of instructing travelers about altitude illness is not to prevent any possibility of getting altitude illness, but to prevent deaths from altitude illness. The onset of symptoms and clinical course are slow enough and predictable enough that there is no reason for someone to die from altitude illness unless trapped by weather or geography in a situation in which descent is impossible. The three rules that travelers should be made aware of to prevent death from altitude illness are:

- Learn the early symptoms of altitude illness and recognize when personally suffering from them.

- Never ascend to sleep at a higher altitude when experiencing any of the symptoms of altitude illness.

- Descend if the symptoms become worse while resting at the same altitude.

Studies have shown that travelers who are on organized group treks to high-altitude locations are more likely to die of altitude illness than travelers who are by themselves. This is most likely the result of group pressure (whether perceived or real) and a fixed itinerary. The most important aspect of preventing severe altitude illness is to refrain from further ascent until all symptoms of altitude illness have disappeared.

Children are as susceptible to altitude illness as adults, and young children who cannot talk can show very nonspecific symptoms, such as loss of appetite and irritability. There are no studies or case reports of harm occurring to a fetus if the mother travels briefly to a high altitude during pregnancy. However, most authorities recommend that pregnant women stay below 3,658 meters (12,000 feet) if possible.

Three medications have been shown to be useful in the prevention and treatment of altitude illness. Acetazolamide (Diamox®) can prevent AMS when taken prior to ascent, and can speed recovery if taken after symptoms have developed. The drug appears to work by acidifying the blood, which causes an increase in respiration and thus aids in acclimatization. The standard dose is 250 milligrams (mg) BID (bis in die, that is, twice daily), usually starting the day prior to ascent. Anecdotal observations support the use of 125 mg BID as being equally effective with fewer side effects. Allergic reactions to acetazolamide are extremely rare, but the drug is related to sulfonamides, and should not be used by sulfa-allergic travelers.

Dexamethasone has been shown to be effective in the prevention and treatment of AMS and HACE. The drug prevents symptoms, but there is no evidence that it aids acclimatization. Thus, there is a risk of a sudden onset of symptoms if the traveler goes off the drug while ascending. It is preferable for the traveler to use acetazolamide to prevent AMS while ascending, and to reserve the use of dexamethasone to treat severe symptoms. The dosage is 4 mg every 6 hours.

Nifedipine has been shown to prevent and ameliorate HAPE in people who are particularly susceptible to HAPE. The dosage is 10 mg every 8 hours.

For the majority of travelers, the best way to avoid altitude illness is to plan a gradual ascent. If this is not possible, acetazolamide may be used prophylactically, and dexamethasone and nifedipine may be carried for emergencies.

# Chapter 24

# *Recommended and Required Vaccinations for Travel*

## *How to Determine Vaccinations That Are Required or Recommended*

The following steps are suggested to determine vaccination requirements.

1. The traveler should be advised to list his or her itinerary in the sequence in which countries will be visited. The length of stay in each country also should be considered. For the purpose of the International Health Regulations, the incubation periods of the quarantinable diseases are:

   - Cholera—5 days

   - Plague—6 days

   - Yellow fever—6 days

---

Text in this chapter is excerpted from *Health Information for International Travel, 2001–2002,* a brochure produced by the Centers for Disease Control and Prevention (CDC). Under the headings "How to Determine Vaccinations That Are Required or Recommended," available online at http://www.cdc.gov/travel/vaccinations/how-to.htm, "General Recommendations on Vaccination and Prophylaxis," available online at http://www.cdc.gov/travel/vaccinations/recommendations.htm, "Vaccination Certificate Requirements," available online at http://www.cdc.gov/travel/vaccinations/cert-requirements1.htm, and "Vaccination Certificate Requirements for Direct Travel From the United States To Other Countries," available online at http://www.cdc.gov/travel/vaccinations/cert-requirements2.htm. 2002.

2. Health care providers should use *Yellow Fever Vaccine Requirements and Information on Malaria Risk and Prophylaxis, by Country* to determine the yellow fever vaccination requirements for each country. Because some countries require vaccination only if a traveler arrives from an infected area, health care providers should check the current biweekly *Summary of Health Information for International Travel* (also known as the Blue Sheet) to determine if any country on the itinerary is currently infected with yellow fever. The Blue Sheet is available both from the Centers for Disease Control and Prevention (CDC) website at http://www.cdc.gov/travel/blusheet.htm and from the CDC Fax Information Service by telephoning 1-888-CDC-FAXX (232-3299) and requesting document number 220022.

Most immunizations are not required under the International Health Regulations, but are recommended to protect the health of the traveler. Health care providers should consider inoculating the traveler for the following diseases: tetanus, diphtheria, pertussis, poliomyelitis, measles, hepatitis A, hepatitis B, varicella, Japanese encephalitis, meningococcal meningitis, rabies, typhoid fever, and yellow fever. For those diseases for which no vaccines are available, specific preventive behaviors or medications are a necessity.

Because the recommendations in this chapter can change because of outbreaks or other events (such as natural disasters), travelers should be advised either to contact the CDC Fax Information Service (request document number 000005) or to consult the CDC Travelers' Health website at http://www.cdc.gov/travel for the most up-to-date information.

## *General Recommendations on Vaccination and Prophylaxis*

The Advisory Committee on Immunization Practices (ACIP) makes immunization recommendations to the U.S. Public Health Service. Benefits and risks are associated with the use of all immunobiologics—no vaccine is completely effective or completely free of side effects. The recommendations are based on scientific evidence of benefits and risks to achieve optimal levels of protection against vaccine-preventable diseases. The recommendations include information on general immunization issues and on the use of specific vaccines. When these recommendations are issued or revised, they are published in the *Morbidity and Mortality Weekly Report*, a publication produced by the

Centers for Disease Control and Prevention, available online at http://www.cdc.gov/mmwr.

Vaccinations against diphtheria, tetanus, pertussis, measles, mumps, rubella, varicella, poliomyelitis, hepatitis B, *Haemophilus influenzae* type b, and pneumococcal invasive disease are routinely administered in the United States, usually in childhood. If people do not have a history of adequate protection against these diseases, immunizations appropriate to their age and previous immunization status should be obtained, whether or not international travel is planned. The childhood vaccination schedule changes annually and recommendations for adolescents and adults change often. Immunization providers should obtain the most current schedules from the National Immunization Program website. For specific vaccines and toxoids, additional details on background, adverse reactions, precautions, and contraindications are found in the appropriate ACIP statements.

## Spacing of Immunobiologics

### Multiple Doses of the Same Antigen

Some vaccines require more than one dose for adequate protection. The use of multiple reduced doses or the use of doses given at less than minimum intervals can lessen the antibody response and is not endorsed or recommended; such doses should not be counted as part of the vaccination series. With the oral typhoid vaccine, it is unnecessary to restart an interrupted series of a vaccine or toxoid or to add extra doses. However, some products (tetanus and diphtheria toxoids) require periodic booster doses to maintain protection.

### Simultaneous Administration

All commonly used vaccines can safely and effectively be given simultaneously (that is, on the same day) without impairing antibody responses or increasing rates of adverse reactions. This is particularly helpful for international travelers for whom exposure to several infectious diseases might be imminent.

In general, inactivated vaccines may be administered simultaneously at separate sites. However, when vaccines commonly associated with local or systemic reactions are given simultaneously, reactions can be accentuated. It is preferable to administer these vaccines on separate occasions.

Simultaneous administration of acellular pertussis (DTaP); inactivated poliovirus (IPV); *Haemophilus influenzae* type b (Hib); measles, mumps, and rubella (MMR); varicella; pneumococcal conjugate; and hepatitis B vaccines is encouraged for those who are the recommended age to receive these vaccines and for whom no contraindications exist at the time. Yellow fever vaccine may be administered simultaneously with all other currently available vaccines.

Limited data suggest that the immunogenicity and safety of Japanese encephalitis (JE) vaccine are not compromised by simultaneous administration with DTaP or whole-cell pertussis (DTP) vaccine. No data exist on the effect of concurrent administration of other vaccines, drugs (for example, chloroquine or mefloquine), or biologicals on the safety and immunogenicity of JE vaccine.

Inactivated vaccines generally do not interfere with the immune response to other inactivated or live virus vaccines. An inactivated vaccine may be given either simultaneously or at any time before or after a different inactivated vaccine or a live virus vaccine.

The immune response to an injected live virus vaccine (for example, MMR, varicella, or yellow fever) might be impaired if administered within 28 days of another live virus vaccine. Whenever possible, injected live virus vaccines administered on different days should be administered at least 28 days apart. If two injected live virus vaccines are not administered on the same day but less than 28 days apart, the second vaccine should be readministered 4 weeks or more later.

Live virus vaccines can interfere with an individual's response to tuberculin testing. Tuberculin testing, if otherwise indicated, can be done on the day that live virus vaccines are administered or 4 to 6 weeks later.

### Vaccination of People with Acute Illnesses

It is important to take every opportunity to provide appropriate vaccinations. The decision to delay vaccination because of a current or recent acute illness depends on the severity of the symptoms and their etiology. Although a moderate or severe acute illness is sufficient reason to postpone vaccination, minor illnesses (such as diarrhea, mild upper respiratory infection with or without low-grade fever, or other low-grade febrile illness) are not contraindications to vaccination. Antimicrobial therapy is not a contraindication to vaccination, except in some circumstances with oral typhoid vaccine (Ty21a). People with moderate or severe acute illness with or without fever should be vaccinated as soon as their condition has improved. This precaution is to avoid superimposing adverse effects from the vaccine on underlying illness or mistakenly attributing a manifestation of underlying illness to the vaccine.

Routine physical examinations or temperature measurements are not prerequisites for vaccinating anyone who appears to be in good health. Asking if a person is ill, postponing a vaccination for someone with moderate or severe acute illness, and vaccinating someone without contraindications are appropriate procedures in immunization programs.

## *Immune Globulin (IG) Preparations*

When MMR and varicella vaccines are given with immune globulin (IG, formerly called immune serum globulin and immunoglobulin) preparations, antibody response can be diminished. IG preparations do not interfere with the immune response to yellow fever vaccine. The duration of inhibition of MMR and varicella vaccines is related to the dose of IG. Administration of MMR or its components and of varicella vaccines should be delayed for 3 to 11 months after IG administration, depending on the type and quantity administered. Recommended intervals are shown in Table 24.1.

Immune globulin administration may become necessary after MMR or its individual components and varicella vaccines have been given, and interference can occur. Vaccine virus replication and stimulation of immunity usually occur within 2 to 3 weeks after vaccination. If the interval between administration of one of these vaccines and the subsequent administration of an IG preparation is at least 14 days, the vaccine need not be readministered. If the interval is less than 14 days, the vaccine should be readministered after the interval shown in Table 24.1, unless serologic testing indicates that antibodies have been produced. If administration of immune globulin becomes necessary, MMR or its components and varicella vaccines can be administered simultaneously with IG, with the recognition that vaccine-induced immunity can be compromised. The vaccine should be administered in a site remote from that chosen for the IG injection. Vaccination should be repeated after the interval noted in Table 24.1, unless serologic testing indicates antibodies have been produced.

When IG is given with the first dose of hepatitis A vaccine (HAV), the proportion of people who develop protective levels of antibody is not affected, but antibody concentrations are lower. Because the final concentrations of anti-HAV are many times higher than those considered protective, this reduced immunogenicity is not expected to be clinically important. IG preparations interact minimally with other inactivated vaccines and toxoids. Therefore, other inactivated vaccines may be given simultaneously or at any time interval after or before an antibody-containing blood product is used. However, such vaccines should be administered at different sites.

### Hypersensitivity to Vaccine Components

Vaccine components can cause allergic reactions in some recipients. These reactions can be local or systemic and can include anaphylaxis or anaphylactic-like responses. The vaccine components responsible can include the vaccine antigen, animal proteins, antibiotics, preservatives, or stabilizers. The most common animal protein allergen is egg protein in vaccines prepared using embryonated chicken eggs (influenza and yellow fever vaccines). Generally, people who are able to eat eggs or egg products safely may receive these vaccines, while people with histories of anaphylactic allergy (for example, hives, swelling of the mouth and throat, difficulty breathing, hypotension, or shock) to eggs or egg proteins ordinarily should not. Screening people by asking whether they can eat eggs without adverse effects is a reasonable way to identify those who might be at risk from receiving yellow fever and influenza vaccines. Recent studies have indicated that there are other components in vaccines in addition to egg proteins (for example, gelatin) that might cause allergic reactions, including anaphylaxis in rare instances. Protocols have been developed for testing and vaccinating people with anaphylactic reactions to egg ingestion.

Some vaccines contain preservatives (for example, thimerosal, a mercury compound) or trace amounts of antibiotics to which people might be allergic. Those administering the vaccine(s) should carefully review the information provided in the package insert before deciding if the rare person with such allergy should receive the vaccine(s). No currently recommended vaccine contains penicillin or penicillin derivatives. Some vaccines (for example, MMR and its individual component vaccines) contain trace amounts of neomycin or other antibiotics; the amount is less than would normally be used for the skin test to determine hypersensitivity. However, people who have experienced anaphylactic reactions to the antibiotic generally should not receive these vaccines. Most often, neomycin allergy is a contact dermatitis—a manifestation of a delayed-type (cell-mediated) immune response—rather than anaphylaxis. A history of delayed-type reactions to neomycin is not a contraindication to receiving these vaccines.

## Reporting Adverse Events Following Immunization

Modern vaccines are extremely safe and effective. However, adverse events following immunization have been reported with all vaccines. These range from frequent, minor, local reactions to extremely rare, severe, systemic illness such as paralysis associated with oral poliovirus (OPV). Information on side effects and adverse events following specific vaccines and toxoids are discussed in detail in each ACIP statement. Health care providers are required by law to report selected adverse events occurring after vaccination with DTaP, diphtheria-tetanus (DT), tetanus-diphtheria (Td), MMR, measles-rubella (MR), measles, OPV, IPV, varicella, Hib, hepatitis B, and yellow fever vaccines. (Reportable events are listed in *MMWR* 1988;37(13):197–200 and, in general, are events usually requiring the recipient to seek medical attention.) These events and all temporally associated events following receipt of all other vaccines severe enough to require the recipient to seek medical attention should be reported to the Vaccine Adverse Event Reporting System (VAERS) (1-800-822-7967) maintained by the Centers for Disease Control and Prevention and the U.S. Food and Drug Administration.

## Vaccination Certificate Requirements

Under the International Health Regulations adopted by the World Health Organization, a country may, under certain conditions, require an International Certificate of Vaccination against yellow fever from international travelers.

The World Health Assembly amended the International Health Regulations in 1973 so that cholera vaccination is no longer required of any traveler. As a result, no country requires a certificate of cholera immunization and, indeed, cholera vaccine is no longer available in the United States.

## Vaccination Certificate Requirements for Direct Travel from the United States to Other Countries

For direct travel from the United States, only the following countries require an International Certificate of Vaccination against yellow fever.

- Benin
- Ghana
- Burkina Faso

**Table 24.1.** Suggested Intervals for Vaccines Containing Live Measles Virus after Administration of Immune Globulin.*

| Indication | Dose | Suggested Interval before Measles Vaccination |
|---|---|---|
| *Tetanus (TIG)* | 250 units (10 mg IgG/kg) IM | 3 months |
| *Hepatitis A (IG)* International Travel | | |
|    3 months or less | 0.02 mL/kg (3.3 mg IgG/kg) IM | 3 months |
|    More than 3 months | 0.06 mL/kg (10 mg IgG/kg) IM | 3 months |
| *Hepatitis B prophylaxis (HBIG)* | 0.06 mL/kg (10 mg IgG/kg) IM | 3 months |
| *Rabies prophylaxis (HRIG)* | 20 IU/kg (22 mg IgG/kg) IM | 4 months |
| *Varicella prophylaxis (VZIG)* | 125 units/10 kg (20–40 mg IgG/kg IM (maximum 625 units) | 5 months |
| *Measles prophylaxis (IG)* | | |
|    Normal contact | 0.25 mL/kg (40 mg IgG/kg) IM | 5 months |
|    Immunocompromised contact** | 0.50 mL/kg (80 mg IgG/kg) IM | 6 months |
| *Blood transfusion* | | |
|    Red blood cells (RBCs), washed | 10 mL/kg negligible IgG/kg) IV | None |
|    RBCs, adenine-saline added | 10 mL/kg (10 mg IgG/kg) IV | 3 months |
|    Packed RBCs (Hct 65%)**** | 10 mL/kg (60 mg IgG/kg) IV | 6 months |
|    Whole blood (Hct 35% to 50%)**** | 10 mL/kg (80–100 mg IgG/kg) IV | 6 months |
|    Plasma/platelet products | 10 mL/kg (160 mg IgG/kg) IV | 7 months |
| *Cytomegalovirus prophylaxis (CMV IGIV)* | 150 mg/kg (maximum) | 6 months |
| *Respiratory syncytial virus (RSV) monoclonal antibody (Synagis™)***** | 15 mg/kg IM | None |
| *RSV prophylaxis (RSV IGIV)* | 750 mg/kg | 9 months |
| *Intravenous Immune Globulin (IGIV)* | | |
|    IGIV, Replacement therapy | 300–400 mg/kg IV | 8 months |
|    IGIV, ITP*** | 400 mg/kg IV | 8 months |
|    IGIV, ITP*** | 1,000 mg/kg IV | 10 months |
|    IGIV, Kawasaki disease | 2 grams/kg IV | 11 months |

Abbreviated forms used in table: mg—milligram; kg—kilogram; Ig—immune globulin; IM—intramuscular; mL—milliliter; IU—international unit; IV—intravenous.

*This table is not intended to be used for determine the correct indications and dosage for the use of IG preparations. Unvaccinated people might not be fully protected against measles during the entire suggested interval, and additional doses of IG or measles, or both, vaccines may be indicated following measles exposure. The concentration of measles antibody in a particular IG preparation can vary by lot. The rate of antibody clearance following receipt of an IG preparation can also vary. The recommended intervals are extrapolated from an estimated half-life of 30 days for passively acquired antibody and an observed interference with the immune response to measles vaccine for 5 months following a dose of 80 mg IgG/kg.

**Notes to Table 24.1 continued on next page.**

- Liberia
- Cameroon
- Mali
- Central African Republic
- Mauritania (for a stay of more than 2 weeks)
- Congo
- Niger
- Côte d'Ivoire
- Rwanda
- Democratic Republic of the Congo
- São Tomé and Príncipe
- French Guiana
- Togo
- Gabon

For travel to and between other countries, individual country requirements should be checked. Currently, no vaccinations are required to return to the United States.

### Exemption from Vaccination

**Age:** Some countries do not require an International Certificate of Vaccination for infants younger than 6 months of age or 1 year of

**Table 24.1.** Suggested Intervals for Vaccines Containing Live Measles Virus after Administration of Immune Globulin.* **_(Notes continued)_**

**Measles vaccination is recommended for children with human immunodeficiency virus (HIV) infection but is contraindicated in patients with congenital disorders of the immune system.

***Immune (formerly, idiopathic) thrombocytopenic purpura.

****Assumes a serum IgG concentration of 16 mg/mL.

*****Contains only antibody to respiratory syncytial virus.

age. Travelers should be advised to check the individual country requirements in Yellow Fever Vaccine Requirements and Information on Malaria Risk and Prophylaxis, by Country.

**Medical Grounds:** If a physician concludes that a particular vaccination should not be administered for medical reasons, the traveler should be given a signed and dated statement of the reasons on the physician's letterhead stationary.

There are no other acceptable reasons for exemption from vaccination.

### Unvaccinated Travelers

Travelers who do not have the required vaccinations upon entering a country might be subject to vaccination, medical followup, or isolation, or a combination of these. In a few countries, unvaccinated travelers are denied entry.

### Travel on Military Orders

Because military requirements may exceed the requirements indicated in this publication, any person who plans to travel on military orders (civilians and military personnel) should be advised to contact the nearest military medical facility to determine the requirements for the trip.

### Authorization to Provide Vaccinations and to Validate the International Certificate of Vaccination

A yellow fever vaccination must be given at an official yellow fever vaccination center as designated by respective state health departments or the Division of Global Migration and Quarantine, Centers for Disease Control and Prevention, and the accompanying certificate must be validated by the center that administers the vaccine. (Other vaccinations may be given under the supervision of any licensed physician.) Validation of the certificate can be obtained at most city, county, and state health departments, or from vaccinating physicians who possess a Uniform Stamp. State health departments are responsible for designated nonfederal yellow fever vaccination centers and issuing Uniform Stamps to be used to validate the International Certificate of Vaccination. Information about the location and hours of yellow fever vaccination centers may be obtained by contacting local or state health departments. Physicians administering vaccine to travelers should emphasize that an International Certificate of Vaccination must be validated to be acceptable to quarantine authorities. Failure to secure validations can cause a traveler to be revaccinated, quarantined, or denied entry.

*People Authorized to Sign the Certificate*

The International Certificate of Vaccination must be signed by a licensed physician or by a person designated by the physician. A signature stamp is not acceptable.

Chapter 25

# *Insurance*

## *Chapter Contents*

# Section 25.1

## *Overview of Travel Insurance*

"Five Travel Insurance Tips for International Travelers," and "The Basics of Travel Insurance." This material is provided by Insure.com. Copyright © 2002 Insure.com, Inc. Reprinted with permission.

### *Five Travel Insurance Tips for International Travelers*

You've got your passport, the tickets are booked, and your luggage is packed. In short, you're all set to take a whirlwind trip around the globe—or are you? Have you thought about what would happen if you were to get hurt or fall ill on your international tour, or if a terrorist attack interrupts your itinerary?

The simple fact is that many international travelers do not have appropriate insurance.

One of the most important reasons to consider buying a travel insurance policy for your overseas trip is the medical coverage and emergency medical evacuation insurance that comes with most travel insurance policies.

"The simple fact is that many international travelers do not have appropriate insurance protection," says Dr. Eliot Heher, chief medical director for HTH (Highway to Health) Worldwide, an insurer specializing in travel insurance and health insurance for Americans on extended stays overseas.

### *You'll Likely Need Travel Health and Accident Insurance*

Government-sponsored health insurance programs rarely cover medical care received in a foreign country, and many private health insurance plans—whether provided through employers or purchased individually—limit overseas coverage to emergencies and it can be up to you to prove the emergency. Do you know the difference between emergency and urgent care under your health insurance plan?

Check with your health insurer to see what is covered before you go overseas. If you're concerned that your health insurance might not be enough on your trip, you might want to buy a travel insurance policy to fill in the gaps. Also remember that in some parts of the world your health insurance might not be accepted as a guarantee of payment, which some hospitals require before they will treat you. So while your insurance might reimburse you after the trip, you could be stuck first paying out of pocket for your medical care. Most travel insurance policies will provide these guarantees and offer the option to pay from the very first dollar in medical expenses you incur.

Along with health and accident insurance, many travel insurers provide a 24-hour assistance telephone line to help international travelers find their way to the local pharmacy, get a replacement set of glasses, and find an English-speaking doctor or reputable hospital.

### Be Sure to Buy Medical Evacuation Coverage

It's the sort of insurance you hope you never have to use, but you sure are glad when you have it. While you're going through your health insurance policy to see what medical care is covered on international trips, also check the limits of your emergency medical evacuation coverage. A typical health insurance policy will cap payments for emergency medical transportation between $500 and $1,000, which is fine if all you need is an ambulance to bring you to your hometown hospital, but it can fall far short of your needs on an international trip, says Dan McGinnity, vice president of communications for the Travel Guard Group Inc.

McGinnity recalls the case of a family vacationing in St. Martin in the West Indies when the 2-year-old daughter was hit by a car. After arriving at the hospital in St. Martin, the family called Travel Guard to arrange for payment. When the Travel Guard doctor contacted the attending physician he was concerned about the quality of care, says McGinnity. Travel Guard sent an air ambulance (a jet with a doctor and medical facilities on board) to the island and brought the entire family back to Miami at a cost of about $25,000—all covered by the travel insurance policy.

If you're going on a cruise, medical evacuation insurance can be even more important. Think about the added price of a helicopter airlift from the cruise ship, on top of the air ambulance flight back to the United States.

### Protect Yourself from the Unexpected

If you become too ill to travel, trip-cancellation insurance will pay for any nonrefundable costs for the trip. If you've ever had a head cold on an airline flight you know that traveling when you're sick is no fun at all. No one wants to take a vacation when they're ill, but your airline, cruise company, or tour operator isn't likely to be sympathetic to your plight. That's where trip-cancellation or interruption coverage as part of a travel insurance policy can come in handy. If you become too ill to travel, or if one of your family members gets sick and you need to stay home to care for them, trip-cancellation insurance will pay for any nonrefundable costs for the trip—from hotel bookings to airline or cruise line cancellation fees.

The same reimbursements would also apply if you fell victim to an illness that wasn't serious enough to require an air ambulance flight but still forced you to cut your trip short and come home.

### Terrorism Coverage May Be a Wise Buy

Most travel insurance policies now include acts of terrorism as a reason to cancel or interrupt an international trip, but before you buy this protection, make sure you know how it works.

If the U.S. State Department issues a travel advisory recommending that Americans avoid a certain country, many travel insurance policies will pay for cancellation fees if you want to cancel your vacation or buy you a ticket home to cut your vacation short.

Other travel insurers focus on the city instead of the country. These types of policies will reimburse you if you cancel or cut short a trip due to an act of terrorism at your destination either while you are there or within 30 days of your scheduled arrival.

Neither of these options is substantially better than the other, but they are different, so you do need to know when you'll be covered by your travel insurance policy, as well as when you won't.

Speaking of not being covered, if a policy you are considering says that it covers acts of terrorism but then has a huge laundry list of exceptions, you might want to look elsewhere. "Some policies have one line describing the coverage and then two paragraphs of exclusions— you're covered unless there is an event with more than 5,000 people in the same city, unless the attack involves a chemical, nuclear, or biological weapon, and so on," says McGinnity. "If you have to say, 'All right, when am I covered?' then how much protection are you really getting?"

### Other Travel Insurance Services Could Come in Handy

Many travel insurers also offer a host of other helpful services through their emergency contact numbers. Often a travel insurer can help you replace lost travel documents and passports, provide translation services, and assist in money transfers. Some even offer legal assistance and bail bond services, says Claudia Fullerton, chief marketing officer for CSA Travel Protection.

"Most people don't know what the laws are in other countries," says Fullerton. "Legal problems in a foreign country can be really scary, especially if you don't speak the language."

Also, most travel insurance policies will bundle in coverage for lost or delayed luggage. Lost or stolen luggage is often covered under a home insurance policy or paid for by your airline, but in some cases having additional coverage as part of a travel insurance policy can make your trip a lot more smooth.

"Travel insurance makes it a lot easier if you need to access that coverage," says Fullerton. "When you're traveling it can be hard to get in contact with your home insurer to file a claim. If you try to purchase each type of coverage separately, you'll find that the whole is a lot less expensive than the sum of the parts."

Fullerton acknowledges that the lost and delayed luggage portions of travel insurance are among the least used—the airlines usually take responsibility for luggage problems—but she says that having the extra funds, usually around $250 per person, can be a godsend.

"Most people don't end up having to use travel insurance," says Fullerton. "But if you don't have it, you could wind up in a real bind. Personally, if I go somewhere outside the United States, I buy a comprehensive travel insurance policy."

Most travel insurance policies are comprehensive, automatically including coverage that might be redundant, for convenience and simplicity, says McGinnity. You have one phone number to call regardless of the type of trouble you encounter on your international trip, and it often comes as a bargain.

"A lot of things are automatically included in a standard travel insurance policy so you don't have to worry about it," says McGinnity. "Also, if you try to purchase each type of coverage separately, you'll find that the whole is a lot less expensive than the sum of the parts."

## The Basics of Travel Insurance

While travel insurance was formerly looked upon as a luxury, consumers concerned about whether their vacations can be canceled by incidents outside their control, or worried about the quality of medical care in the area they are visiting, now view travel insurance as a good value. Generally, a comprehensive travel insurance policy costs 5 to 7 percent of the price of your trip.

Before buying travel insurance, be sure you don't already have sufficient coverage through your home insurance, health insurance, or as a perk on your credit card if you charged your trip.

### *What to Buy*

A travel insurance policy usually offers two coverages—trip cancellation/interruption and emergency medical evacuation. Reimbursements for lost baggage or trip delays are nice if they come bundled with trip cancellation/interruption or emergency medical evacuation, but they're usually not good buys on their own. If you have absolutely no health insurance, or if your health plan won't cover you at all while you're abroad, then you should look into medical or hospital coverage. Be sure to check your health insurance policy carefully.

Trip cancellation/interruption coverage will reimburse you for any nonrefundable deposits you put down on a trip or cruise if it turns out that you won't be able to go after all, or if you have to leave early. The catch? It will only pay out if you have to cancel or leave early because of a covered reason. That's why it's so important to read the fine print. Some policies will cover only medical reasons (say you're admitted to the hospital), and some will not cover pre-existing medical conditions (like an old back injury flaring up).

### *Things to Ask Your Travel Insurance Company*

- What if an old back injury flares up and I can't go after all?
- What if I decide to change resorts/cruises/departure dates after I put down my deposit?
- What if my touring company goes belly-up?
- What if I get called for jury duty and can't go on the trip?
- What if my mother suddenly takes ill in the middle of my cruise and I need to go home?
- What if I break my leg while I'm out on the slopes?
- What if my plane is delayed and I can't meet up with my tour group?
- What if I get sick and need to go to the hospital?
- What if I get sick and need to see a doctor?

Trip cancellation/interruption will pay the difference between what you can get refunded from the cruise line, tour company, or airline, and what you originally paid. That means that you must seek a refund first with the tour company before you file a claim on your trip cancellation/interruption insurance.

Trip cancellation/interruption policies may also cover unforeseen emergencies, such as an accident on the way to the airport, a hijacking, a natural disaster, a fire or flood at your house, or a call to jury duty. However, they probably still won't cover you if you change your plans, if your job forces you to stay in town, or if you can't go because of personal finances. Travel insurance in general also excludes self-inflicted injuries and problems arising from the use of illegal drugs.

If your cruise line or touring company goes out of business, your trip cancellation/interruption policy may cover the loss. If you bought the policy from the tour company itself however, chances are you're out of luck. Your coverage also depends on how the policy is written. Some will only pay out if the company ceases all operations for 10 days or more, or if it files for bankruptcy. But many touring companies never bother to file for bankruptcy—they just disappear. And if your trip operator closes down for just a few days, it can still mess up your plans.

If you're up on top of a mountain and break your leg, or if you're in the depths of the Amazon jungle and you get a fever, emergency medical evacuation coverage will pay for the cost of transporting you to safety and, in some cases, all the way home.

This is coverage for the really big problems such as a helicopter rescue, which can run you as much as $20,000, or the cost of your trip back to states. It makes the most sense to buy this coverage if you're going on an adventure vacation or to an area where you'll be far from modern medical facilities. In such situations, you should make sure you've gotten all the recommended vaccinations. It's also a good idea to bring along an emergency kit with medical supplies. If you are going to be engaging in risky behavior like hunting big game, mountain climbing, or skiing, make sure that your policy covers such situations.

### *Sources for Travel Insurance and Health Care Abroad: Toll-Free Numbers*

Access America International: 800-284-8300

CSA Travel Protection: 800-348-9505

HTH Worldwide: 888-243-2358

Travelex: 800-228-9792

Travel Guard: 800-826-1300

Travel Insured International: 800-826-1300

Health Care Abroad: 800-237-6615

International SOS Assistance: 800-523-8930

Europe Assistance: 800-821-2828

If you have health insurance, find out from your health plan what benefits apply when you're abroad. If you won't have any health coverage while you're traveling, you might want to look for a travel insurance policy that includes medical coverage. You'll probably get the best buy if it's bundled with trip cancellation/interruption or emergency medical evacuation coverage, although there are companies who specialize in health care and general assistance for travelers abroad. You should know whether the policy will actually pay for the medical care up front, whether you have to get approval from the insurance company's medical specialist before you can get care, and if there is a referral line for you to call. Be cautious about sales pitches that play on your fears.

### *How Much Does It Cost?*

Most comprehensive travel insurance policies, which include travel medical coverage, medical evacuation, and trip-cancellation or interruption insurance, cost between 5 and 7 percent of the price of your trip. Prices are based on your age and the cost of your trip—where you're traveling generally doesn't factor into the price—as well as the amount of medical coverage and baggage-replacement insurance you buy.

So, if you're taking a weeklong tour of England or Ireland that costs you about $1,000 per person, you should expect to pay between $50 and $70 each for a travel insurance policy. If, on the other hand, you're planning a two-week cruise of the Caribbean—from $3,000 to $5,000 for a stateroom—it could cost as little as $150 to as much as $350 to insure your vacation.

What about safaris in the Australian outback or the African Serengeti? With tours running upwards of $4,000 and airfare that could top $2,000, you should expect to pay $300 to $420 per person for travel insurance on these adventure getaways.

### *Where to Buy It*

Many travel agencies, cruise lines, and tour companies sell travel insurance directly, but it's not really the best way to buy it. While prices are sometimes better, the coverage is likely to carry more exclusions. Buying insurance through a cruise line or tour company also means you probably won't be able to collect if they go under. In general, it's best to buy travel insurance directly from an insurance company.

## Section 25.2

# *Information about Medical Insurance, Social Security, and Preparing for Medical Emergencies Abroad*

"Medical Information for Americans Traveling Abroad," an undated document from the U.S. Department of State, Bureau of Consular Affairs, available online at http://travel.state.gov/medical.html. Cited November 2002.

If an American citizen becomes seriously ill or injured abroad, a U.S. consular officer can assist in locating appropriate medical services and informing family or friends. If necessary, a consular officer can also assist in the transfer of funds from the United States. However, payment of hospital and other expenses is the responsibility of the traveler.

Before going abroad, learn what medical services your health insurance will cover overseas. If your health insurance policy provides coverage outside the United States, remember to carry both your insurance policy identity card as proof of such insurance and a claim form. Although many health insurance companies will pay customary and reasonable hospital costs abroad, very few will pay for your medical evacuation back to the United States. Medical evacuation can easily cost $10,000 and up, depending on your location and medical condition.

The Social Security Medicare program does not provide coverage for hospital or medical costs outside the U.S.A. Senior citizens may wish to contact the American Association of Retired Persons (AARP) for information about foreign medical care coverage with Medicare supplement plans.

To facilitate identification in case of an accident, complete the information page on the inside of your passport providing the name, address and telephone number of someone to be contacted in an emergency.

A traveler going abroad with any preexisting medical problems should carry a letter from the attending physician, describing the medical condition and any prescription medications, including the generic name of prescribed drugs. Any medications being carried overseas should be left in their original containers and be clearly labeled. Travelers should check with the foreign embassy of the country they are visiting to make sure any required medications are not considered to be illegal narcotics.

A listing of addresses and telephone numbers of U.S. embassies and consulates abroad is contained in Key Officers of Foreign Service Posts. This publication may be obtained through the Superintendent of Documents, U.S. Government Printing Office, Washington, DC 20402. Also available from the Government Printing Office is Health Information for International Travel by the Centers for Disease Control and Prevention (CDC). This contains a global rundown of disease and immunization advice and other health guidance, including risks in particular countries. The CDC maintains the international travelers hotline at 1-877-FYI-TRIP (1-877-394-8747), an automated faxback service at 1-888-CDC-FAXX (1-888-232-3299) and a home page on the Internet at http://www.cdc.gov.

For information about outbreaks of infectious diseases abroad, consult the World Health Organization's (WHO) web site at http://www.who.int/en. The WHO also provides travel health information at http://www.who.int/iht.

For detailed information on physicians abroad, the authoritative reference is *The Official ABMS Directory of Board Certified Medical Specialists* published for the American Board of Medical Specialists and its certifying member boards. This publication should be available in your local library. U.S. embassies and consulates abroad maintain lists of hospitals and physicians. Major credit card companies also can provide the names of local doctors and hospitals abroad. Some countries require foreign visitors to have inoculations or medical tests before entering. Before traveling, check the latest entry requirements with the foreign embassy of the country to be visited. Several private organizations will provide medical information and insurance for overseas travelers. Most charge a fee for this service. The following is provided for informational purposes only and in no way constitutes an endorsement, expressed or implied, by the Department of State.

## Air Ambulance/Med-Evac: U.S.-Based Companies

*Able Jet*
Fort Pierce, FL
Toll-Free: 800-225-3538
Internet: www.ablejet.com

*AirEvac*
2630 Sky Harbor Boulevard
Phoenix, AZ 85034
Toll-Free: 800-421-6111
Internet: www.airevac.com

*Critical Care Med Flight*
P.O. Box 245
Lawrenceville, GA 30046
Toll-Free: 800-426-6557
Fax: 770-513-0249
Internet:
www.criticalcaremedflight.com

*Global Care / Medpass*
6875 Shiloh Rd., East
Alpharetta, GA 30005
Toll-Free: 800-860-1111
Fax: 678-341-1800
Internet: www.globalems.com
E-Mail:
customer.service@globalcare.net

*MedAire*
80 East Rio Salako Pkwy,
Suite 610
Tempe, AZ 85281
Phone: 480-333-3700
Fax: 480-333-3592
Internet: www.medaire.com
E-Mail: info@mediaire.com

## Air Ambulance/Med-Evac: Foreign-Based Companies

*Euro-Flite Ltd.*
P.O. Box 187
FIN-0153, Vantaa, Finland
Phone: 011-358-9-870-2544
Fax: 011-358-9-870-2507
Internet: www.jetflite.fi/8/
frame8.htm

*MedicAir*
35, Rue Jules Ferry
93170—Bognolet
Paris, France
Phone: 011-331-41-72-14-14
Internet: http://
medicair.starnet.fr/uk/
sommaire.html
E-Mail: operations@medic-air.com

*Tyrol Air Ambulance*
P.O. Box 81
A-6026 Innsbruck-Flughafen
Innsbruck, Austria
SITA INNTAXH
AFTN LOWITYWX
Phone: 011-43-512-22422
Internet: www.taa.at
E-Mail: taa@taa.at

### Travel Insurance Companies

*Access America, Inc.*
P.O. Box 90315
Richmond, VA 23286
Phone: 866-807-3982
Internet: www.accessamerica.com
E-Mail:
service@accessamerica.com

*Clements International*
1660 L. Street, NW,
9th Floor
Washington, DC 20036
Toll-Free: 800-872-0067
Phone: 202-872-0060
Fax: 202-466-9064
Internet: www.clements.com
E-Mail: info@clements.com

*InsureMyTrip.com*
50 Motor Parkway
Commack, NY 11725
Toll-Free: 800-487-4722
Phone: 860-290-4850
Fax: 860-282-6158
Internet:
www.InsureMyTrip.com
E-Mail: info@insuremytrip.com

*MultiNational Underwriters, Inc.*
107 S. Pennsylvania Street,
Suite 402
Indianapolis, IN 46204
Toll-Free: 800-605-2282
Phone: 317-262-2132
Fax: 317-262-2140
Internet: www.mnui.com
E-Mail: insurance@mnui.com

*Travel Guard*
1145 Clark Street
Stevens Point, WI 54481
Toll-Free: 800-826-4919
Internet: www.travelguard.cm

*Worldwide Assistance*
1133 15th Street, NW, Suite 400
Washington, DC 20005
Toll-Free: 800-777-8710 ext. 417
Fax: 202-828-5892
Internet:
www.worldwideassistance.com
E-Mail:
info@worldwideassistance.com

## *Executive Medical Services*

*GlobaLifeline*
80 East Rio Salado Parkway,
Suite 610
Tempe, AZ 85281
Toll-Free: 800-890-8209
Internet: www.globalifeline.com
E-Mail: info@globalifeline.com

*Health Quest Travel Inc.*
P.O. Box 1535
Nevada City, CA 95959
Toll-Free: 888-899-0717
Phone: 530-265-2380
Fax: 530-478-1898
Internet:
www.healthquesttravel.com

*World Clinic*
41 Mall Road
Burlington, MA 01805
Toll-Free: 800-636-9186
Phone: 781-744-3170
Internet: www.worldclinic.com
E-Mail: info@worldclinic.com

# Chapter 26

# *Health Risks from Animal and Insect Bites while Traveling Abroad*

## Animal-Associated Hazards

Animals in general tend to avoid human beings, but they can attack, particularly if they are protecting their young or territory. Travelers should be reminded that, in areas of endemic rabies, domestic dogs, cats, or other animals should not be petted, handled, or fed. Wild animals should be avoided; most injuries from wild animals are the direct result of attempting to pet, handle, or feed the animals.

The bites and stings of and contact with some insects cause unpleasant reactions. Travelers should be advised to seek medical attention if an insect bite or sting causes redness, swelling, bruising, or persistent pain. Many insects also transmit communicable diseases. Some insects can bite and transmit disease without the traveler's being aware of the bite, particularly when the traveler is camping or staying in rustic or primitive accommodations. Travelers should be advised to use insect repellents, protective clothing, and mosquito netting when visiting many parts of the world.

Poisonous snakes are hazards in many locations, although deaths from snake bites are relatively rare. The Australian brown snake,

Text in this chapter is excerpted from *Health Information for International Travel, 2001–2002,* a brochure produced by the Centers for Disease Control and Prevention (CDC). Under the headings "Animal-Associated Hazards," available online at http://www.cdc.gov/travel/other/animal-hazards.htm, and "Protection Against Mosquitoes and Other Arthropod Vectors," available online at http://www.cdc.gov/travel/bugs.htm. 2002.

Russell's viper and cobras in southern Asia, carpet vipers in the Middle East, and coral snakes and rattlesnakes in the Americas are particularly dangerous. Most snake bites are the direct result of handling or harassing snakes, which bite as a defensive reaction. Attempts to kill snakes are dangerous, often leading to bites on the fingers. The venom of a small or immature snake can be even more concentrated than that of larger ones; therefore, all snakes should be left alone.

Fewer than half of all snake bite wounds actually contain venom, but travelers should be advised to seek medical attention any time a bite wound breaks the skin. A pressure bandage, ice (if available), and immobilization of the affected limb are recommended first-aid measures while the victim is moved as quickly as possible to a medical facility. Specific therapy for snake bite is controversial, and should be left to the judgment of local emergency medical personnel. Snakes tend to be active at night and in warm weather. As a precaution, boots and long pants should be worn when walking outdoors at night in snake-infested regions. Bites from scorpions can be painful, but seldom are dangerous, except possibly in infants. In general, exposure to bites can be avoided by sleeping under mosquito nets and by shaking clothing and shoes before putting them on, particularly in the morning. Snakes and scorpions tend to rest in shoes and clothing.

## Protection against Mosquitoes and Other Arthropod Vectors

Although vaccines or chemoprophylactic drugs are available against important vector-borne diseases such as yellow fever and malaria, there are none for most other mosquito-borne diseases such as dengue, and travelers still should be advised to use repellents and other general protective measures against arthropods. The effectiveness of malaria chemoprophylaxis is variable, depending on patterns of resistance and compliance with medication. For many vector-borne diseases, no specific preventatives are available.

### *General Preventive Measures*

The principal approach to prevention of vector-borne diseases is avoidance. Tick- and mite-borne infections characteristically are diseases of place; whenever possible, known foci of disease transmission should be avoided. Although many vector-borne infections can be prevented by avoiding rural locations, certain mosquito- and midge-borne arboviral and parasitic infections are transmitted seasonally, and

344

simple changes in itinerary can greatly reduce risk for acquiring certain infections.

Travelers should be advised that exposure to arthropod bites can be minimized by modifying patterns of activity or behavior. Some vector mosquitoes are most active in twilight periods at dawn and dusk or in the evening. Avoidance of outdoor activity during these periods can reduce risk of exposure. Wearing long-sleeved shirts, long pants, and hats will minimize areas of exposed skin. Shirts should be tucked in. Repellents applied to clothing, shoes, tents, mosquito nets, and other gear will enhance protection.

When exposure to ticks or biting insects is a possibility, travelers should be advised to tuck their pants into their socks and to wear boots, not sandals. Permethrin-based repellents applied as directed will enhance protection. Travelers should be advised that, during outdoor activity and at the end of the day, they should inspect themselves and their clothing for ticks. Ticks are detected more easily on light-colored or white clothing. Prompt removal of attached ticks can prevent some infections.

When accommodations are not adequately screened or air conditioned, bed nets are essential to provide protection and comfort. Bed nets should be tucked under mattresses and can be sprayed with a repellent, such as permethrin. The permethrin will be effective for several months if the bed net is not washed. Aerosol insecticides and mosquito coils can help to clear rooms of mosquitoes; however, some coils contain dichlorodiphenyltrichloroethane (DDT) and should be used with caution.

### Repellents

Travelers should be advised that permethrin-containing repellents (such as Permanone®) are recommended for use on clothing, shoes, bed nets, and camping gear. Permethrin is highly effective as an insecticide and acaricide and as a repellent. Permethrin-treated clothing repels and kills ticks, mosquitoes, and other arthropods, and retains this effect after repeated laundering. There appears to be little potential for toxicity from permethrin-treated clothing. The insecticide should be reapplied after every five washings.

Permethrin-containing shampoo (Nix®) and cream (Elimite®), marketed for use against head lice and scabies infestations, potentially could be effective as repellents when applied on the hair and skin. However, they are approved only to treat existing conditions. Most authorities recommend repellents containing N,N-diethylmetatoluamide

(DEET) as an active ingredient. DEET repels mosquitoes, ticks, and other arthropods when applied to the skin or clothing. Formulations containing <35% DEET are recommended because the additional gain in repellent effect with higher concentrations is not significant when weighed against the potential for toxicity. Travelers should be advised to use lower concentrations for children (no more than 10% DEET). Repellents with DEET should be used sparingly on children 2 through 6 years of age and not at all on infants younger than 2 years of age. A microencapsulated, sustained release formulation can have a longer period of activity than liquid formulations at the same concentrations. Length of protection also varies with ambient temperature, extent of perspiration, any water exposure, abrasive removal, and other factors.

DEET is toxic when ingested. High concentrations applied to skin can cause blistering. Rare cases of encephalopathy in children, some fatal, have been reported after cutaneous exposure. Other neurologic side effects also have been reported. Toxicity did not appear to be dose-related in many cases and these might have been idiosyncratic reactions in predisposed individuals. However, a dose-related effect leading to irritability and impaired concentration and memory has been reported.

Travelers should be advised that the possibility of adverse reactions to DEET will be minimized if they take the following precautions: (1) apply repellent sparingly and only to exposed skin or clothing; (2) avoid applying high-concentration products to the skin; (3) do not inhale or ingest repellents or get them in the eyes; (4) avoid applying repellents to portions of children's hands that are likely to have contact with the eyes or mouth; (5) never use repellents on wounds or irritated skin; and (6) wash repellent-treated skin after coming indoors. If a reaction to insect repellent is suspected, travelers should be advised to wash treated skin and seek medical attention.

Bed nets, repellents containing DEET, and permethrin should be purchased before traveling and can be found in hardware, camping, sporting goods, and military surplus stores.

# Part Four

# Protecting Money and Possessions while Traveling

# Chapter 27

# *Avoiding Home Burglary while Away*

## *Lock Crime out of Your Home*

### *Lighting*

Lighting is one of the most cost-effective deterrents to burglary. Indoor lighting gives the impression that a home is occupied. If you are going to be away from your home, consider using automatic timers to switch interior lights on and off at preset times. Outdoor lighting can eliminate hiding places.

Install exterior lighting near porches, rear and side doorways, garage doors, and all other points of entry. Entryways to your home always should be well lighted. Place lights out of reach from the ground so the bulbs cannot be removed or broken. Aim some lights away from the house so you can see if anyone is approaching, or install motion-sensing lights, which turn on automatically as someone approaches.

### *Shrubs and Landscaping*

Your home's walkways and landscaping should direct visitors to the main entrance and away from private areas. The landscaping should provide maximum visibility to and from your house. Trim shrubbery that could conceal criminal activity near doors and windows. Provide light on areas of dense shrubs and trees that could serve

Reprinted with permission from "Lock Crime out of Your Home." © 1998 National Crime Prevention Council.

as hiding places. Cut back tree limbs that could help thieves climb into windows, and keep yard fencing low enough too avoid giving criminals places to hide.

### Exterior Doors

Making your home safer from crime doesn't always mean having to install expensive alarms—effective home security starts with properly locked doors and windows and visible, well-lighted entryways.

All exterior doors should be either metal or solid wood. For added security, use strong door hinges on the inside of the door, with non-removable or hidden pins. Every entry door should be well lighted and have a wide-angle door viewer so you can see who is outside without opening the door.

### Locks

Strong, reliable locks are essential to effective home security. Always keep doors and windows locked—even a five—minute trip to the store is long enough for a burglar to enter your home. Use quality keyed knobs as well as deadbolts—deadbolts can withstand the twisting, turning, prying, and pounding that regular keyed knobs can't.

When choosing a deadbolt, look for such features as a bolt that extends at least one inch when in the locked position, to resist ramming and kicking; hardened steel inserts to prevent the bolt from being sawed off, and a reinforced strike plate with extra long mounting screws to anchor the lock effectively.

Most deadbolts are single-cylinder; they operate from the outside with a key and from the inside with a thumb latches. Double-cylinder deadbolts require a key to open the lock from both outside and inside your home. These locks are especially effective for doors with glass within 40 inches of the lock—an intruder cannot break the glass and unlock the door by reaching through.

Some jurisdictions do not allow these locks—check with your local law enforcement or building code authorities before installing a double cylinder deadbolt. As one alternative, security glazing can be applied to glass panels in or near the door, or shatterproof glass can be installed, though these options can be expensive.

### Sliding Glass Doors

Sliding glass doors can offer easy entry into your home. To improve security on existing sliding glass doors, you can install keyed locking devices that secure the door to the frame; adjust the track clearances on the doors so they can't be pushed out of their tracks; or put a piece of wood or a metal bar in the track of the closed door to prevent the door from opening even if the lock is jimmied or removed.

## *Windows*

Most standard double-hung windows have thumb turn locks between the two window panels. Don't rely on these—they can be pried open or easily reached through a broken pane. Instead, install keyed locking devices to prevent the window from being raised from the outside, but make sure everyone in the house knows where to find the keys in case of an emergency. Some jurisdictions have restrictions on this type of lock—check with your local law enforcement before you install them.

An easy, inexpensive way to secure your windows is to use the "pin" trick. Drill an angled hole through the top frame of the lower window partially into the frame of the upper window. Then insert a nail or eyebolt. The window can't be opened until you remove the nail. Make a second set of holes with the windows partly opened so you can have ventilation without intruders.

The National Citizens' Crime Prevention Council, sponsored by the Crime Prevention Coalition of America, is substantially funded by the Bureau of Justice Assistance, Office of Justice Programs, U.S. Department of Justice. Distribution made possible in part by a grant from ADT Security Services, Inc., a Tyco International Ltd. Company.

# Chapter 28

# *Theft while Traveling*

Your information and valuables are far more vulnerable to theft while traveling abroad than in the United States. Principal targets for theft include:

- Government and business documents of interest to the local intelligence service.

- Personal documents (passport and other ID and travel documents) of interest to criminal organizations, including those that arrange illegal immigration to the U.S.

- Laptop computers are of interest to everyone—for the information on them, for resale, or for personal use.

- Expensive jewelry, cameras, and any other items that are easy to sell.

You have special vulnerabilities in your hotel room, elsewhere in your hotel, while in the airport or on the train, with sensitive equipment

---

This chapter contains "Theft while Traveling," excerpted from the "Counterintelligence Awareness Guide" http://www.nnsi.doe.gov/C/Courses/CI_Awareness_Guide/ Home.htm, produced by the Counterintelligence Training Academy, Nonproliferation and National Security Institute, Department of Energy, cited November 2002. This chapter also contains "Safety and Security," http://www.studyabroad.com/handbook/ safety.html, excerpted with permission from the *StudyAbroad.com Handbook* by Bill Hoffa, © 2000 Educational Directories Unlimited, Inc. For additional information, visit www.studyabroad.com.

in transit, and in any office to which local foreign nationals have unrestricted access.

### Hotel Rooms and Vaults

Bag operations is the term commonly used to describe surreptitious entry into hotel rooms to steal, photograph, or photocopy documents; steal or copy magnetic media; or download from laptop computers. Bag operations are common. In fact, they are routine procedure in quite a few countries.

Bag operations are typically conducted by the host government's security or intelligence service, frequently with cooperation of the hotel staff. Hotel security staffs commonly maintain close contact with the local police and government security service. It is common for retired government security and intelligence officers to obtain employment in the security offices of major hotels and corporations. Bag operations may also be conducted by the corporation you are dealing with or by a competitor company. They may be done during the day while you are out of the room or at night while you are asleep. Yes, they do take the risk of coming into your room while you are sleeping.

Government and business travelers often report that their belongings have been searched while they were absent from their hotel room. In some cases, they have returned to their room soon after departing, to retrieve a forgotten item, and find persons in their room claiming they are there to repair a broken TV, etc. Seldom is anything missing; the purpose is only to copy documents or download information from a traveler's laptop computer. Sometimes there is little effort to conceal the search. Other times it is more subtle. If done correctly, the traveler will not be aware of the search.

Leaving sensitive government or company information in your hotel room, even in a locked briefcase or the safe provided in your room, is an invitation for material to be copied or photographed while you are out. Hotel vaults are not much better. In most cases, foreign intelligence officers can gain access to hotel lockboxes or vaults without you becoming aware of the compromise.

Never leave a laptop computer with sensitive information on it in the room unattended. Keep it in your personal possession at all times or don't take it on the trip. If you must take a laptop, use encryption to protect sensitive files and perform regular backups to ensure no loss of vital information in case of theft.

Suitcase and attaché case locks may delay the trained professional for a few minutes but will not protect your sensitive information.

Nevertheless, it is wise to keep your luggage locked whenever you are out of the room. Although locks will not inhibit the professional thief or intelligence agent, they will keep the curious maid honest. Curious hotel employees are even more likely to remain honest if combination locks are set so that the combination for each piece of luggage is different. For attaché cases with two combination locks, use different combinations for each lock.

The only solution to the security problem is to take as little sensitive information as possible when traveling overseas, and to carry what you must take on your person, possibly on computer media. Computer diskettes and CD-ROMs must also be carried with you at all times.

If you must carry sensitive information, the following suggestions may be helpful.

- While asleep or in the shower, engage both the dead bolt and the privacy latch or chain on the hotel room door. A hotel's emergency keys can override the dead bolt locks, so the latch or chain is your principal source of security. (Note: Many hotel rooms have a door to a connecting room. This is a potential vulnerability, as these doors do not normally have a privacy latch or chain.)

- Utilize a portable or improvised burglar alarm while asleep. Two ash trays and a water glass are quite effective as an alarm when placed on the floor in front of the door into your room. Place a water glass in one ashtray and balance the second ashtray on top of the glass. If a straight chair is available, place it next to the door and put the ash tray/water glass alarm on the edge of the chair where it will fall with enough racket to wake you.

- When leaving the room, make a mental or written note of how your suitcase or other personal property that would not normally be touched by the cleaning personnel was left. Any movement might suggest that others were in the room to examine your belongings. The same procedure is even more effective to check for surreptitious entry while you were asleep.

- Jewelry or other valuables should normally be left at home, but you may need to protect a substantial amount of money. Guidelines for protecting money from thieves are different from those for protecting sensitive information from the local intelligence or security service. Money should not be kept on your person. It should be kept in a safe in a local office or in the hotel's safe deposit box or safe. This is safer than a room safe and may also make the hotel liable for any loss. Liability laws in many countries provide that the hotel is not liable for the loss of guest property unless it is in the care, custody and control of the hotel. Additional protection may be gained by double enveloping all valuables, initialing across the seams, and then taping all edges and seams (over the initials).

- If you determine that an item is missing, conduct a thorough search prior to reporting the incident to hotel security. Do not expect to receive a copy of the security report, as it is an internal document. The incident should be reported to the local police, the security officer at the nearest U.S. Embassy or Consulate, and your insurance carrier. Hotel security can provide a letter verifying that you reported property missing.

### Elsewhere in the Hotel

There are a number of areas of your hotel where you are particularly vulnerable to theft.

- *Rest Rooms:* Female travelers should be careful about placing purses on hangers on the inside of the lavatory doors or on the floor in stalls—two frequent locations for grab and run thefts. On occasion, unauthorized persons use rest rooms for other types of theft or to deal drugs or engage in prostitution.

- *Public Telephones:* Areas around public telephones are often used by criminals to stage pickpocket activity or theft. Keep briefcases and purses in view or in touch while using phones. Safeguard your telephone credit card numbers. Criminals sometimes hang around public telephones to gather credit card numbers and then sell the numbers for unauthorized use.

- *Hotel Bars and Restaurants:* Purse snatchers and briefcase thieves are known to work hotel bars and restaurants waiting for unknowing guests to drape these items on chairs or under tables, only to discover them missing as they are departing. Keep items in view or in touch. Be alert to scams involving an unknown person spilling a drink or food on your clothing. An accomplice may be preparing to steal your wallet, briefcase or purse.

- *Pool or Beach Areas:* These are fertile areas for thieves to take advantage of guests enjoying recreation. Leave valuables in the hotel. Safeguard your room key and camera. Sign for food and beverages on your room bill rather than carry cash.

- *Prostitutes* take advantage of travelers around the world through various ploys, including use of knock out drugs and theft from the victim's room. Avoid engaging persons you do not know and refrain from inviting them to your guest room.

## Airports and Trains

Airports, railroad terminals and trains are easy targets for pick-pockets, thieves, and terrorist bombers. Unattended baggage is an obvious risk. Checked baggage is also at risk and should never contain valuables such as a camera or sensitive papers. It is not unusual for government and business travelers to report broken suitcase locks and rearranged contents.

Theft from sleeping compartments on trains is surprisingly common. Train thieves spray chemicals inside sleeping compartments to render the occupant(s) unconscious in order to enter and steal valuables. Using this technique, valuables can be stolen from under a sleeping person's pillow. A locked door may be helpful but is no guarantee.

Laptop computers are a prime target for theft everywhere, but they are especially vulnerable in airports. They are stolen for the value of the information on them as well as for the value of the computer.

According to Safeware, an insurer of personal computers, 10% of all laptop thefts occur in airports. Airports offer an inviting atmosphere for thieves due to large crowds, hectic schedules, and weary travelers. Laptop thefts commonly occur in places where people set them down—at security checkpoints, pay phones, lounges and restaurants, check-in lines, and restrooms. Two incidents at separate European airports demonstrate the modus operandi of thieves operating in pairs to target laptop computers:

- Airport security at Brussels International Airport reported that two thieves exploited a contrived delay around the security X-ray machines. The first thief preceded the traveler through the security checkpoint and then loitered around the area where security examines carry-on luggage. When the traveler placed his laptop computer onto the conveyer belt of the X-ray machine, the second thief stepped in front of the traveler and set off the metal detector. With the traveler now delayed, the first thief removed the traveler's laptop from the conveyer belt just after it passed through the X-ray machine and quickly disappeared.

- While walking around the Frankfurt International Airport in Germany, a traveler carrying a laptop computer in his roll bag did not notice a thief position himself to walk in front of him. The thief stopped abruptly as the traveler bypassed a crowd of people, causing the traveler also to stop. A second thief, who was following close behind, quickly removed the traveler's laptop computer from his roll bag and disappeared into the crowd.

All travelers, both domestic and international, should be alert to any sudden diversions when traveling, especially when transiting transportation terminals. If victimized, travelers should report the thefts immediately to the authorities and be able to provide the makes, model information, and serial numbers of their laptop computers, or any other items of value.[1]

### Sensitive Equipment in Transit

Sensitive equipment may be stolen so that it can be copied through reverse engineering. For some purposes, it may be sufficient to only gain access to the equipment for a brief period. For example, a cleared company participated in an air show that took place overseas. The company shipped over an operational $250,000 multi-mode radar system that can be used on fighter aircraft. At the conclusion of the air show, the radar system was packaged for return shipping by company personnel, and the radar assembly was actually bolted to the shipping container. The shipping container was routed through a third country with the customs seals intact.

Upon being opened by company personnel, it was discovered that the radar was no longer bolted to the shipping container. As a result, the radar system was damaged beyond repair. It was determined that the radar was properly bolted down at the time it was prepared for shipment. It also was determined that the country that sponsored the air show was keenly interested in the radar's technology. It is not known whether the intruder's failure to re-bolt the radar was an oversight or was done deliberately to destroy evidence of whatever was done to examine the radar.[2]

Lesson learned: The company did not really need to take the entire radar assembly to the air show. A mock-up without the internal mechanisms could have been set up along with photographs of the internal components.

### Overseas Offices

Offices of U.S. Government agencies and U.S. businesses in foreign countries are vulnerable both to burglary and to theft of information by local national employees. For example, the Western European office of a large American corporation was burglarized in an obvious case of industrial espionage. Located on the sixth floor of a 12-story office building, it was entered from the outside window ledge by breaking the window. The thieves ignored the company's expensive computers and other valuable items and went directly to their target—the company's marketing and business data, client and business contact lists, and banking information. Wastebaskets can be a great source of information.

Foreign offices of U.S. Government and business organizations are staffed, in part, by local citizens. In many countries, some of these employees cooperate voluntarily with the local security or intelligence service or are pressured or coerced into doing so.

In one allied Western European country, collecting proprietary information from the offices of American and other foreign corporations with offices in that country is known as economic patriotism. Collected information is provided routinely to local competitors of the U.S. companies. In many countries, local national employees are also debriefed for assessment data about the American personnel.

Foreign intelligence interest is not necessarily determined by an employee's rank in the company. Researchers, key business managers, and corporate executives can all be targets, but so can support employees such as secretaries, computer operators, technicians, and maintenance people. The latter frequently have good, if not the best, access to competitive information. Additionally, their lower pay and rank may provide fertile ground for manipulation by an intelligence agency.

Protection of sensitive information is very difficult under these circumstances. Discussion of all the physical and technical security requirements for protection of proprietary technologies and sensitive commercial information is beyond the scope of this security guide.

## Safety and Security

### Tips for Securing Valuables during Travel

**Packing:** Don't carry everything in one place! Never pack essential documents, medicine—anything you could not do without—in your checked luggage. Put them in your carry-on bag.

**Cash:** Never carry large amounts of cash. American Express travelers checks are a good idea. Have three lists of checks. Leave one at home. Carry one list with your checks and carry one list separately from your checks. Keep two lists up-to-date as you cash checks. Keep the receipts for your checks separate from your travelers checks. For the small amount of cash you need, try using a necklace pouch or a money belt.

**Credit Cards:** Take only the cards you will use on the trip. Keep separate a list of cards, numbers, and emergency replacement procedures.

**Insurance:** Since it may be necessary to contact your insurance agent(s) while abroad, keep all names and phone numbers, as well as your policy number(s), with you in a safe place.

**Luggage:** Mark all luggage, inside and out, with your name and address. If you have an itinerary, put a copy inside each bag. Keep a list of what is in each bag and carry the list with your other documents. Mark your bags in some distinctive way, so they are easily found. Count your pieces of luggage each time you move. Try to travel light, it's safer and less cumbersome.

**Medicines:** Take all you need for the trip. Take copy of your prescription(s), with the generic name of the drug(s). Keep medicines in original drugstore containers. Take extra glasses and your lenses prescription with you.

**Passport:** Carry with you—separate from your passport—two extra passport pictures, passport number, date and place issued, and a certified—not photocopied—copy (not the original) of your birth certificate or an expired passport. If your passport is lost, report to local police; get written confirmation of the police report and, take the above documents to the nearest United States Consulate and apply for a new passport.

**Ticket:** Make a copy of your ticket or, list your ticket number, all flights included, and name and address of issuing agency, and keep this list separate from your ticket.

### Overseas Security Measures to Reduce the Risk of Crime, Violence, and Disease

Overseas study programs recognize their responsibility to do their utmost to provide a secure and unthreatening environment in which you can safely live and learn. Responsible campuses and programs consult regularly with colleagues around the country who are involved in the administration of study abroad programs; with resident program directors of programs; with responsible officials of foreign host universities; with contacts in the U.S. Department of State and other governmental and non-governmental agencies and with other experts, including faculty who are well-informed on issues and events. It is in no one's interest to risk your safety and well-being.

The ability to communicate almost instantaneously worldwide via fax machines and electronic mail enables campuses (and parents) to obtain and share information quickly and accurately, in the event of an overseas emergency that may have repercussions for study abroad programs and students. In short, most campuses and programs have in place an effective system of consultation and consensus—in order to make proactive and reactive decisions concerning the safe operation of their programs.

*Crime, Violence, and Terrorism*

Most countries in the world have less street crime and personal violence than is potentially present in urban and suburban American. Indeed, in many countries U.S. students report when they return that they had never felt safer in their lives. This does not mean that there is no crime and that your safety is assured because of, or in spite of, the fact that you carry a U.S. passport in a perhaps statistically more peaceful local environment.

The simple fact of your being a foreigner and not knowing quite what is and isn't safe behavior—not being certain where and where not to go or how to act—increases, at least somewhat, the possibility that you can be victimized by petty crime, such as fraud, robbery, theft, or even physical attack. Further, in certain places and at certain times, it is very possible to get caught in the midst of forms of political strife which may not be directed at you personally or even at you as an American, but nevertheless can be very dangerous.

With regard to the threat of terrorism, in those few sites where even remote danger might occasionally exist, program directors work with local police and U.S. consular personnel and local university officials in setting up whatever practical security measures are deemed prudent. In such places, you will be briefed during orientation programs and reminded at any times of heightened political tension about being security conscious in your daily activities. Terrorism is a twentieth-century reality and is not likely to diminish (or increase) significantly. To succumb to the threat by reacting in fear may well be the objective that terrorists seek to achieve. Nevertheless, there are certain rather obvious precautions that American students abroad can take. Among these are the following:

**Common sense precautions:** Do your homework, listen and heed the counsel you are given, and remain vigilant. Here are some essential Do's and Don'ts, which will serve you well:

- Keep a low profile and try not to make yourself conspicuous by dress, speech, or behavior, in ways that might identify you as a targetable individual. Do not draw attention to yourself either through expensive dress, personal accessories (cameras, radios, sunglasses, etc.) or careless behavior.

- Avoid crowds, protest groups, or other potentially volatile situations, as well as restaurants and entertainment places where Americans are known to congregate. Keep abreast of local news. Read local newspapers, magazines, etc. and speak with local officials to learn about any potential civil unrest. If there should be any political unrest, do not get involved.

- Be wary of unexpected packages and stay clear of unattended luggage or parcels in airports, train stations, or other areas of uncontrolled public access.

- Report to the responsible authority any suspicious persons loitering around residence or instructional facilities, or following you; keep your residence area locked; use common sense in divulging information to strangers about your study program and your fellow students.

- If you travel to countries beyond your program site and expect to be there for more than a week, register upon arrival at the U.S. consulate or embassy having jurisdiction over the location.

- Make sure the resident director, host family, or foreign university official who is assigned the responsibility for your welfare always knows where and how to contact you in an emergency and your schedule and itinerary of where you are traveling, even if only overnight.

- Develop with your family a plan for regular telephone or mail contact, so that in times of heightened political tension, you will be able to communicate with your parents directly about your safety and well-being.

- The U.S. government monitors the political conditions in every country around the world. For current information, advisories, or warnings contact the State Department in Washington DC (202-647-4000) or the local U.S. embassy or consulate where you are.

- Be aware of local health conditions abroad: especially if you are traveling to remote areas, you should be aware of any public health service recommendations or advisories. For current health conditions abroad contact local officials, or have your parents contact the country desk at the State Department (http://travel.state.gov/travel_warnings.html or 202-647-4000, or the Centers for Disease Control, 404-639-3311).

- Know local laws: laws and systems of justice are not universal. Do not assume that just because it is legal in the United States, that it is legal abroad.

- Use banks to exchange your money: do not exchange your money on the black market, on the street. Do not carry on your person more money than you need for the day. Carry your credit cards, etc. in a very safe place.

- Do not impair your judgment due to excessive consumption of alcohol, and do not fall under the influence of drugs.

- Female travelers are sometimes more likely to encounter harassment, but uncomfortable situations can usually be avoided by taking the following precautions: Dress conservatively. While short skirts and tank tops may be comfortable, they may also encourage unwanted attention. Avoid walking alone late at night or in questionable neighborhoods. Do not agree to meet a person whom you do not know in a non-public place. Be aware that some men from other countries tend to mistake the friendliness of American women for romantic interest.

## References

1. National Counterintelligence Center, *Counterintelligence News and Developments*, March 1996.

2. James Norvell, Assessing Foreign Collection Trends, *Security Awareness Bulletin*, Number 1-98, Department of Defense Security Institute.

# Chapter 29

# *Safeguarding Your Personal Laptop Computer*

Laptop computers are a prime target for theft from your office, your home, or at airports, hotels, railroad terminals and on trains while you are traveling. They are an extremely attractive target for all types of thieves, as they are small, can be carried away without attracting attention, and are easily sold for a good price. They are also a favorite target for intelligence collectors, as they concentrate so much valuable information in one accessible place.

Safeware, the largest insurer of personal computers in the United States, paid claims for the theft of 319,000 laptop computers during 1999.[1] Of course, most laptops are not insured, so this is only a small fraction of the total number of laptop computers that were stolen during that year.

When a laptop is stolen, you don't know whether it was taken for the value of the information on the computer or for the value of the computer itself. This makes it difficult to assess the damage caused by the loss.

This chapter offers guidelines for keeping your laptop from being stolen, discusses technical measures for protecting information on the laptop if it is stolen or entered surreptitiously, and notes special problems relating to traveling overseas with your laptop.

---

"Security of Laptops" is excerpted from the "Counterintelligence Awareness Guide" http://www.nnsi.doe.gov/C/Courses/CI_Awareness_Guide/Home.htm, produced by the Counterintelligence Training Academy, Nonproliferation and National Security Institute, Department of Energy, cited November 2002.

## Protection of Laptops

The basic rule for protecting your laptop is to treat it like your wallet or purse. Your laptop is a more attractive target for thieves than your wallet or purse, and if you lose your laptop, the cost to you in money and inconvenience is probably greater than if you lose your wallet or purse. If your laptop has sensitive government, commercial, or scientific data on it, the loss may be valued in the millions.

Even in your office, unless it is a controlled secure area, it is advisable to keep your laptop out of sight when not in use, preferably in a locked drawer or cabinet. The Washington, DC police recently formed a task force to fight a surge in thefts from downtown offices; laptops were the thieves' preferred target.[2]

Your laptop is especially vulnerable while you are traveling. Here is a summary of basic precautions during travel.

- Disguise your laptop. The distinctive size and shape of a laptop computer make it an easily spotted target for thieves. Carry it in a briefcase or other, preferably grungy-looking, case.

- Never let a laptop out of your sight in an airport or other public area. If you set it down while checking in at the airport counter or hotel registration desk, lean it against your leg so that you can feel its presence, or hold it between your feet.

- When going through the airport security check, don't place your laptop on the conveyor belt until you are sure no one in front of you is being delayed. If you are delayed while passing through the checkpoint, keep your eye on your laptop.

- When traveling by plane or rail, do not ever place the computer (or other valuables) in checked baggage. If your aircraft departure is delayed and you are directed or invited to deplane and wait in the terminal, take your computer and other valuables with you. Don't leave them unattended at your seat or in the overhead.

- Never store a computer in an airport or train station locker. If you must leave it in a car, lock it in the trunk out of sight.

- Avoid leaving your computer in a hotel room, but if you must do so, at least lower the risk of theft by keeping it out of sight. Lock it securely in another piece of luggage. Placing the computer in a hotel vault or room safe should make it secure from theft, but

in some foreign countries it may not be secure from access by local intelligence or security personnel.

- Never keep passwords or access phone numbers on the machine
  or in the case. Do not program your computer's function keys
  with sign-on sequences, passwords, access phone numbers, or
  phone credit card numbers. If the machine is stolen or lost,
  these would be valuable prizes.

- Try to keep only software files on your laptop's hard drive. Store
  your data files on diskettes and carry them separately from the
  computer.

- Back up all files before traveling.

- Beware of power surges. Don't be connected to either power
  lines or a copper phone line during a storm with lightning.

While in any public place, such as an airplane or hotel lobby, don't
have up on your laptop screen anything you don't want the public to
know about. A survey of 600 American travelers found that over one-
third admitted looking at someone else's laptop while flying. Younger
travelers were the worst offenders, with 49 percent of the men and
40 percent of the women under 40 admitting they look at what their
seatmate is working on. Most are checking to see what their fellow
passenger is doing, while others are more interested in who they are
working for.[3]

Be prepared for the airport security check. You may be directed by
airport security personnel to open and turn on your laptop to demonstrate that it is actually a functioning computer. Be sure the battery
is charged or have the power cord handy. If you can't turn your laptop
on, you may not be permitted to take it on board the aircraft. The airport security x-ray machines will usually not affect hard drives. Floppy
diskettes, having less shielding, may be affected. If possible, pass these
to the attendant for hand examination.

It is even more difficult to protect your laptop, and the information on it, when traveling in foreign countries where your laptop may
be targeted as a treasure trove of information.

## Technology for Protecting Information on Your Laptop

Due to the very high risk and high cost of laptop theft, many products are being developed to protect the security of information in your

laptop if it is stolen, prevent the surreptitious entry into files on your laptop, make it more difficult to steal a laptop, or make it easier to find a stolen laptop. Specific products are not discussed here, as the technology is changing so rapidly. The following general types of products are now available.

*Encryption software.* Storing all data files in encrypted form will prevent disclosure of the data even if your computer is stolen.

Software that hides information on your hard drive, so that it is not found by the average thief who steals your laptop or, for example, by an intelligence collector who gains surreptitious access to your laptop in your hotel room.

Various types of locks, keys, and biometric identification devices designed to prevent anyone but you from using the computer, and perhaps to alert you to any unauthorized attempt to use your computer.

Software utilities that wipe the hard disk clean when deleting sensitive data files. These overwrite the deleted data making it totally unrecoverable, as opposed to the normal Delete command that only deletes the pointer that allows the computer to find the file on your hard drive. The file itself is not deleted until it is overwritten by another file.

*Tracers that identify the location of a stolen laptop.* When the stolen laptop is linked to the Internet, it transmits a signal to a monitoring station that identifies the user's telephone number or Internet account.

*Proximity alarms that go off if the laptop gets too far away from its owner or user.* Ask your system administrator or computer security specialist to evaluate which of the available alternatives best meet your needs.

## Traveling Overseas with a Laptop

Your laptop computer is even more vulnerable to theft or unauthorized access while traveling abroad than in the United States. If you are traveling overseas, be aware that some countries have import restrictions on laptops. Check before you leave to avoid delays and possible confiscation. Also some countries do not allow encryption of telecommunications traffic within their borders—because they want to be able to monitor your messages.

When you return to this country, U.S. Customs may try to impose an import tax if they think the computer was purchased abroad. There are several ways to establishing prior ownership. One is to carry with you a bill of sale for the computer and/or insurance policy endorsement showing the serial number. You may carry a property pass from your employer that shows the serial number. Or you may register your laptop and any other valuables that might be mistaken as imports with U.S. Customs prior to leaving the country. You can do this at the Customs Entrance and Clearance Desk at the airport in advance of your flight.

## *References*

1.  Safeware web site at www.safeware.com.

2.  Arthur Santana, Office Thieves Target Laptops, *Washington Post*, Nov. 5, 2000, p. A1.

3.  Rob Lenihan, CNNfn, Laptop peeking takes off, April 12, 2000.

# Chapter 30

# *What to Do If Your Passport Is Stolen*

## *What Should a U.S. Citizens Do If Their Passport Is Lost or Stolen Abroad?*

Contact the nearest U.S. embassy or consulate for assistance. Phone numbers for U.S. embassies and consulates are also available in our Consular Information Sheets and Key Officers handbook. You will need to speak to the American Citizens Services unit of the Consular Section. If you are scheduled to leave the foreign country shortly, please provide the Consular Section with details regarding your departure schedule. Every effort will be made to assist you quickly. You will also be directed to where you can obtain the required passport photos.

If you are notified by a relative or friend that their U.S. passport has been lost/stolen, you may wish to contact Overseas Citizens Services, (202) 647-5225 at the U.S. Department of State in Washington, D.C. providing as much information about possible about the person's who needs passport services abroad. This will assist us in trying to verify the person's previous passport, clearing the person's name through the Department Passport Name Check System, and relaying this information to the U.S. embassy or consulate. Your relative/ friend must apply for a new passport at the nearest U.S. embassy or consulate.

"Lost and Stolen U.S. Passports Abroad." An undated document from the U.S. Department of State. Available online at http://travel.state.gov/lost_passports_abroad.html. Cited November 2002.

## What Are the Requirements to Obtain a Replacement Passport?

You will need to complete a new passport application. The consular officer taking an application for replacement of a lost, stolen, or misplaced passport must be reasonably satisfied as to your identity and citizenship before issuing the replacement. In virtually all cases this can be done through examination of whatever citizenship and identity documents are available, conversations with the applicant, close observation of demeanor and replies to questions asked, and discussions with the applicant's traveling companions or contacts in the United States. Please note the new requirements for passports for minors under the age of 14 and how this will change the way passport applications for minors are handled abroad.

## What Information Will I Need to Provide the Consular Officer?

You will be asked for certain information to assist in verifying your citizenship:

1.   Personal Data: (including, but not limited to)

     • your name

     • date of birth

     • place of birth

     • passport number (if available)

     • date and place where your passport was issued

     If you can provide the U.S. embassy or consulate with a photocopy of your passport identification page, that will make getting a new passport easier since your citizenship and identity information would be more readily available.

2.   Affidavit Regarding Loss/Theft of the Passport/Police Report: When you report the loss, theft, or misplacement of your passport you must execute an affidavit fully describing the circumstances under which it was lost, stolen. U.S. Department of State form DS-64 may be used for this purpose, or you may simply execute a sworn statement before the consular officer describing what happened. A police report is not mandatory

but may be required when the embassy/consulate believes a problem may exist such as possible fraud. An applicant eligible to receive a passport should not be placed in circumstances to miss a plane or unreasonably delay travel to obtain a police report.

3. Citizenship Verification and Name Clearance: The U.S. embassy/consulate will confirm your previous passport issuance through our Passport Verification System or by requesting that Overseas Citizens Services, (202) 647-5225, in the U.S. Department of State retrieve the actual passport application. The consular section will also attempt to clear your name through the U.S. Department of State name check system to ensure there is nothing preventing issuance of a U.S. passport to you (for example: outstanding arrest warrant, court order, etc.).

4. Proof of Identity: You will also be asked for some proof of your identity. If all your personal papers were lost or stolen with your passport, your identity can be established in a number of ways. In most cases the problem of identity is resolved quickly. It should be noted, however, that if there is any indication of possible fraud the consular officer may request additional documentation or other information.

   • Information from Consular Interview: The consular officer may be satisfied as to your identity based on the interview with you, or may require other information.

   • Identifying Witness: Persons traveling with a group or with friends, family or associates in the foreign country can have such a person execute an affidavit of an identifying witness before the consular officer. An identifying witness does not have to be a U.S. citizen.

   • Information from Family, Friends or Associates in the United States: If you are traveling alone and do not know anyone in the foreign country who can attest to your identity, your family, friends, or associates in the U.S. may contact the consular officer by phone or fax confirming your identity. This is usually quite informal. In emergency situations, your contacts may also communicate with the U.S. Department of State, that Overseas Citizens Services, (202) 647-5225.

- Information from Previous Passport Records: If necessary, information about your identity may be obtained from your previous passport application which may have to be retrieved by Overseas Citizens Services, (202) 647-5225, in the U.S. Department of State from the Federal Records Center which is located outside of Washington, DC.

## Will the Replacement Passport Be Issued for the Full 10-Year Validity Period for an Adult?

Replacements for lost passports are normally issued for the full 10-year period of validity for adults. Occasionally, cases will arise in which the consular officer has some lingering doubt because of statements made by the applicant, or other circumstances, but is still reasonably satisfied as to identity and citizenship. If there is not time to request and receive the Department's verification, a passport limited to 3 months may be issued. Limited passports may also be issued in cases in which an applicant has, by mistake, packed the passport with luggage being sent to another location, left the passport at home, perhaps in another country, but has to travel immediately, lost or been robbed of multiple passports in a short time span, etc. When issuing a limited passport in an emergency situation, consular officers will carefully explain to the applicant that the passport is limited for the duration of the present trip only. When the applicant returns to the United States and wishes to travel again internationally, the applicant will have to apply for a replacement passport and pay the regular fee.

## Are Fees Charged for Replacement of Lost/Stolen Passports Abroad?

The normal passport fees are collected from applicants for replacement passports. Applicants will be asked to provide names of persons they feel would be able to assist them financially if there is sufficient time. However, if: the applicant's money and documents have been lost or stolen, or the applicant is a victim of a disaster and the applicant does not have and cannot reasonably be expected to obtain money to pay the fees before continuing travel, no passport fee will be charged and a limited validity passport will be issued. When the person applies for a full validity passport on their return to the United States the regular passport fee will be charged for the replacement passport.

## Can the U.S. Embassy Issue a Replacement Passport over a Weekend or Holiday?

U.S. passports are not routinely issued by U.S. embassies and consulates abroad on weekends and holidays when the embassy/consulate is closed. All U.S. embassies and consulates have an after hours duty officer available to assist with life or death emergencies of U.S. citizens abroad. Contact the nearest U.S. embassy or consulate after hours duty officer for assistance if you have an emergency and need to travel. Phone numbers for U.S. embassies and consulates are also available in our Consular Information Sheets and Key Officers handbook.

If you are scheduled to travel directly to the United States, the duty officer may be able to assist in issuing a transportation letter to the airline and alerting U.S. Customs and Immigration to the fact that you will be attempting to enter the United States without a passport.

Duty officers must focus primary attention on life or death emergencies. Depending on the circumstances and conditions in the foreign country, it is possible that a replacement passport may not be issued until the embassy/consulate reopens for business. At that time the Consular Section will be in a better position to verify your citizenship and identity and clear your name through the Department of State name check system.

# Chapter 31

# *Beware of Con Artists*

## *Safety and Security*

The first rule is: Trust your intuition—if something seems wrong it probably is wrong. If you have been told that a certain area is a good area but you turn the corner and don't feel right, then turn around and go back—no matter what someone told you, trust your instincts.

Buy a good, lightweight, frameless backpack. Do not use a suitcase. The backpack holds more. It can be carried on your back for long distances. It also leaves your hands free for books, maps, food, etc. The frameless pack can move through airport luggage paths without being damaged or damaging the transport system.

When you are on the move from one place to another, consolidate your luggage into one backpack—not two or three small bags. Having more than the pack on your back makes you very vulnerable for a snatch and run. If you can't get it all in one backpack then you have too much stuff —ship some things home.

If you have a camera *do not wear it around your neck*—it is supposed to be a camera not a status symbol. Carry the camera in a small shoulder pack. Only take it out to snap a photo.

Never take photos of people without their permission. It is rude, culturally insensitive—and may get you into trouble. If you feel it is not a problem to take the photo, why wouldn't you ask first?

Reprinted with permission from www.hostelhandbook.com. © 2001 The Hostel Handbook for the U.S.A. and Canada.

## Common Scams

Most people who lose their money are not robbed, per se. They lay their bag down and after a distraction, the bag is missing or they are victimized by 'con artist' (con = confidence, artist = actor). You are much more likely to give your money to a con artist than you are likely to be robbed. There are hundreds of scams and they all depend on two basic features: they trusted you so you must trust them and you're going to make money out of the deal. Keep in mind that you shouldn't give your money to strangers—even one that has convinced you that you can trust them. And, if it seems to good to be true, then it probably isn't true.

### The Lost Purse

A very nonthreatening person (older woman or apparent invalid) approaches you on the street for the time or directions. In the course of the brief conversation, this person spots a purse on the sidewalk or in a garbage can and involves you in an investigation. You find some papers, personal items, etc. in the purse and this person convinces you that the two of you should telephone a number in the papers to see if the purse is stolen. You telephone and discover that the purse was stolen and (your lucky day) there is a reward. The person on the phone will give you $300 if you will bring the purse to their apartment. Wow! But then, your new friend tells you that they don't have the time to accompany you—but...you are such a nice person, "why don't you give me whatever cash you have on you and you go collect the $300?" By this time, you are in too deep—when you arrive at the (fake) address for your reward, you realize it's a con and you have given a stranger all your cash.

### Three Card Monte

At some point you will walk along a street and see a crowd gathered around a game of cards. The dealer has three cards face down on a box. He moves the cards around quickly. The player is supposed to pick out the King (or Ace or whatever). An apparent idiot is playing the game with him and cannot see that the King is slightly worn from use. But you can. You get sucked into playing this game and a couple of people in the crowd are really impressed with your skill. After you win a little money, the dealer begs you for the opportunity to win some of the money back—a double or nothing routine. Your cheering

378

section in the crowd encourages you, "you can't lose—you're good." You take out more money, certain that only you can see the difference in the cards—and that you are about to make big bucks.

Full of hubris, you take your winnings, double it with more of your money and you pick the same worn card—but, what's this, it's no longer the King. You lose. The dealer takes it all. The old switcheroo. You can shout and complain but the same people in the crowd who before said you were skilled and amazing now accuse you of being a bad loser.

You see, they are all in it together: the dealer, the first player, and some of the audience (plus a couple of people standing on the corner watching for the police and probably another couple picking pockets in the crowd around the excitement). Don't go near this scene. You can't win.

### *The Pig in a Poke*

As you walk down the street, someone whistles and points at a box under his arm. It appears to be a video camera—new, so new it is still in a vacuum-wrapped box. He whispers that it's hot or that it fell off a truck—slang for stolen. He says that it is your lucky day—he has to get rid of it quickly. He explains that you can't look at it because the police might come by. He will sell it to you for only $50. Wow! An $800 dollar camera for only $50. Back at the hostel, you open the box and it's three well-wrapped bricks.

There are lots of others and I have seen them in every major city around the world. Remember this; if it is too good to be true, then it probably isn't true. At the moment you find yourself in the position of giving money to someone you just met, STOP. Repeat these words to yourself: I don't give money to strangers—even if I think I can trust them and I'm going to make loads of money.

# Chapter 32

# *If You've Had Food or Souvenirs Taken Away by a Customs Inspector*

## *Why Are You Taking My...?*

If you've had food or souvenirs taken away by an inspector of the U.S. Department of Agriculture (USDA) while entering the United States at an airport, border station, or seaport, it is important that you understand why.

USDA restricts certain items brought into the United States from foreign countries. Prohibited items can harbor foreign animal and plant pests and diseases that could seriously damage America's crops, livestock, pets, and the environment.

Because of this threat, you are required to declare on a U.S. Customs form any meats, fruits, vegetables, plants, animals, and plant and animal products in your possession. This declaration must cover all items carried in your baggage and hand luggage. You will also be asked to indicate whether you have visited a farm or ranch outside the United States. Officers of USDA's Animal and Plant Health Inspection Service (APHIS) inspect passenger baggage for undeclared agricultural products. At some ports, APHIS personnel use beagle dogs to sniff out hidden items. APHIS inspectors also use low-energy x-ray machines adapted to reveal concealed fruits and meats. Travelers who

"Why Are You Taking My...?", a fact sheet from the Animal and Plant Health Inspection Service, U.S. Department of Agriculture, September 2001. "Know Before You Go" is a brochure from U.S. Customs and Border Protection, 2001. The complete text of "Know Before You Go" is available online at http://www.customs.gov/xp/cgov/travel/vacation/know_brochure/.

fail to declare a prohibited item can be fined up to $1,000 on the spot and have their items confiscated.

Travelers are often surprised to hear that a single piece of fruit or meat can cause serious damage. In fact, one pest-infested or disease-infected item carelessly discarded can wreak havoc on American crops and livestock. The extra cost for controlling agricultural pests and diseases ripples down from farmers to consumers in the form of higher food prices. Taking prohibited agricultural items from travelers helps prevent outbreaks that could affect everyone.

### Fresh Fruit

It may look luscious and wholesome, but fruit you bring into the United States from abroad could carry agricultural pests and diseases. Oranges, for example, could harbor the Mediterranean fruit fly (Medfly)—a devastating pest of more than 200 fruits, nuts, and vegetables. In fact, it is possible that individual travelers carried in the infested fruit that brought the Medfly to California in 1979 and to Florida in 1997. Medfly infestations can cause billion-dollar losses to the citrus industry.

### Meat and Meat Products

Regulations prohibit you from bringing in fresh, dried, and canned meats and meat products from most foreign countries. If any meat is used in preparing a product, that product is prohibited. Commercially canned meat is allowed if the inspector can determine from the label that the meat was cooked in the can after it was sealed to make it shelf-stable without refrigeration.

Animal disease organisms can live for months in sausage and other meat, including many types of canned hams sold abroad. Foot-and-mouth disease and African swine fever are just two of several dreaded foreign livestock diseases that could cost the U.S. livestock industry billions to eradicate, cause higher food prices, and eliminate export markets.

### Plants in Soil

Some of the most notorious and varied pest hitchhikers are micro-scopic insects, disease agents, and weed seeds that lurk in soil and plant parts. These organisms could cause extensive harm to our crops and forests.

You can import many plants legally and safely, provided you follow USDA guidelines and buy plants from reputable dealers. For informa-tion and permit applications, write USDA, APHIS, Plant Protection and

Quarantine, 4700 River Road, Unit 136, Riverdale, MD, 20737-1236, Attn: Permit Unit. You can visit the PPQ permit Web site at http://www. aphis.usda.gov/ppq/permits. In addition, APHIS' Import Authorization System currently allows customers to submit applications to import fruits & vegetables and animal products, organisms, and vectors online, as well as check the status of an existing application and submit revisions to an existing application. To apply for a permit online, visit https://web01.aphis.usda.gov/IAS.nsf/Mainform?OpenForm.

## Exotic Birds

Sometimes without even showing signs of illness, parrots, parakeets, and other birds brought to the United States from other countries can carry and spread serious diseases, such as exotic Newcastle disease. Therefore, birds are subject to specific rules. Restrictions include a minimum 30-day quarantine stay in a USDA-operated import facility, which requires advance reservations and related fees. Birds must also be tested for exotic diseases while in quarantine.

To avoid confiscation of pet birds, know current restrictions and guidelines. For information, contact USDA, APHIS, Veterinary Services, 4700 River Road, Unit 39, Riverdale, MD, 20737-1231, Attn: National Center for Import/Export. Also, visit the traveler's website for travel tips including importing exotic birds at http://www.aphis.usda.gov/oa/pubs/usdatips.pdf.

## Hunting Trophies

The entry of hunting trophies into the United States—as well as game animal carcasses, hides, dairy products, and other animal products and byproducts—is severely restricted and in many instances prohibited. These articles can also harbor livestock disease organisms. When the product involves endangered species, restrictions of the U.S. Department of the Interior's Fish and Wildlife Service apply. For information, contact U.S. Fish and Wildlife Service, Office of Management Authority, 4401 North Fairfax Dr., Arlington, VA 22203 or visit their Web site at http://www.fws.gov.

## Packing Material

Insects and even diseases can hide in packing material made from agricultural products like straw and burlap. Straw from wheat, if infected with an exotic wheat smut, for example, could do billions of dollars of damage to American wheat fields. Straw hats or other decorative items made from straw may be forbidden entry into the United States if derived from prohibited material.

You may be surprised to hear that some agricultural pests can live on packing material for long stretches of time without any source of food. One such pest is the khapra beetle, a tiny, brownish-black pest of grain. It can hide in the folds of burlap and can survive there, without feeding, for up to 3 years. But when the beetle reaches a supply of grain, it goes on a rampage. A colony reproduces so fast and eats so much that an infested grain bin literally comes alive with wriggling larvae. A khapra beetle infestation in the United States and Mexico in the 1950s cost about $11 million to eradicate.

### *Live Snails*

No live snails may be brought into the mainland United States without a permit obtained from USDA. In 1966, a small boy brought two giant African snails into Florida from Hawaii. He eventually discarded them, and shortly thereafter these voracious consumers of foliage and fruit were infesting a 16-block area near his home. It took years and half a million dollars to eradicate them.

### *Do Your Part*

Please do your part to help protect American agriculture and ensure that we continue to enjoy a healthy and abundant food supply. If you have questions about APHIS' inspection procedures or whether particular agricultural products can be brought into the United States, contact APHIS' Plant Protection and Quarantine (PPQ). Look in the phone book under U.S. Department of Agriculture for the nearest PPQ office.

## Know before You Go

"Duty" and "dutiable" are words you will find frequently throughout this chapter: Duty is the amount of money you pay on items coming from another country. It is similar to a tax, except that duty is collected only on imported goods. Dutiable describes items on which duty may have to be paid. Most items have specific duty rates, which are determined by a number of factors, including where you got the item, where it was made, and what it is made of.

To "declare" means to tell the Customs officer about anything you're bringing back that you did not have when you left the United States. For example, you would declare alterations made in a foreign country

384

to a suit you already owned, and you would declare any gifts you acquired overseas.

### When You Return to the United States

When you come back, you'll need to declare everything you brought back that you did not take with you when you left the United States. If you are traveling by air or sea, you may be asked to fill out a Customs declaration form. This form is almost always provided by the airline or cruise ship. You will probably find it easier and faster to fill out your declaration form and clear Customs if you do the following:

- Keep your sales slips! As you read this chapter, you'll understand why this is especially important for international travelers.

- Try to pack the things you'll need to declare separately.

- Read the signs in the Customs area. They contain helpful information about how to clear Customs.

Be aware that under U.S. law, Customs inspectors are authorized to examine luggage, cargo, and travelers. Under the search authority granted to Customs by the U.S. Congress, every passenger who crosses a U.S. border may be searched. To stop the flow of illegal drugs and other contraband into our country, we need your cooperation. If you are one of the very few travelers selected for a search, you will be treated in a courteous, professional, and dignified manner. If you are searched and you believe that you were not treated in such a manner, or if you have any concerns about the search for any reason whatsoever, please contact U.S. Customs' Executive Director, Passenger Programs.

### What You Must Declare

- Items you purchased and are carrying with you upon return to the United States.

- Items you received as gifts, such as wedding or birthday presents.

- Items you inherited.

- Items you bought in duty-free shops or on the ship or plane.

- Repairs or alterations to any items you took abroad and then brought back, even if the repairs/alterations were performed free of charge.

- Items you brought home for someone else.

385

- Items you intend to sell or use in your business.

- Items you acquired (whether purchased or received as gifts) in the U.S. Virgin Islands, American Samoa, Guam, or in a Caribbean Basin Economic Recovery Act country (please see section on $600 exemption for a list of these countries) that are not in your possession when you return. In other words, if you acquired things in any of these island nations and asked the merchant to send them to you, you must still declare them when you go through Customs. (This differs from the usual procedure for mailed items.)

You must state on the Customs declaration, in United States currency, what you actually paid for each item. The price must include all taxes. If you did not buy the item yourself—for example, if it is a gift—get an estimate of its fair retail value in the country where you received it. If you bought something on your trip and wore or used it on the trip, it's still dutiable. You must declare the item at the price you paid or, if it was a gift, at its fair market value.

*Joint Declaration*

Family members who live in the same home and return together to the United States may combine their personal exemptions. This is called a joint declaration. For example, if Mr. and Mrs. Smith travel overseas and Mrs. Smith brings home a $1,000 piece of glassware, and Mr. Smith buys $600 worth of clothing, they can combine their $800 exemptions on a joint declaration and not have to pay duty.

Children and infants are allowed the same exemption as adults, except for alcoholic beverages.

*Register Items before You Leave the United States*

If your laptop computer was made in Japan—for instance—you might have to pay duty on it each time you bring it back into the United States, unless you could prove that you owned it before you left on your trip. Documents that fully describe the item—for example, sales receipts, insurance policies, or jeweler's appraisals—are acceptable forms of proof.

To make things easier, you can register certain items with Customs before you depart—including watches, cameras, laptop computers, firearms, and tape recorders—as long as they have serial numbers or other unique, permanent markings. Take the items to the nearest Customs Office and request a Certificate of Registration (Customs

Form 4457). It shows Customs that you had the items with you before leaving the U.S. and all items listed on it will be allowed duty-free entry. Customs inspectors must see the item you are registering in order to certify the certificate of registration. You can register items with Customs at the international airport from which you're departing. Keep the certificate for future trips.

### *Duty-Free Exemption*

The duty-free exemption, also called the personal exemption, is the total value of merchandise you may bring back to the United States without having to pay duty. You may bring back more than your exemption, but you will have to pay duty on it. In most cases, the personal exemption is $800, but there are some exceptions to this rule, which are explained below.

### *Exemptions*

Depending on the countries you have visited, your personal exemption will be $600, $800, or $1,200. (The differences are explained in the following section.) There are also limits on the amount of alcoholic beverages, cigarettes, cigars, and other tobacco products you may include in your duty-free personal exemption.

The duty-free exemptions ($600, $800, or $1,200) apply if:

- The items are for your personal or household use.

- They are in your possession (that is, they accompany you) when you return to the United States. Items to be sent later may not be included in your $800 duty-free exemption.

- They are declared to Customs. If you do not declare something that should have been declared, you risk forfeiting it. If in doubt, declare it.

- You are returning from an overseas stay of at least 48 hours. For example, if you leave the United States at 1:30 p.m. on June 1, you would complete the 48-hour period at 1:30 p.m. on June 3. This time limit does not apply if you are returning from Mexico or from the U.S. Virgin Islands. (See the section on the $200 exemption.)

- You have not used your exemption, or any part of it, in the past 30 days. If you use part of your exemption—for example, if you go to England and bring back $150 worth of items—you must wait another 30 days before you are allowed another $800 exemption. (However, see the section on the $200 exemption.)

- The items are not prohibited or restricted as discussed in the section on Prohibited and Restricted Items. Note the embargo prohibitions on products of Cuba.

*$200 Exemption*

If you can't claim other exemptions because you've been out of the country more than once in a 30-day period or because you haven't been out of the country for at least 48 hours, you may still bring back $200 worth of items free of duty and tax. As with the exemptions discussed earlier, these items must be for your personal or household use.

Each traveler is allowed this $200 exemption, but, unlike the other exemptions, family members may not group their exemptions. Thus, if Mr. and Mrs. Smith spend a night in Canada, each may bring back up to $200 worth of goods, but they would not be allowed a collective family exemption of $400.

Also, if you bring back more than $200 worth of dutiable items, or if any item is subject to duty or tax, the entire amount will be dutiable. Let's say you were out of the country for 36 hours and came back with a $300 piece of pottery. You could not deduct $200 from its value and pay duty on $100. The pottery would be dutiable for the full value of $300.

You may include with the $200 exemption your choice of the following: 50 cigarettes and 10 cigars and 150 milliliters (5 fl. oz.) of alcoholic beverages or 150 milliliters (5 fl. oz.) of perfume containing alcohol.

*$800 Exemption*

If you are returning from anywhere other than a Caribbean Basin country or a U.S. insular possession (U.S. Virgin Islands, American Samoa, or Guam), you may bring back $800 worth of items duty-free, as long as you bring them with you (this is called accompanied baggage).

Duty on items you mail home to yourself will be waived if the value is $200 or less. (See sections on "Gifts" and "Sending Goods to the United States.") Antiques that are at least 100 years old and fine art may enter duty-free, but folk art and handicrafts are generally dutiable.

This means that, depending on what items you're bringing back from your trip, you could come home with more than $800 worth of gifts or purchases and still not be charged duty. For instance, say you received a $700 bracelet as a gift, and you bought a $40 hat and a $60 color print. Because these items total $800, you would not be charged duty, because you have not exceeded your duty-free exemption. If you had also bought a $500 painting on that trip, you could bring all $1300 worth of merchandise home without having to pay duty, because fine art is duty-free.

*Tobacco Products*

Passengers/travelers may import previously exported tobacco products only in quantities not exceeding the amounts specified in exemptions for which the traveler qualifies. Any quantities of previously exported tobacco products not permitted by an exemption will be seized and destroyed. These items are typically purchased in duty-free stores, on carriers operating internationally, or in foreign stores. These items are usually marked "Tax Exempt. For Use outside the U.S.," or "U.S. Tax Exempt for Use outside the U.S."

For example, a returning resident is eligible for the $800 exemption, which includes not more than 200 cigarettes and 100 cigars. If the resident declares 400 previously exported cigarettes, the resident would be permitted 200 cigarettes, tax-free under the exemption and the remaining 200 previously exported cigarettes would be confiscated. If the resident declares 400 cigarettes, of which 200 are previously exported and 200 not previously exported, the resident would be permitted to import the 200 previously exported cigarettes tax free under the exemption and the resident would be charged duty and tax on the remaining 200 not previously exported cigarettes.

The tobacco exemption is available to each person. Tobacco products of Cuban origin, however, are prohibited unless you actually acquired them in Cuba and are returning directly or indirectly from that country on licensed travel. You may not, for example, bring in Cuban cigars purchased in Canada. Persons returning from Cuba may bring into the U.S. no more than $100 worth of goods.

*Alcoholic Beverages*

One liter (33.8 fl. oz.) of alcoholic beverages may be included in your exemption if:

- You are 21 years old.
- It is for your own use or as a gift.
- It does not violate the laws of the state in which you arrive.

Federal regulations allow you to bring back more than one liter of alcoholic beverage for personal use, but, as with extra tobacco, you will have to pay duty and Internal Revenue Service tax. While federal regulations do not specify a limit on the amount of alcohol you may bring back for personal use, unusual quantities are liable to raise suspicions that you are importing the alcohol for other purposes, such as for resale. Customs officers are authorized by Alcohol Tobacco and Firearms (ATF) make on-the-spot determinations that an importation is for commercial purposes, and may require you to obtain a permit to import the alcohol before leasing to you. If you intend to bring back a substantial quantity of alcohol for your personal use you should contact the Customs port you will be re-entering the country through, and make prior arrangements for entering the alcohol into the U.S.

Having said that, you should be aware that state laws may limit the amount of alcohol you can bring in without a license. If you arrive in a state that has limitations on the amount of alcohol you may bring in without a license, that state law will be enforced by Customs, even though it may be more restrictive than Federal regulations. We recommend that you check with the state government before you go abroad about their limitations on quantities allowed for personal importation and additional state taxes that might apply.

In brief, for both alcohol and tobacco, the quantities discussed in this booklet as being eligible for duty-free treatment may be included in your $800 (or $600 or $1,200) exemption, just as any other purchase would be. But unlike other kinds of merchandise, amounts beyond those discussed here as being duty-free are taxed, even if you have not exceeded, or even met, your personal exemption. For example, if your exemption is $800 and you bring back three liters of wine and nothing else, two of those liters will be dutiable. Federal law prohibits shipping alcoholic beverages by mail within the United States.

### $600 Exemption

If you are returning directly from any one of the following 24 Caribbean Basin countries, your customs exemption is $600:

- Antigua and Barbuda
- El Salvador
- Nicaragua
- Aruba
- Grenada
- Panama
- Bahamas
- Guatemala
- Saint Kitts and Nevis
- Barbados

- Guyana
- Saint Lucia
- Belize
- Haiti
- Saint Vincent and the Grenadines
- British Virgin Islands
- Honduras
- Trinidad and Tobago
- Costa Rica
- Jamaica
- Dominica
- Montserrat
- Dominican Republic
- Netherlands, Antilles

You may include two liters of alcoholic beverages with this $600 exemption, as long as one of the liters was produced in one of the countries listed above (see section on Unaccompanied Purchases from Insular Possessions and Caribbean Basin Countries).

*Travel to More Than One Country*

If you travel to a U.S. possession and to one or more of the Caribbean countries listed above (for example, on a Caribbean cruise), you may bring back $1,200 worth of items without paying duty. But only $600 worth of these items may come from the Caribbean country(ies); any amount beyond $600 will be dutiable unless you acquired it in one of the insular possessions.

For example, if you were to travel to the U.S. Virgin Islands and Jamaica, you would be allowed to bring back $1,200 worth of merchandise duty-free, as long as only $600 worth was acquired in Jamaica. (Keeping track of where your purchases occurred and having the receipts ready to show the Customs inspectors will help speed your clearing Customs.)

If you travel to any of the Caribbean countries listed above and to countries where the standard personal exemption of $800 applies—for example, a South American or European country—up to $800 worth of merchandise may come from the non-Caribbean country. For instance, if you travel to Venezuela and Trinidad and Tobago, your exemption is $600, only $200 of which may have been acquired in Venezuela.

*$1,200 Exemption*

If you return directly or indirectly from a U.S. Insular possession (U.S. Virgin Islands, American Samoa, or Guam), you are allowed a $1,200 duty-free exemption. You may include 1,000 cigarettes as part of this exemption, but at least 800 of them must have been acquired in an insular possession. Only 200 cigarettes may have been acquired elsewhere. For example, if you were touring the South Pacific and you stopped in Tahiti, American Samoa, and other ports of call, you could bring back five cartons of cigarettes, but four of them would have to have been bought in American Samoa.

Similarly, you may include five liters of alcoholic beverages in your duty-free exemption, but one of them must be a product of an insular possession. Four may be products of other countries (see section on Unaccompanied Purchases from Insular Possessions and Caribbean Basin Countries).

*Gifts*

Gifts you bring back from a trip abroad are considered to be for your personal use. They must be declared, but you may include them in your personal exemption. This includes gifts people gave you while you were out of the country, such as wedding or birthday presents, and gifts you've brought back for others. Gifts intended for business, promotional, or other commercial purposes may not be included in your duty-free exemption.

Gifts worth up to $100 may be received, free of duty and tax, by friends and relatives in the United States, as long as the same person does not receive more than $100 worth of gifts in a single day. If the gifts are mailed or shipped from an insular possession, this amount is increased to $200. When you return to the United States, you don't have to declare gifts you sent while you were on your trip, since they won't be accompanying you.

By federal law, alcoholic beverages, tobacco products, and perfume containing alcohol and worth more than $5 retail may not be included in the gift exemption.

Gifts for more than one person may be shipped in the same package, called a consolidated gift package, if they are individually wrapped and labeled with each recipient's name. Here's how to wrap and label a consolidated gift package:

Be sure to mark the outermost wrapper with:

- The words "UNSOLICITED GIFT" and the words "CONSOLIDATED GIFT PACKAGE";

- The total value of the consolidated package;

- The recipients' names; and

- The nature and value of the gifts inside (for example, tennis shoes, $50; shirt, $45; toy car, $15).

If any item in the consolidated gift parcel is subject to duty and tax or worth more than the $100 gift allowance, the entire package will be dutiable.

You, as a traveler, cannot send a "gift" package to yourself, and people traveling together cannot send "gifts" to each other. But there would be no reason to do that anyway, because the personal exemption for packages mailed from abroad is $200, which is twice as much as the gift exemption. If a package is subject to duty, the United States Postal Service will collect it from the addressee along with any postage and handling charges. The sender cannot prepay duty; it must be paid by the recipient when the package is received in the United States. (Packages sent by courier services are not eligible for this duty waiver.)

For more information about mailing packages to the United States, please contact your nearest Customs office and ask for our pamphlet "International Mail Imports."

### Duty-Free or Reduced Rates

*Items from Certain Countries*

The United States gives duty preferences—that is, free or reduced rates—to certain developing countries under a trade program called the Generalized System of Preferences (GSP). Some products that would otherwise be dutiable are not when they come from a GSP country. For details on this program, as well as the complete list of GSP countries, please ask your nearest Customs office for a copy of our pamphlet "Gsp & The Traveler."

Similarly, many products of Caribbean and Andean countries are exempt from duty under the Caribbean Basin Initiative, Caribbean Basin Trade Partnership Act, and Andean Trade Preference Act. Most products of certain sub-Saharan African countries are exempt from duty under the African Growth and Opportunity Act. Most products of Israel may also enter the United States either free of duty or at a reduced rate. Check with Customs for details on these programs.

The North American Free Trade Agreement (NAFTA) went into effect in 1994. If you are returning from Canada or Mexico, your goods are eligible for free or reduced duty rates if they were grown, manufactured, or produced in Canada or Mexico, as defined by the Act. Again, check with Customs for details.

*Personal Belongings*

Your personal belongings can be sent back to the United States duty-free if they are of U.S. origin and if they have not been altered or repaired while abroad. Personal belongings like worn clothing can be mailed home and will receive duty-free entry if you write the words "American Goods Returned" on the outside of the package.

*Household Effects*

Household effects include furniture, carpets, paintings, tableware, stereos, linens, and similar household furnishings. Tools of trade, professional books, implements, and instruments that you've taken out of the United States will be duty-free when you return.

You may import household effects you acquired abroad duty-free if:

- You used them for at least one year while you were abroad.

- They are not intended for anyone else or for sale.

Clothing, jewelry, photography equipment, portable radios, and vehicles are considered personal effects and cannot be brought in duty-free as household effects.

However, the amount of duty collected on them will be reduced according to the age of the item.

## Unaccompanied Purchases from Insular Possessions and Caribbean Countries

Unaccompanied purchases are goods you bought on a trip that are being mailed or shipped to you in the United States. In other words, you're not carrying them with you when you return. If your unaccompanied purchases are from an insular possession or a Caribbean Basin country and are being sent directly from those locations to the United States, you may enter them as follows:

- Up to $1,200 worth will be duty-free under your personal exemption if the merchandise is from an insular possession.

- Up to $600 worth will be duty-free if it is from a Caribbean Basin country.

- Of these amounts ($1,200 or $600), up to $800 worth will be duty-free if the merchandise was acquired elsewhere than the insular possessions or the Caribbean Basin. However, merchandise that qualifies for the $800 exemption must be in your possession when you return (must accompany you) in order for you to claim the duty-free exemption. The duty-free exemptions for unaccompanied baggage apply only to goods from the insular possessions and the Caribbean Basin countries listed earlier.

- An additional $1,000 worth of goods will be dutiable at a flat rate if they are from an insular possession, or from a Caribbean Basin country.

- If you are sending back more than $2,200 from an insular possession or more than $1,600 from a Caribbean Basin country, the duty rates in the Harmonized Tariff Schedules of the United States will apply. The Harmonized Tariff Schedule describes different rates of duty for different commodities; linen tablecloths, for example, will not have the same duty rates as handicrafts or plastic toy trucks.

### *Prohibited and Restricted Items*

The Customs Service has been entrusted with enforcing some 400 laws for 40 other government agencies, such as the Fish and Wildlife Service and the Department of Agriculture. These other agencies have great interest in what people bring into the country, but they are not always at ports of entry, guarding our borders. Customs is always at ports of entry—guarding the nation's borders is what we do.

The products we want to keep out of the United States are those that would injure community health, public safety, American workers, children, or domestic plant and animal life, or those that would defeat our national political interests. Sometimes the products that cause injury, or have the potential to do so, may seem fairly innocent. But, as you will see from the material that follows, appearances can be deceiving.

Before you leave for your trip abroad, you might want to talk to Customs about the items you plan to bring back to be sure they're not prohibited or restricted. Prohibited means the item is forbidden by law to enter the United States, period. Examples are dangerous toys, cars that don't protect their occupants in a crash, or illegal substances like absinthe and Rohypnol. Restricted means that special licenses or permits are required from a federal agency before the item is allowed to enter the United States. Examples are firearms and certain fruits, vegetables, pets, and textiles. [Below is a list of items that may be either restricted or prohibited. Contact U.S. Customs if you plan on bringing back items in any of the below categories.]

- Cultural Artifacts and Cultural Property (Art/Artifacts).
- Absinthe.
- Automobiles.
- Trademarked and Copyrighted Articles.
- Ceramic Tableware.
- Dog and Cat Fur.
- Drug Paraphernalia.
- Firearms.
- Fish and Wildlife.
- Game and Hunting Trophies.
- Food Products.
- Meats, Livestock, and Poultry.
- Fruits and Vegetables.
- Plants.
- Gold.
- Medication.
- Merchandise from Embargoed Countries.
- Pets.
- Textiles and Clothing.

# Part Five

# Other Travel Security Concerns

# Chapter 33

# *Travel Safety for Women while Abroad*

## *Her Own Way: Advice for the Woman Traveler*

From the young to businesswomen to energetic grandmothers, women are traveling like never before. They're traveling solo, in pairs, with their children and as members of interest groups. And while women travel for many of the same reasons as men do, their social concerns, as well as their health and safety needs, are very, very different.

Female travelers are directly affected by the religious and societal beliefs of the countries they visit. As they make their way around the globe, chances are they'll be called upon to adapt the way they dress or the manner in which they interact with the male population. They might even find that, in some places, it's inappropriate to be outdoors after sundown. The more that women prepare themselves for these differing attitudes, the richer and safer their traveling experiences will be. Whether you're a breast-feeding mother, a busy executive or an older traveler, as a woman you'll have a unique set of health concerns

---

This chapter includes excerpts from "Her Own Way: Advice for the Woman Traveler," published by the Department of Foreign Affairs and International Trade, Ottawa, ON, Canada, April 2002, and "Pregnancy, Breast-Feeding, and Travel: Factors Affecting the Decision to Travel," excerpted from *Health Information for International Travel, 2001-2002*, produced by the Centers for Disease Control and Prevention (CDC), available online at http://www.cdc.gov/travel/pregnant.htm.

to contend with on the road. A bit of pre-planning and research in this area will prove to be invaluable once you're on your way.

Everyone knows that, when traveling, a woman must be extra vigilant in terms of safety and security. What steps can she take to avoid possible sexual harassment? How can she make her hotel room secure? This chapter is filled with practical tips specifically of interest to the female traveler. Its prime objective is to inform and inspire women to travel safely.

## *Lessening the Culture Shock*

Knowledge itself is power. A smart traveler is one who finds out everything she can about the culture and customs, and the role of women, in the places she'll be visiting. It makes sense to learn what to expect and prepare yourself for as many eventualities as possible. One of your best sources of travel information is other women. Connect with them; ask for their advice. Note their recommendations on hotels, bed and breakfasts (B&Bs) and restaurants. Find out if they have friends or know of organizations or bookstores for you to contact at your destination. Tips and information from these sources can be invaluable.

In Southeast Asia, signs are posted at religious landmarks asking women not to enter if they're menstruating. Ask other women if you may read parts of their travel journals. If they don't mind sharing, this is a wonderful way of acquainting yourself with other cultures from a woman's point of view. It will also prepare you for the emotional highs and lows that may occur on your journey.

Don't count on mainstream media to present information specifically relevant to the female traveler. Instead, supplement your reading with travel books, newsletters, magazines and Web sites for women. They address, with appropriate empathy, the most important health, safety, cultural and emotional issues experienced by females on the road.

Surf the Net. Post your queries on on-line bulletin boards. You could get responses from helpful travelers around the world. But beware of those who may be using the Net for unsavory purposes. Seek out women in your community who were born and raised in the places you plan to visit. They are the perfect guides to appropriate behavior and dress for women within their culture. Get them to teach you a few key words and phrases in their mother tongue, too. Consider investing in a self-defense course designed for women. You'll embark on your journey with added confidence.

## Travel Light, Travel Smart

It's a good idea to travel light. As a woman alone, you'll be far less vulnerable and much more independent if you're not loaded down with heavy luggage and extra bags. Depending on your style of travel, a small suitcase on wheels or a backpack is a good luggage choice. Try to make sure you have at least one hand free at all times.

A few days before your departure, you might want to try some test walks. Pack your bag and make your way around the block. Visualize yourself climbing subway stairs or getting on and off a train unassisted. You'll probably go home and reduce the bag's contents by half. A fanny pack, tote bag or small day pack is useful for shorter excursions. If you plan to do a lot of shopping, you'll need an extra lightweight bag to bring your souvenirs home.

It's smart to keep your luggage locked at all times. Carry several small locks and two sets of keys. Avoid expensive-looking camera bags. They may only serve to identify you as a wealthy tourist. Be creative. Try using a diaper bag instead.

Luggage tags with flaps that hide your name and address from inquiring eyes are a smart idea. They protect your anonymity and thwart would-be thieves who may try to identify the empty home you've left behind.

Taking a handbag? One that has zippered inner compartments for added security and a thick shoulder strap that goes over your head as well as your shoulder is ideal. The best way to carry your handbag is in front of you, next to your stomach. This way, it isn't easily accessible to pickpockets.

## Extra Security Makes Sense

In your handbag or fanny pack, carry only those necessities that are lightweight and that you can afford to lose or have stolen. You should conceal those items that are not easily replaceable and are crucial to your travel arrangements—your passport, traveler's checks, cash, medical prescriptions, contact numbers for your doctor and a copy of your insurance policy—by carrying them close to your body.

You can use a cotton money belt that you wear around your waist or a cotton pouch that hangs around your neck and is concealed by loose-fitting clothes. Another excellent option is a security half-slip worn under a skirt or dress. Hidden under the hem are three zippered compartments perfect for holding travel documents, cash and credit cards. If you plan to spend time at the beach, consider buying a waterproof pack worn around the waist. It's a practical method of keeping your valuables safe and dry.

Be sure to make duplicate copies of all your important travel documents. Store these in your suitcase and, if the originals are lost or stolen, you'll have a workable backup system. It's also a good idea to leave copies of these documents with a family member or friend.

If you'll be traveling in developing countries, pack a small flashlight. Power failures can be frequent. Consider carefully whether to accept food or drink from strangers. Understand that drugging is always a possibility.

In any country you visit, avoid sightseeing in isolated places.

If you plan to rent a car, consider traveling with a cellular phone. If you do, make sure you have an emergency telephone number in case you experience a mechanical breakdown or find yourself in a dangerous situation. Never pick up hitchhikers. And never get out of your car if someone bumps into it; wait for the police to arrive.

### Air Travel

Remember that, when you're flying, your body has to adapt to changes in cabin pressure, the air you're breathing and different time zones. Traveling in comfortable, casual clothes that don't restrict body movement is a good idea. Also remember that your feet are bound to swell. Avoid traveling in pull-on boots; shoes with laces make the most sense. Lip balm and moisturizer can help to combat the dryness of aircraft cabins. Shoes are never worn in Muslim mosques and Buddhist temples. Travelers should pack a pair of heavy socks.

If you use contraceptive pills, be sure to take them every 24 hours. Don't be misled by crossing time zones.

A good way to minimize jet lag is to drink a glass of water for every hour you're in the air. Chewing gum will help relieve the pressure that builds up in your ears, especially during the plane's final descent.

### Accommodation

Choose your accommodation carefully. You may wish to consider small hotels, B&Bs or homestay exchanges. Their size generally allows for caring, personal attention. To avoid extra stress, travel early in the day, especially if you don't have reservations. This gives you time to find a place you like before it gets dark.

Whether the accommodation is a hotel, a B&B or a hostel, always ask to see the room before you take it. Is it clean enough? Does the door lock properly? Does it feel safe? Trust your intuition. Don't stay anywhere unless you feel entirely comfortable with both the accommodation and its location. Never accept a room if the check-in clerk calls out your name or room number. Others within hearing distance may use this information to try to call you or gain access to your room.

You should avoid ground-floor rooms or any room that has easy access from outside, such as from a balcony or fire escape. Book a room that is close to an elevator and away from exits. Stairwells allow troublemakers to hide and to come and go undetected.

Never open your door to anyone without taking the necessary precautions. Even if your visitor claims to be a member of the staff, you should check with the front desk to verify the person's need to enter your room. Consider investing in a small, lightweight, portable smoke detector, as well as a deadbolt that can easily be installed on any inward-opening door. These items are perfect if you plan to stay in very simple accommodation.

### Networking along the Way

For those who would like to connect with other women on the road, here are some suggestions:

- As soon as you begin your journey, start plugging into the female network. Finding a good source may lead you to many others. Local women are usually as pleased to meet you as you are to meet them.

- Carry referrals from women back home. Take advantage of the contacts they made when they traveled.

- In larger cities, make a quick check of local directories under the headings female, woman or travel. This can produce wonders. You'll probably find listings for craft collectives, women's bookstores, women's entrepreneurial councils and women's organizations.

- Check with the embassy or consulate for any listings of women's expatriate clubs and organizations. Members of these groups can sometimes be an excellent source of information. They might even invite you to one of their cultural events. Think about joining a female-guided walking tour. It's not only a wonderful way to learn about a place, but it's also a perfect way to meet other female travelers. Be sure to chat with the leader; she'll be a worthwhile source of female-friendly information.

- In less populated places, the person who runs the place where you're staying will probably know everyone in the village and will be ready to provide advice and introductions. Carry a small notepad and colored pencils. While children might not understand the language you speak, they'll delight in drawings you make for them.

- Pack photographs of your home and family. They're perfect icebreakers wherever you travel. If you can't make yourself understood in the local language, seek out female teenagers. Chances are they're studying some English at school and will take pride in being your translator.

### Dress Sense

When visiting a religious site, a woman should always dress conservatively. A woman traveler should carry a scarf in case she needs to cover her head. Give some thought to how you dress. At home, you'll encounter few, if any, clothing restrictions, but it still makes sense to dress conservatively. Leave your valuables at home.

If you travel into developing countries and male-dominated societies, make every effort to dress modestly. In some places, customs based on religious and moral beliefs strongly influence the way the women dress. For you to blatantly break these rules would be considered irreverent and might put you in jeopardy. Why not adapt your clothing to fit the customs of the host country? It becomes an interesting and educational challenge.

Outside North America, a one-piece swimsuit is always a safer choice than a bikini. In some countries, local women might swim entirely clothed, in accordance with their religious beliefs.

### Avoiding Harassment

Unfortunately, the potential for sexual harassment and intimidation is a reality around the world. Be prepared. Do your networking and research before you leave. Find out as much as you can about the roles of both women and men in the places you plan to visit. Avoid wearing provocative, form-fitting clothing.

In the Pacific Islands, a woman's thighs are considered an erotic part of her body and should not be exposed in public. A woman alone may be considered fair game. Understand this and prepare yourself mentally for any propositions, suggestive comments or catcalls. Then simply ignore them.

In some male-dominated cultures, it's considered incorrect for a woman to travel solo. For these and other potentially challenging destinations, you might want to team up with a companion. Two women traveling together might have an easier time.

In some cultures, making eye contact with a man is a sign that you want his company. Some women solve this problem by wearing dark glasses. Be aware that you'll probably be openly stared at. In countries where you look very different from everybody else, both men and women will make no attempt to hide their curiosity.

Behave confidently. When you're out, try to look as if you know exactly where you're going and what you're doing. Take your cue from the local women. As a general rule, if they don't sit in cafes alone, you shouldn't either. If they aren't wearing sleeveless dresses, neither should you.

Never accept car rides or hitchhike. Ask the local hotels to recommend reputable taxis and, whenever possible, try to double up with someone you know when traveling by cab.

In India, a female's upper arms are considered sensual areas of the body and therefore must never be exposed in public.

Crowded trains and buses can be perfect breeding grounds for antisocial behavior. Some men will use this opportunity to touch or pinch the female passengers standing close to them. If this happens to you, make a fuss. Point at the offender and chastise him in a loud voice. He'll probably slink away. However, to avoid these types of advances, consider choosing reserved seating. In countries where it is available, take advantage of the female-only section in buses, trains and subways. Use this excellent opportunity to communicate with local women and their children.

### Alone after Sundown

Women rightly tend to be more cautious about going out after sundown. However, that doesn't mean that you shouldn't go out at all. Simply take precautions. For example, in planning an evening out, arrange in advance to have a taxi take you there and back. When deciding where to eat dinner, choose a restaurant that is close to where you're staying.

In Saudi Arabia, a woman must wear an abbaya (a long black dress that covers the body from the shoulders to the toes). A scarf should be carried at all times to cover the head when requested.

Since it's always interesting to experience the sights and rhythms of a place after dark, consider joining a sightseeing group. Check with the local tourism center for any appropriate tours or cultural events that are available. Make sure that the tour bus picks you up and drops you off at your hotel or hostel.

Alternatively, you may appreciate matinee performances, which are far less expensive and may give you an opportunity to meet others. If you're not comfortable eating alone in the evening, have your main meal at lunchtime when even the finest restaurants offer their specialties at more reasonable prices.

During the day, why not stop at a market or supermarket and shop alongside the local women? You can learn about the food specialties of the area and put together a meal to eat as a picnic in your room. Even with wine, it's less expensive than eating out every night.

Understand that, in some parts of the world, respectable women don't go out alone in the evening. In these places, a flagrant rejection of this custom could very well put you in jeopardy. Instead, after a long day of sightseeing, welcome the opportunity to rest, relax and rejuvenate yourself, so you can be ready to enjoy another full day of new experiences.

### Maintaining Connections

You should maintain contact with at least one person back home, especially if you're traveling solo. By letter, fax, e-mail or telephone, let that person know where you are and where you're heading next.

Off traveling for the day? You should leave a note in your room explaining where you're going. If you run into trouble, at least there will be clues to follow. Always carry a business card from your hotel or B&B. If you get lost, approach another woman on the street and show her the address on the card. She may be able to point you in the right direction.

### Staying Healthy

Not all travel books deal with uniquely female health needs. You can augment what you read with the experienced advice of other women travelers. It's a good idea to carry your doctor's phone and fax numbers as well as copies of prescriptions for medication you might require along the way. You won't always be able to eat properly. Consider carrying multivitamins to supplement your diet. Your regular brand of contraceptive pill may not be available at your destination. Take enough with you to last the whole trip.

Major stomach upsets (diarrhea or vomiting) cause your body to lose its ability to absorb the contraceptive pill. It's wise to use condoms to guard against unwanted pregnancy. You may want to pack a supply of condoms to protect yourself against sexually transmitted diseases, too.

When traveling to developing countries, carry a supply of tampons and sanitary napkins. They tend to be difficult to find and may be expensive. It's not unusual for women to stop menstruating when they're traveling for a long time. If there are no other symptoms and you're not concerned that you might be pregnant, don't worry.

If you're prone to yeast infections, they're more likely to recur in warm, moist climates. Wearing loose-fitting cotton underwear and skirts rather than pants may help. Carry appropriate medication in your first-aid kit; it might not be available where you're traveling.

Cystitis is an infection of the urinary tract and bladder. Drinking a lot of purified water, especially in hotter climates, may help to reduce your chances of suffering from this problem.

If you wear contact lenses, consider using disposables. Storing and cleaning your lenses can become a nuisance if you're going to be on an extended journey.

It's definitely inadvisable to have ear-piercing, acupuncture, tattooing or manicures while you're on the road. Instruments that are not properly sterilized can carry hepatitis B or AIDS.

If you absolutely must have dental work, injections or an internal examination, contact the nearest embassy or consulate abroad. Officials there can often recommend appropriate local medical practitioners.

### *Getting Medical Advice*

Your risk of acquiring a disease while traveling depends on several factors. These include your age, your current state of health and immunization status, your itinerary, the duration and style of your trip, and anticipated activities (including contact with animals, exposure to fresh water, sexual contact), as well as the local disease situation.

Your travel plans should include contacting a travel medicine clinic or your physician six to eight weeks before departure. Based on an individual risk assessment, a health care professional can determine your need for immunizations and medication and can advise you on what precautions to take to avoid disease while traveling.

Consider joining the International Association for Medical Assistance to Travelers (IAMAT). This organization provides information on immunization requirements, health and climatic conditions, tropical diseases such as malaria, food and water sanitation, and maintains a list of English-speaking physicians around the world who have agreed to treat travelers.

If you have a pre-existing medical condition that could present a problem while you are traveling, it is wise to wear a MedicAlert® bracelet. Through the MedicAlert® Foundation, your vital medical facts are stored in a database that can be accessed 24 hours a day from anywhere in the world.

Make sure you don't leave without adequate health insurance for travelers. Review your policy thoroughly so that you know exactly what your coverage entails. For example, does your policy provide an in-house worldwide emergency hotline that you can call if you're in trouble? Does the policy pay foreign hospital and related medical costs? If so, does it pay up-front or expect you to pay and be reimbursed later? Carry proof of your coverage with you.

### Coping with Foreign Bathrooms

Modern bathrooms as we know them in North America do exist around the world, but not everywhere. As a traveler, you'll come across everything from outhouses to simple holes in the ground where squatting is a necessity. Some toilets will flush, but many won't. In developing countries, some cubicles are enclosed. However, as you venture further into the countryside, you might have to make do with little or no privacy.

To cope with the vagaries of foreign bathrooms, consider wearing a long, full skirt. This will allow for some modesty in situations where you have to go outdoors. Always carry a supply of toilet paper with you. In some parts of the world, it's either very scarce or too coarse to be usable. In parts of Asia and Africa, expect a jug of water, left beside the toilet, in lieu of paper.

The smell in toilets is sometimes overpowering. Try dabbing some mentholated ointment or lip balm under your nose to help mask the odors while you use the facilities. Carry your own antiseptic wipes or a small bar of soap. These are generally not readily available.

### Traveling with Children

When traveling by air with an infant, carry a bottle or pacifier for the baby to suck on during takeoff and landing. This helps to equalize ear pressure and keeps the baby more comfortable. If you're breast-feeding, take your cues from local women, since cultural practices vary from country to country. However, when in doubt, try to breast-feed in private.

Never leave a young child unattended. Always keep some form of identification in your child's pocket in case you accidentally become separated.

For emergency identification purposes, take along several recent photographs of your child. You may also wish to leave extra copies of those photographs with a family member. Teach your child never to open the door of your hotel room to anybody. When entering or leaving a hotel elevator, keep your child right beside you. If the doors close too quickly, he or she could be stranded.

If your child is under 16 and is not listed on your passport, you must have a certified document from the child's father giving permission for the child to travel. If you're traveling to another country with your child and there is a possibility of a custody dispute developing while you're away, talk to a lawyer before leaving home.

### The Older Traveler

This is a wonderful time in your life to be traveling. In most cultures, age brings respect. Children will gravitate to you. Local women will be protective, and you'll suffer less from unsolicited male advances.

Check your library for the many travel books written especially for the older adult. They contain valuable information about obtaining discounts, avoiding single supplements, educational holidays and the many group travel opportunities available for those of mature age.

Planning an adventure holiday involving hiking or a lot of walking? If you're not already involved in fitness activities, consider beginning an appropriate exercise program at least a month before your departure.

Expecting to carry a backpack? You might want to do a few training walks to get used to it. You can start light and work your way up to carrying the full capacity.

If you're experiencing the hot flashes of menopause, pack a wardrobe of layers that can easily be adjusted to your fluctuating body temperature.

A small magnifying glass is perfect for reading the tiny print on maps.

Make very sure that you have adequate health and travel insurance.

### Businesswomen Abroad

In many parts of the world, a woman's traditional role is in the home. The concept of a woman as a business executive is much less common. Understanding the customs and proper business protocol at your destination is imperative. Learn to greet your business host in his or her language. This show of respect and consideration is always appreciated. Always meet your business contacts in the lobby of your hotel. Avoid giving out your room number.

Print your business cards in English on one side and in the language of the host country on the other. Especially in countries where women generally don't hold key corporate positions, this will eliminate any misunderstanding about the rank and position you hold within your profession. Find out the correct way to give and receive business cards. In China (including Hong Kong) and Japan, you're expected to use both hands. However, in parts of the Middle East, you must never use your left hand, as that hand is considered unclean.

Dress appropriately. If local women don't wear trousers to the office, you shouldn't either. Wear sensible shoes that allow you to stand for long periods and to move quickly if necessary. Learn how to decline food graciously during business dinners so that no one will be insulted. For example, in Asia, leave some food in your bowl. This implies that your hosts have fed you well and you're no longer hungry.

Understand that, in some countries, even if you do business with men during the day, you may be seated separately, with women only, for evening dining. In certain cultures, businessmen may consider it acceptable to proposition or to flirt with visiting businesswomen. Don't be offended. A simple and direct no is appropriate.

Before offering gifts to your hosts, make sure that the type of present and even the color of the wrapping paper are culturally acceptable.

## Pregnancy, Breast-Feeding, and Travel: Factors Affecting the Decision to Travel

When deciding to travel, a pregnant woman should be advised to consider the potential problems associated with international travel, as well as the quality of medical care available at her destination and during transit. According to the American College of Obstetrics and Gynecology, the safest time for a pregnant woman to travel is during the second trimester (18 through 24 weeks) when she usually feels best and is in least danger of experiencing a spontaneous abortion or premature labor. A woman in the third trimester should be advised to stay within 300 miles of home because of concerns about access to medical care in case of problems such as hypertension, phlebitis, or false premature labor. Pregnant women should be advised to consult with their health care providers before making any travel decisions.

(See Table 33.1 for information on relative contraindications to international travel during pregnancy.)

## General Recommendations for Travel

Once a pregnant woman has decided to travel, a number of issues need to be considered prior to her departure. For instance, a pregnant woman should be advised to travel with at least one companion; she should also be advised that, during her pregnancy, her level of comfort might be adversely affected by traveling. Following are some guidelines for the pregnant traveler with regard to medical considerations.

### Guidelines for the Pregnant Traveler

The pregnant traveler should be advised to:

- Make sure, before traveling, that her health insurance is valid while abroad and during pregnancy, and that the policy covers a newborn should delivery take place. Also, a supplemental travel insurance policy and a prepaid medical evacuation insurance policy should be obtained, though most might not cover pregnancy-related problems.

- Check medical facilities at her destination. For a woman in the last trimester, medical facilities should be able to manage complications of pregnancy, toxemia, and cesarean sections.

- Determine beforehand whether prenatal care will be required abroad and, if so, who will provide it. The pregnant traveler should also make sure prenatal visits requiring specific timing are not missed.

- Determine, prior to traveling, whether blood is screened for human immunodeficiency virus (HIV) and hepatitis B at her destination. The pregnant traveler and her companion(s) also should be advised to know their blood types.

Motor vehicle accidents are a major cause of morbidity and mortality for pregnant women. When available, safety belts should be fastened at the pelvic area. Lap and shoulder restraints are best; in most accidents, the fetus recovers quickly from the safety belt pressure. However, even after seemingly blunt, mild trauma, a physician should be consulted.

411

Typical problems of pregnant travelers are the same as those experienced by pregnant nontravelers: fatigue, heartburn, indigestion, constipation, vaginal discharge, leg cramps, increased frequency of urination, and hemorrhoids. Signs and symptoms that indicate the need for immediate medical attention are bleeding, passing tissue or clots, abdominal pain or cramps, contractions, ruptured membranes, excessive leg swelling, headaches, or visual problems.

Hepatitis E (HEV), which is not vaccine preventable, can be especially problematic for pregnant women, for whom there is a case fatality rate of 17% to 33%. Therefore, pregnant women should be advised the best preventive measures are to avoid potentially contaminated water and food, as with other enteric infections.

### Breast-Feeding and Travel

The decision to travel internationally while nursing produces its own challenges. However, breast-feeding has nutritional and anti-infective advantages that serve an infant well while traveling.

Therefore, breast-feeding should be advised. Moreover, exclusive breast-feeding relieves concerns about sterilizing bottles and about availability of clean water. Supplements are usually not needed by breast-fed infants younger than 6 months of age, and breast-feeding should be maintained as long as possible. If supplementation is considered necessary, powdered formula that requires reconstitution with boiled water should be carried. For short trips, it may be feasible to carry an adequate supply of pre-prepared canned formula.

Nursing women may be immunized for maximum protection, depending on the travel itinerary, but consideration needs to be given to the neonate who cannot be immunized at birth and who would not gain protection against many infections (for example, yellow fever, measles, and meningococcal meningitis) through breast-feeding.

Neither inactivated nor live virus vaccines affect the safety of breast-feeding for mothers or infants. Breast-feeding does not adversely affect immunization and is not a contraindication to the administration of any vaccines, including live virus vaccines, for breast-feeding women. Although rubella vaccine virus may be transmitted in breast milk, the virus usually does not infect the infant and, if it does, the infection is well tolerated. Breast-fed infants should be vaccinated according to routine recommended schedules.

Nursing women should be advised that their eating and sleeping patterns, as well as stress, will inevitably affect their milk output. They need to increase their fluid intake; avoid excess alcohol and caffeine; and, as much as possible, avoid exposure to tobacco smoke.

## Specific Recommendations for Pregnancy and Travel

### Routine Immunizations

Because of the theoretical risks to the fetus from maternal vaccination, the risks and benefits of each immunization should be carefully reviewed. Ideally, all women who are pregnant should be up to date on their routine immunizations. In general, pregnant women

**Table 33.1.** Risk Factors for International Travel during Pregnancy

**Travelers with Obstetrical Risk Factors**

History of miscarriage.

Incompetent cervix.

History of ectopic pregnancy (ectopic with present pregnancy should be ruled out prior to travel).

History of premature labor or premature rupture of membranes.

History of or existing placental abnormalities.

Threatened abortion or vaginal bleeding during present pregnancy.

Multiple gestation in present pregnancy.

History of toxemia, hypertension, or diabetes with any pregnancy.

Primigravida at 35 years of age or older or 15 years of age or younger.

Valvular heart disease.

**Travelers with General Medical Risk Factors**

History of thromboembolic disease.

Severe anemia.

Chronic organ system dysfunction that requires frequent medical interventions.

**Travelers Contemplating Travel to Potentially Hazardous Destinations**

High altitudes.

Areas endemic for or with ongoing outbreaks of life-threatening food- or insect-borne infections.

Areas where chloroquine-resistant Plasmodium falciparum is endemic.

Areas where live virus vaccines are required and recommended.

should be advised to avoid live vaccines and to avoid becoming pregnant within 3 months of having received one; however, no harm to the fetus has been reported from the accidental administration of these vaccines during pregnancy (see Table 33.2).

**Diphtheria-Tetanus:** The combination diphtheria-tetanus immunization should be given if the pregnant traveler has not been immunized within 10 years, although preference would be for its administration during the second or third trimester.

**Measles, Mumps, and Rubella:** The measles vaccine, as well as the measles, mumps, and rubella (MMR) vaccines in combination, are live virus vaccines and are contraindicated in pregnancy. However, in cases in which the rubella vaccine was accidentally administered, no complications have been reported. Because of the increased incidence of measles in children in developing countries, and because of the disease's communicability and its potential for causing serious consequences in adults, it is advisable to recommend that nonimmune women delay traveling until after delivery, when immunization can be given safely. If a pregnant woman has a documented exposure to measles, immune globulin should be given within a 6-day period to prevent illness.

**Poliomyelitis:** It is important for the pregnant traveler to be protected against poliomyelitis. Paralytic disease can occur with greater frequency when infection develops during pregnancy. Anoxic fetal damage has also been reported, with up to 50% mortality in neonatal infection. If not previously immunized, a pregnant woman should be advised to have at least two doses of vaccine before travel (day 0 and at 1 month). Despite being a live virus vaccine, the oral poliovirus vaccine (OPV) was recommended in the past when immediate protection was needed. However, OPV is no longer available. There is no convincing evidence of adverse effects of inactivated poliovirus vaccine (IPV) in pregnant women or developing fetuses. However, it is prudent to avoid polio vaccination of pregnant women unless immediate protection is needed.

Breast-feeding does not interfere with successful immunization against polio.

**Hepatitis B:** The hepatitis B vaccine may be administered during pregnancy. Pregnant travelers should be advised to consult with their health care providers.

414

**Influenza:** The influenza and pneumococcal vaccines should be given to pregnant women with chronic diseases or pulmonary problems. In general, women with serious underlying illnesses should be advised not to travel to developing countries when pregnant.

*Travel-Related Immunization during Pregnancy*

**Yellow Fever:** The yellow fever vaccine should not be given to a pregnant woman unless travel to an endemic or epidemic area is unavoidable. In these instances, the vaccine can be administered. Although concerns exist, no congenital abnormalities have been reported after administration of this vaccine to pregnant women.

If traveling to or transiting regions within a country where the disease is not a current threat but where policy requires a yellow fever vaccination certificate, pregnant travelers should be advised to carry a physician's waiver, along with documentation (of the waiver) on the immunization record.

In general, pregnant women should be advised to postpone until after delivery (when vaccine can be administered without concern of fetal toxicity) travel to areas where yellow fever is a risk. However, a nursing mother should also delay travel because the neonate cannot be immunized because of the risk of vaccine-associated encephalitis.

**Hepatitis A:** Pregnant women without immunity to hepatitis A virus (HAV) need protection before traveling to developing countries. HAV is usually no more severe during pregnancy than at other times and does not affect the outcome of pregnancy. There have been reports, however, of acute fulminant disease in pregnant women during the third trimester, when there is also an increased risk of premature labor and fetal death. These events have occurred in women from developing countries and might have been related to underlying malnutrition. HAV is rarely transmitted to the fetus, but this can occur during viremia or from fecal contamination at delivery. Immune globulin is a safe and effective means of preventing HAV, but immunization with one of the HAV vaccines gives a more complete and prolonged protection. The effect of these inactivated virus vaccines on fetal development is unknown, but the production methods for the vaccines are similar to that for IPV, which is considered safe during pregnancy.

**Typhoid:** The safety of the oral Ty21a typhoid vaccine in pregnancy is not known. It is not absolutely contraindicated during pregnancy, according to the Advisory Committee on Immunization Practices

415

(ACIP). Nonetheless, the Vi capsular polysaccharide vaccine (ViCPS) injectable preparation is the vaccine of choice during pregnancy because it is inactivated and requires only one injection. With either of these, the vaccine efficacy (about 70%) needs to be weighed against the risk of disease.

**Meningococcal Meningitis:** The polyvalent meningococcal meningitis vaccine can be administered during pregnancy if the woman is entering an area where the disease is epidemic. Studies of vaccination during pregnancy have not documented adverse effects among either pregnant women or neonates. Based on data from studies involving the use of meningococcal vaccines and other polysaccharide vaccines administered during pregnancy, altering meningococcal vaccination recommendations during pregnancy is unnecessary.

**Rabies:** The cell-culture rabies vaccines may be given during pregnancy for either pre- or post-exposure prophylaxis.

**Japanese Encephalitis:** No information is available on the safety of Japanese encephalitis vaccine during pregnancy. It should not be routinely administered during pregnancy, except when a woman must stay in a high-risk area. If not mandatory, travel to such areas should be delayed.

**Miscellaneous:** Bacille Calmette-Guerin (BCG) vaccine for the prevention of tuberculosis can theoretically cause disseminated disease and, thus, affect the fetus. The vaccine is not recommended. Skin testing for tuberculosis exposure before and after travel is preferable when the risk is high.

## *Malaria during Pregnancy*

Malaria in pregnancy carries significant morbidity and mortality for both the mother and the fetus. Pregnant women should be advised to avoid travel to malarious areas if possible. Because no antimalarial agent is 100% effective, if pregnant women do travel to malarious areas, they should be advised to use personal protection measures. Pregnant women should remain indoors between dusk and dawn; however, if they are outdoors at night, they should wear light-colored clothing, long sleeves, long pants, and shoes and socks. Pregnant women should sleep in air-conditioned quarters or use screens and permethrin-impregnated bed nets.

**Table 33.2.** Vaccination during Pregnancy

| Vaccine | | Use |
|---|---|---|
| Hepatitis A | Inactivated virus | Data on safety in pregnancy are not available; the theoretical risk of vaccination should be weighed against the risk of disease. |
| Hepatitis B | Recombinant or plasma-derived | If indicated |
| Immune globulins, pooled or hyperimmune | Immune globulin or specific globulin preparations | If indicated |
| Influenza | Inactivated whole virus or subunit | If indicated |
| Japanese encephalitis | Inactivated virus | Data on safety in pregnancy are not available; the theoretical risk of vaccination should be weighed against the risk of disease. |
| Measles | Live attenuated virus | Contraindicated |
| Meningococcal meningitis | Polysaccharide | If indicated |
| Mumps | Live attenuated virus | Contraindicated |
| Pneumococcal | Polysaccharide | If indicated |
| Polio, inactivated | Inactivated virus | If indicated |
| Rabies | Inactivated virus | If indicated |
| Rubella | Live attenuated virus | Contraindicated |
| Tetanus-diphtheria | Toxoid | If indicated |
| Typhoid (ViCPS) | Polysaccharide | If indicated |
| Typhoid (Ty21a) | Live bacterial | Data on safety in pregnancy are not available. |
| Varicella | Live attenuated virus | If indicated |
| Yellow fever | Live attenuated virus | If indicated |

Pyrethrum-containing house sprays or coils may also be used indoors if insects are a problem. Insect repellents containing N,N-diethylmetatoluamide (DEET) (<35%) as recommended for adults should be used sparingly. Nursing mothers should advised to carefully to wash repellents off their hands and breast skin prior to handling infants.

For pregnant women who travel to areas without chloroquine-resistant *Plasmodium falciparum*, chloroquine has been used for malaria chemoprophylaxis for decades with no documented increase in birth defects. For pregnant women who travel to areas with chloroquine-resistant *P. falciparum*, mefloquine should be recommended for chemoprophylaxis during the second and third trimesters. For women in their first trimester, experience suggests that mefloquine causes no significant increase in spontaneous abortions or congenital malformations if taken during this period.

Because of evidence that chloroquine and mefloquine are not associated with congenital defects, the Centers for Disease Control and Prevention (CDC) do not recommend that women planning pregnancy need to wait a specific period of time after their use before becoming pregnant. However, if women or their health care providers wish to decrease the amount of antimalarial drug in the body before conception, Table 33.3 provides information on the half-lives of selected antimalarial drugs. After 2, 4, and 6 half-lives, approximately 25%, 6%, and 2% of the drug remains in the body.

Nursing mothers should be advised to take the usual adult dose of antimalarial appropriate for the country to be visited. The amount of medication in breast milk will not protect the infant from malaria. Therefore, the breast-feeding child needs his or her own prophylaxis.

Any pregnant traveler returning with malaria should be treated as a medical emergency. Women who have traveled to areas that have chloroquine-resistant strains of *P. falciparum* should be treated as if they have illness due to chloroquine-resistant organisms. Because of the serious nature of malaria, quinine or intravenous quinidine should be used and should be followed by Fansidar®, or even doxycycline, despite concerns regarding potential fetal problems. Frequent glucose levels and careful fluid monitoring often require intensive care supervision.

### *Travelers' Diarrhea during Pregnancy*

Pregnant travelers should be advised to exercise dietary vigilance while traveling during pregnancy because dehydration from travelers' diarrhea (TD) can lead to inadequate placental blood flow. They should also boil potentially contaminated water and avoid long-term use of iodine-containing purification systems. Iodine tablets can probably be used for travel up to several weeks, but congenital goiters have been reported in association with administration of iodine-containing drugs during pregnancy. Pregnant travelers should eat only well-cooked meats and pasteurized dairy products, while avoiding pre-prepared salads; this will help to avoid diarrheal disease, as well as infections such as toxoplasmosis and listeria, which can have serious sequelae in pregnancy. Pregnant women should be advised not to use prophylactic antibiotics for the prevention of TD.

Oral rehydration is the mainstay of TD therapy. Bismuth subsalicylate compounds are contraindicated because of the theoretical risks of fetal bleeding from salicylates and teratogenicity from the bismuth. The combination of kaolin and pectin may be used, but loperamide should be used only when necessary. The antibiotic treatment of TD during pregnancy can be complicated. An oral third-generation cephalosporin may be the best option for treatment if an antibiotic is needed.

Breast-feeding is desirable during travel and should be continued as long as possible because of its safety and the resulting lower incidence of infant diarrhea. A nursing mother with TD should not stop breast-feeding, but should increase her fluid intake.

### Air Travel during Pregnancy

Commercial air travel poses no special risks to a healthy pregnant woman or her fetus. The lowered cabin pressures (kept at the equivalent

**Table 33.3.** Half-Lives of Selected Antimalarial Drugs

| Drug | Half-Life |
| --- | --- |
| Chloroquine | Can extend from 6 to 60 days |
| Mefloquine | 2 to 3 weeks |
| Doxycycline | 12 to 24 hours |
| Atovaquone | 2 to 3 days |
| Proguanil | 14 to 21 hours |
| Primaquine | 4 to 7 hours |
| Sulfadoxine | 150 to 200 hours |
| Pyrimethamine | 80 to 95 hours |

of 1,524 to 2,438 meters [5,000 to 8,000 feet]) affect fetal oxygenation minimally because of the fetal hemoglobin dissociation curve. Severe anemia (hemoglobin, 0.5 grams per deciliter [g/dL]), sickle-cell disease or trait, a history of thrombophlebitis, or placental problems are relative contraindications to flying; however, supplemental oxygen can be ordered in advance. Each airline has policies regarding pregnancy and flying; it is always safest to check with the airline when booking reservations because some will require medical forms to be completed. Domestic travel is usually permitted until the pregnant traveler is in her 36th week of gestation, and international travel may be permitted until the 32nd week. A pregnant woman should be advised always to carry documentation stating her expected date of delivery.

An aisle seat at the bulkhead will provide the most space and comfort, but a seat over the wing in the midplane region will give the smoothest ride. A pregnant woman should be advised to walk every half hour during a smooth flight and flex and extend her ankles frequently to prevent phlebitis. The safety belt should always be fastened at the pelvic level. Fluids should be taken liberally because of the dehydrating effect of the low humidity in aircraft cabins.

Women traveling with neonates or infants should be advised to check with their pediatricians regarding any medical contraindications to flying. Infants are particularly susceptible to pain with eustachian tube collapse during pressure changes. Breast-feeding during ascent and descent relieves this discomfort.

## *The Travel Health Kit during Pregnancy*

Additions and substitutions to the usual travel health kit need to be made during pregnancy and nursing. Talcum powder, a thermometer, oral rehydration salts (ORS) packets, multivitamins, an antifungal agent for vaginal yeast, acetaminophen, insect repellent containing a low percentage of DEET, and a sunscreen with a high SPF should be carried. Women in their third trimesters may be advised to carry a blood pressure cuff and urine dipsticks so they can check for proteinuria and glucosuria, both of which would require attention. Antimalarial and antidiarrheal self-treatment medications should be evaluated individually, depending on the traveler, her trimester, the itinerary, and her health history. Most medications should be avoided, if possible.

# Chapter 34

# *Security for Elderly Travelers*

International travel can be a rich and rewarding adventure. Whether you have waited a lifetime to take the perfect trip or are an experienced world traveler, we would like to offer some advice to help you plan a safe and healthy trip.

American consuls at U.S. embassies and consulates abroad are there to help if you encounter serious difficulties in your travels. They are happy to meet you if you come in to register your passport at the Consular Section of the U.S. embassy or consulate. But it is also their duty to assist American citizens abroad in times of emergency—at hospitals or police stations, for instance. This chapter is written in the hopes that it will help you to prevent such emergencies from arising.

## *Preparation for Your Trip*

**Start early.** Apply for your passport as soon as possible. Three months before your departure date should give you plenty of time.

**Learn about the countries you plan to visit.** Before you go, read up on the culture, people, and history for the places you will travel. Bookstores and libraries are good resources. Travel magazines

---

"Travel Tips for Older Americans," 1996 U.S. Department of State, Bureau of Consular Affairs, publication number 10377. Cited November 2002. Available online at http://travel.state.gov/olderamericans.html. Despite the age of this document, readers seeking travel tips for older Americans will find this information useful.

and the travel sections of major newspapers tell about places to visit and also give advice on everything from discount airfares to international health insurance. Many travel agents and foreign tourist bureaus provide free information on travel abroad.

For up-to-date travel information on any country in the world that you plan to visit, obtain the Department of State's Consular Information Sheet. They cover such matters as health conditions, unusual currency and entry regulations, crime and security conditions, drug penalties, and areas of instability. In addition, the State Department issues travel warnings when it recommends Americans defer travel to a country because of unsafe conditions. Travel warnings are under continuous review by the Department of State and are removed when conditions warrant. The Department of State also issues public announcements as a means to disseminate information quickly about relatively short-term and/or trans-national conditions which would pose significant risks to the security of American travelers.

### *How to Access Consular Information Sheets, Travel Warnings and Public Announcements*

Consular Information Sheets, Travel Warnings and Public Announcements are available at any of the 13 regional passport agencies, field offices of the Department of Commerce, and U.S. embassies and consulates abroad, or, by sending a self-addressed, stamped envelope and indicating the desired country to the Office of Overseas Citizens Services, Bureau of Consular Affairs, Room 4811, U.S. Department of State, Washington, DC 20520-4818.

**By fax:** From your fax machine, dial (202) 647-3000, using the handset as you would a regular telephone. The system prompts you on how to proceed.

**By internet:** Information about travel and consular services is now available on the Internet's World Wide Web. The address is http://travel.state.gov. Visitors to the web site will find Travel Warnings, Public Announcements and Consular Information Sheets, passport and visa information, travel publications, background on international adoption and international child abduction services, international legal assistance, and the Consular Affairs mission statement. There is also a link to the State Department's main site on the Internet's World Wide Web that provides users with current foreign affairs information. The address is http://www.state.gov.

**Consular Affairs Bulletin Board (CABB):** If you have a personal computer, modem and communication software, you can access the Consular Affairs Bulletin Board (CABB). This service is free of charge. To view or download the documents from a computer and modem, dial the CABB on (301) 946-4400.

## Leave a Detailed Itinerary

Give a friend or relative your travel schedule. Include names, addresses, and telephone numbers of persons and places to be visited; your passport number and the date and place it was issued; and credit card, travelers check, and airline ticket numbers. Keep a copy of this information for yourself in a separate place from your purse or wallet. If you change your travel plans—for example, if you miss your return flight to the United States or extend your trip—be sure to notify relatives or friends at home.

## Don't over-Program

Allow time to relax and really enjoy yourself. Even if this is your once-in-a-lifetime trip, don't feel you have to fill every available minute. If you are visiting a country such as China, where physical activity can be quite strenuous and sudden changes in diet and climate can have serious health consequences for the unprepared traveler, consult your physician before you depart.

## What to Pack

Carefully consider the clothing you take. Don't pack more than you need and end up lugging around heavy suitcases. Wash-and-wear clothing and sturdy walking shoes are good ideas. Consider the climate and season in the countries you will visit and bring an extra outfit for unexpectedly warm or cool weather. A sweater or shawl is always useful for cooler evenings and air-conditioned planes and hotels. Dress conservatively—a wardrobe that is flashy or too causal may attract the attention of thieves or con artists.

Include a change of clothing in your carry-on luggage. Otherwise, if your bags are lost, you could be wearing the same clothes you were traveling in during the entire time it takes to locate your luggage— an average of 72 hours.

Do not pack anything that you would hate to lose such as valuable jewelry, family photographs, or objects of sentimental value.

## Passports and Visas

### Passports

It is a good idea to apply 3 months before you plan to travel. If you also need visas, allow more time as you must have a valid passport before applying for a visa. If this is your first passport, you must apply in person, bringing with you proof of U.S. citizenship (usually a certified copy of your birth certificate, previous U.S. passport, a naturalization certificate, or a Consular Report of Birth Abroad); 2 identical recent front-view photos (2" x 2"); a completed passport application (Form DS-11); proof of identity, such as a valid drivers license or other photo or physical-description I.D.; and the appropriate fee for a passport valid for 10 years.

You may apply at any passport agency or at one of the many clerks of court or post offices designated to accept passport applications. Your birth certificate or other documents will be returned to you by mail, along with your new passport.

You may be eligible to apply for a passport by mail. If you have had a passport issued within the past 12 years and you are able to mail that passport with your application, you can use Form DS-82, "Application for Passport by Mail," to apply. Obtain this form from any office that accepts passport applications or from your travel agent. Follow the instructions on the back of the form.

If you are leaving on an emergency trip within two weeks, apply in person at the nearest passport agency and present your tickets and itinerary from an airline, as well as the other required items. Or, apply at a court or post office and arrange to have the application sent to the passport agency through an overnight delivery service of your choice. (You should also include a self-addressed, pre-paid envelope for the return of the passport by express mail.) Be sure to include your dates of departure, travel plans on your application and all appropriate fees (including the $35 expedite fee).

When you receive your passport, be sure to sign it on page 1 and to pencil in on page 4 the requested information. This will help us notify your family or friends in case of an accident or other emergency. Do not designate your traveling companion as the person to be notified in case of an emergency.

### Visas

Many countries require a visa—an endorsement or stamp placed in your passport by a foreign government that permits you to visit that country for a specified purpose and a limited time. A number of countries require you to obtain a visa from the embassy or consular office nearest to your residence. The addresses of foreign consular offices can be found in telephone directories of large cities or in the Congressional Directory, available in most libraries; or you may write to the appropriate embassy in Washington, D.C. and request the address of their consulate that is nearest to you. You can also obtain the Department of State booklet, *Foreign Entry Requirements*, which lists visa and other entry requirements and locations of all foreign embassies and consulates in the U.S. Apply for your visa directly to the embassy or consulate of each country you plan to visit or ask your travel agent to assist you with visas. U.S. passport agencies cannot obtain visas for you.

An increasing number of countries are establishing entry requirements regarding AIDS testing, particularly for long-term residents and students. Check with the embassy or consulate of the countries you plan to visit for the latest information.

## Health

Health problems sometimes affect visitors abroad. Information on health precautions can be obtained from local health departments or private doctors. General guidance can also be found in the Centers for Disease Control and Prevention's (CDC) book, Health Information for International Travel, available from the Superintendent of Documents, U.S. Government Printing Office, Washington, D.C. 20402, or the CDC's international travelers hotline at (404) 332-4559.

### Health Insurance

It is wise to review your health insurance policy before you travel. In some places, particularly at resorts, medical costs can be as high or higher than in the United States. If your insurance policy does not cover you abroad, it is strongly recommended that you purchase a policy that does. There are short-term health insurance policies designed specifically to cover travel. If your travel agent cannot direct you to a medical assistance company, look for information in travel magazines. The U.S. government cannot pay to have you medically evacuated to the United States.

The Social Security Medicare program does not provide for payment of hospital or medical services obtained outside the United States. However, some Medicare supplement plans offer foreign medical care coverage at no extra cost for treatments considered eligible under Medicare. These are reimbursement plans. You must pay the bills first and obtain receipts for submission them later for compensation. Many of these plans have a dollar ceiling per trip.

Review your health insurance policy. Obtaining medical treatment and hospital care abroad can be expensive. If your Medicare supplement or other medical insurance does not provide protection while traveling outside the United States, we strongly urge you to buy coverage that does. The names of some of the companies offering short-term health and emergency assistance policies are listed in the Bureau of Consular Affairs flyer, *Medical Information for Americans Traveling Abroad*. The flyer is available by sending a stamped, self-addressed envelope to Bureau of Consular Affairs, Room 6831, U.S. Department of State, Washington, DC 20520-4818.

### *Trip Insurance*

One sure way to ruin a vacation is to lose money because an emergency forces you to postpone or cancel your trip. Except for tickets on regularly scheduled airlines, almost any travel package you purchase will have a penalty for cancellation and some companies will give no refund at all. Regularly scheduled airlines usually give a refund if an illness or death in the family forces you to cancel. Airlines require a note from the doctor or a death certificate. Take careful note of the cancellation penalty for any other large travel purchase you make, such as a tour package, charter flight, or cruise. Unless you can afford to lose the purchase amount, protect yourself by buying trip insurance. If you invest in trip insurance, make sure your policy covers all reasonable possibilities for having to cancel. For instance, if an emergency with a family member would force you to cancel, insure against that as well.

Some trip insurance policies will give a refund if the company goes out of business or otherwise does not make good on its offering. The best insurance against company default is to choose a reputable company that guarantees a refund if they do not provide the services procured. If, however, you are tempted to purchase a tour at a great bargain price and you can't find a guarantee of delivery in the fine print, protect yourself by purchasing trip insurance that covers company default.

Shop around for the trip insurance policy that offers the most benefits. Some credit card and traveler's check companies offer travel protection packages for an additional fee. Benefits may even include accident and illness coverage while traveling.

### Immunizations

Information on immunizations and health precautions for travelers can be obtained from local health departments, the Centers for Disease Control and Prevention's international travelers hotline at (404) 332-4559, private doctors, or travel clinics. General guidance can also be found in the U.S. Public Health Service book, *Health Information for International Travel*. Immunizations are normally recommended against diphtheria, tetanus, polio, typhoid, and hepatitis A for travelers. Generally, these immunizations are administered during childhood.

### Medical Assistance Programs

One strong advantage of medical assistance programs is that they also cover the exorbitant cost of medical evacuation in the event of an accident or serious illness. As part of the coverage, these companies usually offer emergency consultation by telephone. They may refer you to the nearest hospital or call directly for help for you. If you need an interpreter, they may translate your instructions to a health care worker on the scene. Another benefit that is normally part of such coverage is payment for the return of remains to the United States in case of death.

If your regular health insurance already covers you for medical expenses abroad, you can buy a medical assistance program that offers all the consultative and evacuation services listed above except for the health insurance itself. Cost of medical assistance coverage is usually inexpensive without health insurance coverage or a little more for the complete medical assistance program including health insurance. On the other hand, escorted medical evacuation can cost thousands of dollars.

If your travel agent cannot direct you to a medical assistance company, look for information on such services in travel magazines. Once you have adequate coverage, carry your insurance policy identity cards and claim forms with you when you travel.

### Medication

If you require medication, bring an ample supply in its original containers. Do not use pill cases. Because of strict laws concerning narcotics throughout the world, bring along copies of your prescriptions and, if possible, carry a letter from your physician explaining your need for the drug. As an extra precaution, carry the generic names of your medications with you because pharmaceutical companies overseas may use different names from those used in the United States.

If you wear eyeglasses, take an extra pair with you. Pack medicines and extra eyeglasses in your hand luggage so they will be available in case your checked luggage is lost. To be extra secure, pack a backup supply of medicines and an additional pair of eyeglasses in your checked luggage. If you have allergies, reactions to certain medications, foods, or insect bites, or other unique medical problems, consider wearing a medical alert bracelet. You may also wish to carry a letter from your physician explaining desired treatment should you become ill.

## Medical Assistance Abroad

If you get sick, you can contact a consular officer at the nearest U.S. embassy or consulate for a list of local doctors, dentists, and medical specialists, along with other medical information. If you are injured or become seriously ill, a consul will help you find medical assistance and, at your request, inform your family or friends. The list of English speaking doctors is also available before you travel by writing to the Office of Overseas Citizens Services, Room 4811, 2201 C Street, NW, Washington, DC 20520. Please specify to which country you will be traveling.

## Health Precautions

Air pollution abroad may sometimes be severe. Air pollution and high altitudes are a particular health risk for the elderly and persons with high blood pressure, anemia, or respiratory or cardiac problems. If this applies to you, consult your doctor before traveling.

In high altitude areas most people need a short adjustment period. If traveling to such an area, spend the first few days in a leisurely manner with a light diet and reduced intake of alcohol. Avoid strenuous activity, this includes everything from sports to rushing up the stairs. Reaction signs to high altitude are lack of energy, a tendency to tire easily, shortness of breath, occasional dizziness, and insomnia.

If possible, drink only bottled water or water that has been boiled for 20 minutes. Be aware of ice cubes that may not have been made with purified water. Vegetables and fruits should be peeled or washed in a purifying solution. A good rule to follow is if you can't peel it or cook it, do not eat it. Diarrhea may be treated with antimicrobial treatment which may be prescribed or purchased over the counter. Travelers should consult a physician, rather than attempt self-medication, if the diarrhea is severe or persists several days.

### Charter Flights

Before you pay for a charter flight or travel package, read your contract carefully and see what guarantee it gives that the company will deliver the services that it is trying to sell you. Tour operators sometimes go out of business in the middle of a season, leaving passengers stranded, holding unusable return tickets and unable to obtain a refund for the unused portion of their trip. Unless you are certain a company is reputable, check its credentials with your local Better Business Bureau (BBB). The BBB maintains complaint files for a year.

## Money and Valuables

*Don't take your money in cash.* Bring most of your money in traveler's checks. Have a reasonable amount of cash with you, but not more than you will need for a day or two. Convert your traveler's checks to local currency as you use them rather than all at once.

You may also wish to bring at least one internationally-recognized credit card. Before you leave, find out what your credit card limit is and do not exceed it. In some countries, travelers who have innocently exceeded their limit have been arrested for fraud. Leave unneeded credit cards at home.

ATMs (Automated Teller Machines) are becoming increasingly popular in some of the more modern countries abroad. Often these ATMs can be accessed by your local bank card depending on which service is available. The exchange rates are comparable to the going rate of exchange. Check with your local bank to find out which ATM service is available in the country you plan to visit. Because ATMs may not always be available, this should be used as only a backup method and not depended on solely for all your financial transactions abroad.

If you must take jewelry or other valuables, use hotel security vaults to store them. It is wise to register such items with U.S. Customs before leaving the United States to make customs processing easier when you return.

It is a violation of law in some countries to enter or exit with that country's currency. Check with a travel agent or the embassy or consulate of the countries you plan to visit to learn their currency restrictions. Before departing from the U.S., you may wish, if allowed, to purchase small amounts of foreign currency and coins to use for buses, taxis, telephone calls, and other incidentals when you first arrive in a country. You may purchase foreign currency from some banks or from foreign exchange dealers. Most international airports also have money exchange facilities.

Once you are abroad, local banks generally give more favorable rates of exchange than hotels, restaurants, or stores for converting your U.S. dollars and traveler's checks into foreign currency.

## Your Trip

*Driving.* U.S. auto insurance is usually not valid outside of the United States and Canada. When you drive in any other country, be sure to buy adequate auto insurance in that country. When renting a car abroad, make certain that adequate insurance is part of your contract; otherwise, purchase additional coverage in an amount similar to that which you carry at home. Also, prior to driving in a foreign country, familiarize yourself with the metric system since countries abroad display speed limits in kilometers per hour. Remember: If you plan to rent a car, keep in mind which side of the road traffic moves. Unlike the U.S., many countries drive on the left hand side of the road.

*Flying.* On overseas flights, break up long periods of sitting. Leave your seat from time to time and also do in-place exercises. This will help prevent you from arriving tired and stiff-jointed. Also, get some exercise after a long flight. For example, take a walk or use your hotel's exercise room.

*Reconfirm.* Upon arrival at each stopover, reconfirm your onward reservations. When possible, obtain a written confirmation. International flights generally require confirmation 72 hours in advance. If your name does not appear on the reservation list, you could find yourself stranded.

*Register.* If you plan to be in a location for 2 weeks or more or in an area where there is civil unrest or any other emergency situation, register with the nearest U.S. embassy or consulate. This will help in locating you, should someone in the United States wish to confirm your safety and welfare or need to contact you urgently.

## Practical Safety Precautions

*Respect the local laws and customs.* While abroad, you are subject to the laws and regulations of your host country and are not protected by the U.S. Constitution. If you should be detained by local authorities, ask them to notify a U.S. consular officer. Under international agreements and practice, you have a right to contact an American consul. Although U.S. consuls cannot act as your attorney or get you out of jail, they can provide you with a list of local attorneys and inform you of your rights under local laws. They will also monitor the status of detained Americans and make sure they are treated fairly under local laws.

*Guard your passport.* Your passport is the most valuable document you carry abroad. It confirms that you are an American citizen. Do not carry your passport in the same place as your money or pack it in your luggage. Remember to keep your passport number in a separate location in case it is lost or stolen. In some countries, you may be required to leave your passport overnight or for several days with the hotel management. This may be local practice—do not be concerned unless the passport is not returned as promised. If your passport is lost or stolen abroad, immediately report it to the local police, obtain a copy of the report, and contact the nearest U.S. embassy or consulate to apply for a new passport.

*Be alert.* Move purposefully and confidently. If you should find yourself in a crowded area, such as in an elevator, subway, marketplace, or in busy tourist areas, exercise special caution to avoid theft.

*Robbery.* Help prevent theft by carrying your belongings securely. Carry purses tucked under an arm and not dangling by a strap. Carry valuables hidden in an inside front pocket or in a money belt, not in a hip pocket. You may wish to wrap your wallet with rubber bands to make it more difficult for someone to slip it from your pocket unnoticed. Money belts or pouches that fit around your shoulder, waist or under clothing are available through some luggage shops and department stores.

## Assistance from U.S. Embassies and Consulates

*Emergencies.* If you encounter serious legal, medical, or financial difficulties or other problems abroad, contact the nearest U.S. embassy or consulate for assistance. Although consular officers cannot serve as attorneys, they can help you find legal assistance. Consular officers cannot cash checks, lend money, or act as travel agents. However, in an emergency, consular officers can help you get in touch with your family back home to inform them on how to wire funds to you and to let them know of your situation. Consular officers can also provide you with the latest information about adverse conditions abroad.

*Nonemergencies.* Consular officers also provide nonemergency services such as information on absentee voting and acquisition or loss of U.S. citizenship. They can arrange for the transfer of Social Security and other benefits to Americans residing abroad, provide U.S. tax forms, notarize documents, and advise U.S. citizens on property claims.

*Safeguarding your health.* If you are injured or become seriously ill abroad, a U.S. consular officer will assist you in finding a physician or other medical services, and, with your permission, will inform your family members or friends of your condition. If needed, consular officers can assist your family in transferring money to the foreign country to pay for your treatment.

*Death abroad.* Each year, about 6,000 Americans die abroad. Two thirds of them are Americans who live overseas, but approximately 2,000 Americans per year die while visiting abroad. Consular officers will contact the next of kin in the United States and will explain the local requirements. It is a worthwhile precaution to have insurance that covers the cost of local burial or shipment of remains home to the United States. Otherwise, this cost must be borne by your next of kin and can be extremely expensive. The U.S. government cannot pay for shipment of remains to the United States.

## *Shopping—Some Things to Avoid*

Beware of purchasing souvenirs made from endangered wildlife. Many wildlife and wildlife products are prohibited either by U.S. or foreign laws from import into the United States. You risk confiscation and a possible fine if you attempt to import such things. Watch out for and avoid purchasing the following prohibited items:

- All products made from sea turtles.

- All ivory, both Asian and African.

- Furs from spotted cats.

- Furs from marine mammals.

- Feathers and feather products from wild birds.

- All live or stuffed birds from Australia, Brazil, Colombia, Costa Rica, Ecuador, Guatemala, Mexico, Paraguay, Venezuela, and some Caribbean countries.

- Most crocodile and caiman leather.

- Most coral, whether in chunks or in jewelry.

### When You Return

*Be prepared.* On arrival in the United States, have your passport ready when you go through immigration and customs controls. Keep receipts for any items you purchased abroad. U.S. citizens may bring back and orally declare $400 worth of merchandise duty free. The next $1000 is taxed at a flat rate of 10%. Check with U.S. Customs for further information.

*Currency.* There is no limit on the amount of money or negotiable instruments which can be brought into or taken out of the United States. However, any amount over $10,000 must be reported to U.S. Customs on Customs Form 4790 when you depart from or enter into the United States.

*Foreign produce.* Don't bring home any fresh fruits or vegetables. Such items will be confiscated.

### Other Useful Travel Publications

For the official word on immunizations, customs, what you can legally bring into the United States, and how to protect yourself from business fraud, you may order one of the following U.S. Government publications:

- *Health Information for International Travel* is a comprehensive listing of immunization requirements of foreign governments. In addition, it gives the Centers for Disease Control and Prevention's recommendations on immunizations and other health precautions for international travelers. Copies are available from the Superintendent of Documents, U.S. Government Printing Office, (202) 512-1800.

- *Know before You Go, Customs Hints for Returning U.S. Residents* gives detailed information on U.S. Customs regulations, including duty rates. Single copies are available free from any local Customs office or by writing to the U.S. Customs Service, http://www.customs.gov.

- *Don't Pack a Pest* lists the regulations on bringing agricultural items into the United States from most parts of the world. Fresh fruits and vegetables, meat, potted plants, pet birds, and other items are prohibited or restricted. Obtain the publication free from the Animal and Plant Health Inspection Service, U.S. Department of Agriculture, 732 Federal Bldg., 6505 Belcrest Road, Hyattsville, Maryland 20782.

- *Buyer Beware!* is prepared by the World Wildlife Fund. This publication provides information about restrictions on importing wildlife and wildlife products. For a free copy, write to the Publications Unit, U.S. Fish and Wildlife Service, Department of the Interior, Washington, DC 20240.

- *Tips for Business Travelers to Nigeria* is designed to help U.S. citizens doing business in Nigeria identify business scams, and provide them with information about what the U.S. Government can or cannot do to assist them. The booklet is free by sending a self-addressed, stamped envelope to CA/OCS/ACS/AF, Room 4811, U.S. Department of State, Washington, DC 20520-4818.

The following publications from the Department of State may be ordered for $1–$1.50 each from the Superintendent of Documents, U.S. Government Printing Office (GPO), Washington, DC 20402; tel. (202) 512-1800. (Prices and availability are subject to change without notice. Check pricing information with the GPO before ordering.)

- *Your Trip Abroad* provides basic travel information—tips on passports, visas, immunizations, and more. It will help you prepare for your trip and make it as trouble-free as possible.

- *A Safe Trip Abroad* gives travel security advice for any traveler, but particularly for those who plan trips to areas of high crime or terrorism.

- *Tips for Americans Residing Abroad* is prepared for the more than 3 million Americans who live in foreign countries.

The following publications are also from the Department of State:

- *Foreign Entry Requirements* lists visa and other entry requirements of foreign countries and tells you how to apply for visas and tourist cards. Order this publication from the Consumer Information Center, Pueblo, CO 81009.

- *Key Officers of Foreign Service Posts* gives addresses and telephone, telex, and fax numbers for all U.S. embassies and consulates abroad.

- *Background Notes* are brief, factual pamphlets on all countries in the world. They give current information on each country's people, culture, geography, history, government, economy, and political condition and include a factual profile, brief travel notes, a country map, and suggested reading list. For information on their price and to order copies contact: U.S. Government Printing Office at (202) 512-1800. You may also obtain select issues by fax by calling the State Department's Bureau of Public Affairs Fax on Demand at (202) 763-7720 from your fax machine.

# Chapter 35

# *Safety for Students Traveling Internationally*

## *Travel Tips for Students: Preparing for Your Trip Abroad*

*Apply early for your passport and, if necessary, any visas.* Passports are required to enter and/or depart most countries around the world. Apply for a passport as soon as possible. Some countries also require U.S. citizens to obtain visas before entering. Most countries require visitors who are planning to study or work abroad to obtain visas before entering. Check with the embassy of the foreign country that you are planning to visit for up-to-date visa and other entry requirements. (Passport and visa information is available on the Internet at http://travel.state.gov.)

*Learn about the countries that you plan to visit.* Before departing, take the time to do some research about the people and their culture, and any problems that the country is experiencing that may affect

This chapter contains "Travel Tips for Students," Bureau of Consular Affairs, United States Department of State, September 2000, available online at http://travel.state.gov/student_tips_brochure.html; "Tips for Students," an undated document from the Bureau of Consular Affairs, United States Department of State, cited November 2002, available online at http://travel.state.gov/studentinfo.html. This chapter also includes "Maintaining Mental and Emotional Health," © 1999. Rhodes, Gary M., Ph.D. (Editor), Center for Global Education, University of Southern California, SAFETI Clearinghouse, www.usc.edu/globaled/safeti. This material is adapted by Dr. Rhodes from "Maintaining Strong Mental and Emotional Health," *Pre-Service Health Training for Volunteers Binder*, Peace Corps Office of Medical Services.

your travel plans. The Department of State publishes *Background Notes* on about 170 countries. These brief, factual pamphlets contain information on each country's culture, history, geography, economy, government, and current political situation. *Background Notes* are available at http://www.state.gov.

*Read the consular information sheet.* Consular information sheets provide up-to-date travel information on any country in the world that you plan to visit. They cover topics such as entry regulations, the crime and security situation, drug penalties, road conditions, and the location of the U.S. embassy, consulates, and consular agencies.

*Check for travel warnings and public announcements.* Travel warnings recommend U.S. citizens defer travel to a country because of dangerous conditions. Public announcements provide fast-breaking information about relatively short-term conditions that may pose risks to the security of travelers.

*Find out the location of the nearest U.S. embassy or consulate.* If you are traveling to a remote area or one that is experiencing civil unrest, find out the location of the nearest U.S. embassy or consulate and register with the consular section when you arrive. (U.S. embassy and consulate locations can be found in the country's consular information sheet.) If your family needs to reach you because of an emergency, they can pass a message to you through the Office of Overseas Citizens Services at 202-647-5225. This office will contact the embassy or consulate in the country where you are traveling and pass a message from your family to you. Remember consular officers cannot cash checks, lend money or serve as your attorney. They can, however, if the need arises, assist you in obtaining emergency funds from your family, help you find an attorney, help you find medical assistance, and replace your lost or stolen passport.

*Find out what information your school offers.* Find out whether your school offers additional information for students who are planning to study, travel, or work abroad. Many student advisors can provide you with information about studying or working abroad. They may also be able to provide you with information on any travel benefits for students (e.g. how to save money on transportation and accommodations, and other resources.)

*Before committing yourself or your finances, find out about the organization and what it offers.* The majority of private programs for vacation, study or work abroad are reputable and financially sound. However, some charge exorbitant fees, use deliberately false educational claims, and provide working conditions far different from those advertised. Even programs of legitimate organizations can be poorly administered.

### How to Access Consular Information Sheets, Travel Warnings, and Public Announcements

There are four ways to obtain consular information sheets, travel warnings, and public announcements:

- Internet: http://travel.state.gov

- Telephone: Dial the Office of Overseas Citizens Services at 202-647-5225.

- Fax-on-demand: From your fax machine dial 202-647-3000, using the handset as you would a regular phone. The system prompts you on how to proceed.

- Mail: Send a self-addressed, stamped business-size envelope to: Overseas Citizens Services, Room 4811, Department of State, Washington, DC 20520-4818. On the outside envelope, write the name of the country or countries needed in the lower left corner.

- Also available at http://travel.state.gov: passport applications and procedures, foreign and U.S. visa information, travel publications (including the pamphlet *Travel Warning on Drugs Abroad*), links to several U.S. embassy and consulate web sites worldwide, and other sources of information for students.

### Top Ten Travel Tips for Students

1. Make sure you have a signed, valid passport and visas, if required. Also, before you go, fill in the emergency information page of your passport.

2. Read the consular information sheets (and public announcements or travel warnings, if applicable) for the countries you plan to visit.

3. Leave copies of your itinerary, passport data page and visas with family or friends at home, so that you can be contacted in case of an emergency. Keep your host program informed of your whereabouts.

4.  Make sure you have insurance that will cover your emergency medical needs (including medical evacuation) while you are overseas.

5.  Familiarize yourself with local laws and customs of the countries to which you are traveling. Remember, while in a foreign country, you are subject to its laws.

6.  Do not leave your luggage unattended in public areas and never accept packages from strangers.

7.  While abroad, avoid using illicit drugs or drinking excessive amounts of alcoholic beverages, and associating with people who do.

8.  Do not become a target for thieves by wearing conspicuous clothing and expensive jewelry and do not carry excessive amounts of cash or unnecessary credit cards.

9.  Deal only with authorized agents when you exchange money to avoid violating local laws.

10. When overseas, avoid demonstrations and other situations that may become unruly or where anti-American sentiments may be expressed.

## More Tips for Students

The Department of State offers the following information for student advisors and for their students who plan to travel and/or study abroad. (This is an official U.S. Government source. Inclusion of non-U.S. Government links does not imply endorsement of contents.)

### Students Should Learn as Much as Possible about the Countries in Which They Plan to Travel or Study

Students should read the State Department's consular information sheet for the country in which they plan to study or visit, and check any public announcements or travel warnings that may pertain to that particular country. A consular information sheet is available for every country in the world and provides an overview of conditions pertaining to travel in each country.

Students should learn about the history, culture, politics and customs of the country/countries in which they travel and study, and to respect the country's customs, manners, rules and laws. For instance, various countries and cultures respect certain manners and dress codes. American students should also abide by these manners and dress codes as much as possible.

It is a good idea for students to learn as much as they can of the language of the country in which they plan to travel or study. Learning basic phrases of the language can be helpful, and it indicates a willingness on the part of students to make an effort to communicate in the language of the country.

The Department of State publishes *Background Notes* on countries worldwide. These are brief, factual pamphlets with information on each country's culture, history, geography, economy, government and current political situation. *Background Notes* are available for approximately 170 countries. They often include a reading list, travel notes and maps.

It is important that students learn about the local laws abroad and obey them. Remember, while in a foreign country, you are subject to its laws. This year, the State Department has issued two press releases: a press release for college newspapers on travel safety abroad for students and a press release on spring break in Cancun, reminding students about drug laws and drunk and disorderly conduct during spring and summer breaks.

### What Students Need to Know about Obtaining Passports and Visas to Travel, Study and or Work Abroad

Students must have a signed, valid passport and visas, if required. Students studying abroad must be sure that they have the proper visa to study there. A visitors visa or entry without a visa may not allow one to study.

Students should remember to fill in the emergency information page of their passport.

It is a good idea for relatives of students abroad to obtain and maintain a valid passport as well, in case of an emergency requiring them to travel.

Students who wish to work part-time in conjunction with their studies or when their studies are finished, should make sure that they understand the laws that apply and comply with them.

The United States requires student visas for study in the United States.

Students should make copies of their passport's data page and any visas. They should keep a copy separately from the originals while traveling and leave one at home with their family and with their student advisor. This will help to obtain a replacement passport in the event that a passport is lost or stolen.

Students are encouraged to travel with extra photos, in case they need to get a new passport quickly.

### Students Should Learn about Medical Insurance and Evacuation Insurance in Case of a Medical Emergency Abroad

Every year, hundreds of students become ill or suffer injuries overseas. It is essential that students have medical insurance and medical evacuation insurance that would cover a medical emergency abroad.

### Students Are Encouraged to Know the Location of the Nearest U.S. Embassy or Consulate and to Register

If students are going to be in a country for more than a couple of weeks, they should to register at the American Embassy or Consulate. This is helpful to students and their families, if there is need to locate family members in the event of an emergency.

### What U.S. Consular Officers Can and Cannot Do to Help U.S. Citizens Abroad

If students find themselves in trouble overseas, the Consular Officer at the nearest U.S. embassy or consulate can provide certain assistance and advice. Consular Officers can also help in the event of illness, injury, natural catastrophe, evacuations, destitution, or death.

In the United States, the Office of Overseas Citizens Services can also assist American students abroad and their families in the USA in emergency cases. There is a 24 hour number to call 202-647-5225.

There are certain things that consular officers at American embassies can not do for American citizens abroad. For example, they can not cash checks, lend money or serve as your attorney.

### General Precautions That Students Should Take while Traveling or Studying Abroad

Remember not to leave luggage unattended and not to carry packages for anyone. The packages could contain drugs or other illegal items.

Do not become a target for thieves by wearing conspicuous clothing and expensive looking jewelry.

There are restrictions on photography in certain countries. Students should check the consular information sheet for the countries where they plan to visit or travel.

Students should avoid demonstrations or civil disturbances, which could turn violent. Demonstrations could also turn anti-American.

The Department of State is engaged in outreach efforts to education-related organizations to publicize road safety risks in other countries. Students, who may chose less expensive, often less reliable methods of local travel while in foreign countries, should be aware of the potential danger.

## *Maintaining Strong Mental and Emotional Health*

Students may have previously been through various transitions, and already have many of the skills, techniques, and instincts needed to adjust to a new country. It is useful for them to review the coping mechanisms they have applied in the past, those that worked, and those that did not.

### *Assessing Current Stress Levels*

It is important to be able to identify what the source of stress is. It is natural for student to feel overwhelmed from time to time. Just pinning down what the matter is can be something of a relief.

#### *Manifestation of Stress*

Many emotions and reactions are to be expected when you are stressed. Some common manifestations are:

- Irritability over small things.
- Difficulty concentrating.
- Difficulty falling asleep or staying asleep.
- Queasy stomach.
- Desire to run away.
- Constant feeling or tiredness.
- Psychosomatic illness.
- Excessive criticism of others.
- Poor work performance.

- Difficulty making decisions.
- Being unusually introspective.
- Feelings of guilt, worry and anxiety.

### *Coping Choices Students Make*

When a student is in a low mood, he or she is vulnerable, and thus more likely to make poor choice for coping. Examples of poor coping choices include:

- Resorting to heavy alcohol use.
- Staying in bed 12–14 hours a day.
- Staying in your living quarters all day.
- Eating excessively.
- Avoiding friends and neighbors.
- Escaping into sexual relationships.

The more coping strategies a student has identified and thought about before his/her struggles begin, the more likely he/she is to make good choices. Based on feedback from numerous students, the following six basic techniques are especially helpful in dealing with the stresses and strains of adjustment:

- Immerse yourself in study/reading that is satisfying.
- Find a local person with whom you can talk regularly.
- Practice your faith through prayer, meditation, reading, etc.
- Write letters/e-mails (or make audiotapes) to family and friends.
- Visit fellow students.
- Meet with Resident Director/faculty to talk about the stress.

### *Predictable Stages of Adjustment for Students*

Experience tells us that there are some fairly predictable stages that most students go through during participation in study abroad. Knowing about them may help the student prepare and react more effectively:

- Orientation and honeymoon.
- Initial culture shock/confrontation.

- Adjustment-crisis/depression-frustration-to adjustment (cycle).
- Recovery-integration into host culture.
- Re-entry and reverse culture shock.

## *Managing Expectations*

The difference between what you expect and what you actually experience may determine the level of distress you feel. It is helpful, therefore, to review students' expectations and visualizations so that they are not surprised-or even shocked-by what they find.

## *Understanding Intercultural Skills*

Students should understand that among the many intercultural skills required for successful adjustment in a different culture, intercultural specialists believe that being aware of one's own culture is most important. Understanding the culture you bring with you overseas helps you see the one you find much more clearly. Other intercultural skills include:

- Being aware of one's limitations.
- Respecting the other culture.
- Learning from interacting.
- Being non-judgmental.
- Avoiding stereotypes.
- Being able to communicate.
- Listening and observing.
- Tolerating ambiguity.
- Being persistent.

## *Seeking Help*

It is normal to experience stress in adjusting to being a student, and all students will have to cope with stresses, strains, low moods, etc.—such struggles are natural. However, whenever your usual coping mechanisms are not working for you or you find yourself making coping choices that are not in your best interest, realize that you may need more support, and seek help.

Students need to be aware of whether a discussion will be confidential and of all the available counseling and support services providers.

(This could include resident director, local counseling and health professionals at private or host institution health center, as well as program administration representative and health counseling center at the home campus.)

Signs of a serious problem, recognized in yourself or in a fellow student, which require intervention include:

- Prolonged depression.
- Marked changes in eating or sleeping patterns.
- Excessive anxiety that interferes with the ability to function.
- Self-destructive or violent behavior.
- Alcohol or substance abuse.
- Failure to comply with medical recommendations.

# Chapter 36

# *International Child Abduction*

## *Introduction*

Parental child abduction is a tragedy. When a child is abducted across international borders, the difficulties are compounded for everyone involved. This chapter is designed to assist the adult most directly affected by international child abduction, the left-behind parent.

## *Prevention: How to Guard against International Child Abduction*

### *How Vulnerable Is Your Child?*

You and your child are most vulnerable when your relationship with the other parent is troubled or broken, the other parent has close ties to another country, and/or the other country has traditions or laws that may be prejudicial against a parent of your gender or to non-citizens in general. However, anyone can be vulnerable.

### *Cross-Cultural Marriages: Should You or Your Child Visit the Country of the Other Parent?*

Many cases of international parental child abduction are actually cases in which the child traveled to a foreign country with the approval

Excerpted from "International Parental Child Abduction," U.S. Department of State, Pub. No. 10862, http://travel.state.gov/int'lchildabduction.html, revised July 2001.

of both parents, but was later prevented from returning to the United States. Sometimes the marriage is neither broken nor troubled, but the foreign parent, upon returning to his or her country of origin, decides not to return to the U.S. or to allow the child to do so. A person who has assimilated a second culture may find a return to his or her roots disturbing and may feel pulled to shift loyalties back to the original culture. Furthermore, a person's behavior may change when he or she returns to the culture where he or she grew up.

In some societies, children must have their father's permission and a woman must have her husband's permission to travel. If you are a woman, to prevent your own or your child's detention abroad, find out about the laws and traditions of the country you plan to visit or plan to allow your child to visit, and consider carefully the effect that a return to his traditional culture might have on your child's father; in other societies, children need the permission of both parents to travel and the refusal of one parent to give that permission may prevent the departure of a child from that country. For detailed advice in your specific case, you may wish to contact an attorney in your spouse's country of origin. Many U.S. Embassies/Consulates list attorneys on their web-sites, accessible via http://travel.state.gov.

### Precautions That Any Parent Should Take

In international parental child abduction, an ounce of prevention is worth a pound of cure. Be alert to the possibility and be prepared:

- Keep a list of the addresses and telephone numbers of the other parent's relatives, friends, and business associates both here and abroad.

- Keep a record of important information about the other parent, including: physical description, passport, social security, bank account, and driver's license numbers; and vehicle description and plate number.

- Keep a written description of your child, including hair and eye color, height, weight, fingerprints, and any special physical characteristics.

- Take full-face color photographs and/or videos of your child every six months—a recent photo of the other parent may also be useful.

If your child should be abducted, this information could be vital in locating your child.

In addition, the National Center for Missing and Exploited Children (NCMEC), suggests that you teach your child to use the telephone, memorize your home phone number, practice making collect calls, and instruct him or her to call home immediately if anything unusual happens. Discuss possible plans of action with your child in the case of abduction. Most important, however, if you feel your child is vulnerable to abduction, seek legal advice. Do not merely tell a friend or relative about your fears.

### The Importance of a Custody Decree

Under the laws of the United States and many foreign countries, if there is no decree of custody prior to an abduction, both parents may be considered to have equal legal custody of their child. Even though both parents may have custody of a child, it still may be a crime for one parent to remove the child from the United States against the other parent's wishes. If you are contemplating divorce or separation, or are divorced or separated, or even if you were never legally married to the other parent, ask your attorney, as soon as possible, if you should obtain a decree of sole custody or a decree that prohibits the travel of your child without your permission or that of the court. If you have or would prefer to have a joint custody decree, you may want to make certain that it prohibits your child from traveling abroad without your permission or that of the court.

### How to Draft or Modify a Custody Decree

A well-written custody decree is an important line of defense against international parental child abduction. NCMEC, in its publication *Family Abduction: How to Prevent an Abduction and What to Do If Your Child Is Abducted*, makes several recommendations to help prevent the abduction of your child if your spouse is a legal permanent resident alien or a U.S. citizen with ties to a foreign country. For instance, it may be advisable to include court-ordered supervised visitation and a statement prohibiting your child from traveling without your permission or that of the court. If the country to which your child might be taken is a member of the Hague Convention on the Civil Aspects of International Child Abduction (Hague Convention), your custody decree should state that the terms of the Hague Convention apply if there is an abduction or wrongful retention. The American Bar Association (ABA) also suggests having the court require the non-citizen parent or the parent with ties to a foreign country to post a bond. This may be useful both as a deterrent to abduction and, if forfeited because of an abduction, as a source of revenue for you in your efforts to locate and recover your child.

Obtain several certified copies of your custody decree from the court that issued it. Give a copy to your child's school and advise school personnel to whom your child may be released.

## U.S. Passports

The Department of State's Passport Lookout Program can help you determine if your child has been issued a U.S. passport. You may also ask that your child's name be entered into the State Department's Children's Passport Issuance Alert Program. This will enable the Department to notify you or your attorney if an application for a U.S. passport for the child is received anywhere in the United States or at any U.S. embassy or consulate abroad. If you have a court order that either grants you sole custody, joint legal custody, or prohibits your child from traveling without your permission or the permission of the court, the Department may also refuse to issue a U.S. passport for your child. The Department may not, however, revoke a passport that has already been issued to the child. There is also no way to track the use of a passport once it has been issued, since there are no exit controls of people leaving the U.S.

To inquire about a U.S. passport or to have your child's name entered into the passport alert program, complete the request form found at http://travel.state.gov/int'lchildabduction.html and mail or fax it to:

### Office of Children's Issues
Children's Passport Issuance Alert Program (CPIAP)
2201 C Street, NW, SA22, Room 2100
Washington, DC 20520-4818
Phone: 202-736-7000
Fax: 202-312-9743

### Change in Passport Regulations

A new law, which took effect in July 2001, requires the signature of both parents prior to issuance of a U.S. passport to children under the age of 14.

*Requirements*

Both parents, or the child's legal guardians, must execute the child's passport application and provide documentary evidence demonstrating that they are the parents or guardians; or the person executing the application must provide documentary evidence that such person has sole custody of the child; has the consent of the other parent to the issuance of the passport; or is acting in place of the parents and has the consent of both parents, of a parent with sole custody over the child, or of the child's legal guardian, to the issuance of the passport.

*Exceptions*

The law does provide two exceptions to this requirement: (1) for exigent circumstances, such as those involving the health or welfare of he child, or (2) when the Secretary of State determines that issuance of a passport is warranted by special family circumstances. For additional information, see the Bureau of Consular Affairs home page on the Internet at http://travel.state.gov.

## *Foreign Passports—the Problem of Dual Nationality*

Many United States citizen children who fall victim to international parental abduction possess, or may have a claim to dual nationality. While the Department of State will make every effort to avoid issuing a United States passport if the custodial parent has provided a custody decree, the Department cannot prevent embassies and consulates of other countries in the United States from issuing their passports to children who are also their nationals. You can, however, ask a foreign embassy or consulate not to issue a passport to your child. Send the embassy or consulate a written request, along with certified complete copies of any court orders you have which address custody or the overseas travel of your child. In your letter, inform them that you are sending a copy of this request to the United States Department of State. If your child is only a United States citizen, you can request that no visa for that country be issued in his or her United States passport. No international law requires compliance with such requests, but some countries may comply voluntarily.

The United States government does not have exit controls at the border. There is no way to stop someone with valid travel documents at the United States border. The U.S. government does not check the names or the documents of travelers leaving the United States. Many foreign countries do not require a passport for entry. A birth certificate is sufficient to enter some foreign countries. If your child has a valid passport from any country, he or she may be able to travel outside the United States without your consent.

## What the State Department Can and Cannot Do When a Child Is Abducted Abroad

When a United States citizen child is abducted abroad, the State Department's Office of Children's Issues (CA/OCS/CI) works with United States embassies and consulates abroad to assist the child and left-behind parent in a number of ways. Despite the fact that children are taken across international borders, child custody disputes remain fundamentally civil legal matters between the parents involved, over which the Department of State has no jurisdiction. If a child custody dispute cannot be settled amicably between the parties, it often must be resolved by judicial proceedings in the country where the child is located.

### *What the State Department Can Do*

- Act as the primary point of contact for left-behind parents.

- Act as a liaison with federal and state agencies, including law enforcement officials.

- In cases where the Hague Convention on the Civil Aspects of International Child Abduction applies, assist parents in filing an application with foreign authorities for return of or access to the child.

- Attempt to locate, visit, and report on the child's general welfare.

- Provide the left-behind parent with information on the country to which the child was abducted, including its legal system, custody laws, and a list of local attorneys willing to accept American clients.

- Inquire as to the status of judicial or administrative proceedings overseas.

- Assist parents in contacting local officials in foreign countries or contact them on the parent's behalf.

- Provide information concerning how federal warrants against an abducting parent, passport revocation, and extradition from a foreign country may affect return of a child to the United States.

- Alert foreign authorities to any evidence of child abuse or neglect.

- If the child is in the Children's Passport Issuance Alert Program, contact the left-behind parent when application is made for a new U.S. passport for the child.

### *What the State Department Cannot Do*

- Intervene in civil legal matters between the parents.

- Enforce an American custody agreement overseas (United States custody decrees are not automatically enforceable outside of United States boundaries).

- Force another country to decide a custody case or enforce its laws in a particular way.

- Assist the left-behind parent in violating foreign laws or re-abducting the child to the United States.

- Pay legal or other expenses.

- Act as a lawyer, give legal advice, or represent parents in court.

- Take custody of the child.

- Revoke the child's passport.

## How to Search for a Child Abducted Abroad

### *Where to Report Your Missing Child*

1. If your child is missing or has been abducted, file a missing person report with your local police department and request that your child's name and description be entered into the "missing person" section of the National Crime Information Center (NCIC) computer. This is provided for under the National Child Search Act of 1990. The abductor does not have to be charged with a crime when you file a missing person report. It is not always a good idea to file criminal charges against the abducting parent at the same time you file a missing person report, although local law enforcement authorities may urge you to do so. In addition, through INTERPOL, the international police organization, your local police can request that a search for your child be conducted by the police in the country where you believe your child may have been taken. If your local law enforcement is unaware of the legal requirements for

immediate entry into NCIC please contact the Office of Children's Issues at 202-736-7000.

2. Contact the National Center for Missing and Exploited Children (NCMEC) at 1-800-THE LOST/1-800-843-5678. With the searching parent's permission, the child's photograph and description may be circulated to the media in the country to which you believe the child may have been taken.

3. Request information about a possible United States passport and have your child's name entered into the United States Children's Passport Issuance Alert Program. A United States passport for a child under 16 years expires after 5 years. If you do not know where your child is, but information about the child is in the name check system, it may be possible to locate him or her through the passport application process. All United States passport agencies and United States embassies and consulates are on-line with the name check system.

### After Your Child Is Located

A consular officer overseas, working with this information, will try to confirm the location of your child. If the consular officer is unable to find the child based on the information provided, he or she may also request information from local officials on your child's entry or residence in the country. Please note, however, that most countries do not maintain such records in a retrievable form, and some countries will not release such information.

The Department of State may also ask you for photographs of both your child and the abducting parent because these are often helpful to foreign authorities trying to find a missing child.

The Department of State, when requested to do so, may conduct visits to determine the welfare and whereabouts of American citizens abroad. The Office of Children's Issues communicates such requests to the United States embassy or consulate responsible for the area to which you believe your child has been abducted. A welfare and whereabouts visit cannot be conducted if the abducting parent refuses access.

### Further Steps to Take in Your Search

It is possible that none of the institutions mentioned (the police, the NCMEC, or the Department of State) will succeed in locating your child right away and you will need to carry on the search on your own. As you search, you should, however, keep these institutions informed of your actions and progress.

- One of the best ways to find your child overseas is through establishing friendly contact with relatives and friends of the other parent, either here or abroad. You may have more influence with such persons than you suspect, and their interest in your child's welfare may lead them to cooperate with you.

- The United States Department of Health and Human Services, Office of Child Support Enforcement maintains the Federal Parent Locator Service (FPLS). The primary purpose of this service is to locate parents who are delinquent in child support payments, but the service will also search for parental abductors when requested to do so by an authorized person. Generally speaking, an authorized person is a state court judge, police officer, prosecutor, or other state official seeking to enforce a child custody order. Please ask your local law enforcement to request a search. To learn how to access the services of the FPLS, contact your local or state Child Support Enforcement office. These offices are listed under government listings in your telephone directory.

- You can contact the principal of the school to obtain information on requests that may have been made by the abductor to your child's school for the transfer of your child's records.

- You can find out from the National Center for Missing and Exploited Children how to prepare a poster on your child. A poster may assist foreign authorities in attempting to locate your child.

- You can ask your district attorney to contact the United States Postal Inspection Service to see if a "mail cover" can be put on any address that you know of in the United States to which the abductor might write.

- It may be possible for local law enforcement authorities to obtain, by subpoena or search warrant, credit card records that may show where the abductor is making purchases. Check with state and local authorities if anything can be done. In the same manner, you can try to obtain copies of telephone bills of the abductor's friends or relatives who may have received collect calls from the abductor. Law enforcement may also be able to track usage of a cell phone or e-mail the abductor may be sending.

## The Best Solution: Settling out of Court

### Promoting Communication between Parents and Children

Legal procedures can be long and expensive. You may have greater success negotiating with the abducting parent. In some cases, friends or relatives of the abductor may be able to help you reach a compromise with the abductor. A decrease in tension might bring about the return of your child, but, even if it does not, it can increase your chances of being able to visit the child and participate in some way in the child's upbringing. In some cases compromise and some kind of reconciliation are the only realistic option.

### Obtaining Information on Your Child's Welfare

If you know your child's location and your child is a United States citizen you can request that a United States consular officer attempt to visit your child. If the consul obtains the other parent's permission to visit the child, he or she will do so and report back to you about your child. Sometimes consular officers are also able to send you letters or photos from your child. Contact the Office of Children's Issues (CA/OCS/CI) at 202-736-7000 to request such a visit.

### Working with Foreign Authorities

In child abduction cases, consular officers routinely maintain contact with local child welfare and law enforcement officers. If there is evidence of abuse or neglect of the child, the United States embassy or consulate may request that local authorities become involved.

### The Question of Desperate Measures/Re-Abduction

Consular officers cannot take possession of a child abducted by a parent or aid parents attempting to act in violation of the laws of a foreign country. Consular officers must act in accordance with the laws of the country to which they are accredited. The Department of State strongly discourages taking desperate and possibly illegal measures to return your child to the United States. Attempts to use self-help measures to bring an abducted child to the United States from a foreign country may endanger your child and others, prejudice any future judicial efforts you might wish to make in that country to stabilize the situation, and could result in your arrest and imprisonment in that country. In imposing a sentence, the foreign court will not necessarily give weight to the fact that the would-be abductor was the custodial parent in the United States or otherwise had a valid claim under a United States court order (e.g., failure of the foreign parent to honor the terms of a joint custody order). Should you be arrested, the United States Embassy will not be able to secure your release.

If you do succeed in leaving the foreign country with your child, you and anyone who assisted you may be the target of arrest warrants and extradition requests in the United States or any other country where you are found. Even if you are not ultimately extradited and prosecuted, an arrest followed by extradition proceedings can be very disruptive and disturbing for both you and your child.

Finally, there is no guarantee that the chain of abductions would end with the one committed by you. A parent who has re-abducted a child may have to go to extraordinary lengths to conceal his or her whereabouts, living in permanent fear that the child may be re-abducted again. Please consider how this might affect the child.

If you are contemplating such desperate measures, you should read the information available from the National Center for Missing and Exploited Children (NCMEC) about the emotional trauma inflicted on a child who is a victim of abduction and re-abduction. The NCMEC advises against re-abduction not only because it is illegal, but also because of possible psychological harm to the child.

## One Possible Solution: The Hague Convention

One of the most difficult and frustrating elements for a parent of a child abducted abroad is that United States laws and court orders are not automatically recognized abroad and therefore are not directly enforceable abroad. Each country has jurisdiction within its own territory and over people present within its borders. No country can tell another country how to decide cases or enforce laws. Just as foreign court orders are not automatically enforceable in the United States, United States court orders are not automatically enforceable abroad.

At the Hague Conference on Private International Law in 1976, 23 nations agreed to draft a treaty to deter international child abduction. Between 1976 and 1980, the United States was a major force in preparing and negotiating the Hague Convention on the Civil Aspects of International Child Abduction (Hague Convention or the Convention).

The Convention was incorporated into U.S. law and came into force for the United States on July 1, 1988. As of July 2001, the Convention is in force between the United States and 50 other countries. The Convention applies to wrongful removals or retentions that occurred on or after the date the treaty came into force between those two countries. The dates vary for each country and more countries are considering signing on to the Convention all the time. Check the most recent list prepared by the Office of Children's Issues to learn whether the Convention was in force in a particular county at the time of the wrongful removal or retention. You can find the list on the Department of State web site, http://travel.state.gov.

### What Is Covered by the Convention

The Hague Convention is a civil legal mechanism available to parents seeking the return of, or access to, their child. As a civil law mechanism, the parents, not the governments, are parties to the legal action.

The countries that are party to the Convention have agreed that a child who is habitually resident in one party country, and who has been removed to or retained in another party country in violation of the left-behind parent's custodial rights, shall be promptly returned to the country of habitual residence. The Convention can also help parents exercise visitation rights abroad.

There is a treaty obligation to return an abducted child below the age of 16 if application is made within one year from the date of the wrongful removal or retention, unless one of the exceptions to return apply. If the application for return is made after one year, the court may use its discretion to decide that the child has become resettled in his or her new country and refuse return of the child. In any case, a court may refuse to order a child returned if any of the following conditions apply (note: interpretation of these exceptions varies from country to country):

- A grave risk that the child would be exposed to physical or psychological harm or otherwise placed in an intolerable situation in his or her country of habitual residence.

- If the child objects to being returned and has reached an age and degree of maturity at which the court can take account of the child's views (the treaty does not establish at what age children reach this level of maturity: that age and the degree of weight given to children's views varies from country to country).

- If the return would violate the fundamental principles of human rights and freedoms of the country where the child is being held.

## *How to Use the Hague Convention*

The Convention provides a legal mechanism for you to seek return of your child or exercise your visitation rights. You do not need to have a custody decree to use the Convention. However, to apply for the return of your child, you must have had and been actually exercising a "right of custody" at the time of the abduction, and you must not have given permission for the child to be removed, or, in the case of a retention, to be retained beyond a specified, agreed-upon period of time. The Convention defines "rights of custody" as including "rights relating to the care of the person of the child and, in particular, the right to determine the child's place of residence." This right need not be sole custody. If there was no court order in effect at the date of the abduction, these "rights of custody" may be established by the law in the state in which your child was living before his or her removal. In some cases it may be advisable to get a determination in your local court that 1) you have a right of custody to your child, and 2) the removal or retention was wrongful. Use of the Convention is not restricted to U.S. citizens.

An application should be submitted as soon as possible after an abduction or wrongful retention has taken place. As stated above, there is a time factor of one year involved. Do not wait until you get a custody order. That order would be irrelevant anyway. Copies of the application form can be found at http://travel.state.gov/int'lchild abduction.html.

Each country that is party to the Convention has designated a Central Authority to carry out specialized duties under the Convention. The Central Authority for the United States is the Department of State's Office of Children's Issues (CA/OCS/CI). You may submit your application directly to the Central Authority or foreign court of the country where the child is believed to be held, but, in order to ensure that you receive all available assistance it is best to submit your application to the U.S. Central Authority.

# Chapter 37

# *Personal Security Guidelines for the American Business Traveler Overseas*

Effective security precautions require a continuous and conscious awareness of one's environment as well as the need to exercise prudence, judgment, and common sense. This is especially true where the traveler must adapt to new cultures, customs, and laws. Personal security cannot be delegated to others; it is a responsibility of each one of us, as we promote American economic and commercial interests around the globe.

## Travel Preparation

### *Travel Itinerary*

Do not publicize your travel plans, but limit that knowledge to those who need to know. Leave a complete itinerary (including contact numbers, if known) with your office and with family or a friend.

### *Your Passport*

- At least 6 months remaining validity?
- 3 copies of the page containing your photograph:

---

"Personal Security for the American Business Traveler Overseas," a brochure by the Bureau of Diplomatic Security, Overseas Security Advisory Council (OSAC), November 1995, available online at http://www.pueblo.gsa.gov/cic_text/travel/business-overseas/travel.html. Despite the age of this document, readers seeking information about security for American business travelers will find this information useful.

- Place one in carry-on bag.
- Place one in luggage.
- Leave one with office or family.

## *Your Visas*

- Current/appropriate visa(s) (tourist/business).
- Visa application information must be accurate. False information may be grounds for incarceration.

## *Other Documents*

- Take only the credit cards you need.
- Carry only the documents you will need in a wallet or purse.
- Realize all business documents might be subject to search, seizure, or copying.
- Carry a U.S. driver's license with your photo on it.
- Make two copies of the numbers of credit cards and traveler's checks, and telephone numbers to report loss, and air ticket numbers and store in your wallet or briefcase. (These items should be stored in separate locations to preclude loss of all the information.)

## *Health Related Issues*

- Carry a copy of prescriptions and an ample supply of any prescription medications, in original containers if possible.
- Bring an extra set of eyeglasses or contact lenses. Carrying your prescription with you will expedite the procurement of replacements.
- Carry an international shot record that certifies appropriate inoculations.
- List with your blood type, allergies, medical conditions and special requirements. (Medical alert bracelets are a good idea.)
- If you do not have comprehensive medical coverage, consider enrolling in an international health program. (Hospitals in foreign countries do not take credit cards and most will not honor U.S.-based medical insurance plans.)

- Keep your personal affairs up-to-date. Have an up-to-date will and insurance policy. Leave a power of attorney with a family member or friend should anything happen to you.

- While traveling, eat moderately and drink plenty of water to avoid dehydration.

- If possible, before you travel, make an effort to adjust your sleep patterns.

- Sleep as much as possible during the flight.

- Carry air sickness medication with you. Even the best traveler sometimes experiences air sickness.

- Avoid a demanding schedule upon arrival. Give yourself a chance to adjust to your surroundings.

### *Sources of Information*

- Talk with people who have visited the country recently.

- Check with the U.S. State Department, Bureau of Consular Affairs for traveling conditions and warnings. Dial 202-647-5225.

- Use airlines, hotels, and car rental companies that are recommended by your travel agent.

- If renting a car, will you need an international driver's permit for the country you plan to visit?

- Items of value, such as cameras and laptop computers, can be registered with Customs before departing the United States.

- The embassy of the country you plan to visit can provide a list or pamphlet describing customs restrictions or banned materials. (Minimize the possibility of an encounter with the local authorities.)

### *Luggage*

- Hand carry sensitive information.

- Be sure that your luggage is tagged with covered tags.

- Put your name and address inside each piece of luggage and be sure it is secured.

- The locks on your luggage are not secure. For added security, run a strip of nylon filament tape around the suitcase.

- On luggage, use your business address and telephone number.

- Check with the airline and your personal insurance company regarding coverage for lost luggage.

- Use sturdy luggage and do not over pack.

- Do not transport items for other people. Any gifts received from a foreign business contact should be thoroughly inspected before being placed in your luggage. If you are asked by airline personnel if you are carrying gifts or other items, respond affirmatively and allow the item to undergo security inspection.

- Leave all expensive and heirloom jewelry at home.

- Never place your valuables (money or traveler's checks) in your checked luggage.

- Never leave your bags unattended. Be especially alert to luggage thieves who target airline and railway terminals as well as car rental agency counter areas.

- If available, obtain a modest amount of foreign currency before you leave your home country. (Criminals may watch for and target international travelers purchasing large amounts of foreign currency at airport banks and currency exchange windows.)

## Transportation Hub Security

To diminish the risks of becoming a victim of a terrorist attack and reduce your exposure to the criminal threat, remember the following when checking into a transportation hub:

- Go in the opposite direction of any disturbance. DO NOT GET INVOLVED.

- Always be aware of where you are in relation to exits. If an incident occurs, you need to know how to avoid it and get out of the area.

- Check in early; avoid last minute dashes to the airport.

- Go directly to the gate or secure area after checking your luggage.

- Avoid waiting rooms and shopping areas outside the secure areas.

- At many airports, security personnel will ask you questions about your luggage. Know what items you are carrying and be able to describe all electrical items.

- Cooperate with security personnel.

- Do not exchange items between bags while waiting for security screening or immigration or customs processing.

- Cooperate if a conflict should arise while undergoing the screening process. Discuss the matter with a supervisor from the appropriate air carrier afterwards.

- At most airports, X-ray will not damage film, video tapes, or computer equipment. Therefore, such items can be cleared in this way without being handled by a screener.

- Arrange to be met upon your arrival whenever possible.

- Alternately, consider transportation to and from the airport by a hotel vehicle.

- Declare all currency and negotiable instruments as required by law.

- NEVER leave your luggage or briefcase unattended at anytime.

- Dress casually when traveling to avoid attention.

- Always reconfirm onward flights at least 72 hours in advance.

- DO NOT accept or deliver letters, packages, or anything else from anyone unknown to you. It could result in your being arrested for illegally exporting a prohibited item.

## Hotel Security

Use hotels recommended by the corporate travel agency, where possible.

### Reservations

- Make your own reservations when practical and consistent with company policies. (The fewer people who become involved in your travel and lodging arrangements, the better.)

- If traveling abroad, especially in high threat areas, consider making reservations using your employer's street address, without identifying the company, and using your personal credit card.

Again, the less known about your travel itinerary, and who you represent, the better.

- If arriving in mid afternoon, ensure that reservations are guaranteed.

- Request information about hotel parking arrangements before renting an automobile.

- Be aware that credit card information may be compromised by hotel, rental car, and restaurants. Always audit monthly credit card statements to ensure that unauthorized use has not been made of your account.

- Join frequent travelers' programs. They are available with many lodging companies. These programs enable upgrades to executive or concierge floors where security is generally better.

### Arriving at and Departing from the Hotel

The most vulnerable part of your journey is traveling between the point of debarkation and embarkation and the hotel.

- Disembark as close to a hotel entrance as possible and in a lighted area. Before exiting the vehicle, ensure there are no suspicious persons or activities.

- Do not linger or wander unnecessarily in the parking lot, indoor garage, or the public space around hotel.

- Parking garages are difficult to secure. Avoid dimly lit garages that are not patrolled and do not have security telephones or intercoms.

- Watch for distractions that may be staged to set up a pickpocket, luggage theft, or purse snatch.

- Stay with your luggage until it is brought into the lobby or placed in your taxi.

- Use the bellman. Luggage in the care, custody, and control of the hotel causes the hotel to be liable for your property. Keep claim checks, they are your evidence.

- Due to hotel liability limits, personal travel documents, laptop computers, valuables, and sensitive documents should be hand carried and personally protected.

- Valets should receive only the ignition key.

- Women travelers should consider requesting an escort to their vehicles.

## *Check-in*

- In some countries, your passport may be held by the hotel for review by the police or other authorities. If so, retrieve it at the earliest possible time.

- Position luggage against your leg during registration, but place a briefcase or a purse on the desk or counter in front of you.

- Request a room between the second and seventh floor. Most fire departments do not have the capability to rescue people above the seventh floor level with external rescue equipment (i.e., ladders).

- Avoid low-level rooms with sliding glass doors and easy window access. Depending upon the situation, area, and security coverage, exercise a higher level of security if assigned a ground-level room.

- Request rooms that are away from the elevator landing and stairwells. This is to avoid being caught by surprise by persons exiting the elevator with you or hiding in the stairwell.

- Accept the bellman's assistance upon check-in. Allow the bellman to open the room's door, turn the lights on, and check the room to ensure that it is vacant and ready for your stay.

- Inquire how guests are notified if there is an emergency.

- Find the nearest fire stairwell.

- Note the location of fire alarms, extinguishers, and hoses, and read any fire safety information available in your room.

- Check outside your room window to ascertain if there is a possible escape route that would be feasible in an extreme emergency.

- Find the nearest house telephone in case of an emergency.

- Note how hotel staff are uniformed and identified. Verify hotel employees with the front desk before permitting entry to your room.

- While in the room, keep the door closed and engage the deadbolt and privacy latch or chain. A limited number of hotel emergency keys can override the deadbolt locks.

- Guests should always place money or valuables in the safe deposit box at the front desk of the hotel. Guest room safes are not secure.

- Stay only at hotels that have smoke detectors and/or sprinklers installed in all rooms and provide information about fire and safety procedures.

### *In Case of a Fire*

- Keep calm.

- Do not panic.

- Call the front desk and notify them of the location of the fire.

- Check your door by placing your palm on the door and then on the door knob. If either feels hot, do not open the door.

- If it is safe to exit from your room, head for the stairs. Take your room key with you; you may have to return to your room.

- If the corridor is full of smoke, crawl to the exit and again check the door before opening it to see if it is hot. The fire could be in the stairwell.

- Do not use the elevator.

- If you cannot leave your room or the stairwells are unsafe and you must return to your room, notify the front desk that you are in your room awaiting rescue.

- Open a window for fresh air. Do not break the window as you may need to close it again if smoke starts to enter from the outside.

- Fill the tub and sink with water. Soak towels and blankets as necessary to block vents and openings around doors to keep the smoke and fumes out.

- Attempt to keep the walls, doors, and towels covering vents and cracks cool and wet.

- A wet towel swung around the room will help clear the room of smoke.

- Cover your mouth and nose with a wet cloth.

- Stay low, but alert to any signs of rescue from the street or the halls. Let the firefighters know where you are by waving a towel or sheet out the window.

## *Personal Security in a Foreign Country*

- All hotel rooms and telephones are not bugged; however, your business purpose will be more secure if you act as if they are.

- Keep your hotel room key with you at all times, if possible.

- At night, secure your passport and other valuables.

- Do not divulge the name of your hotel or room number to strangers.

### *Street Smarts*

- Invest in a good map of the city. Note significant points on the map such as your hotel, embassies, and police stations. Make a mental note of alternative routes to your hotel or local office should your map become lost or stolen.

- Be aware of your surroundings. Look up and down the street before exiting a building.

- Learn how to place a local telephone call and how to use coin telephones. Make sure you always have extra tokens or coins for telephone use.

- Areas around public telephones are often used by criminals to stage pickpocket activity or theft. Keep briefcases and purses in view or in touch while using phones. Caution is urged in safeguarding telephone credit card numbers. Criminals wait for callers to announce credit card numbers on public phones and then sell the numbers for unauthorized use.

- Avoid jogging or walking in cities you are not familiar with. If you must jog, be aware of the traffic patterns when crossing public streets. (Joggers have been seriously injured by failing to understand local traffic conditions.)

- Speak with the bellman, concierge, and front desk regarding safe areas around the city to jog, dine, or sight see. Ask about local customs and which taxi companies to use or avoid.

- Avoid renting vehicles or driving unless you are familiar with the local traffic laws and customs.

- Valuables should normally be left at home. The rule of thumb is if you neither want nor can afford to lose them, do not take them. However, if you must carry valuables, the best way to protect them is to secure them in your local offices. Second best is the hotel safe.

- Keep your passport with you at all times. Only relinquish it to the hotel if required by law when registering, or if you are required to identify yourself to local authorities for any reason.

- Vary the time and route by which you leave and return to the hotel. Be alert for persons watching your movements.

- Be cautious when entering public restrooms.

- Purse snatchers and briefcase thieves are known to work hotel bars and restaurants waiting for unknowing guests to drape these items on chairs or under tables only to discover them missing as they are departing. Keep items in view or in touch.

- Be alert to scams involving an unknown person spilling a drink or food on your clothing. An accomplice may be preparing to steal your wallet, purse, or briefcase.

- Pools or beaches are attractive areas for thieves. Leave valuables in the hotel, but carry a token sum to placate violent thieves. Sign for food and beverages on your room bill rather than carry cash.

- Avoid persons you do not know. Prostitutes—both men and women—take advantage of travelers through various ploys: knock out drugs, confederates, and theft from the victim's room.

### *Workplace Security*

- Safeguard all sensitive or proprietary papers and documents; do not leave them lying around in the office or on top of a desk.

- Guard your conversations so that unauthorized personnel are not able to eavesdrop on discussions pertaining to proprietary information, personnel issues, or management planning or problems. In many countries, local employees are debriefed by the intelligence or security services in an effort to learn as much as possible about activities of American companies and their personnel.

- Be careful of all communications. Be aware that the monitoring of telephone, telegraph, and international mail is common in many countries.

## Personal Conduct

Hostile and even friendly intelligence organizations are always on the lookout for sources who are vulnerable to coercion, addictions, greed, or emotional manipulation. To eliminate, or at least reduce, the possibility of inadvertently doing something that would bring your activities to the special attention of one of these agencies:

- Do not do anything that might be misconstrued, reflect poorly on your personal judgment, or be embarrassing to you or your company.

- Do not gossip about character flaws, financial problems, emotional relationships, or the marital difficulties of anyone working for the company, including yourself.

- Do not carry, use, or purchase any narcotics, marijuana, or other abused drugs. Some countries have very stringent laws covering the import or use of medications and other substances. If you are using a prescribed medication that contains any narcotic substance or other medication that is subject to abuse, such as amphetamines or tranquilizers, carry a copy of the doctor's prescription for all medications and check local restrictions and requirements prior to departure. Some countries may require additional documentation or certification from your doctor.

- Do not let a friendly ambiance and alcohol override your good sense and capacity when it comes to social drinking.

- Do not engage in black-market activities such as the illegal exchange of currency or the purchase of religious icons or other local antiquities.

- Do not carry any political or religious tracts or brochures or publications likely to be offensive in the host country, such as pornography or radical magazines.

- Do not photograph anything that appears to be associated with the military or internal security of the country, including airports, ports, or restricted areas such as military installations, antennae, or government buildings.

- Do not purchase items that are illegal to import into the United States or other countries such as endangered species or agricultural products.

471

## *Arrested—What Do I Do Now?*

Foreign police and intelligence agencies detain persons for a myriad of reasons or for no other reason than suspicion or curiosity. The best advice is to exercise good judgment, be professional in your demeanor, and remember these suggestions:

- Ask to contact the nearest embassy or consulate representing your country. As a citizen of another country you have this right, but that does not mean that your hosts will allow you to do so right away. Continue to make the request periodically until they accede and let you contact your embassy or consulate.

- Stay calm, maintain your dignity, and do not provoke the arresting officer(s).

- Admit nothing; volunteer nothing.

- Sign nothing. Often, part of the detention procedure is to ask or tell the detained to sign a written report. Decline politely until such time as the document is examined by an attorney or an embassy or consulate representative.

- Accept no one at face value. When the representative from the embassy or consulate arrives, request some identification before discussing your situation.

- Do not fall for the ruse of helping those detaining you in return for your release. They can be very imaginative in their proposals on how you can be of assistance to them. Do not sell yourself out by agreeing to anything. If there appears to be no other way out, tell them that you will think it over and let them know. Once out of their hands, contact the affiliate or your embassy for assistance in getting out of the country.

### *Targeting Recognition*

Persons traveling abroad on business should be aware that they could be targeted by an intelligence agency, security service, terrorists, criminals, or a competitor if they are knowledgeable of, or carrying, sensitive or proprietary information. In the course of doing business abroad, there are indicators that should be recognized as potential hazards and indicate unwarranted interest in your activities:

- Repeated contacts with a local or third-country national who is not involved in your business interests or the purpose of your visit, but as a result of invitations to social or business functions, appears at each function. This individual's demeanor may indicate more than just a passing interest in you and your business activities.

- A close social relationship with a representative of a host government is often unavoidable for business reasons. Be cautious and do not allow the relationship to develop any further than the business level.

- Accidental encounters with an unknown local national who strikes up a conversation and wants to:
    - Practice English or another language.
    - Talk about your country of origin or your employment.
    - Buy you a drink because he or she has taken a liking to you.
    - Talk to you about politics.
    - Use other excuses to begin a friendly relationship.

## Surveillance Recognition

Foreign intelligence, security services, terrorists, and criminals use surveillance for operational preparation prior to taking action. The main terrorist threat to a traveler is that of being at the wrong place at the wrong time and becoming an inadvertent victim of a terrorist act.

Be observant and pay attention to your sixth sense. If you get the funny feeling that something is not right or that you are being watched, pay attention. Report your suspicions or any information to the general manager of the local affiliate or your embassy or consulate just in case something does occur.

If you have reason to believe that you are under surveillance, continue to act naturally. Do not try to slip away, lose, or embarrass the surveillance as this may anger and alert them. It also may cause them to question whether you are, in fact, just a business person.

In your hotel room, do not play investigator and start looking for electronic listening devices. Ensure that you do not say or do anything in your hotel room that you would not want to see printed on the front page of *The New York Times*.

473

# Chapter 38

# *Avoid Being a Target for Foreign Intelligence Agencies*

## *Risks during Foreign Travel*

The risk of becoming an intelligence target increases greatly during foreign travel. As an American government official, scientist, or business traveler with access to useful information, you can become the target of a foreign intelligence or security service at anytime in any country. The threat is certainly not limited to so-called unfriendly countries.

Never think, "They wouldn't dare risk something like that against me. They have too much at stake." Many countries do risk it, routinely, because the potential benefits are great and the risks are very low when an intelligence service is operating on its home turf. Even U.S. Government cabinet level officials and corporate CEOs have been assigned to bugged hotel rooms and had all their documents secretly photographed or their laptop computers accessed.

Conversely, never think you are too low-ranking to be of interest. Secretaries, file clerks and cleaning crew are targeted because they can often provide access to valuable information. Foreign government scrutiny of you while visiting another country may occur by design or chance for any of the following reasons:

"Risks During Foreign Travel," "Avoiding and Recognizing Foreign Intelligence Interest," "Overseas Communications," and "Bugging Hotel Rooms," excerpted from the "Counterintelligence Awareness Guide" http://www.nnsi.doe.gov/ C/Courses/CI_Awareness_Guide/Home.htm, produced by the Counterintelligence Training Academy, Nonproliferation and National Security Institute, Department of Energy, cited November 2002.

- You have government, business, scientific, or technical information of potential value to a foreign government or a local industry.

- You have relatives or organizational affiliations or speak the local language fluently in the country you are visiting.

- You fit a terrorism, narcotic trafficking, criminal, or other profile.

- You buy or sell on the black-market.

- The local government discovers on your person or in your luggage literature that is banned or strictly controlled.

- You are associating with individuals the host government considers as political dissidents.

Following are some of the common methods that may be used. Most activities directed against you will be conducted in an unobtrusive manner that you are very unlikely to notice. Others are sometimes conducted in a rather crude manner that is observable. Brief summaries of many cases in which American travelers have reported such observations are found in *In the Line of Fire: American Travelers Abroad.*

### Methods

**Assessment:** Friendly discussion with local contacts who assess whether you have information of value and seek to identify any personal attitudes, beliefs, problems or needs that could be exploitable.

**Elicitation:** A ploy whereby seemingly normal conversation is contrived to extract intelligence information of value. Advantages of this technique are that it:

- Puts someone at ease to share information.

- Is difficult to recognize as an intelligence technique.

- Is easily deniable.

**Eavesdropping:** Listening to other peoples' conversations to gather information.

- Frequently done in social environments where attendees feel comfortable and secure and, therefore, are more likely to talk about themselves or their work.

- Frequent venues include restaurants, bars, and public transportation.

476

- Eavesdropping can occur in a radius of six to eight seats on public transportation or 10–12 feet in other settings.

**Technical eavesdropping:** Use of audio and visual devices, usually concealed.

- Relatively cost efficient and low risk.

- Concealed devices can be installed in public and private facilities—such as hotel rooms, restaurants, offices, and automobiles.

**Bag operations:** Surreptitious entry into someone's hotel room to steal, photograph, or photocopy documents; steal or copy magnetic media; or download from laptop computers.

- Often conducted or condoned by host government intelligence or security services or by operatives for local corporations.

- Frequently done with cooperation of hotel staff.

**Surveillance:** Following you to determine your contacts and activities.

- Labor intensive if done correctly. Not usually done unless you are suspected of improper activity or a target of great interest.

**Theft of information:** Stealing documents, briefcases, laptop computers or sensitive equipment.

- Laptop computers are especially vulnerable as they may contain a treasure trove of information.

- Theft of laptops from hotel rooms and while transiting airports is especially common.

- Foreign service has plausible denial, as the laptop may have been stolen for the value of the laptop rather than value of the information it contained. You may never know whether the information was compromised or not.

**Intercepting electronic communications:** Telephones, fax, telex, and computers can all be monitored electronically.

- You are particularly vulnerable while communicating to, from or within foreign countries, as most foreign telecommunications systems cooperate with their country's security service.

- Office, hotel, and portable telephones (including cellular) are key targets.

### How to Protect Yourself

Common sense and basic counterintelligence (CI) awareness can effectively protect you against foreign attempts to collect sensitive, proprietary, and other privileged information. Following are a few tips.

- Arrange a pre-travel briefing from your security office.

- Maintain physical control of all sensitive documents or equipment at all times. Do not leave items that would be of value to a foreign intelligence service unattended in hotel rooms or stored in hotel safes.

- Limit sensitive discussions—hotel rooms or other public places are rarely suitable to discuss sensitive information.

- Do not use computer or facsimile equipment at foreign hotels or business centers for sensitive matters.

- Do not divulge information to anyone not authorized to hear it.

- Ignore or deflect intrusive inquiries or conversation about business or personal matters.

- Keep unwanted material until it can be disposed of securely. Burn or shred paper and cut floppy disks in pieces and discard.

- Keep your laptop computer as carry-on baggage—never check it with other luggage and, if possible, remove or control storage media.

- If secure communications equipment is accessible, use it to discuss business matters.

- Report any CI incident to the relevant U.S. Government agency and/or your local security office.

## Avoiding and Recognizing Foreign Intelligence Interest

While traveling abroad, you are on the other country's home turf where the local security and intelligence services have many resources available. They can monitor and, to some extent, control the environment in which you live and work. You, in turn, may be at a disadvantage, because you are on unfamiliar territory.

Allied as well as hostile intelligence and security organizations use their home field advantage to look for potential sources who can be developed and exploited based on greed, manipulation of psychological or emotional weaknesses, conflicting loyalties, addiction, or coercion. The local services routinely monitor black market activities, dissident groups, prostitution, certain bars, gay hangouts, gambling establishments, and other areas where human weaknesses may be observable.

Many Americans possess personality traits that increase their vulnerability to the classic routines of espionage.

**Sociability:** Americans characteristically want to be liked. In order to gain approval we tend to be social and gregarious even with casual contacts.

**Candor and trust:** Americans generally place a high value on candor and on trust. We tend to be open and trustful and to accept others at face value.

**Pride:** As Americans, we are proud of our phenomenal accomplishments in science, business, war, and world leadership. We tend to underestimate people from other cultures, including their ability to conduct successful intelligence operations against us.

**Ambition:** Americans tend to be ambitious, oriented toward job advancement and professional recognition. Success is often measured by money and status.

These personality traits make many of us vulnerable to manipulation by people who offer friendship, understanding and flattery, or who offer opportunities for money or professional recognition, but who may have an ulterior motive for doing so.

### *Avoiding Intelligence Interest*

To eliminate, or at least reduce, the possibility of your doing something inadvertent that may mark you as a person of special interest to one of these agencies, here are some do not's to remember:

- DO NOT do anything which might be misconstrued or reflect poorly on your personal judgment, professional demeanor, or be embarrassing to you, your employer, or your country.

- DO NOT gossip about character flaws, financial problems, emotional relationships or marital difficulties of any co-workers, or yourself. This type of information is eagerly sought after by those who would like to exploit you or another employee.

- DO NOT carry, use, or purchase any narcotics, marijuana, or other abused drugs. Some countries have very stringent laws covering the import or use of medications and other substances. If you are using a prescribed medication that contains any narcotic substance or other medication that is subject to abuse, such as amphetamines or tranquilizers, carry a copy of the doctor's prescription for all medications and check for local restrictions and requirements prior to departure. Some countries may require additional documentation/certification from your doctor.

- DO NOT let a friendly ambiance and alcohol override your good sense and capacity when it comes to social drinking. In some countries, heavy drinking in the form of toasting is quite common, and very few westerners can keep up with a local national when it comes to drinking the national brew. If you are not careful, you could easily embarrass yourself, your employer, and/or your country. An accident while driving under the influence could lead to serious trouble.

- DO NOT engage in black market activities such as the illegal exchange of currency, or the purchase of religious icons or other local antiquities that may be stolen or otherwise not authorized for export.

- DO NOT accept or deliver letters, packages or anything else from or to anyone you do not know. You have no way of knowing what you are carrying and it could result in your being arrested for illegally importing a prohibited item.

- DO NOT engage in any type of political or religious activity, or carry any political or religious tracts or brochures, or publications likely to be offensive in the host country, such as pornography or weapons.

- DO NOT photograph anything that appears to be associated with the military or internal security of the country, including airports, ports, or restricted areas such as military installations.

- DO NOT ask the local government for any special favors or permits, such as permission to travel to a restricted area or a special benefit for a relative or friend.

- If in doubt, DO NOT.

## *Recognizing Intelligence Interest*

Several scenarios that are particularly common while traveling abroad are mentioned here. The following situations should be closely scrutinized and usually avoided, if possible.

- Repeated contacts with a local or third country national who is not involved in the business or other purpose of your visit, but who appears at each social or business function to which you are invited. This individual's demeanor may indicate more than just a passing interest in you or your work.

- A close personal and social relationship with a foreign national of a hostile host government is often unavoidable for business reasons. In these instances, don't let your guard down. Don't assume that this is a true friendship.

- Be skeptical of the accidental encounter with an unknown local national who strikes up a conversation and wants to practice English, talk about your country or your employment, buy you a drink because they have taken a liking to you, talk to you about politics, or who uses any other pretext to begin a friendly relationship.

If any of the these situations or anything else occurs which just does not ring true, be skeptical. It may be innocent, but exercise prudence and good judgment. If you become aware that you are under physical or technical surveillance, this is a strong indication that someone is interested in monitoring your activities and learning more about you. Physical surveillance refers to following you on foot or by car. Technical surveillance refers to bugging your hotel room, using a concealed camera to observe your behavior in your hotel room, or monitoring your phone calls.

Although obviously worrisome, surveillance is no cause for panic. It may be a routine search for information that can be used against you, initiated solely on the basis of the sensitive information to which you are presumed to have access. You may be followed only because you met with someone who happens to be under surveillance. The bug in your hotel room may be left over from a previous operation, or be a permanent installation that is activated only when the room is occupied by a more important target than you.

If you possess sensitive information, either in your head or in documents on your person, you should assume that you may be followed and behave accordingly. Do not do or say anything that could be used against you or that might increase interest in you as a target. Although you should be alert at all times, DO NOT do anything that suggests you are either looking for or are trying to avoid surveillance. This would suggest that you are engaged in illegal or improper activities and make you an even more important target.

In your hotel room, assume that the room and telephone are being monitored. DO NOT try to play investigator and start looking for electronic listening devices. This again could send the wrong signal to whoever is behind the surveillance. Just act normally and make sure that you do not say or do anything in your hotel room that you would not want to see printed on the front page of the local newspaper. And do not do or say anything that suggests you know or suspect someone is listening. Taunting the local security service is always wrong, as it is definitely counterproductive.

If you have any reason to believe that you are being targeted by an intelligence or security service or any criminal or terrorist group, there is only one course of action to follow. Report your suspicions to the American Embassy or Consulate or to your employer and follow their guidance. Report only to an American citizen, not to a local national. And report only in person, not by telephone, fax, or electronic mail, as such communications to the American Embassy or Consulate may be monitored.

## Overseas Communications

Many foreign telecommunications companies are owned or controlled by the government. Even those not government-owned or controlled are regulated by the government and will normally cooperate when their government requests assistance in monitoring specific lines.

Under these circumstances, it is easy to intercept and monitor telephone, fax, e-mail, computer, and any other form of electronic communications. A typical communications monitoring scenario might be as follows:

- A foreign intelligence service rents an office near the targeted office or home or in another location selected to provide easy access to telecommunications facilities or transmissions from the target.

- An electronic listening post is set up in the office and manned around the clock. The listening post eavesdrops on telephone, fax, telex, and computer communications.

- Computers screen all communications and pick out those that are potentially valuable by identifying key words such as the name of a company, person, technology, product, project, or anything else that may identify a topic of interest to the monitoring organization or its customers.

- Interesting communications are recorded and screened manually for the preparation of written reports. In many countries, a principal goal is to support national businesses by providing them with information on such things as their foreign competitors' technology, marketing plans, prices, bids, and negotiating strategies.

Government programs to intercept foreign telecommunications are now standard practice in many countries. Global economic competition, the great increase in global telecommunications, and the development of computer search engines to screen massive amounts of electronic material make it cost-effective for an increasing number of countries to develop extensive intercept programs.

The cost and technology for developing a significant intercept capability is now well within the capability of many corporations, criminal syndicates, or terrorist groups in addition to foreign governments. The equipment for this can be obtained easily by almost anyone.

### *Security Countermeasures*

You must assume that all overseas telecommunications that would be valuable to another government, company, or group will be intercepted, recorded, organized into reports, and reviewed by the persons for whom that information has value. Although that will not be true in every case, the likelihood is sufficiently great that you cannot afford to assume otherwise if compromise of the information would be a significant loss. In most cases, it is virtually impossible to detect when telecommunications are being intercepted and monitored. This leaves three alternatives:

- Encrypt all telecommunications that you cannot afford to have compromised. However, some countries do not allow encryption of telecommunications traffic within their borders.

- Communicate by courier.
- Accept the loss of confidentiality and plan accordingly.

Access to telephones, fax machines and computers should be controlled to reduce the possibility of tampering. Telephones can be adjusted so that they act as transmitters even after they are hung up. Conversations near a phone may be transmitted to the foreign country's phone system switching facility and can be monitored from anywhere between the phone and that facility. Computers and fax machines can be tampered with to facilitate monitoring that bypasses the encryption system.

Security procedures should be followed carefully when operating any computer linked to an outside network or telephone system.

## Bugging Hotel Rooms

It is sometimes said that all hotel rooms abroad are bugged for audio and visual surveillance. Of course it is not true that all of them are bugged, but a great many are—especially in major hotels frequented by foreign business and government travelers. To maintain an adequate level of security awareness while conducting business abroad, you must operate on the assumption that your hotel room conversations are being monitored. If you are an active target who is known to pick up local women, you could also be filmed by a concealed camera.

The goal of surreptitious monitoring may be to learn your business or negotiating strategy, identify your local contacts, assess your vulnerabilities, or obtain evidence that can be used to accuse you of improper activities or to pressure you to cooperate.

It is noteworthy that legal restrictions against technical surveillance that apply in the United States have not been adopted by other countries with which we have close trading ties. The overseas operations of American companies engaged in international commerce are particularly vulnerable.

Most foreign security and intelligence services have various means of screening incoming visitors to identify persons of potential intelligence interest. They also have well-established contacts with the hotels that commonly host conferences and meetings with international participation. For convenience, some even maintain permanent offices within the largest hotels. If the local intelligence service considers you a significant intelligence target, it may arranged for you to be assigned a room that is already prepared for the desired monitoring.

Some luxury hotels offer a baby monitoring service to guests who wish to use the club or guest services, while still minding the toddlers asleep in their hotel room. This service is an integral part of the hospitality features incorporated into the hotel phone system. That means it is possible from a central location to activate the microphone within the telephone set within any room at any time. Consider how this might be used by the local security service.

Even without such a built-in system, it takes only a minute or two for someone to enter a hotel room and bug the telephone so that all room conversations can be monitored from a line connected to the hotel switchboard.

# Chapter 39

# *Discrimination Abroad*

Students participating in study abroad programs worldwide have expressed concern in recent years about how they will be viewed and received in other societies. The range of their concerns encompasses ethnicity, gender, religion, nationality, sexual orientation, and physical disabilities as well as reactions abroad to U.S. government policies and widely-held stereotypes about Americans. Sometimes students are surprised and dismayed to discover that other societies do not necessarily share prevailing American approaches to these issues or U.S. values about such matters.

Encounters with prejudice can be painful for students who feel very strongly that their views are correct and that the prevailing views in the host society are wrong. Because students are guests in the universities and residence halls of other countries, their internal conflicts can sometimes become intensely difficult for them. Therefore it is crucial that each student give serious thought before departure to the question of how to respond to attitudes and behaviors abroad that may be considered unacceptable.

One strategy for dealing with behaviors that would be labeled in the U.S. as sexist, racist, or discriminatory is to be analytical rather than emotional. Try not to take these things personally or to feel hurt or angry. Try instead to seek some intellectual understanding of the

---

From "Encountering Intolerance Abroad," © 2002 University of California Education Abroad Program. Reprinted with permission. For additional information, visit http://www.eap.ucop.edu.

behavior you observe and try to understand it even though you may strongly disagree.

Another strategy is to remove yourself from the source of the offensive behavior but to discuss it later with members of the host society whom you trust, and with other Americans, staff, or fellow students. If an explanation is offered, try not to dismiss it by making judgments based on your personal or home country standard, but rather try to understand the historical and social forces that maintain the values of the host society in the face of pressures for change. Many actions or words that we might immediately interpret in a negative light may be more understandable in their host country context. Societies are, after all, highly complex, interactive, and continuously evolving systems that elude simplistic explanations. Indeed, it is precisely when simplistic, stereotypic explanations hold sway in a society (for example, "all our problems are the fault of ___") that the greatest intolerance occurs.

In recent years, Europe and Asia have been undergoing rapid and far-reaching change which has strained the patience and good will of many, especially those who have not shared in the prosperity and privilege that the region's success has engendered. Like violent crime in the U.S., extremist views and resulting actions are disturbing developments that the world community is watching very closely. Nevertheless, students should not be deterred from going about their lives and their business in a normal fashion. Facing such matters thoughtfully, with personal resolve and with compassion for any victim of prejudice is a far more constructive response than fear, anger, and withdrawal.

We encourage you to read about social and political issues abroad, to think about and discuss these issues before departure, to practice personal tolerance, and to be mature and realistic in your expectations. However, students should report serious or repeated instances of verbal or physical aggression to their director or other representative as soon as they occur. All relevant details should be provided at that time. The director has been instructed to provide counsel and to pursue appropriate action within the local cultural and/or institutional context.

Chapter 40

# Safety in Rental Cars

## Renting a Car

Renting a car can be confusing and expensive if you don't understand industry terms and how fees are calculated. If you have a poor driving record, renting a car may be next to impossible. This chapter will outline some points to consider and questions to ask when you reserve a rental car.

### Choosing a Rental Car Company

Before you reserve a car, think about the size you want or need and how much you're willing to spend. This will help you avoid making a hasty or expensive decision that you may regret later. At the same time, be aware that vehicle classification systems vary. The terms compact, mid-size, and luxury sometimes differ among companies.

Call several rental car companies for price estimates, or check rates through your travel agent. Ask about specials geared to the length of time you need the vehicle. Many companies offer weekly or weekend

This chapter contains U.S. Federal Trade Commission fact sheets, "Renting a Car," (produced in cooperation with the American Society of Travel Agents), 1996, http://www.ftc.gov/bcp/conline/pubs/autos/carrent.htm; "Rental Cars," 2002, http://www.ftc.gov/bcp/conline/audio/rental_cars.htm, "Rental Car Additional Driver Charges," 2002, http://www.ftc.gov/bcp/conline/audio/vacation_rental_car.htm; and "Rental Car Extra Charges," 2002, http://www.ftc.gov/bcp/conline/audio/rental_car_extra_charge.htm.

deals. If your plans are flexible, you may be able to save money by renting a car when price breaks are available. But be sure to ask about restrictions on special offers, including blackout dates when an advertised price may not be available.

Ask if the rental car company checks the driving records of potential customers. Many companies now check driving records when customers arrive at the counter. Some reject customers whose driving records don't meet company standards. Even if you have a confirmed reservation, you may be disqualified from renting a car for moving violations within the last few years; seat belt law violations; accidents, regardless of fault; convictions for Driving While Intoxicated (DWI), Driving Under the Influence (DUI), reckless driving, or leaving the scene of an accident; or driving with an invalid, suspended or revoked license. Ask your travel agent or the rental car company in advance whether your driving record will be checked.

Ask if there may be charges that could increase an advertised base rate, such as Collision Damage Waiver (CDW) fees (in states that allow them); a deposit or refundable charge; airport surcharges and drop-off fees; fuel charges; mileage fees; taxes; additional-driver fees; underage-driver fees; out-of-state charges; and equipment-rental fees (for items such as ski racks and car seats).

## Understanding the Terms and Charges

Ask about charges before you sign your rental agreement. The information may help you save money and avoid disputes when the time comes to pay your bill.

**Collision Damage Waiver (CDW)**, in states that allow it, is an optional charge of $9 to $13 a day. Rental car agents may urge you to buy this option. Although they call it collision damage coverage, it's not technically collision insurance. Rather, it is a guarantee that the rental company will pay for damages to your rented car. By declining the waiver, you accept responsibility for any damages. However, under CDW, the company will not pay for bodily injuries or damages to your personal property. If you do not buy CDW coverage or are not covered by your personal auto insurance policy, you could be liable for the full value of the car. Some rental companies may hold you liable only for the first $1,000 or $2,000.

Some CDWs exclude coverage under certain circumstances. For example, coverage may be revoked if you damage the car when driving it in a negligent manner, on unpaved roads, or out of the state in which you rented the vehicle. Some companies void their CDW coverage if a driver drinks alcohol or if a non-authorized driver operates the car.

The coverage offered by rental car companies may duplicate insurance you have through your auto and homeowner's policies. Coverage under your medical plan would offer protection that CDW coverage lacks. Read your insurance policies and medical plan for specifics. If you're not sure about the coverage, call your insurers. If you're traveling on business, your employer may have insurance that covers you. Also, some credit card companies and motor clubs provide members with free rental protection when you use their cards to pay for rentals.

In addition to CDW coverage, a rental car company also may offer:

- Personal Accident Insurance (PAI). At a daily cost of $1.50 to $4, it pays a death benefit and a portion of your medical expenses if you're in an accident.

- Personal Effects Coverage (PEC) or Personal Effects Protection (PEP). At an average daily cost of $1.25, it safeguards your luggage against damage. If your homeowner's policy covers your luggage and other belongings while you travel, you may not need this protection.

A refundable charge may be required when you pick up your rental car. The charge varies, but may be hundreds of dollars. Most rental companies make the charge to your credit card but do not process the amount unless you do not return the car as specified in your rental contract. Until you return the car, however, your spending limit on your credit card may be reduced by the amount of the deposit. This may be important if you plan to charge other items to your credit card and are near your credit limit. If you do not have a major credit card, or you do not want to charge the deposit, companies may ask for the deposit in cash.

Airport surcharges and drop-off fees can increase the base rental rate considerably. Surcharges apply when airport authorities impose fees for airport use even when rental car companies shuttle you to an off-airport site. Drop-off fees refer to charges that some companies impose to allow you to drop off the car at a different location from the pick-up point.

A fuel charge is the amount many rental car companies add to your bill for gasoline. Some companies give you a half-tank at a charge of $10 to $15 and tell you to return the car empty; others fill the tank and charge for the amount of gas you use. Companies that do not charge for the initial tank may ask you to return the car with a full tank. If you don't, you'll be charged the rental company's price for gasoline. It's often much higher than a local station.

Mileage fees usually are assessed on a cents-per-mile basis or as a flat fee when you exceed the allotted free mileage cap. Knowing approximately how far you will drive will allow you to select the company that offers the most favorable mileage terms.

Taxes are levied by states and some municipalities. You may be able to avoid the higher tax rate of an urban pick-up site if you pick up your rental car at a suburban location. Additional-driver fees and underage-driver fees are costs a company assesses when you share the driving with another person or when a driver is under a certain age (often 25).

Out-of-state charges are assessed when you drive the car out of the state in which it was rented. Equipment-rental fees are imposed when you order extras such as ski racks and car seats. If these items are important to you, make sure you reserve them in advance.

## Rental Cars

You're at the rental car check-out counter and you've just been told that the total cost for the vehicle will be 35% greater than the daily rate you were quoted when you made the reservation. What happened?

The daily of weekly rental rate is the first thing most of us ask when we are renting a car. But that number is only part of what you'll actually pay. When you make the reservation, ask for a complete accounting of all the charges, including rental sales tax, airport tax, surcharges, and so on.

*Consumer Reports Travel Letter* surveyed 16 cities and found that a car rented at Logan Airport in Boston had the highest add-on fees and New York City the lowest. In Boston, the final cost for a vehicle was 38.6% above the initial rental fee, whereas in New York, the charges came to 12.9% above the daily rate.

In order to avoid an unpleasant surprise when you arrive at the car rental counter, ask for all charges, no just the daily rate, when you make the reservation.

## Rental Car Additional Driver Charges

You're taking the family on a driving vacation using a rental car. But charges for an extra driver may give you an unpleasant surprise at the car rental counter.

Most car rental companies let your spouse or immediate family members drive without additional cost, but a few charge extra for relatives who also use the car. Many more charge for each additional driver other than the spouse of immediate family member.

There's no rational economic reason for an additional driver charge; the exception being high-risk younger drivers. It's just another way to inflate your car rental bill.

Another gambit is to charge the extra driver fee for the entire length of the rental, even though the other person may only be driving for a couple of days. But it's better to avoid the additional driver gouge than to evade it. Failure to have an additional driver sign up with the rental company is a violation of your contract and might negate your insurance protection, which is bad news if you're in an accident.

## *Rental Car Extra Charges*

If you are renting a car, there's an important question you should ask at the check-out counter.

The question: when must I return the car to avoid extra charges? For example, in a short-term rental, you may be surprised to find you have to pay for two full days, even if you rent the vehicle one afternoon and return it the next morning.

If you rent for the week and go over a few hours or days, you may have to pay a higher daily rate than you would expect based on the weekly charges. However, some companies do give you an hour's grace period. And you may be able to pay for the extra time on an hourly rate rather than for the whole day, which may turn out to be a better deal. But it's very important to establish the ground rules before you drive away from the rental lot.

Chapter 41

# Train and Subway Safety

In many countries, railroads continue to offer a safe, reliable and comfortable means of travel between major metropolitan areas. Other countries, however, operate rail systems that use antiquated equipment, are often over crowded and seldom run on time. As a general rule, the more advanced (socially and economically) a country is, the more modern and reliable will be its rail service. Frequently, rail travel provides a more economical method of travel than other modes of transportation, and frequently it is the only available transportation to smaller cities and towns. However, rail travel can present some security risks to the traveler, just like other means of travel.

Railroads are soft targets for several types of criminal or terrorist attacks. They operate over open ground and are easily accessible to the public. The tracks on which the trains operate are in the open for most of the distance they cover. This easy accessibility provides an inviting target for bombings and other forms of sabotage.

The railroad terminals and stations are like self-contained cities, open to the public, frequently for 24 hours a day. They provide a fertile ground for pickpockets, purse snatchers, baggage thieves, bombers and other criminals to operate.

Likewise, trains themselves offer similar opportunities to criminals and terrorists. A train is like a hotel on wheels, offering temporary accommodations, such as restaurants, sleeping space, bars and lounges. All of these can be, and often times are, subject to criminal

"Traveling by Train and Driving Abroad," an undated document produced by the U.S. Department of State. Cited November 2002.

activities including robbery, thievery, bombing and even, albeit rarely, hostage taking.

## Security Risks

Generally, railroad terminals and trains are easy targets for the following types of attacks: bombing and other forms of sabotage to railroad tracks, terminals and trains; robberies and burglaries; theft of unattended baggage on board trains and in rail terminals; and thefts from sleeping compartments.

Just as air travel calls for planning and preparation to lessen the risks of unfortunate experiences while traveling, rail travel also requires certain preventive measures in order to lessen the likelihood of the traveler becoming a victim. Some of these simple, yet effective, precautions can help make a rail trip a comfortable and convenient means of moving between or within many countries of the world.

## Some Precautionary Measures

**Prior to departure:** It should be noted that many cities have more than one railroad station. Travelers should confirm in advance from which station your train will depart. Make certain that you use the right one.

Make reservations in advance so that you do not have to stand in the frequently long lines at the rail station ticket counters. This is where pickpockets, baggage thieves and purse snatchers like to operate. Your hotel concierge can assist in making your reservations and picking up your ticket.

Travel light and always keep your luggage under your control. In the time it takes to set down your luggage to check a timetable, a baggage thief can make off with it.

Watch your tickets. Keep them in an inside pocket or purse to lessen the chance that they can be stolen. Do not discard your train ticket until completion of your trip and you have left the arrival area. In some countries you will be required to show your ticket at the exit of the arrival station. If you do not have it, you may be required to purchase another one. Hold on to your ticket, whether or not a conductor checks it.

Make certain that you board the right car and that it is going to your intended destination. Find out in advance if your car will have to be switched to another train en route, when and where this will occur, and the name of the stop just prior to the switching point; be prepared accordingly.

If you have to transfer to another train to reach your destination, determine this in advance and know where you will make the transfer, the time of transfer, and the train number and departure time of your connecting train (and the track number if possible).

Learn how to tell if you are in the correct car and if it goes to your destination. Name boards on the side of the car will tell you this. For example, a name board may appear like this:

VENEZIA
Bologna Firenze
ROMA

This shows that the car began in Venice, stops in Bologna and Florence, and terminates in Rome. Next to the steps leading into the car you should see the numeral 1 or 2, or both. The 1 indicates First Class; the 2 indicates Second Class; and 1at one end of the car and 2 at the other indicates one part of the car is First Class and the other is Second Class.

Make certain you know how to spell and pronounce the name of your destination city so you can recognize it when announced.

Be alert to train splitting. This occurs when part of the train is split off and attached to another train while the remainder of the original train then continues on its way. Check with the ticket agent or on board conductor to determine this.

Try not to schedule a late night or early morning arrival. You might find yourself stranded at a rail station with no public transportation. Arrange to be met at your arrival point whenever possible.

### On Board the Train

If possible, check unneeded luggage into the baggage car. Keep your luggage with you at all times. If you must leave your seat, either take the luggage with you or secure it to your seat or the baggage rack with a strong cable-lock.

Try to get a window seat. This provides a quick means of escape in the event of an accident.

Have necessary international documents, including your passport, handy and ready for inspection by immigration officials at each border crossing.

Always keep your camera and other valuables with you at all times. If you have a private compartment, keep the door locked and identify anyone wishing to gain access. Know the names of your porters and ask them to identify themselves whenever entering your compartment.

When in your compartment, be aware that some train thieves will spray chemicals inside to render the occupant(s) unconscious in order to enter and steal valuables. A locked door will at least keep them out. If you become suspicious of anyone, or someone bothers you, notify the conductor or other train personnel.

If you feel you must leave the train temporarily at a stop other than your destination, make certain that you are not left behind. An understanding of military time (the so-called 24-hour clock) will make it easier for you to understand the train schedule.

Make certain you have currency from each of the countries through which you will be traveling. In some lesser developed countries (and on some trains) it may be advisable to carry your own food and water.

## Upon Arrival

Make certain that you depart from the train at the correct location. Use only authorized taxis for transportation to your hotel or other destination. Be alert to criminals such as pick pockets, baggage thieves and/or unauthorized taxi drivers/guides.

If you do not have a hotel reservation, go to the in-station hotel services and reservations desk for help in obtaining a hotel room.

Chapter 42

# Safety and
# Security on Cruises

## Cruise Ship Travel: Preventive Measures

International cruise ship travelers often are uncertain about the
vaccines and prevention behaviors applicable to their particular cruise
itineraries. Cruise ships often visit international ports and passengers
disembark to sightsee and to experience the local culture; however,
among cruise ship passengers, risk of exposure to geographic-specific
infectious diseases is difficult to quantify because of limited data.
Because of this difficulty, the Centers for Disease Control and Prevention (CDC) recommends following those prevention and vaccine
recommendations that apply to each country visited (as detailed in this
text and at CDC's Travelers' Health website at http://www.cdc.gov/travel).
The traveler should be advised to consult with a travel health advisor
or a primary health care provider who may choose to modify the recommendations depending on the length of the traveler's visit ashore.

### *Sanitation*

In 1975, because of several major disease outbreaks on cruise vessels,
the Centers for Disease Control and Prevention (CDC) established the

---

"Cruise Ship Travel: Preventive Measures," excerpted from *Health Information for International Travel, 2001-2002*, produced by the Centers for Disease Control, available online at http://www.cdc.gov/travel/cruise.htm; "Cruise Ship Travel:
Health Recommendations," Centers for Disease Control, September 2002, available online, http://www.cdc.gov/travel/other/cruiseship_recommend.htm;
"Cruise Ship Consumer Fact Sheet," United Sates Coast Guard, 1998, http://
www.uscg.mil/hq/g-m/cruiseship.htm.

Vessel Sanitation Program (VSP) as a cooperative activity with the cruise ship industry. This joint program strives to achieve and maintain a level of sanitation on passenger vessels that will lower the risk of gastrointestinal disease outbreaks and provide a healthful environment for passengers and crews. CDC addresses the program goals by encouraging the industry to establish and maintain a comprehensive sanitation program and overseeing of its success through an inspection process. Every vessel having a foreign itinerary and carrying 13 or more passengers is subject to twice yearly unannounced inspections and, when necessary, reinspections. Inspections, conducted only at ports under U.S. control, cover such environmental aspects as:

- Water supply, storage, distribution, backflow protection, and disinfection.

- Food handling during storage, preparation, and service, and product temperature control.

- Potential contamination of food, water, and ice.

- Employee practices and personal hygiene.

- General cleanliness, facility repair, and vector control.

- Training programs in general environmental and public health practices.

A score of 86 or higher at the time of the inspection indicates that the ship is providing an acceptable standard of sanitation. In general, the lower the score, the lower the level of sanitation; however, a low score does not necessarily imply an imminent risk of an outbreak of gastrointestinal disease or other illness related to environmental sanitation. Each ship is required to document a plan for corrective action following each inspection. Inspectors will recommend a ship not sail if they detect an imminent health hazard aboard ship (for example, inadequate facilities for maintaining safe food temperatures or a contaminated drinking water system). Full information on inspection criteria can be obtained by writing to the VSP office. At any time, the Director of CDC may determine that failure to implement corrective actions presents a threat of communicable disease being introduced into the United States and may take additional action, including detaining the ship in port.

The scores and inspection reports for each ship are available via the Internet at http://www.cdc.gov/nceh/vsp. Scores are also published biweekly in the *Summary of Sanitation Inspections of International Cruise Ships*, commonly known as the *Green Sheet*. This sheet is distributed to travel-related services worldwide and is a way to communicate a ship's compliance with VSP recommendations both to the cruise ship industry and to the consumer. The *Green Sheet* is also available via the Internet site, as well as the CDC fax information service (1-888-232-6789; request information on Cruise Ship Sanitation Inspection Updates). Information can also be requested by sending an e-mail to vsp@cdc.gov or by writing to the Vessel Sanitation Program, National Center for Environmental Health, CDC, 4770 Buford Highway, NE, Mailstop F-16, Atlanta, Georgia 30341-3724.

## Cruise Ship Travel: Health Recommendations

Travel by cruise ship often congregates large groups of people from different parts of the U.S. and the world. In such settings, diseases can spread from person-to-person contact (e.g. measles, rubella, certain respiratory illnesses such as, influenza and certain gastrointestinal illnesses such as, Norwalk-like virus). Additionally, if a ship stops and passengers disembark to sightsee, they may be at risk for diseases in the geographic areas they visit, although such risk is difficult to quantify. It is also important to note, certain diseases can be transmitted before symptoms are apparent and that some people who become ill while on a cruise ship may have been infected prior to travel.

Anyone who becomes ill while on a cruise ship should seek medical attention on board and see a health care provider upon returning home. Ill persons should limit contact with the general population on board as much as possible to reduce further spread of disease. Ship authorities report infectious diseases of public health significance to state or federal health officials.

People planning cruise ship travel, especially anyone older than 65 years of age, anyone with acute or chronic illnesses or pregnant women should consult with a health care provider prior to travel for advice and possible preventive medication. Other measures to prevent the spread of infectious diseases on cruise ships include frequent hand washing and obtaining appropriate immunizations prior to travel.

# Cruise Ship Consumer Facts

## *Ocean Cruise Ships*

**Vessel safety.** Ocean-going cruise ships of U.S. registry must meet a comprehensive set of Coast Guard safety regulations and be inspected annually by the Coast Guard to check for compliance. The safety regulations cover such things as hull structure, watertight integrity, structural requirements to minimize fire hazards, equipment requirements for lifesaving, firefighting, and vessel control, and requirements pertaining to the safe navigation of the ship. If the ship passes its annual inspection, it is issued a Coast Guard Certificate of Inspection valid for one year. The certificate must be displayed where passengers can see it.

Today, nearly all the ocean cruise lines employ passenger ships registered under flags of various foreign countries. (Note: The law requires that cruise-ship advertising in the U.S. disclose the country of registry.) Each ship is subject to the vessel inspection laws of the country in which it is registered. However, as a condition of permitting the vessels to take on passengers at U.S. ports, the U.S. Coast Guard requires the ships to meet the International Convention for the Safety of Life at Sea (referred to as SOLAS.) SOLAS and other international regulations also require compliance with stringent regulations regarding structural fire protection, firefighting and lifesaving equipment, watercraft integrity and stability, vessel control, navigation safety, crewing and crew competency, safety management and environmental protection.

To insure compliance with SOLAS, the Coast Guard examines the ship when it first goes into service at a U.S. port, with quarterly checks thereafter. The examinations emphasize structural fire safety and proper lifesaving equipment. Fire and abandon ship drills conducted by the ship's crew are witnessed, and operational tests are made on key equipment such as steering systems, fire pumps, and lifeboats. The Coast Guard has the authority to require correction of any deficiencies before allowing the ship to take on passengers at the U.S. port. The records of these examinations (called Control Verification Examinations) are open to the public at the Coast Guard Marine Safety Office (MSO) which conducted the examination. To do a search for a specific vessel, contact our Port State Information Exchange web site at: http://psix.uscg.mil.

**Crewmember competency.** On U.S. passenger vessels, licensed individuals and crew must meet standards for experience and training set forth in Coast Guard regulations. The Coast Guard can revoke or suspend the individual's license or merchant mariner's document for acts of misconduct or incompetence. On foreign-flag cruise ships trading in the U.S., SOLAS requires the vessel to be sufficiently and efficiently manned. The officers' licenses and the vessel's compliance with manning standards are checked as part of the Control Verification Examination.

Medical care and services are not covered coast guard regulations and SOLAS generally focus on requirements for the safe navigation and design of the cruise ship itself. There are many aspects of the daily care of passengers and their on-board accommodation that are not covered by Government regulation. One example of this is medical care. The Coast Guard does not require that passenger vessels carry a ship's doctor. Most, if not all ocean-going passenger vessels today do provide a doctor and medical facilities in order to offer attractive and competitive service. Passengers should realize that the quality of their medical care is not guaranteed by Coast Guard regulations. If you are concerned about this aspect of life aboard a cruise ship, contact the cruise line or travel agent for the particulars of medical services provided, both at sea and while visiting foreign ports.

**Emergency drills.** Coast Guard regulations and SOLAS require that the master of an ocean cruise ship periodically hold fire and life-boat drills. They are intended not only to give the crew practice, but also to show the passengers how to act in the event of an emergency at sea. Passengers should participate fully in these drills. The timing and frequency of the drills depends in large part on the length of the voyage. On voyages that will last more than one week, the first drill will be held before the ship gets underway (passengers who embark at the last minute sometimes miss this drill), with additional drills at least once a week thereafter. On voyages of one week or less, the drills must be held within 24 hours after leaving port.

Coast Guard and international regulations also require a notice to be posted conspicuously in each passenger cabin or stateroom. The notice explains the following: How to recognize the ship's emergency signals (alarm bells and whistle signals are normally supplemented by announcements made over the ship's public address system); the location of life preservers provided for passengers in that stateroom (special life preservers for children will be provided, if necessary, by the room steward); instructions and pictures explaining how to put on the life preserver; and the lifeboat to which passengers in that stateroom are assigned. (Note: Passengers need not be alarmed if they discover that the total number of person's on board a cruise ship (passengers + crew) exceeds the total capacity of the ship's lifeboats. Modern cruise ships carry a variety of survival craft. Passengers are invariably assigned to lifeboats or similar survival craft. The total capacity of all the survival craft on board will exceed the total number of persons on the vessel).

When fire and lifeboat drills are held, crew members from the stewards department are generally responsible for assisting and directing passengers in the drill. Direction signs showing the path to reach lifeboats are posted in passageways and stairways throughout the ship. The crewmember in charge of each lifeboat will muster the passengers assigned to that lifeboat, and give passengers any final instructions necessary in the proper method of donning and adjusting their life preservers. If there is any portion of the emergency procedures the passenger doesn't understand, they should question the crew until the instructions are clear and completely understood.

**Sanitation and cleanliness.** Oversight of sanitary conditions on passenger vessels is the responsibility of the U.S. Public Health Service (USPHS). The USPHS conducts both scheduled and surprise inspections of passenger vessels in U.S. ports. The inspections focus on proper sanitation for drinking water, food storage, food preparation and handling, and general cleanliness. The USPHS will provide the public with results of inspections on individual vessels, and take reports of unsanitary conditions on individual vessels.

Vessels are responsible for proper trash disposal. As part of its mission to protect the marine environment, the Coast Guard enforces regulations regarding ocean dumping from vessels. The regulations make it illegal to dump plastic refuse and garbage mixed with plastic into any waters, and restrict dumping of non-plastic trash and other forms of garbage. These regulations apply to all U.S. vessels wherever they operate (except in waters under exclusive jurisdiction of a State), and to foreign vessels operating in U.S. waters out to and including the Exclusive Economic Zone (200 miles off shore).

**Terminal security.** In accordance with Federal regulations, terminal operators and cruise lines share the primary responsibility for shoreside and shipboard security of passengers. The Coast Guard examines all security plans and can require improvements in their security measures. Passengers embarking on international voyages may expect to have their baggage searched or passed through screening devices before boarding. The terminal operator and cruise line have strict procedures for passenger identification and visitor control. Passengers who wish to have friends visit the ship prior to sailing should check with the cruise line well in advance. All these security measures are designed to prevent the introduction of unauthorized weapons and persons on the cruise ship.

**Financial responsibility.** The Federal Maritime Commission requires that operators of passenger vessels carrying 50 or more passengers from a U.S. port must be financially capable of reimbursing their customers if the cruise is cancelled. The Commission also requires proof of ability to pay claims arising out of passenger injuries or death for which the ship operator may bear some liability. It is important to understand that the Commission does not have the legal authority to automatically secure these financial settlements for individual consumers. If a cruise is cancelled, or there is an injury incurred during the cruise, the consumer will have to initiate action on his or her own behalf against the cruise line.

## How to Complain

**Vessel safety:** Persons who wish to complain about a safety-related matter they have observed on a cruise ship should contact the Coast Guard Marine Safety Office (MSO) responsible for the Control Verification Examination of the ship. Interested persons can get a referral to the appropriate MSO by calling the Coast Guard toll-free Consumer Hotline: 1-800-368-5647. The most popular ports for cruise ships are Miami, FL; Juneau, AK, and San Juan, PR. The Coast Guard MSO telephone numbers are: (305) 535-8705 (Miami); (907) 463-2450 (Juneau), and (787) 729-6800 (San Juan).

**Sanitary conditions:** Reports of unsanitary conditions on a cruise ship can be made to: U.S. Public Health Service, Chief, Vessel Sanitation Program, National Center for Environmental Health, 1850 Eller Dr., Suite 101, Ft. Lauderdale, FL, 33316. Telephone: 954-356-6650.

**Illegal dumping:** Passengers on cruise ships who observe any dumping of plastic at sea should report it to the National Response Center by calling 1-800-424-8802 or the nearest Coast Guard MSO (to locate, call the Coast Guard Hotline.) A written report can be mailed to:

Commandant (G-MOR-3)
Response Operations Division
U.S. Coast Guard Headquarters
2100 Second Street SW
Washington, DC 20593-0001

**Terminal security:** Persons who wish to complain about security procedures in a terminal, or report lax security should contact the Coast Guard Marine Safety Office. Interested persons can get a referral to the appropriate MSO by calling the Coast Guard toll-free hotline: 1-800-368-5647.

**Cruise cancellation and financial reimbursements:** The Federal Maritime Commission cannot order a cruise line to reimburse passengers for cruise cancellations, or to pay claims for injuries or fatal accidents. However, to the extent they are able, Commission staff will try to assist individual consumers who are having trouble obtaining financial settlements in these areas.

# Part Six

# Additional Help and Information

Chapter 43

# Glossary of Terms
# Related to Travel Security

**alien:** Any person not a citizen or national of the United States.

**ATM:** Automated teller machine.

**aviation safety reporting system (ASRS):** Administered by NASA (National Aeronautics and Space Administration) for the FAA (Federal Aviation Administration), the ASRS receives, processes, analyzes, interprets and reports safety data provided voluntarily by pilots, controllers, flight attendants, mechanics and other users of the national airspace system. Reports may not be used for enforcement action by the FAA. The database information may be considered for making systemic safety changes.

**baggage:** Property necessary for the purpose of travel.

**commercial carrier:** Any firm furnishing commercial transportation. This includes airplanes, trains, ships, and buses.

**con:** The intentional misrepresentation of existing fact or condition, or the use of some other deceptive scheme or device, to obtain money, goods, or other things of value.

---

Terms from this glossary were compiled from the following government sources: Federal Aviation Administration; Federal Bureau of Investigation; Immigration and Naturalization Service, U.S. Department of Justice; National Institute of Environmental Health Sciences, National Institutes of Health; U.S. Army.

509

**continental United States (CONUS):** The 48 contiguous States and the District of Columbia.

**controlled flight into terrain (CFIT):** CFIT occurs when an aircraft is under control but the pilots lose their sense of where the plane is in relation to terrain features. CFIT accounts for about one-fourth of worldwide commercial air accidents.

**courier:** A cleared employee designated by the contractor, whose principal duty is to transmit classified material to its destination. The classified material remains in the personal possession of the courier except for authorized overnight storage.

**credit card/ATM fraud:** The unlawful use of a credit (or debit) card or automatic teller machine for fraudulent purposes.

**foreign government:** Any national governing body organized and existing under the laws of any country other than the United States and its possessions and trust territories and any agent or instrumentality of that government.

**foreign interest:** Any foreign government, agency of a foreign government, or representative of a foreign government; any form of business enterprise or legal entity organized, chartered, or incorporated under the laws of any country other than the U.S. or its possessions and trust territories, and any person who is not a citizen or national of the United States.

**foreign nationals:** Any person who is not a citizen or national of the United States.

**fraud:** The intentional perversion of the truth for the purpose of inducing another person or other entity in reliance upon it to part with some thing of value or to surrender a legal right.

**frequent flyer benefits:** Mileage points accumulated using the airlines frequent flyer mileage programs which results in free airline tickets.

**full-time student:** A student who attends undergraduate school a minimum of 12 equivalent semester hours, or meets the minimum requirements of the school to maintain a full time status.

**high risk personnel:** Personnel who are more likely to be terrorist or criminal targets because of their grade, assignment, symbolic value, vulnerabilities, location, or specific threat.

**hostage:** Any person held against his or her will as security for the performance of specific actions.

**impersonation:** Falsely representing one's identity or position, and acting in the character or position thus unlawfully assumed, to deceive others and thereby gain a profit or advantage, enjoy some right or privilege, or subject another person or entity to an expense, charge, or liability which would not have otherwise been incurred.

**infrequent traveler:** Individuals that travel less than two times per year.

**intelligence:** Intelligence is the product resulting from the collection, evaluation, analysis, integration, and interpretation of all available information, that concerns one or more aspects of foreign nations or of areas of foreign operations, and that is immediately or potentially significant to military planning and operations.

**national security:** The national defense and foreign relations of the United States.

**national:** A person owing permanent allegiance to a state.

**naturalization:** The conferring, by any means, of citizenship upon a person after birth.

**negotiations:** A dialogue between authorities and offenders which has as the ultimate goal the safe release of hostages and surrender of the offenders.

**passport:** Internationally recognized travel document issued under the authority of the Secretary of State attesting to the identity and nationality of the bearer. A passport indicates that its bearer is entitled to receive the protection and assistance of the diplomatic and consular offices of their country while abroad. In essence, it is a request on the part of the issuing government that officials of foreign governments permit the bearer to travel or sojourn in their territories and afford them lawful aid and protection. A passport does not constitute authority to enter any country; however, many countries have procedures which permit U.S. citizens to enter their territory without further documentation upon presentation of a U.S. passport.

**runway incursions:** Any occurrence at an airport that involves an aircraft, vehicle, person, or object on the ground that creates a collision hazard or results in loss of separation with an aircraft taking off, intending to take off, landing, or intending to land.

**soldier:** U.S. Army officers, warrant officers, and enlisted personnel.

**terrorism:** The calculated use of violence or the threat of violence to attain political, religious, or ideological goals. Terrorists intimidate, coerce, and instill fear. Terrorism involves a criminal act that is often symbolic in nature and intended to influence an audience beyond the immediate victims.

**unaccompanied baggage:** Baggage which can be shipped in conjunction with the traveler to the authorized destination, but will not accompany the traveler.

Chapter 44

# International Embassies and Travel Warnings Resources

The following embassies can be contacted to obtain information about passports, visas, immunizations, AIDs/HIV testing, and other subjects necessary for ensuring security and health when traveling to these areas.

For obtaining specific travel warnings related to these countries, contact the U.S. Department of State using the information below. The Department of State also keeps an updated, extensive listing of travel warnings on the Web at http://travel.state.gov/travel_warnings.html.

### U.S. Department of State
2201 C Street NW
Washington, DC 20520
Phone: 202-647-4000
Hotline for American Travelers: 202-647-5225

### Embassy Contact Information

**Afghanistan**
Embassy of Afghanistan
2000 L Street, N.W.
Washington, DC 20036
Phone: 202-416-1620

**Albania**
Embassy of the Republic of Albania
2100 S. Street, N.W.
Washington, DC 20008
Phone: 202-223-4942

---

Embassy contact information excerpted from "Foreign Entry Requirements," U.S. Department of State, Bureau of Consular Affairs, Office of Public Affairs and Policy Coordination, May 2002 (online at http://travel.state.gov/foreignentryreqs.html). Addresses verified and updated in November 2002.

## Algeria

Embassy of the Democratic and Popular Republic of Algeria
2137 Wyoming Ave., N.W.
Washington, DC 20008
Phone: 202-265-2800
Internet: http://www.algeria-us.org

## Angola

Embassy of Angola
2100 16ᵗʰ Street, N.W.
Washington, DC 20009
Phone: 202-452-1042
Internet: http://www.angola.org

## Antigua and Barbuda

Embassy of Antigua and Barbuda
3216 New Mexico Ave., N.W.
Washington, DC 20016
Phone: 202-362-5122

## Argentina

Argentine Embassy
1718 Connecticut Ave., N.W.
Washington, DC 20009
Phone: 202-238-6460
Regional Consulate: CA 213-954-9155, FL 305-373-7794, GA 404-880-0805, IL 312-819-2620, NY 212-603-0400 or TX 713-871-8935
Internet: http://www.uic.edu/orgs/argentina

## Armenia

Embassy of the Republic of Armenia
2225 R Street, N.W.
Washington, DC 20008
Phone: 202-319-2983
Consulate General in Beverly Hills, CA: 310-657-6102
Internet: http://www.armeniaemb.org

## Aruba

Embassy of the Netherlands
Phone: 202-244-5300
Consulate General: CA 310-266-1598, IL 312-856-0110, NY 212-246-1429 or TX 713-622-8000

## Australia

Embassy of Australia
1601 Mass. Ave., N.W.
Washington, DC 20036
Phone: 202-797-3145 or Consulate General: CA 310-229-4840
Internet: http://www.immi.gov.au or http://www.austemb.org

## Austria

Embassy of Austria
3524 International Court, N.W.
Washington, DC 20008
Phone: 202-895-6767 or nearest Consulate General: CA 310-444-9310, IL 312-222-1515, or NY 212-737-6400

## Azerbaijan

Embassy of the Republic of Azerbaijan
2741 34ᵗʰ Street, N.W.
Washington, DC 20008
Phone: 202-337-3500

## Azores

Contact the Embassy of Portugal
Phone: 202-332-3007

## Bahamas

Embassy of the Commonwealth of the Bahamas
2220 Massachusetts Ave., N.W.
Washington, DC 20008
Phone: 202-319-2660 or nearest Consulate: FL 305-373-6295 or NY 212-421-6420

## Bahrain

Embassy of the State of Bahrain
3502 International Drive, N.W.
Washington, DC 20008
Phone: 202-342-0741 or:
The Permanent Mission to the
U.N.
866 Second Ave., 14th Floor
New York, NY 10017
Phone: 212-223-6200
Internet: http://www.bahrain
embassy.org

## Bangladesh

Embassy of the People's Republic of Bangladesh
3510 International Drive., N.W.
Washington, DC 20008
Phone: 202-244-0183, or the
Bangladesh Mission in New
York at 212-867-3434
Internet: http://www.
bangladoot.org

## Barbados

Embassy of Barbados
2144 Wyoming Ave., N.W.
Washington, DC 20008
Phone: 202-939-9200, or
Consulate General in New York
212-867-8435

## Belarus

Embassy of the Republic of
Belarus
1619 New Hampshire Ave., N.W.
Washington, DC 20009
Phone: 202-986-1606
Consulate General
708 3rd Ave., 21st Floor
New York, NY 10017
Phone: 212-682-5392

## Belgium

Embassy of Belgium
3330 Garfield St., N.W.
Washington, DC 20008
Phone: 202-333-6900, or nearest
Consulate General: CA 323-857-
1244, GA 404- 659-2150, IL 312-
263-6624, or NY 212-586-5110

## Belize

Embassy of Belize
2535 Massachusetts Ave., N.W.
Washington, DC 20008
Phone: 202-332-9636, or the
Belize Mission in New York at
212-599-0233

## Benin

Embassy of the Republic of
Benin
2737 Cathedral Ave., N.W.
Washington, DC 20008
Phone: 202-232-6656

## Bermuda

Contact the British Embassy
Phone: 202-588-7800
(See United Kingdom)

## Bhutan

Bhutan Mission to the U.N.
2 United Nations Plaza
27th Floor
New York, NY 10017
Phone: 212-826-1919 or:
The Bhutan Travel Service
120 E 56th Street, Suite 1130
New York, NY 10022
Toll Free: 800-950-9908
Phone: 212-838-6382

## Bolivia

Embassy of Bolivia (Consular Section)
3014 Mass. Ave., N.W.
Washington, DC 20008
Phone: 202-232-4827, or nearest Consulate General: CA 415-495-5173, FL 305-358-3450, NY 212-687-0530, or

## Bosnia and Herzegovina

Consulate General
866 U.N. Plaza, Suite 580
New York, NY 10017
Phone: 212-593-0264
Internet: http://www.bhembassy.org

## Botswana

Embassy of the Republic of Botswana
531 New Hampshire Ave., N.W.
Washington, DC 20036
Phone: 202-244-4990, or nearest Honorary Consulate: CA 213-626-8484, or TX 713-680-1155

## Brazil

Brazilian Embassy (Consular Section)
3009 Whitehaven St., N.W.
Washington, DC 20008
Phone: 202-238-2828, or nearest Consulate: CA 323-651-2664 or 415-981-8170, FL 305-285-6200, IL 312-464-0244, MA 617-542-4000, NY 917-777-7777 or TX 713-961-3063
Internet: http://www.brasilemb.org

## Brunei Darussalam

Embassy of Brunei Darussalam
3520 International Court, N.W.
Washington, DC 20008
Phone: 202-342-0159 or:
Brunei Darussalam Permanent Mission to the U.N.
711 United Nations Plaza
New York, NY 10017
Phone: 212-697-3465

## Bulgaria

Embassy of the Republic of Bulgaria
1621 22nd St., N.W.
Washington, DC 20008
Phone: 202-387-7969 or:
The Bulgarian Consulate in New York
Phone: 212-935-4646
Internet: http://www.bulgaria-embassy.org

## Burkina Faso

Embassy of Burkina Faso
2340 Mass. Ave., N.W.
Washington, DC 20008
Phone: 202-332-5577, or Honorary Consulate in CA 310-575-5555 or LA 504-945-3152
Internet: http://burkinaembassy-usa.org

### Burma (Myanmar)
Burmese Embassy (Embassy of the Union of Myanmar)
2300 S St., N.W.
Washington, DC 20008
Phone: 202-332-9044, or:
The Myanmar Consulate
General Office
10 East 77th St.
New York, NY 10021
Phone: 212-535-1310

### Burundi
Embassy of the Republic of Burundi
2233 Wisconsin Ave.
Suite 212, N.W.
Washington, DC 20007
Phone: 202-342-2574, or
Permanent Mission of Burundi to the U.N. 212-499-0001

### Cambodia
Royal Embassy of Cambodia
4500 16th Street, N.W.
Washington, DC 20011
Phone: 202-726-7742
Internet: http://
www.embassy.org/Cambodia

### Cameroon
Embassy of the Republic of Cameroon
2349 Mass. Ave., N.W.
Washington, DC 20008
Phone: 202-265-8790

### Canada
Canadian Embassy
501 Pennsylvania Ave., N.W.
Washington, DC 20001
Phone: 202-682-1740, or nearest
Consulate General: CA 213-346-2701, MI 313-567-2085, NY 212-596-1700 or 716-858-9501, or WA 206-443-1375
Internet: http://www.cic.gc.ca

### Cape Verde
Embassy of the Republic of Cape Verde
3415 Mass. Ave., N.W.
Washington, DC 20007
Phone: 202-965-6820, or:
Consulate General
535 Boylston St., 2nd Floor
Boston, MA 02116
Phone: 617-353-0014
Internet: http://
www.capeverdeusembassy.org

### Cayman Islands
(See West Indies, British)

### Central African Republic
Embassy of Central African Republic
1618 22nd St., N.W.
Washington, DC 20008
Phone: 202-483-7800

### Chad
Embassy of the Republic of Chad
2002 R St., N.W.
Washington, DC 20009
Phone: 202-462-4009
Internet: http://
www.chadembassy.org

## Chile

Embassy of Chile
1732 Mass. Ave., N.W.
Washington, DC 20036
Phone: 202-785-1746, or nearest
Consulate General: CA 310-785-
0113 and 415-982-7662, FL 305-
373-8623, IL 312-654-8780, PA
215-829-9520, NY 212-355-0612,
TX 713-621-5853
Internet: http://www.chile-usa.org

## China, People's Republic of

Chinese Embassy
2201 Wisconsin Avenue, N.W.
Washington, DC 20007
Phone: 202-338-6688, or nearest
Consulate General: CA 213-807-
8018 and 415-563-4857, IL 312-
803-0098, NY 212-330-7409, TX
713-524-4311
Internet: http://www.china-
embassy.org/eng

## Colombia

Colombian Consulate
1875 Conn. Ave., N.W.
Suite 218
Washington, DC 20009
Phone: 202-332-7476, or nearest
Consulate General: CA 323-653-
4299 or 415-495-7195, FL 305-
448-5558 or 441-0437, GA
404-255-3038, IL 312-923-1196,
LA 504-525-5580, MA 617-536-
6222, NY 212-949-9898, or TX
713-527-8919
Internet: http://www.
colombiaemb.org

## Comoros Islands

Embassy of the Federal and
Islamic Republic of Comoros
336 East 45th St.
2nd Floor
New York, NY 10017
Phone: 212-972-8010

## Congo, Democratic Republic of the (formerly Zaire)

Embassy of the Democratic
Republic of the Congo
1800 New Hampshire Ave., N.W.
Washington, DC 20009
Phone: 202-234-7690 or:
Permanent Mission to the U.N.
747 Third Ave.
New York, NY 10017

## Congo, Republic of the

Embassy of the Republic of the
Congo
4891 Colorado Ave., N.W.
Washington, DC 20011
Phone: 202-726-5500

## Cook Islands

Consulate for the Cook Islands
Kamehameha Schools, #16
Kapalama Heights
Honolulu, HI 96817
Phone: 808-847-6377

## Costa Rica

Embassy of Costa Rica
2112 S St. N.W.
Washington, DC 20008
Phone: 202-234-2945
 or nearest Consulate General:
(see next page)

CA 415-392-8488, GA 404-951-7025, FL 305-371-7485, IL 312-263-2772, LA 504-887-8131, NY 212-425-2620, or TX 713-266-1527
Internet: http://costarica-embassy.org

### Côte d'Ivoire (Ivory Coast)
Embassy of the Republic of Côte d'Ivoire
2424 Mass. Ave., N.W.
Washington, DC 20008
Phone: 202-797-0300, or
Honorary Consulate: CA 415-391-0176

### Croatia
Embassy of Croatia
2343 Massachusetts Ave., N.W.
Washington, DC 20008
Phone: 202-588-5899, or the nearest Consulate General in CA 310-477-1009, OH 440-951-4246, or NY 212-599-3066
Internet: http://www.croatiaemb.org

### Cuba
Contact the Embassy of Switzerland
Cuban Interests Section
2630 16th Street, N.W.
Washington, DC 20009
Phone: 202-797-8518
Spanish Speakers: 202-797-8609

### Curacao
(See Netherlands Antilles)

### Cyprus
Embassy of the Republic of Cyprus
2211 R St., N.W.
Washington, DC 20008
Phone: 202-462-5772, or the Consulate General in New York 212-686-6016, or the nearest Honorary Consulate: AR 602-264-9701, CA 310-397-0771, FL 904-953-2802, GA 770-941-3760, IL 847-296-0064, IN 219-481-6897, LA 504-568-9300, MA 617-497-0219, MI 313-582-1411, NC 910-353-2115, OR 503-248-0500, PA 215-728-6980, TX 713-928-2264, VA 757-481-3583, or WA 425-827-1700

### Czech Republic
Embassy of the Czech Republic
3900 Spring of Freedom St., N.W.
Washington, DC 20008
Phone: 202-274-9123, or the nearest Consulate General: Los Angeles, CA 310-473-0889, or New York, NY 212-717-5643
Internet: http://www.mzv.cz/Washington

### Denmark (including Greenland)
Royal Danish Embassy
3200 Whitehaven St., N.W.
Washington, DC 20008
Phone: 202-234-4300, or nearest Consulate General: CA 310-443-2090, Chicago 312-787-8780, or New York 212-223-4545
Internet: http://www.denmarkemb.org

## Djibouti

Embassy of the Republic of
Djibouti
1156 15ᵗʰ St., N.W.
Suite 515
Washington, DC 20005
Phone: 202-331-0270, or:
The Djibouti Mission to the U.N.
866 United Nations Plaza
Suite 4011
New York, NY 10017
Phone: 212-753-3163

## Dominica

Consulate of the Commonwealth
of Dominica
3216 New Mexico Avenue, N.W.
Washington, DC 20016
Phone: 202-364-6791

## Dominican Republic

Embassy of the Dominican
Republic
1715 22ⁿᵈ St., N.W.
Washington, DC 20008
Phone: 202-332-6280, or nearest
Consulate General: AL 334-342-
5648, CA 510-864-7777, FL 305-
375-9537 or 904-346-0909,
HI 808-396-5702, GA 404572-
4814, IL 847-441-1831, LA 504-
522-1843, MD 410-560-2101,
MA 617-482-8121, MI 248-559-
0684, MN 612-339-7566,
NY 212-768-2480, PA 215-923-
3006, or TX 713-266-0165
Internet: http://www.domrep.org

## Ecuador (including the Galapagos Islands)

Embassy of Ecuador
2535 15ᵗʰ St., N.W.
Washington, DC 20009
Phone: 202-234-7166, or nearest
Consulate General: CA 323-658-
6020 or 415-957-5921, FL 305-
539-8214, IL 312-329-0266,
LA 504-523-3229, MA 617-738-
9465, NJ 201-985-2959, NY 212-
808-0211, or TX 713-572-8731

## Egypt

Embassy of the Arab Republic of
Egypt
3521 International Court, N.W.
Washington, DC 20008
Phone: 202-895-5400, or nearest
Consulate General: CA 415-346-
9700, IL 312-828-9162, NY 212-
759-7120, or TX 713-961-4915
Internet: http://
www.touregypt.net

## El Salvador

Consulate General of
El Salvador
1424 16ᵗʰ St., N.W.
Suite 200
Washington, DC 20036
Phone: 202-331-4032, or nearest
Consulate: CA 213-383-5776,
415-781-7924 or 714-542-3250,
FL 305-371-8850, LA 504-522-
4266, MA 617-577-9111,
NY 212-889-3608, or TX 713-
270-6239 or 214-637-1018
Internet: http://
www.elsalvador.org

## England
(See United Kingdom)

## Equatorial Guinea
Embassy of the Republic of
Equatorial Guinea
2020 16th Street, N.W.
Washington DC 20009
Phone: 202-518-5700

## Eritrea
Embassy of Eritrea
1708 New Hampshire Ave., N.W.
Washington, DC 20009
Phone: 202-319-1991

## Estonia
Consulate General of Estonia
600 Third Avenue
26th Floor
New York, NY 10016
Phone: 212-883-0636
Internet: http://www.estemb.org

## Ethiopia
Embassy of Ethiopia
3506 International Dr., N.W.
Washington, DC 20008
Phone: 202-364-1200
Internet: http://
www.ethiopianembassy.org

## Federal Republic of Yugoslavia
(See Serbia and Montenegro)

## Fiji
Embassy of the Republic of the
Fiji Islands
2233 Wisconsin Ave., N.W.
#240
Washington, DC 20007
Phone: 202-337-8320
Internet: http://www.bulafiji.com

## Finland
Embassy of Finland
3301 Massachusetts Ave., N.W.
Washington, DC 20008
Phone: 202-298-5800, or nearest
Consulate General: CA 310-203-
9903, or NY 212-750-4400
Internet: http://www.finland.org

## Former Yugoslav Republic of Macedonia
Embassy of the Former Yugoslav
Republic of Macedonia
3050 K St., N.W.
Suite 210
Washington, DC 20007
Phone: 202-337-3063, or:
The Consulate General
866 United Nations Plaza
Suite 4018
New York, NY 10017
Phone: 212-317-1727

## France

Consulate General of France
4101 Reservoir Rd., N.W.
Washington, DC 20007
Phone: 202-944-6200, or nearest
Consulate: CA 310-235-3200 or
415-397-4330, FL 305-372-9799,
GA 404-495-1660, IL 312-787-
5359, LA 504-523-5772, MA 617-
542-7374, NY 212-606-3644, or
TX 713-572-2799
Internet: http://www.info-france-
usa.org

## French Guiana

Consulate General of France
4101 Reservoir Rd., N.W.
Washington, DC 20007
Phone: 202-944-6200
Internet: http://www.france-
consulat.org

## French Polynesia

Consulate General of France
Phone: 202-944-6200
Internet: http://www.france-
consulat.org

## Gabon

Gabonese Republic
2034 20th St., Suite 200, N.W.
Washington, DC 20009
Phone: 202-797-1000 or:
The Permanent Mission of the
Gabonese Republic to the UN
18 East 41st St., 6th Floor
New York, NY 10017
Phone: 212-686-9720

## Galapagos Islands

Contact the Embassy of Ecuador
Phone: 202-234-7166

## Gambia

Embassy of the Gambia
1155 15th St., N.W.
Washington, DC 20005
Phone: 202-785-1399 or:
Permanent Mission of The
Gambia to the U.N.
820 2nd Ave., 9th Floor
New York, NY 10017
Phone: 212-949-6640
Internet: http://
www.gambia.com

## Georgia

Embassy of the Republic of
Georgia
1615 New Hampshire Ave.,
N.W., Suite 300
Washington, DC 20009
Phone: 202-393-6060

## Germany

Embassy of the Federal
Republic of Germany
4645 Reservoir Rd., N.W.
Washington, DC 20007
Phone: 202-298-4393, or nearest
Consulate General: CA 415-775-
1061 or 213-930-2703, FL 305-
358-0290, GA 404-659-4760,
IL 312-580-1199, MA 617-536-
4414, MI 313-962-6526, NY 212-
610-9700, TX 713-627-7770, or
WA 206-682-4312
Internet: http://www.germany-
info.org

## Ghana

Embassy of Ghana
3512 International Drive, N.W.
Washington, DC 20008
Phone: 202-686-4520, or:
Consulate General
19 East 47<sup>th</sup> St.
New York, NY 10017
Phone: 212-832-1300
Internet: http://www.ghana-embassy.org

## Gibralter

Contact the British Embassy
Phone: 202-588-7800
(See United Kingdom)

## Gilbert Islands

(See Kiribati)

## Great Britain and Northern Ireland

(See United Kingdom)

## Greece

Embassy of Greece
2221 Mass. Ave., N.W.
Washington, DC 20008
Phone: 202-939-5818 or 5800, or
nearest Consulate: CA 310-826-5555 or 415-775-2102, GA 404-261-3313IL 312-335-3915,
LA 504-523-1167, MA 617-543-0100, NY 212-988-5500, or
TX 713-840-7522
Internet: http://
www.greekembassy.org

## Greenland

Contact the Royal Danish Embassy
Phone: 202-234-4300

## Grenada

Consulate General of Grenada
1701 New Hampshire Ave., N.W.
Washington, DC 20009
Phone: 202-265-2561, or:
Permanent Mission of Grenada
to the U.N.
Phone: 212-599-0301

## Guadeloupe

(See West Indies, French)

## Guatemala

Embassy of Guatemala
2220 R St., N.W.
Washington, DC 20008-4081
Phone: 202-745-4952, or nearest
Consulate: CA 213-365-9251 or
415-788-5651, FL 305-443-4828,
IL 312-332-3170, NY 212-686-3837, or TX 713-953-9531
Internet: http://www.guatemala-embassy.org

## Guiana, French

(See French Guiana)

## Guinea

Embassy of the Republic of
Guinea
2112 Leroy Pl., N.W.
Washington, DC 20008
Phone: 202-483-9420

## Guinea-Bissau

Embassy of Guinea-Bissau
1511 K Street, NW
Suite 519
Washington, DC 20005

## Guyana
Embassy of Guyana
2490 Tracy Pl., N.W.
Washington, DC 20008
Phone: 202-265-6900, or Consulate General: 212-527-3215

## Haiti
Embassy of Haiti
2311 Mass. Ave., N.W.
Washington, DC 20008
Phone: 202-332-4090, or nearest Consulate: FL 305-859-2003, MA 617-266-3660, NY 212-697-9767, PR 809-764-1392, or IL 312-922-4004
Internet: http://www.haiti.org

## Holland
(See Netherlands)

## Holy See, Vatican City State
Apostolic Nunciature
3339 Mass. Ave., N.W.
Washington, DC 20008
Phone: 202-333-7121

## Honduras
Embassy Honduras
1528 K Street, N.W., 2nd Floor
Washington, DC 20006
Phone: 202-737-2972, or nearest Consulate General: CA 213-383-9244 and 415-392-0076, FL 305-447-8927, IL 773-342-8281, LA 504-522-3118, NY 212-269-3611, or TX 713-622-7911
Internet: http://www.hondurasemb.org

## Hong Kong
Special Administrative Region
Embassy of the People's
Republic of China
Phone: 202-338-6688
Internet: http://www.china-embassy.org/eng

## Hungary
Embassy of the Republic of Hungary
3910 Shoemaker Street, N.W.
Washington, DC 20008
Phone: 202-362-6730, or the nearest Consulate General: CA 310-473-9344 or NY 212-752-0661
Internet: http://www.hungaryemb.org

## Iceland
Embassy of Iceland
1156 15th Street, N.W.
Suite 1200
Washington, DC 20005
Phone: 202-265-6653, or Consulate General in NY 212-593-2700
Internet: http://www.iceland.org/us

## India
Embassy of India
2536 Mass. Ave., N.W.
Washington, DC 20008
Phone: 202-939-9806, or nearest Consulate General: CA 415-668-0683, IL 312-595-0405, TX 713-626-2355, or NY 212-774-0600
Internet: http://www.indianembassy.org

## Indonesia
Embassy of the Republic of
Indonesia
2020 Massachusetts Ave., N.W.
Washington, DC 20036
Phone: 202-775-5200 or nearest
Consulate General: CA 213-383-
5126 or 415-474-9571, IL 312-
595-1777, NY 212-879-0600, or
TX 713-785-1691

## Iran, Islamic Republic of
Embassy of Pakistan
Iranian Interests Section
2209 Wisconsin Ave., N.W.
Washington, DC 20007
Phone: 202-965-4990
Internet: http://www.daftar.org

## Iraq
Iraqi Interests Section
1801 P Street, N.W.
Washington, DC 20036
Phone: 202-483-7500

## Ireland
Embassy of Ireland
2234 Mass. Ave., N.W.
Washington, DC 20008
Phone: 202-462-3939, or nearest
Consulate General: CA 415-392-
4214, IL 312-337-1868, MA 617-
267-9330, or NY 212-319-2555
Internet: http://www.ireland
emb.org

## Israel
Embassy of Israel
3514 International Dr., N.W.
Washington, DC 20008
Phone: 202-364-5527, or nearest
Consulate General: CA 323-852-
5500 and 415-844-7500, FL 305-
925-9400, GA 404-487-6500,
IL 312-297-4800, MA 617-535-
0200, NY 212-499-5400, PA 215-
546-5556, or TX 713-627-3780
Internet: http://
www.israelemb.org

## Italy
Embassy of Italy
Whitehaven Street, N.W.
Washington, DC 20008
Phone: 202-612-4400, or nearest
Consulate General: CA 310-820-
0622 or 415-931-4924, FL 305-
374-6322, TX 713-850-7520, IL
312-467-1550, MA 617-542-
0483, MI 313-963-8560, NY 212-
737-9100, PA 215-592-7329, or
TX 713-850-7520
Internet: http://www.italy
emb.org

## Jamaica
Embassy of Jamaica
1520 New Hampshire Ave., N.W.
Washington, DC 20036
Phone: 202-452-0660, or nearest
Consulate: CA 310-559-3822 or
510-266-0072, FL 305-374-8431,
IL 312-663-0023, NY 212-935-
9000, MA 617-266-8604, TX 713-
774-2229, or WA 253-872-8950

## Japan

Embassy of Japan
2520 Mass. Ave., N.W.
Washington, DC 20008
Phone: 202-238-6800, or nearest
Consulate General: AK 907-279-8428, CA 213-617-6700 or 415-777-3533, FL 305-530-9090, GA 404-892-2700, HI 808-543-3111, IL 312-280-0400, LA 504-529-2101, MA 617-973-9772, MI 313-567-0120, MO 816-471-0111, NY 212-371-8222, OR 503-221-1811, TX 713-652-2977, or WA 206-682-9107
Internet: http://www.embjapan.org

## Jordan

Embassy of the Hashemite
Kingdom of Jordan
3504 International Dr., N.W.
Washington, DC 20008
Phone: 202-966-2664, or nearest
Consulate General: CA 415-546-1155, MI 248-557-4377, NY 212-832-0119, or TX 713-224-2911
Internet: http://www.jordanembassyus.org/new

## Kazakhstan

Embassy of the Republic of
Kazakhstan
1401 16th Street, N.W.
Washington, DC 20036
Phone: 202-232-5488, or:
Consulate
866 UN Plaza
Suite 586 A
New York, NY 10017
Phone: 212-888-3024

## Kenya

Embassy of Kenya
2249 R St., N.W.
Washington, DC 20008
Phone: 202-387-6101, or Consulate General: CA 310-274-6635, or NY 212-486-1300
Internet: http://www.kenyaembassy.com

## Kiribati (formerly Gilbert Islands)

Contact the Embassy of Fiji
Phone: 202-337-8320

## Korea, Democratic People's Republic of (North Korea)

Office of Foreign Assets Control
Department of the Treasury
1331 G St., N.W.
Washington, DC 20220
Phone: 202-622-2480
Internet: http://www.ustreas.gov/offices/enforcement/ofac

## Korea, Republic of (South Korea)

Embassy of the Republic of Korea
Consular Division
2320 Massachusetts Ave., N.W.
Washington, DC 20008
Phone: 202-939-5663, or nearest
Consulate General: CA 213-385-9300 and 415-921-2251, FL 305-372-1555, GA 404-522-1611, HI 808-595-6109, IL 312-822-9485, MA 617-348-3660, NY 212-752-1700, TX 713-961-0186, or WA 206-441-1011

## Kuwait

Embassy of the State of Kuwait
2940 Tilden St., N.W.
Washington, DC 20008
Phone: 202-966-0702, or:
Consulate
321 East 44th St.
New York, NY 10017
Phone: 212-973-4318
Internet: http://www.kuwait-info.org

## Kyrgyz Republic (Kyrgyzstan)

Embassy of the Kyrgyz Republic
1732 Wisconsin Ave., N.W.
Washington, DC 20007
Phone: 202-338-5143
Internet: http://www.kyrgyzstan.org

## Laos

Embassy of the Lao People's
Democratic Republic
2222 S St., N.W.
Washington, DC 20008
Phone: 202-667-0076
Internet: http://www.visit-laos.com

## Latvia

Embassy of Latvia
4325 17th St., N.W.
Washington, DC 20011
Phone: 202-726-8213
Internet: http://www.latvia-usa.org

## Lebanon

Embassy of Lebanon
2560 28th St., N.W.
Washington, DC 20008
Phone: 202-939-6300, or
nearest Consulate General:
CA 323-467-1253, MI 313-567-0233, or NY 212-744-7905

## Leeward Islands

(See Virgin Islands, British)

## Lesotho

Embassy of the Kingdom of
Lesotho
2511 Mass. Ave., N.W.
Washington, DC 20008
Phone: 202-797-5533

## Liberia

Embassy of the Republic of
Liberia
5201 16th Street, N.W.
Washington, DC 20011
Phone: 202-723-0437
Internet: http://www.liberiaemb.org

## Libya

Office of Foreign Assets Control
Department of the Treasury
1331 G St., N.W.
Washington, DC 20220
Phone: 202-622-2480
Internet: http://www.ustreas.gov/offices/enforcement/ofac

*Liechtenstein*
Contact the Embassy of Switzerland
2900 Cathedral Ave., N.W.
Washington, DC 20008
Phone: 202-745-7900, or the nearest Consulate General: CA 310-575-1145 or 415-788-2272, GA 404-870-2000, IL 312-915-0061, NY 212-599-5700, or TX 713-650-0000
Internet: http://www.eda.admin.ch/washington_emb/e/home

*Lithuania*
Embassy of Lithuania
2622 16th St., N.W.
Washington, DC 20009
Phone: 202-234-5860, or
Consulate General in New York
420 Fifth Avenue
New York, NY 10018
Phone: 212-354-7849

*Luxembourg*
Embassy of Luxembourg
2200 Mass. Ave., N.W.
Washington, DC 20008
Phone: 202-265-4171, or the nearest Consulate: CA 415-788-0816, or NY 212- 888-6664

*Macau*
Special Administrative Region
Chinese Embassy
2201 Wisconsin Avenue, N.W.
Washington, DC 20007
Phone: 202-338-6688, or the nearest Chinese Consulate General: (see next page)

CA 213-807-8018 or 415-563-4857, IL 312-803-0098, NY 212-330-7409, or TX 713-524-4311 or
Macau Tourist Information Bureau
77 Seventh Avenue, Suite 2R
New York, N.Y. 10011
Phone: 212-206-6828
Internet: http://www.macau.gov.mo

*Macedonia*
(See Former Yugoslav Republic of Macedonia)

*Madagascar, Republic of*
Embassy of the Democratic Republic of Madagascar
2374 Mass. Ave., N.W.
Washington, DC 20008
Phone: 202-265-5525, or:
U.N. Mission in New York, 212-986-9491
Internet: http://www.embassy.org/Madagascar

*Malawi*
Embassy of Malawi
2408 Mass. Ave., N.W.
Washington, DC 20008
Phone: 202-797-1007, or:
Malawi Mission to the U.N.
600 3rd Ave.
New York, NY 10016
Phone: 212-949-0180

*Malaysia*
Embassy of Malaysia
2401 Mass. Ave., N.W.
Washington, DC 20008
Phone: 202-328-2700
or (see next page)

nearest Consulate: CA 213-892-1238, or NY 212-490-2722
Internet: http://www.undp.org/missions/Malaysia

## Maldives
Maldives Mission to the U.N. in New York
Phone: 212-599-6195

## Mali
Embassy of the Republic of Mali
2130 R St., N.W.
Washington, DC 20008
Phone: 202-332-2249

## Malta
Embassy of Malta
2017 Conn. Ave., N.W.
Washington, DC 20008
Phone: 202-462-3611, or nearest Consulate: CA 415-468-4321, MI 313-525-9777, MO 816-833-0033, MN 612-228-0935, NY 212-725-2345, PA 610-664-7475, or TX 713-428-7800 or 214-777-4463

## Marshall Islands, Republic of the
Embassy of Marshall Islands
2433 Massachusetts Avenue, N.W.
Washington, DC 20008
Phone: 202-234-5414, or:
Permanent Mission to the U.N.
220 East 42nd St.
New York, NY 10017
Phone: 212-983-3040, or the Consulate General in Hawaii
808-545-7767
Internet: http://www.rmiembassyus.org

## Martinique
(See West Indies, French)

## Mauritania
Embassy of the Republic of Mauritania
2129 Leroy Pl., N.W.
Washington, DC 20008
Phone: 202-232-5700

## Mauritius
Embassy of Mauritius
4301 Conn. Ave., N.W.
Suite 441
Washington, DC 20008
Phone: 202-244-1491, or the Honorary Consulate:
Los Angeles 818-788-3720

## Mayotte Island
Contact the Embassy of France
Phone: 202-944-6000
Internet: http://www.france-consulat.org

## Mexico
Embassy of Mexico
2827 16th St., N.W.
Washington, DC 20009-4260
Phone: 202-736-1000, or nearest Consulate General: AZ 602-242-7398, CA 213-351-6800, 415-392-5554 and 619-231-8414, CO 303-331-1110, FL 305-716-4977, GA 404 266 1913, IL 312 855-1380, LA 504-522-3596, NY 212-689-0460, or TX 210-227-1085, 214-630-7341, 713-542-2300, 512-478-9031 and 915-533-4082

## Micronesia, Federated States of (Chuuk, Kosrae, Pohnei, and Yap)
Embassy of the Federated States of Micronesia
1725 N St., N.W.
Washington, DC 20036
Phone: 202-223-4383, or nearest
Consulate: Hawaii 808-836-4775
Internet: http://www.fsm
gov.org

## Miquelon Island
Contact the Embassy of France
Phone: 202-944-6000
Internet: http://www.france-consulat.org

## Moldova
Embassy of the Republic of Moldova
2101 S Street, N.W.
Washington, DC 20008
Phone: 202-667-1130
Internet: http://
www.moldova.org

## Monaco
Contact the Embassy of France
Phone: 202-944-6000, or
nearest Honorary Consulate of
the Principality of Monaco:
CA 213-655-8970 or 415-362-5050, IL 312-642-1242, LA 504-522-5700, NY 212-759-5227
Internet: http://www.france-consulat.org

## Mongolia
Embassy of Mongolia
2833 M Street, N.W.
Washington, DC 20007
Phone: 202-333-7117, or:
UN Mission of Mongolia
6 East 77th St.
New York, NY 10021
Phone: 212-861-9460
Internet: http://www.un.int/
Mongolia

## Montserrat
(See West Indies, British)

## Morocco
Embassy of Morocco
1601 21st St., N.W.
Washington, DC 20009
Phone: 202-462-7734, or Consulate General in New York 212-213-9644

## Mozambique
Embassy of the Republic of Mozambique
1990 M St., N.W., Suite 570
Washington, DC 20036
Phone: 202-293-7146, or:
Mozambique Consulate
420 East 50th St.
New York, NY 10022
Phone: 212-644-5965

## Myanmar
(see Burma)

## Namibia
Embassy of Namibia
1605 New Hampshire Ave., N.W.
Washington, DC 20009
Phone: 202-986-0540

## Nauru
Consulate of the Republic of
Nauru in Guam
Ada Professional Bldg.
Marine Dr., 1st Floor
Agana, Guam 96910

## Nepal
Royal Nepalese Embassy
2131 Leroy Pl., N.W.
Washington, DC 20008
Phone: 202-667-4550, or
Consulate General in New York
212-370-3988
Internet: http://www.undp.org/
missions/Nepal

## Netherlands
Embassy of the Netherlands
4200 Linnean Ave., N.W.
Washington, DC 20008
Phone: 202-244-5300, or nearest
Consulate General: CA 310-268-
1598, IL 312-856-0110, NY 212-
246-1429, or TX 713-622-8000
Internet: http://
www.netherlands-embassy.org

## Netherlands Antilles
(Islands include Bonaire,
Curacao, Saba, St.
Eustatius, St. Maarten)
Contact the Embassy of the
Netherlands
Phone: 202-244-5300
Internet: http://
www.netherlands-embassy.org

## New Caledonia
(See French Polynesia)

## New Zealand
Embassy of New Zealand
37 Observatory Circle, N.W.
Washington, DC 20008
Phone: 202-328-4800, or the
Consulate General in
Los Angeles 310-207-1605
Internet: http://www.nzemb.org

## Nicaragua
Consulate of Nicaragua
1627 New Hampshire Ave., N.W.
Washington, DC 20009
Phone: 202-939-6531, or the
nearest Consulate in CA 213-
252-1170 or 415-765-6821,
FL 305-220-6900, LA 504-523-
1507, NY 212-983-1981, or TX
713-272-9628

## Niger
Embassy of the Republic of
Niger
2204 R St., N.W.
Washington, DC 20008
Phone: 202-483-4224

## Nigeria
Embassy of the Republic of
Nigeria
2201 M Street, N.W.
Washington, DC 20037
Phone: 202-822-1500, or the
Consulate General in New York
212-715-7200

## Niue
Contact the Embassy of New
Zealand
Phone: 202-328-4800
Internet: http://nzemb.org

## Norfolk Island
Contact the Australian Embassy
Phone: 202-797-3000
Internet: http://www.
austemb.org or http://
www.pitcairners.org

## Norway
Royal Norwegian Embassy
2720 34th St., N.W.
Washington, DC 20008
Phone: 202-333-6000, or nearest
Consulate General: CA 415-986-
0766, FL 305-358-4386, MN 612-
332-3338, NY 212-421-7333, or
TX 713-521-2900
Internet: http://www.norway.org

## Oman
Embassy of the Sultanate of
Oman
2535 Belmont Rd., N.W.
Washington, DC 20008
Phone: 202-387-1980

## Pakistan
Embassy of Pakistan
2315 Mass. Ave., N.W.
Washington, DC 20008
Phone: 202-939-6295, or CA 310-
441-5114, or NY 212-879-5800
Internet: http://www.pakistan-
embassy.com

## Palau, The Republic of
Representative Office
1150 18th St., N.W.
Suite 750
Washington, DC 20036
Phone: 202-452-6814

## Panama
Embassy of Panama
2862 McGill Terrace, N.W.
Washington, DC 20008
Phone: 202-483-1407, or the
nearest Consulate: CA 415-391-
4268, FL 305-371-7031 or 813-
831-6685, LA 504-525-3458, NY
212-840-2450, PA 215-574-2994,
or TX 713-622-4451

## Papua New Guinea
Embassy of Papua New Guinea
1779 Massachusetts Ave., N.W.,
#805
Washington, DC 20036
Phone: 202-745-3680, or:
Papua New Guinea Honorary
Consulate
P.O. Box 893133
Mililani, Honolulu, Hawaii 96789
Phone: 808-623-8144
Internet: http://
www.pngembassy.org

## Paraguay
Embassy of Paraguay
2400 Mass. Ave., N.W.
Washington, DC 20008
Phone: 202-483-6960
Internet: http://
www.usembparaguay.gov.py

## Peru
Consulate General of Peru
1625 Mass. Ave., N.W., Suite 605
Washington, DC 20036
Phone: 202-462-1084, or nearest
Consulate: CA 213-252-5910 and
415-362-5185, FL 305-374-1305,
IL 312-853-6174, NY 212-481-
7410, or TX 713-355-9438

## Philippines

Embassy of the Philippines
1600 Mass. Ave., N.W.
Washington, DC 20036
Phone: 202-467-9300, or nearest
Consulate General: CA 213-639-
0980 and 415-433-6666, HI 808-
595-6316, NY 212764-1330
Internet: http://www.
philippineembassy-usa.org

## Poland

Embassy of the Republic of Poland
2224 Wyoming Ave., N.W.
Washington, DC 20008
Phone: 202-234-3800, or:
Consulate General
1530 North Lakeshore Dr.
Chicago, IL, 60610
Phone: 312-337-8166
Consulate General
12400 Wilshire Blvd., Suite 555
Los Angeles, CA, 90025
Phone: 310-442-8500
Consulate General
233 Madison Ave.
New York, NY, 10016
Phone: 646-237-2100
Internet: http://
www.polandembassy.org

## Portugal (Includes travel to the Azores and Madeira Islands)

Embassy of Portugal
2310 Tracy Pl., N.W.
Washington, DC 20008
Phone: 202-332-3007, or the
nearest Consulate: CA 415-346-
3400, MA 617-536-8740 and 508-
997-6151, NJ 973-643-4200, NY
212-246-4580, or RI 401-272-2003

## Qatar

Embassy of the State of Qatar
4200 Wisconsin Ave., N.W.
Suite 200
Washington, DC 20016
Phone: 202-274-1603

## Reunion

Contact the Embassy of France
Phone: 202-944-6200
Internet: http://www.france-consulat.org

## Romania

Embassy of Romania
1607 23rd St., N.W.
Washington, DC 20008
Phone: 202-332-4851, or the
nearest Consulate General:
New York 212-682-9120, or
Los Angeles 310-444-0043
Internet: http://
www.roembus.org

## Russia

Embassy of Russia
2641 Tunlaw Road, N.W.
Washington, DC 20007
Phone: 202-939-8907, or the
nearest Consulate General:
NY 212-348-0926, CA 415-928-
6878, or WA 206-728-1910
Internet: http://
www.russianembassy.org

## Rwanda

Embassy of the Republic of
Rwanda
1714 New Hampshire Ave., N.W.
Washington, DC 20009
Phone: 202-232-2882, or:
The Permanent Mission of
Rwanda to the U.N.
124 East 39th Street
New York, NY 10016
Phone: 212-696-0644, or the
nearest Consulate General in
Chicago 708-205-1188, or
Denver 303-321-2400

## Saint Kitts and Nevis

Embassy of Saint Kitts and
Nevis
3216 New Mexico Ave., N.W.
Washington, DC 20016
Phone: 202-686-2636, or
The Permanent Mission to the
U.N.
414 East 75th St., Fifth Floor
New York, NY 10021
Phone: 212-535-1234
Internet: http://
www.stkittsnevis.org

## Saint Lucia

Embassy of Saint Lucia
3216 New Mexico Ave.
Washington, DC 20016
Phone: 202-364-6792, or:
The Permanent Mission to the U.N.
820 Second Ave., Suite 900E
New York, NY 10017
Phone: 212-697-9360

## St. Martin (St Maarten)

(See West Indies, French or
Netherlands Antilles)

## St. Pierre

Contact the Embassy of France
Phone: 202-944-6000
Internet: http://www.france-
consulat.org

## Saint Vincent and The Grenadines

Embassy of Saint Vincent and
The Grenadines
3216 New Mexico Ave.
Washington, DC 20016
Phone: 202-364-6730, or:
Consulate
801 Second Ave., 21st Floor
New York, NY 10017
Phone: 212-687-4490

## Samoa

Independent State of Samoa
Mission to the U.N.
820 2nd Avenue, Suite 800
New York, NY
Phone: 212-599-6196, or the
Honorary Consul in Hawaii 808-
677-7197

## San Marino

Honorary Consulate of the Republic of San Marino
1899 L St., N.W., Suite 500
Washington, DC 20036
Phone: 202-223-3517, or MI 313-
528-1190, or NY 516-242-2212

## Sao Tome and Principe

Permanent Mission of Sao Tome
and Principe to the U.N.
400 Park Avenue, 7th Floor
New York, NY 10022
Phone: 212-317-0533

## Saudi Arabia
Royal Embassy of Saudi Arabia
601 New Hampshire Ave., N.W.
Washington, DC 20037
Phone: 202-342-3800, or nearest
Consulate General: CA 213-479-
6000, NY 212-752-2740, or TX
713-785-5577
Internet: www.saudiembassy.net

## Scotland
(See United Kingdom)

## Senegal
Embassy of the Republic of Senegal
2112 Wyoming Ave., N.W.
Washington, DC 20008
Phone: 202-234-0540

## Serbia and Montenegro
Embassy of Serbia and Montenegro
2134 Kalorama Rd., NW
Washington, DC 20008
Phone: 202-332-0333
Internet: www.yuembusa.org

## Seychelles
Permanent Mission of
Seychelles to the U.N.
800 Second Ave., Suite 400
New York, NY 10017
Phone: 212-972-1785

## Sierra Leone
Embassy of Sierra Leone
1701 19th St., N.W.
Washington, DC 20009
Phone: 202-939-9261

## Singapore
Embassy of Singapore
3501 International Pl., N.W.
Washington, DC 20008
Phone: 202-537-3100

## Slovak Republic
Embassy of the Slovak Republic
3523 International Court, N.W.
Washington, DC 20008
Phone: 202-237-1054
Internet: http://
www.slovakembassy-us.org

## Slovenia
Embassy of the Republic of
Slovenia
1525 New Hampshire Ave., N.W.
Washington, DC 20036
Phone: 202-667-5363, or the
Consulate General of Slovenia
in New York 212-370-3006

## Solomon Islands
Solomon Islands Mission to the
U.N.
820 2nd Ave.
Suite 800A
New York, NY 10017
Phone: 212-599-6192

## Somalia
Consulate of the Somali Demo-
cratic Republic in New York
Phone: 212-688-9410

## South Africa
Embassy of South Africa's
Consular Office
3051 Massachusetts Ave., N.W.
Washington, DC 20008
Phone: 202-232-4400, or the
nearest Consulate in CA 323-
651-0902, IL 312-939-7929, or
NY 212-213-4880
Internet: http://
www.southafrica.net

## Spain

Embassy of Spain
2375 Pennsylvania Ave., N.W.
Washington, DC 20037
Phone: 202-452-0100, or nearest
Consulate General in CA 415-
922-2995 and 213-938-0158,
FL 305446-5511, IL 312-782-
4588, LA 504-525-4951, MA 617-
536-2506, NY 212-355-4080, or
TX 713-783-6200
Internet: http://
www.spainemb.org

## Sri Lanka

Embassy of Sri Lanka
2148 Wyoming Ave., N.W.
Washington, DC 20008
Phone: 202-483-7954, or the
Consulate in CA 323-634-0479
and 323-634-1079, or the near-
est Honorary Consul General:
GA 404-881-7164,
LA 504-455-7600, or NY 212-
966-7040
Internet: http://
www.srilankaembassyusa.org

## Sudan

Embassy of the Republic of the
Sudan
2210 Mass. Ave., N.W.
Washington, DC 20008
Phone: 202-338-8565, or:
Consulate General
655 Third Ave., 5th Floor
New York, NY 10017
Phone: 212-573-6033
Internet: sudanembassyus.org

## Suriname

Embassy of the Republic of
Suriname
4301 Connecticut Ave., N.W.,
Suite 460
Washington, DC 20008
Phone: 202-244-7488, or the
Consulate in Miami 305-593-2697

## Swaziland

Embassy of the Kingdom of
Swaziland
1712 New Hampshire Ave., N.W.
Washington, DC 20009
Phone: 202-234-5002

## Sweden

Embassy of Sweden
1501 M St., N.W.
Washington, DC 20005-1702
Phone: 202-467-2600, or nearest
Consulate General: CA 310-445-
4008, New York 212-583-2550
Internet: http://
www.swedeninfo.com

## Switzerland

Embassy of Switzerland
2900 Cathedral Ave., N.W.
Washington, DC 20008
Phone: 202-745-7900, or the
nearest Consulate General:
CA 310-575-1145 or 415-788-
2272, GA 404-870-2000, IL 312-
915-0061, NY 212-599-5700, or
TX 713-650-0000
Internet: http://
www.eda.admin.ch/
washington_emb

## Syria
Embassy of the Syrian Arab
Republic
2215 Wyoming Ave., N.W.
Washington, DC 20008
Phone: 202-232-6313

## Tahiti
(See French Polynesia)

## Taiwan
Taipei Economic and Cultural
Representative Office
4201 Wisconsin Avenue, N.W.
Washington, DC 20016-2137
Phone: 202-895-1800
or Taipei Economic and Cultural Office in CA 213-389-
1215 or 415-362-7680, FL
305-443-8917, GA 404-872-
0123, HI 808-595-6347, IL 312-
616-0100, MA 617-737-2050,
MO 816-531-1298, NY 212-317-
7300, TX 713-626-7445, or WA
206-441-4586
Internet: http://www.taipei.org
or http://www.boca.gov.tw

## Tajikistan
Contact the Embassy of Russia
Phone: 202-939-8907
Internet: http://
www.russianembassy.org

## Tanzania
Embassy of Tanzania
2139 R St., N.W.
Washington, DC 20008
Phone: 202-939-6125, or:
Tanzanian Permanent Mission
to the U.N.
205 East 42nd St., 13th Floor
New York, NY 10017
Phone: 212-972-9160

## Thailand
Royal Thai Embassy
1024 Wisconsin Ave., N.W.
Washington, DC 20007
Phone: 202-323-3600, or the nearest Consulate General: IL 312-
664-3129, or NY 212-754-1770
Internet: http://
www.thaiembdc.org

## Togo
Embassy of the Republic of Togo
2208 Mass. Ave., N.W.
Washington, DC 20008
Phone: 202-234-4212

## Tonga
Consulate General of Tonga
360 Post St., Suite 604
San Francisco, CA 94108
Phone: 415-781-0365

## Trinidad and Tobago
Embassy of Trinidad and Tobago
1708 Mass. Ave., N.W.
Washington, DC 20036
Phone: 202-467-6490, or the
nearest Consulate General: FL
305-374-2199, or NY 212-682-
7272

## Tunisia
Embassy of Tunisia
1515 Mass. Ave., N.W.
Washington, DC 20005
Phone: 202-862-1850, or nearest
Consulate: CA 415-922-9222, or
NY 212-272-6962

## Turkey
Consular Office of the Embassy
of the Republic of Turkey
2525 Massachusetts Ave., N.W.
Washington, DC 20008
Phone: 202-612-6740, or nearest
Consulate: CA 323-937-0118,
IL 312-263-0644, NY 212-949-
0160, or TX 713-622-5849
Internet: http://www.turkey.org

## Turkmenistan
Embassy of Turkmenistan
2207 Massachusetts Ave., N.W.
Washington, DC 20008
Phone: 202-588-1500
Internet: http://
www.turkmenistanembassy.org

## Turks and Caicos
(See West Indies, British)

## Tuvalu
Contact the British Embassy
Phone: 202-588-7800
(See United Kingdom)

## Uganda
Embassy of the Republic of Uganda
5911 16th St., N.W.
Washington, DC 20011
Phone: 202-726-7100, or:
Permanent Mission to the U.N.
Phone: 212-949-0110

## Ukraine
Consular Office of the Embassy
of Ukraine
3350 M St., N.W.
Washington, DC 20007
Phone: 202-333-7507, or the
Consulate in Chicago 312-642-
4388, or the Consulate General
in New York 212-371-5690
Internet: http://
www.ukremb.com

## United Arab Emirates
Embassy of the United Arab
Emirates
3522 International Court, N.W.
Washington, DC 20008
Phone: 202-243-2400

## United Kingdom (England, Northern Ireland, Scotland, and Wales)
British Embassy
19 Observatory Circle, N.W.
Washington, DC 20008
Phone: 202-588-7800, or nearest
Consulate General: CA 310-477-
3322, IL 312-346-1810, or
NY 212-745-0200
Internet: http://
www.britainusa.com

## Uruguay
Consulate of Uruguay
2715 M St., N.W., 3rd Floor
Washington, DC 20007
Phone: 202-331-4219, or nearest
Consulate General: CA 310-394-
5777, FL 305-443-7453, or NY
212-753-8191
Internet: http://
www.embassy.org/Uruguay

## Uzbekistan

Embassy of the Republic of
Uzbekistan
1746 Massachusetts Ave., N.W.
Washington, DC 20008
Phone: 202-530-7284, or:
The Uzbekistan Consulate
866 United Nations Plaza
Suite 327A
New York, NY 10017
Phone: 212-754-6178
Internet: http://
www.uzbekconsul.org

## Vanuatu

Vanuatu Mission to the U.N.
Phone: 212-593-0144

## Vatican

(See Holy See)

## Venezuela

Embassy of Venezuela
1099 30ᵗʰ Street, N.W.
Washington, DC 20007
Phone: 202-342-2214, or the
nearest Consulate: CA 415-955-
1982, FL 305-577-4214, IL 312-
236-9655, LA 504-522-3284,
MA 617-266-9368, NY 212-826-
1660, or TX 713-961-5166
Internet: http://www.embavenez-
us.org

## Vietnam

Embassy of Vietnam
1233 20ᵗʰ St., N.W., Suite 400
Washington, DC 20036
Phone: 202-861-2293
Internet: http://
www.vietnamembassy-usa.org

## Virgin Islands (British Islands include Anegarda, Jost van Dyke, Tortola and Virgin Gorda)

Contact the British Embassy
Phone: 202-588-7800
(See United Kingdom)

## Wales

(See United Kingdom)

## West Indies (British Islands include Anguilla, Montserrat, Cayman Islands, Turks and Caicos)

Contact the British Embassy
Phone: 202-588-7800
(See United Kingdom)

## West Indies (French Islands include Guadeloupe, Isles des Saintes, La Desirade, Marie Galante, Saint Barthelemy, St. Martin and Martinique)

Contact the Embassy of France
Phone: 202-944-6200
Internet: http://www.france-
consulat.org

## Western Samoa

(See Samoa)

## Yemen, Republic of

Embassy of the Republic of Yemen
2600 Virginia Ave., N.W., Suite 705
Washington, DC 20037
Phone: 202-965-4760, or:
Yemen Mission to the U.N.
866 United Nations Plaza, Rm. 435
New York, NY 10017
Phone: 212-355-1730

## Zaire

(See Congo, Democratic
Republic of )

## Zambia

Embassy of the Republic of
Zambia
2419 Mass. Ave., N.W.
Washington, DC 20008
Phone: 202-265-9717

## Zanzibar

(See Tanzania)

## Zimbabwe

Embassy of Zimbabwe
1608 New Hampshire Ave., N.W.
Washington, DC 20009
Phone: 202-332-7100

Chapter 45

# Other Travel
# Security Resources

## Consumer Affairs Contacts for Popular Airlines

### Alaska Airlines
Manager, Consumer Affairs
PO Box 68900, SEAZI
Seattle, WA 98168-0900
Phone: 206-870-6062
Internet: http://
www.alaskaair.com

### America West Airlines
Director, Customer Relations
4000 E. Sky Harbor Boulevard
Phoenix, AZ 85034
Phone: 480-693-6719
Fax: 480-693-2300
Internet: http://
www.americawest.com

### American Airlines
Managing Director
Customer Relations
P.O. Box 619612 M/D 2400
DFW Airport, TX 75261-9612
Phone: 817-967-2000
Fax: 817-967-4162
Internet: http://www.aa.com

### Continental Airlines
Director, Customer Care
P.O. Box 4607, HQS-CR
Houston, TX 77210-4607
Toll Free: 800-932-2732
Internet: http://
www.continental.com

Resources verified November 2002.

541

### Delta Air Lines
Director, Customer Care
P.O. Box 20980
Atlanta, GA 30320-2980
Phone: 404-715-1450
Internet: http://www.delta.com

### Federal Aviation Administration
Consumer Hotline
AOA-20, FAA
800 Independence Ave., S.W.
Washington, DC 20591
Internet: http://www2.faa.gov
E-Mail: 9-awa-aoa-consumer@faa.gov

### Northwest Airlines
Director, Customer Relations
P.O. Box 11875 M/S C6590
St. Paul, MN 55111-3034
Phone: 612-726-2046
Internet: http://www.nwa.com

### Southwest Airlines
VP, Customer Relations/Rapid Rewards
P.O. Box 36647
Dallas, TX 75235-1647
Phone: 214-792-4223
Internet: http://www.southwest.com

### United Airlines
Director, Customer Relations
P.O. Box 66100
Chicago, IL 60666
Toll Free: 877-228-1327
Fax: 877-406-1059 (Toll Free)
Internet: http://www.ual.com

### U.S. Airways
Managing Director, Corporate and Consumer Affairs
P.O. Box 1501
Winston-Salem, NC 27102
Phone: 336-661-0061
Internet: http://www.usairways.com

## U.S. Government Travel Resources

### Office of Aviation Enforcement and Proceedings
400 Seventh Street, SW
Room 4107
Washington, DC 20590
Phone: 202-366-9342
Internet: http://www.dot.gov/ost/ogc/org/aviation

### U.S. Customs and Border Protection
1300 Pennsylvania Ave., N.W.
Washington, DC 20229
Phone: 202-354-1000
Internet: http://www.cbp.gov

### U.S. Department of Homeland Security
Washington, DC 20528
Internet: www.dhs.gov

### U.S. Department of Transportation
400 7th Street, S.W.
Washington, DC 20590
Phone: 202-366-4000
Internet: http://www.dot.gov

# Contact Information for Filing Airline Complaints

## *Aviation Consumer Protection Division*
U.S. Department of Transportation
400 7th Street, S.W.
Room 4107
Washington, DC 20590
Phone: 202-366-2220
TTY: 202-366-0511
Internet: http://airconsumer.ost.dot.gov/problems.htm
E-Mail: airconsumer@ost.dot.gov

Complaints alleging discriminatory treatment by air carrier personnel (e.g., pilots, flight attendants, gate agents or check in counter personnel) should be directed to the Department of Transportation's Aviation Consumer Protection Division. This office provides complaint forms for consumers to download and print on its website and accepts complaints via e-mail or standard mail.

## *Department of Treasury*
Office of Internal Affairs
U.S. Customs Service
P.O. Box 14475
1200 Pennsylvania Avenue, N.W.
Washington, DC 20044
Toll Free: 877-422-2557 (24 hours/day)
Phone: 202-927-1016
Fax: 202-927-4607

Complaints alleging discriminatory treatment by Customs Service officials should be directed to the Department of Treasury's Office of Internal Affairs. The Department of Treasury's Office of Internal Affairs accepts complaints via phone or mail.

## *Federal Aviation Administration*
Office of Civil Rights
800 Independence Ave., S.W.
Room 1030
Washington, DC 20591
Internet: http://www2.faa.gov

Complaints alleging discriminatory treatment by airport personnel (e.g., airport police) should be directed by mail to the Federal Aviation Administration's Office of Civil Rights.

## Immigration and Naturalization Service (INS)

*Office of the Inspector General*
U.S. Department of Justice
950 Pennsylvania Ave., N.W.
Suite 4706
Washington, DC 20530
Toll Free: 800-869-4499
Fax: 202-616-9881
Internet: http://www.usdoj.gov/oig
E-Mail: oig@hotline@usdoj.gov

*Office of Internal Audit*
U.S. Department of Justice
425 I Street, N.W.
Room 3260
Washington, DC 20536

Complaints alleging discriminatory treatment by Immigration and Naturalization Service (INS) personnel of the Department of Justice, including Border Patrol personnel, should be directed to the Department of Justice's Office of the Inspector General and/or the Immigration and Naturalization Service's Office of Internal Audit. The Office of the Inspector General accepts complaints via e-mail, phone, or via fax, as well as standard mail.

## National Guard Bureau

Equal Employment Office
Director, EEO Division
National Guard Bureau
Jefferson Plaza 1
Room 2400
1411 Jefferson Davis Highway
Arlington, VA 22202-3231
Internet: http://www.ngb.dtic.mil

Complaints alleging discriminatory treatment by members of the National Guard should be directed by mail to the National Guard Bureau's Equal Employment Office.

### Office of Professional Responsibility

U.S. Department of Justice
935 Pennsylvania Ave., N.W.
Washington, DC 20535
Internet: http://www.usdoj.gov/opr

Complaints alleging discriminatory treatment by Federal Bureau of Investigation (FBI) personnel should be directed to the Department of Justice's Office of the Inspector General and/or the Federal Bureau of Investigation's Office of Professional Responsibility. The Office of the Inspector General accepts complaints via e-mail, phone, as well as standard mail.

### Office of the Inspector General

U.S. Department of Justice
950 Pennsylvania Ave., N.W.
Suite 4706
Washington, DC 20530
Toll Free: 800-869-4499
Fax: 202-616-9881
Internet: http://www.usdoj.gov/oig
E-Mail: oig@hotline@usdoj.gov

### Transportation Security Administration (TSA-1)

U.S. Department of Transportation
400 Seventh St., S.W.
Washington, DC 20590
Phone: 866-289-9673
Internet: http://www.tsa.gov
E-Mail: TSA-ConsumerResponse@tsa.dot.gov

Complaints alleging discriminatory treatment by Federal security screeners (e.g., personnel screening and searching passengers and carry-on baggage at airport security checkpoints) should be directed by mail to the Department of Transportation's Transportation Security Administration.

## Resources for Travel Health Issues

**American Red Cross National Headquarters**
431 18th Street, N.W.
Washington, DC 20006
Toll Free: 877-272-7337
Phone: 202-639-3520
Internet: http://www.redcross.org

**American Society of Tropical Medicine and Hygiene (ASTMH)**
60 Revere Drive, Suite 500
Northbrook, IL 60062
Phone: 847-480-9592
Fax: 847-480-9282
Internet: http://www.astmh.org
E-Mail: astmh@astmh.org

**APHIS (Animal and Plant Health Inspection Service)**
U.S. Department of Agriculture
Deputy Administrator
4700 River Road, Unit 84
Riverdale, MD 20737-1234
Toll Free: 866-SAFGUARD (recorded traveler information)
Phone: 301-734-4981
Fax: 301-734-5786
Internet: http://www.aphis.usda.gov

**FEMA (Federal Emergency Management Agency)**
500 C Street, S.W.
Washington, DC 20472
Toll Free: 800-480-2520
Phone: 202-566-1600
Internet: http://www.fema.gov

**International Society of Travel Medicine (ISTM)**
P.O. Box 871089
Stone Mountain, GA 30087-0028
Phone: 770-736-7060
Fax: 770-736-6732
Internet: http://www.istm.org
E-Mail: istm@istm.org

**PAHO (Pan American Health Organization)**
525 23rd Street, N.W.
Washington, DC 20037
Phone: 202-974-3000
Fax: 202-974-3663
Internet: http://www.paho.org
E-Mail: publinfo@paho.org

**U.S. Department of State**
Overseas Citizens Services
Office of American Citizen Services and Crisis Management
Department of State
2201 C Street N.W.
Room 4817, N.S.
Washington, DC 20520
Phone: 202-647-5225 or 202-647-5226
Internet: http://travel.state.gov/overseas_citizens.html

**WHO Headquarters**
Avenue Appia 20
1211 Geneva 27
Switzerland
Phone: 011-41-22-791-2111
Fax: 011-41-22-791-3111
Internet: http://www.who.int
E-Mail: info@who.int

# Passport Resources

**Boston Passport Agency**
Thomas P. O'Neill Fed. Bldg.,
Room 247
10 Causeway Street
Boston, Massachusetts 02222-1094
Phone: 617-565-6990
Internet: http://travel.state.gov/ppt_bn.html

**Chicago Passport Agency**
Kluczynski Federal Bldg.
Suite 380
230 South Dearborn Street
Chicago, Illinois 60604-1564
Phone: 312-341-6020
Internet: http://travel.state/gov/ppt_cg.html

**Department of State**
Passport Services, Correspondence Branch
1111 19th Street, N.W.
Suite 510
Washington, DC 20522-1705
Phone: 202-955-0219
Internet: http://www.state.gov

**Honolulu Passport Agency**
Prince Jonah Kuhio
Kalanianaole Federal Building
300 Ala Moana Blvd.
Suite I-330
Honolulu, Hawaii 96850
Phone: 808-522-8283
Internet: http://travel.state.gov/ppt_hh.html

## Office of Children's Issues

Children's Passport Issuance
Alert Program (CPIAP)
2201 C Street, N.W.
SA22, Room 2100
Washington, DC 20520-4818
Phone: 202-736-7000
Fax: 202-312-9743

## Other Travel Resources

**American Society of Travel Agents (ASTA)**
1101 King St.
Alexandria, VA 22314
Phone: 703-739-2782
Fax: 703-684-8319
Internet: http://www.astanet.com

**Amtrak**
Toll Free: 800-USA-RAIL
Internet: http://www.amtrak.com
E-Mail: service@sales.Amtrak.com

**Federal Railroad Administration**
1120 Vermont Avenue, N.W.
Washington, DC 20590
Phone: 202-493-6395
Internet: http://www.fra.dot/gov

**Greyhound Lines, Inc.**
Customer Service, Customer Assistance, or Refunds
P.O. Box 660689, MS 490
Dallas, TX 75266-0689
Phone: 214-849-8966
Internet: http://www.greyhound.com

**Hostelling International**
733 15ᵗʰ Street, N.W., Suite 840
Washington, DC 20005
Phone: 202-783-6161
Fax: 202-783-6171
Internet: http://www.hiayh.org
E-Mail: hostels@hiayh.org

**Office of Children's Issues**
Overseas Citizens Services
Bureau of Consular Affairs
Room 4817
Washington, DC 20520
Phone: 202-647-7000

**Overseas Security Advisory Council**
Bureau of Diplomatic Security
U.S. Department of State
Washington, DC 20522-1003
Phone: 202-663-0533
Fax: 202-663-0868
Internet: http://ww.ds-osac.org
E-Mail: osac@dsmail.state.gov

Chapter 46

# References for
# Additional Reading

## Sources of Air Travel Information

The following publications can be ordered from the sources listed. Availability and prices are subject to change.

### Consumer Information Center

To order any of the following publications, write to the Consumer Information Center, P.O. Box 100, Pueblo, CO 81002.

* Fly Rights: Information on how to cope with delayed and canceled flights, overbooking, baggage problems, air fares, frequent-flyer programs, and other air service issues. 58 pp. $1.75.

* Fly Smart—An Air Traveler's Guide: Air safety information for passengers. Free.

* New Horizons for the Air Traveler with a Disability. 40 pp. Free.

---

This chapter includes information excerpted from "Sources of Air Travel Information," Office of Aviation Enforcement and Proceedings, U.S. Department of Transportation, July 2000, updated May 2003. The full text is available online at http://airconsumer.ost.dot.gov. Additional resources listed under the headings "Selected Books of Interest to Travelers" and "Information and Updates on the Internet" were compiled from multiple sources deemed reliable. Inclusion does not constitute endorsement.

- Foreign Entry Requirements: Visa and other requirements for many foreign countries. 50 cents.

- Passports: Applying for Them the Easy Way. 50 cents.

### Superintendent of Documents

To order any of the following publications, write to the Superintendent of Documents, P.O. Box 371954, Pittsburgh, PA 15250-7954.

- A Safe Trip Abroad: Precautions against robbery, terrorism. $1.25.

- Health Information for International Travelers: Information on travelers diarrhea, risks from food and water, medical care abroad (including advice about blood transfusions), and more. $20.00 (220 pp.).

### Federal Aviation Administration

To order the following publication write to the Consumer Hotline, AOA-20, FAA, 800 Independence Ave. S.W., Washington, DC 20591.

- Tips for Parents Using Child Restraints on Aircraft. Free.

### U.S. Department of Transportation (DOT) Research and Special Programs Administration

To order the following publication, write to the U.S. Department of Transportation, R.S.P.A., DHM-50, Washington, DC 20590.

- These Fly . . . These May Not: Hazardous materials that you should avoid bringing on airlines. Free.

### Federal Trade Commission

To order the following publication write to the Federal Trade Commission, 6th & Pennsylvania Ave. N.W., Room 130, Washington, DC 20580

- Telemarketing Travel Fraud: Travel scams marketed by phone. Free.

### U.S. Department of Agriculture (USDA)

To order any of the following publications, write to USDA/APHIS Public Information, 4700 River Road, Unit 1-A01, Riverdale, MD 20737.

- Travelers' Tips—Bringing Plant and Animal Products into the U.S.: Free.

- Traveling By Air with Your Pet. Free.

### ECPAT-USA
### (End Child Prostitution, Child Pornography and Trafficking of Children)

To order the following publication, write to ECPAT-USA, 157 Montague Street, Brooklyn, NY 11021.

- What You Should Know about Sex Tourism before You Go Abroad. Free

## Selected Books of Interest to Travelers

The following books include security information that may be of interest to general travelers. They are listed alphabetically by title. Check your local library or bookstore for availability.

### Complete Terrorism Survival Guide: How to Travel, Work and Live in Safety
Author: Juval Aviv
Publisher: Juris Publishing, Inc., 2003
ISBN: 1578231302

### Executive's Guide to Personal Security
Authors: David S. Katz and Ilan Caspi
Publisher: Wiley, John & Sons, Inc., 2003
ISBN: 0471449873

### Frommer's Fly Safe, Fly Smart: The Insider's Guide to a Hassle-Free Flight, Second Edition
Authors: Sascha Segan and Maureen Clarke
Publisher: Wiley, John & Sons, Inc., 2002
ISBN: 076456613X

### Jungle Travel and Survival
Authors: John B. Walden
Publisher: Lyons Press, 2001
ISBN: 158574249X

*Safe Air Travel Companion*
Authors: Clinton McKinnon and Dan McKinnon
Publisher: McGraw-Hill Professional, 2002
ISBN: 0071399186

*Textbook of Travel Medicine and Health, Second Edition*
Authors: Herbert L Dupont and Robert Steffen
Publisher: B.C. Decker, 2001
ISBN: 1550091379

*Worst-Case Scenario Survival Handbook: Travel Handbook*
Authors: Joshua Piven and David Borgenicht
Publisher: Chronicle Books, 2001
ISBN: 0811831310

## Information and Updates on the Internet

*Background Notes* provide information on the culture, history, geography, economy, government, and current political situation for about 170 countries around the world. They are updated periodically and made available by the Office of Electronic Information and Publications of the Bureau of Public Affairs, U.S. Department of State. You can access them at http://www.state.gov/r/pa/ei/bgn/.

**"Don't Be Afraid: Be Ready"** an online publication of the U.S. Department of Homeland Security is available at www.ready.gov. Additional information from can also be found at www.dhs.gov/dhspublic/.

**"Foreign Entry Requirements"** explains passports, visas, and other requirements by country; it is available online at http://travel.state.gov/foreignentryreqs.html.

**"Know Before You Go!"** an online brochure available from U.S. Customs and Border Protection is available at http://www.cbp.gov/xp/cgov/travel/vacation/know_brochure/.

**The National Transportation Library**, a service of the U.S. Department of Transportation, offers information on a list of topics, including air, rail, and car transportation through its "Frequently Asked Questions" at http://ntl.bts.gov/faq/index.html. The "Ask a Librarian" service at http://ntl.bts.gov/cgi-bin/ref/ref.cgi can help with other, more specific inquiries.

**Passports Services and Information** offers updated information from the U.S. Department of State at http://travel.state.gov/passport_ services.html.

**Recreation.gov** provides up-to-date information about recreation areas around the U.S. The website is available at http://www. recreation.gov/.

**"Taxi and Bus Passenger Safety Checklist"** is available from the Association for Safe International Road Travel at http://www.asirt.org/ StudyAbroad/TaxiBusPassengerSafetyChecklist.pdf. An index of other publications is available at http://www.asirt.org/publication.htm.

**Travel Tips and Publications,** including information about your rights and responsibilities during air travel are available from the Office of Aviation Enforcement and Proceedings at http://airconsumer. ost.dot.gov/pubs.htm.

**Travel Warnings and Consular Information Sheets** from the Bureau of Consular Affairs, U.S. Department of State are available online at http://travel.state.gov/travel_warnings.html.

**"Travelers and Consumers: Are You Prepared for Takeoff?"** an online guide prepared by the U.S. Transportation Security Administration (TSA), available at http://www.tsa.gov/public/theme_ home1.jsp.

**Traveler's Health,** a service of the Centers for Disease Control and Prevention (CDC), provides updated information about international health risks, vaccination requirements for foreign travel, and other travel-related tips; online at http://www.cdc.gov/travel/.

# Index

# Index

# H

HACE *see* high-altitude cerebral edema

Hague Convention
child abduction 457–59
described 116

Haiti, embassy contact information 524

Halfan (halofantrine) 249–50

halofantrine 249–50

Hansen's disease 293

HAPE *see* high-altitude pulmonary edema

Havrix 235–37

hazardous materials, described 29–30

"Health and Nutrition" (Hoffa) 215n

health care
airline travel 81–92
business travelers 462–63
international travel 215–23
overseas resources 341–42
toll-free telephone numbers 337–38

Health Care Abroad, contact information 338

*Health Information for International Travel 2001-2002* (CDC) 225n, 232n, 234n, 239n, 252n, 255n, 260n, 269n, 282n, 284n, 304n, 305n, 313n, 319n, 343n, 399n

health insurance *see* insurance coverage

Health Quest Travel, Inc., contact information 342

Heher, Eliot 332

helminth parasites, described 300–301

HEPA filters *see* high-efficiency particulate air

hepatitis
pregnancy 412, 414
travelers risk 234–38
travel tips 217
vaccine 323, 415

"Hepatitis, Viral, Type A" (CDC) 234n

"Hepatitis, Viral, Type E" (CDC) 234n

"Her Own Way: Advice for the Woman Traveler" (Canada Department of Foreign Affairs and International Trade) 399n

Herzegovina *see* Bosnia and Herzegovina

high-altitude cerebral edema (HACE) 315

high-altitude pulmonary edema (HAPE) 315

high-efficiency particulate air (HEPA filters), tuberculosis 89

high risk personnel, defined 511

hijackers, airline travel 50

histidine 309

HIV *see* human immunodeficiency virus

Hoffa, Bill 146n, 215n, 353n

Holland *see* Netherlands

home burglary avoidance 349–51

Honduras, embassy contact information 524

Hong Kong
embassy contact information 524
prisoner transfer treaties 155

Honolulu Passport Agency, contact information 547

hookworms 300

hostage, defined 511

Hostelling International, contact information 547

hotels
business travelers 465–68
safety checklist 20, 22
surveillance methods 477–78, 484–85
theft avoidance 354–57
women travelers 402–3

"How Airport Security Works" (How Stuff Works, Inc.) 3n

How Stuff Works, Inc., airport security publication 3n

"How to Determine Vaccinations That Are Required or Recommended" (CDC) 319n

HTH Worldwide, contact information 337

human immunodeficiency virus (HIV)
influenza vaccine 288–89
travel information 269–81
travel tips 221–23
yellow fever 258

# Titles in the Security

## Child & Youth Security Sourcebook

*Basic Information for General Readers about Protecting Children and Youth from Drug and Substance Abuse, Sexual and Violent Crime, Family Offenses, Peer Conflict, Mental Health Risks, Juvenile Delinquency, and School and Campus Unrest, including Information for Students, Resources for Parents, and Strategies for Educators*

*Along with Statistics, Recovery Programs for Young Victims of Violence, a Glossary of Related Terms, and Resources for Further Information*

Edited by Chad T. Kimball. 646 pages. Index. 2003. 0-7808-0613-1. $68.

R ecent reports show that one in five young people are afraid of attending school because of the threat of various crimes. Seven out of ten crimes committed against young people occur at school, in their home neighborhood, or at a nearby park or playground. In addition to these dangers, many children face threats of abuse and other offenses at home.

This *Sourcebook* provides important information for students, parents, and educators about protecting children and youth from social harm, crime, violence, and substance abuse in schools and in the community. The book presents important material about juvenile delinquency, gangs, school and campus unrest, and peer conflict. It also offers information about dangers to children and youth in the home, including abuse and neglect, child care mistreatment, and child witnesses of sexual and violent crimes. Other chapters furnish material about managing emotional and mental health issues, including anxiety disorders, depression, aggression, and suicidal tendencies.

## Communications Security Sourcebook

*Basic Information for General Readers about Cell Phone and Wireless Communication Security, Telephone Company Security Issues, Telephone Slamming and Cramming, Long Distance Telephone Scams, Telemarketing Fraud and Other Nuisances, Wiretapping and Eavesdropping, and More*

*Along with a Glossary of Related Terms and Resources for Further Information*

Edited by Wilma R. Caldwell. 375 pages. Index. 2003. 0-7808-0646-8. $68.

T oday's communications market has more options for consumers than ever before. However, security concerns associated with advanced telecommunications technologies —such as fraud, theft, privacy invasion, and government surveillance—are rising. Cell phone theft is reaching epidemic proportions. In addition, law enforcement authorities say that there are over one million crank calls placed each year in this country.

The *Communications Security Sourcebook* provides basic consumer information about telecommunications security, wireless communication security, telephone security, and information privacy. It furnishes consumers with the information they need to protect themselves from communication-related fraud and theft as well as to deal with other issues related to modern telecommunications.